BUDDHISM
AND
GANDHĀRA ART

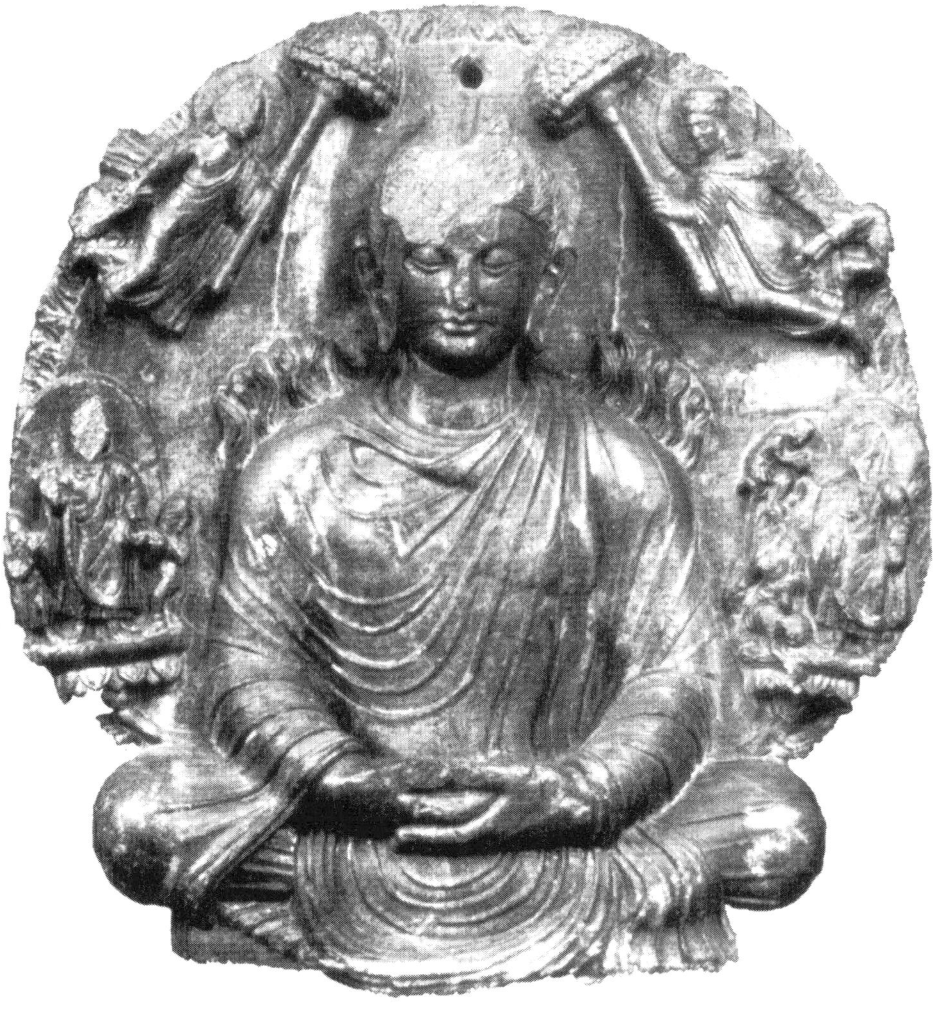

BUDDHISM
AND
GANDHĀRA ART

Editor

R.C. SHARMA

Associate Editor

PRANATI GHOSAL

Indian Institute of Advanced Study

Shimla

Jñāna-Pravāha

Varanasi

Aryan Books International

New Delhi

BUDDHISM AND GANDHĀRA ART

ISBN: 978-81-7305-264-4

First Published: 2004

Reprinted: 2022

This volume constitutes the proceedings of the International Seminar held at Jñāna-Pravāha, Varanasi, from 1st-6th November, 2001. The views expressed in this volume are those of the authors and are not necessarily those of the editors or the publishers.

Published by:

Indian Institute of Advanced Study
Shimla - 171 005

Jñāna-Pravāha
Varanasi - 221 005
and

Aryan Books International
Pooja Apartments, 4B, Ansari Road, New Delhi - 110 002 (India)
Tel.: 91-11-23287589, 23255799; Fax: 91-11-23270385
E-mail: aryanbooks@gmail.com
www.aryanbooks.com

Printed in India

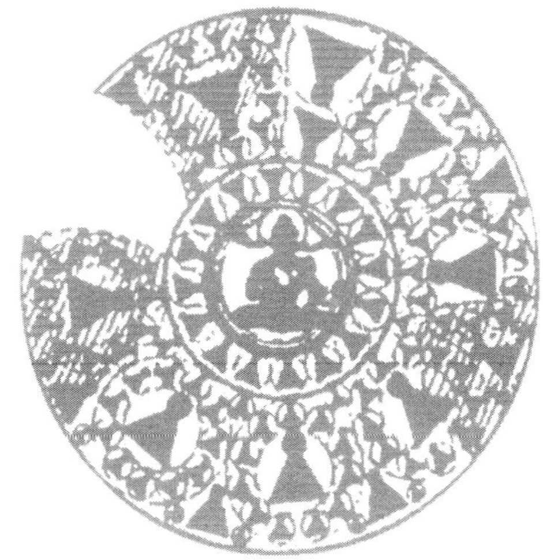

Dedicated to the memory of those
splendid treasures of Gandhāra art
which were either lost or destroyed
deliberately in Afghanistan

PREFACE

The International Seminar on Buddhism and Gandhāra art was the result of fierce attack and demolition of the wonderful cultural heritage in Afghanistan under the instructions of the then Taliban government. Not only the Buddhist world was taken aback by the demolition of the Bamiyan Buddhist statues, but the academicians were also extremely hurt due to this catastrophic event. The authorities of Jñāna-Pravāha, Varanasi and the Indian Institute of Advanced Study, Shimla, proposed to convene an event in which the scholars could pay their tributes to the creators of Gandhāra art and also appreciate the merits of this great style of sculptural art. Owing to the turbulent situation and crisis followed by the attack on the World Trade Center towers in New York, many scholars were not allowed to leave their countries by their respective governments, although they were keen to participate. The seminar on the whole went off well and several important aspects were covered. It coincided with the inauguration of the new building of Jñāna-Pravāha, *Pratīcī* and it was again a very happy coincidence that the conference was held on an important theme of the Art of *Pratīcī* (Western Region).

The founder of Jñāna-Pravāha, Smt. Bimla Poddar, extended immense support in convening the Gandhāra conference and offered valuable suggestions during the preparation of the press copy of the proceedings. The assistance rendered by Dr. Niraj Kumar Pandey and Sri Chandraneel Sharma of Jñāna-Pravāha is also appreciated.

We are indebted to the scholars who graced the occasion and presented their research papers on the subject assigned to them. It is hoped, the proceedings of the seminar on 'Buddism and Gandhāra Art' organized from 1st to 6th November 2001, as incorporated in this volume will be received well by the scholars and students engaged in the study of Buddhism and Gandhāra Art.

R.C. Sharma
Pranati Ghosal

CONTENTS

LIST OF CONTRIBUTORS

Prof. R.C. Sharma

88, Saket Nagar, Varanasi - 221 005.

Dr. Saifur Rahman Dar

Ex-Director, Lahore Museum, 83-G, Marghazar Colony, P.O. - Awan Town, Multan Road, Lahore - 54780 (Pakistan).

Prof. T.P. Verma

397 A, Ganga Pradushan Road, Bhagwanpur, Varanasi 221 005.

Dr. Pranati Ghosal

B 29/32, Saket Nagar, Varanasi - 221 005.

Dr. V.K. Sharma

7B, Geeta Enclave, Bank Colony, Mathura - 281 004.

Sri Kranti Kumar

19, Pratap Nagar, Mavaiya, Sarnath, Varanasi - 221 007.

Dr. Amar Singh

MM - 260, Sector - D, Aliganj Scheme, Lucknow - 226 024.

Prof. C. Willemen

Belgian Royal Academy of Sciences, Royal Academy of Science, PB 656, 8400 Oostende, Belgium.

Dr. S.P. Gupta

Chairman, Indian Archaeological Society, B - 17, Qutab Institutional Area, New Delhi - 110 016.

Prof. Farid Khan

House No. 3, Street - 1, Sector J - 3, Phase - II, Hayatabad (Pakistan).

Dr. B.R. Mani

B - 82, Pandara Road, New Delhi - 110 003.

Dr. Pushpa Tiwari

36/A, Balrampur House, Allahabad - 211 002.

Dr. Anasua Das

Senior Technical Assistant, Indian Museum, 27, Jawaharlal Nehru Road, Calcutta - 700 016.

Prof. V.C. Srivastava

18 - A, Nyaya Marg, Allahabad - 211 001.

Dr. Usha Rani Tiwari

Lecturer, Department of Ancient History, K.N. Govt. Postgraduate College, Gyanpur.

Dr. I.K. Sarma

Former Director, A.S.I., Flat No. 4, 2nd Floor, Latha Apartments, Vidyanagar, Hyderabad - 500 044.

Dr. N.P. Joshi

CK - 1/13, Patani Tola, Bhonsla Mandir, Bhonsla Ghat, Varanasi - 221 001.

Dr. Preety A. Trivedi

36, Bajaj Nagar, Nagpur - 440 001.

Dr. S.D. Trivedi

B 1/7, Sector - G, Aliganj, Lucknow - 226 020.

Prof. Kamal Giri

D - 51/45, Daya Dham, Suraj Kund, Varanasi - 221 010.

Dr. Anamika Roy

29/31, Lajpat Rai Road, New Katra, Allahabad.

Prof. Vibha Tripathi

22, Sankat Mochan Colony, Lanka, Varanasi - 221 005.

Dr. T.K. Biswas

Joint Director, Bharat Kala Bhavan, Banaras Hindu University, Varanasi - 221 005.

Dr. Savita Sharma

Banaras Hindu University, Varanasi - 221 005.

Sri Vidya Nand Singh

Director, Government Museum & Art Gallery, Sector 10 - C, Chandigarh - 160 011.

Prof. Kiran Kumar Thaplyal

B 1 - 18/1, Sector - K, Aliganj, Lucknow - 226 024.

Sri Devendra Handa

Fellow, Indian Institute of Advanced Study, Rashtrapati Nivas, Shimla - 171 005.

1

INTRODUCTION

Keynote*

R.C. SHARMA

Holding of this Seminar in Varanasi or Kāśī is quite befitting for the fact that the core region of Gandhāra, i.e. Uḍyāna and Kāśī both were known for textiles in ancient times. While the former produced beautiful blankets, the latter was known for weaving fine quality clothes, particularly the silk fabrics. This reputation finds place in *Mahāvaṇika Jātaka* of about 2nd century BC :

काशिकानी च वत्थानि उड्डाने च कम्बले [1]

We are not aware of the present state of affairs of Uḍyāna but Kāśī continues to retain its ancient glory in the silk sarees although the trade is not at its peak now.

REGION

The region of Gandhāra has been defined repeatedly by the scholars but a fully satisfactory solution is yet awaited. In a colloqui held in February 1991 at the Indian Museum, Calcutta after considering various facts, suggested that the region of Gandhāra from the cultural and artistic viewpoint has two components. One is the heartland or the core area and the other is the greater Gandhāra. The heartland is somewhat triangular piece of rocky region surrounded by the hills between the present day Afghanistan and the northern Pakistan and roughly measures 100 km from east to west and about 70 km from north to south. Bifurcated into two distinct parts by the Indus, the land was known in the ancient times as Apara Gandhāra (western side) with Puṣkalāvati (modern Charsadda) on the confluence of Indus and Kabul rivers as capital and Pūrva Gandhāra (eastern side) with Takṣaśilā as the headquarter. The greater Gandhāra, however, commanded a vast land as it influenced the art productions in the periphery of several hundred kilometres.

The derivation of name is not certain. We know that the *gandharvas* were well versed in performing arts, i.e. music and dance. The ladies were beautiful, looking like nymphs (*apsaras*). On the other hand, the word *Kandhāra* may be derived from 'Skandhāvāra',[2] i.e.

---

* This is the Keynote Address delivered by the author at the International Seminar held at Jñāna-Pravāha, Varanasi from 1st-6th November, 2001.

military regiment centre as the land was known for fighters and warriors who were employed by the ambitious rulers and invaders. When Chandragupta Maurya annexed it from Selucus, it was transformed into a military regiment, i.e. Skandhāvāra. Among the Greeks it was well known as Arackosia. A locality near Kandahar is even now known as Daṇḍa which means army.[3]

Culture has much more larger dimension than history, geography, politics and even religion. Same is the case with the Gandhāra region which remained culturally associated with India for long. The Indians particularly those who are conversant with this cultural significance feel emotionally attached and affected with the incidents in the region. In ancient time, there was a large common Orient in which several countries of modern times behaved like family members. India and Afghanistan specially Gandhāra region also shared this affinity.

DESTRUCTION

The brutal attack on the Buddhist antiquarian wealth in Afghanistan by some uncivilized persons shook the entire world. It was a real paradox that the country which was the foremost to honour the apostrophe of peace severely assaulted his spirit. The destruction of Buddhist remains was an act of dismantling principles of peace and this really hurt the peace and coexistence or *pañcaśīla* as propagated by the Master. While necessary precautions against such barbarity were taken by the world community, the academicians also raised their voice and endeavoured to restore the heritage as far as possible.

EARLY REFERENCES

The earliest scripture of India, i.e. *Ṛgveda* does mention the Gandhāra region in a somewhat strange context but of course appreciates its important characteristic of producing quality wool.[4] The later Vedic literature also remembers Gandhāra and further details are mentioned in the epics specially the *Mahābhārata* and several names of the area are met with. The heated discussion between Karṇa and Śalya furnishes detailed information about the Gandhāra country and its people.[5] The ties between two countries were further cemented from the time of the Buddha. As the literary traditions inform the two merchants Tapassu and Bhallika came to pay their respects to the Buddha in the eighth week after the Enlightenment. They are reported to have come from Ukkala in the Gandhāra region and offered *madhugolaka* (the sweet balls) to the Master who in exchange offered his eight handfuls of hair for worship.[6] They are considered the first lay devotees. The arrival of these merchants covering about two thousand kilometres is really a remarkable incident in the history of two countries. The texts further inform that they were brothers, Tapassu being elder and Bhallika younger and were sons of a trader leader, Sārthavāha of Pokkharvatī town. Their second visit to the Master was at Rajgṛha and this time the Buddha preached them. Deeply elated by the sermon, Tapassu and Bhallika became devout Buddhists and entered the *saṅgha*.[7]

The *Lalitavistara* records that the two merchants came from Uttarāpatha and passed through Bodh Gaya to offer honey and pieces of sugarcane to the Buddha. The *Mahāvastu* also narrates the incident and informs that honey and *ghee* were the gifts of these two devotees. Subsequently, Hiuen Tsang in the early 7th century says that these two followers on return erected *stūpas* at Asitanjana near Balkha.[8]

We come across a reference where a surgeon and physician, Jīvaka Kumārābhṛtya of Magadha is said to have received his training at Taxila and many students from Kāśī also went to Taxila to study under Jīvaka.[9] The mention is also made of migration of some Śākyas when they were massacred by Virūdha of Kośala and they took shelter in several countries and one prince went to Uḍyāna in the Gandhāra region. His son Uttarsena was able to obtain the relics of Buddha after *Mahāparinirvāṇa* and erected a *stūpa* which was seen by Hiuen Tsang. A. Stein located this in the Swat Valley. Both Fa Hien and Hiuen Tsang wrote about the visit of the Buddha to the country of Uḍyāna (Gandhāra) but this seems to be the outburst of their emotions and the Master never went there. Hiuen Tsang recorded the visit of Buddha to several places but a close scrutiny of facts does not confirm such statement.[10] Of course, the erection of *stūpas* remained a pious act and several spots were chosen for it. Hiuen Tsang mentions another Śākya king who was responsible for building a *stūpa* at Bamiyan.

CARAVANS AND MONKS

We also find numerous references when the monks used to travel with the *Sārthavāhas* (merchants). This must have been in the mutual interest of the traders and the monks. On one hand, the caravan felt safe with the fellow travellers and on the other, the monks must got necessary provisions from the caravan. The spiritual discourses and discussion were also befitting and entertaining. Fa Hien mentions the deposition of skull bone of the Buddha enshrining a *stūpa* near Jalalabad (Uḍyāna). The place probably is, therefore, known as Haḍḍā derived from *haḍḍi* meaning bone.[11] Both the Chinese travellers testify their visit and worship to this sacred place. Hiuen Tsang informs that the eyeballs, tooth, bowl, etc., of the Buddha were also installed for worship. The *stūpa* where the tooth of the Master was deposited became famous as *Dauranta,* i.e. Dantārāma in Jalalabad.[12]

All these references directly or indirectly suggest that there was a good deal of interaction between India and Gandhāra region even before the invasion of Alexander in the 4th century BC. Afghanistan may be considered as the first region to receive the message of the Buddha. When the *saṅgha* was divided into different branches, there were five groups of monks of *mahāsāṅghika* settled in the Gandhāra region in the pre-Christian century. These were Ekavyavahārika, Kaukalika, Bahuśrutiya, Prajñaptivādin and Lokottaravādin.[13]

THE COUNCILS

While the interaction between India and Gandhāra in the realm of art started towards the close of 1st century AD, the thought process had commenced much earlier. It is gathered from the texts that a monk Sambhūta Sāṇavāsi who belonged to Mathurā and attended the second Buddhist Council after hundred years of the Great Demise, went to Kipin (Kapiśā) to check the growing influence of *mahāsāṅghikas* and to propagate the real message of Master of Theravāda.[14] Sambhūta was able to convince the Buddhist Council that *vibhajjavāda* was the essence of Buddha's thought and the same was later upheld by the Third Council also which was convened in the time of Aśoka. The learned monk, however, did not succeed much as the *mahāsāṅghikas* were rapidly increasing their strength and he ultimately returned to Mathurā and breathed his last.

As resolved in the Third Council in the 3rd century BC, several missionaries were despatched for the propagation of *dhamma* to a number of countries and places.[15] Of these two went to north and west, i.e. Thera Majjhantika to Kashmir and Gandhāra and Thera Mahārakṣita to Yona. This may be pointed out here that both these regions were the part of the Aśokan empire. Yona was next to Gandhāra where the Bactrians had settled after the departure of Alexander. Selucus had ceded this territory to Candragupta Maurya in the 4th century BC.

A very interesting fact is that the implementation of the resolution of the Third Buddhist Council for selecting a monk from the Yona country to preach in Aparānta (Koṅkaṇa) in the western part of India.[17] This suggests that the Buddhist scholar Yonaka Dhammarakṣita who participated in the Council was a great scholar and devout Buddhist. Before coming to India he must have undergone vigorous scriptural and religious training in his own country and on the basis of his background, he was asked to preach *dhamma* in India itself. We can, therefore, presume that the teachings of the Buddha had started attracting foreigners even before the Mauryan period. Yona Dhammarakshita was fully conversant with Pālī texts and he preached Aggi Khanḍopama Sutta from the *Aṅguttara Nikāya*.[18] This part lays stress on leading a disciplined and pure life by the monks. Thus, a foreign monk was held in high esteem not only for learning but also for his conduct. As the result of this 37,000 persons received *pabajjā* (monkhood). We are informed by the *Mahāvaṁśa* that same Sūtra was delivered by Mahendra who went to Siṁhal (Śrī Laṅkā) on the same mission.[19]

KUṢĀṆAS

We now come down to the dawn of the Christian era and find a gold plate from a *stūpa* Ekakūṭa from the Uḍyāna region which records in the Kharoṣṭī inscription the name of the king as Senaverma and also the two early Kuṣāṇa kings, i.e. Kuzul Kadphises and Devaputra Sadakṣaṇa (Wema Kadphises).[20] This was the time when the Indian rulers although exercised their sway in the Gandhāra region yet were being uprooted by the powerful Kuṣāṇa invaders who were advancing with speed and reached the heartland of India like Mathurā and even beyond. An inscription from Mathurā informs about the monk Jīvaka from Uḍyāna or Oḍḍīyāna donating a pillar to the Mahārājā Rājātirājā Devaputra Huviṣka Vihāra in the year 59 corresponding to AD 137.[21]

Later

It appears that in the 5th century AD the territory of Uḍyāna was bifurcated into Nagarhāra and Uḍyāna. The kings of the Indian origin or Hindus sometimes appear on scene and in the 8th century AD, the Hindu Śāhīs shifted their capital to Udbhāṇḍapur[22] (Unda near Attok in Pakistan) due to the pressure of the Chinese and the Turks. An inscription on the image of Gaṇeśa mention Khingil Shahi as Otyata Shahi, i.e. Śāhī of Uḍyāna.[23]

Despite a turbulent situation, Jalalabad or the region of Uḍyāna retained its cultural glory and was known as Nagarhāra, i.e. the ornament of Uttarāpatha. There was an exchange of scholars also and we find Bhikṣu Vira Deva who graduated from Kaniṣka Mahāvihār at Peshawar under Ācārya Sarvajñāna Śānti became the head of Nālandā Mahāvihāra.[24]

There are numerous places in the Gandhāra region which find adequate place in the Indian texts. Kabul finds place in the Vedas and the river Kubha is also mentioned.[25] An inscription unearthed about 30 miles west of Kabul (Wardak) belonging to 2nd century AD mentions *Mahāsāṅghikas*. The language is Prākṛt Sanskrit and the script is Kharoṣṭī.[26] It is recorded on the reliquary of the Buddha. This archaeological evidence from the vicinity of Kabul is probably the earliest evidence mentioning *Mahāsāṅghika*.

Similarly, Śalātura on the confluence of river Kabul and Indus (modern Lahore) is known as the birth place of Pāṇini,[27] the great grammarian who belongs to 5th-6th century BC. Another remarkable incident which took place here was the discussion between Thera Nāgasena, a well-known Buddhist monk with the Greek king Menander in the 2nd century BC. The king was much impressed with the arguments of the monk and as a result of this he embraced Buddhism and erected several *stūpas*.[28]

ARCHAEOLOGY

The archaeological evidence generally corroborates the scriptural references but these start from the Mauryan period. From about the middle of the 6th century BC, the region was the part of Achaemenian empire in the time of Cyrus, the Great.[29] Later, in an inscription of Darius, the people of Gandhāra are mentioned as subjects of his empire and that the soldiers of this place fought on the side of Xerxes against Greeks in 480-479 BC.[30] The land remained under the Persian domination until it was conquered by Alexander in 326-27 BC. As pointed out earlier, Candragupta Maurya annexed Gandhāra from Selucus in 305 BC and during the reign of his grandson Aśoka, the process of spread of Buddhism began. Towards the beginning of the 2nd century BC, the Mauryan empire disintegrated, as a result of which several groups of foreign rulers exercised their sway and these included Greeks, Bactrians, Scythians or Śakas, Ausakas, Pārthians and then Kuṣāṇas. We have to depend mainly on the numismatic sources for the reconstruction of the history of the region.

ART STYLE

It was at this point that Gandhāra became the melting pot of several cultural currents and the result of which a mixed school of sculptural style emerged which is known as Gandhāra School of Sculpture. At the same time it maintained the distinct features which bespeak an independent language of artistic evolution.[31] The geographical and historical factors are of course important for assessing the nature and features of this school. It, of course, had the origin in the pre-Kuṣāṇa era but as a well-established and dominating school, it functioned under the patronage of Kuṣāṇas. Unfortunately, the history and chronology of the Kuṣāṇa dynasty is a complicated issue. Although the scholars have been studying this from the mid-19th century yet the issues have not been fully sorted out so far.

An art historian often endeavours to study and suggest the chronology of a style of art. In several cases the efforts have met the desired success and it has been possible to project a reasonable time frame for some important art schools. The case is rather different for the Gandhāra sculptures. This complex nature is suggested by various names given to it like Gandhāra, Indo-Greek, Indo-Hellenistic, Graeco-Buddhist, Indo-Iranian, Indo-Roman, etc. One can infer that not one but several ateliers were functioning in different places simultaneously and these represented some distinct features of their own.

The problem becomes more critical when we are confronted with the paucity of inscribed material. Even in case of date, the era for reckoning is not certain. So far only eight dated sculptures of Gandhāra School have been recovered but the date given does not lead to a definite conclusion for the fact that these represent different eras.

The workshops of Gandhāra School were spread over a large zone and the regional characteristics were bound to creep in. Only one binding factor is prominent and that is the Buddhist theme. Almost 90 per cent of the sculptures illustrate the Buddha, the Buddhist pantheon, the Buddhist devotees, etc. The remaining represent Brāhmanical and alien subjects. Balarāma and Kṛṣṇa are seen on the coin of Agathocles from Ai-khanum in the 2nd century BC.[32] It was the meeting place of Hellenism and Orientalism. Śiva, Skanda, Mātṛkās and later Gaṇeśa were installed at different places. Coins also illustrate some deities.[33] It appears that the Gandhāra products were at the service of Buddhist monks for the dissemination of Buddhism. The narration of life scenes and allied events was a favourite subject matter and prolification of the postures gained momentum. Under the impact of the worldly detached Buddhist monks, the Gandhāra art although handled mostly by the foreign artists, remained unsensual.

At the beginning of the School, Jātaka and symbols dominated but by the passage of time, the figure excelled. It appears that due to canonical prohibition the artist of Gandhāra were depending on the canonical theme and when the restrictions were relaxed the anthropomorphic figure of Buddha was introduced. Soon it attracted the society and his forms were carved in multiple ways. The origin of the Buddha image is a matter of controversy and the champions of Gandhāra and Mathurā Schools have expressed their divergent views on the subject and both have strong arguments in their favour.[34]

The interaction between the two schools of arts, i.e. Mathurā and Gandhāra is also a fascinating subject.[35] The establishment of two *devakulas*—one at Māṭ near Mathurā and the other at Surkhkotal in Afghanistan where live or heroic size portraits of Kuṣāṇa kings were installed, hints to the process of assimilation of two societies. The study of these portraits is a very interesting subject in itself. The findspot is locally known as Õkrī or Iṭokrī ṭīlā and the word seems to have derived from Tukhāra meaning a foreigner.[36] The epithet is justified for the Kuṣāṇas. These are to be compared with the portraits on the coins. There are several trends which travelled from Mathurā to Gandhāra and vice versa.[37] The interaction was not only in trade and art but is also seen at the religious, ritual and mystic level. The copy of an epigraph from a well in Shakardarra in the Gandhāra region was prepared and was set up in a well at Rawal near Mathurā. This was probably done with the hope to transform the brackish water into sweet water.[38] There was a time when Mathurā School was dominated with the Gandhāra impact but after some time, probably towards the end of the reign of Vāsudeva the situation changed and the earlier convention revived. This intermixing of artistic traits bespeaks of the fusion of two cultural currents and subsequently a feeling of repulsion arose and this resulted in the disintegration of the Kuṣāṇa empire.

The region of Gandhāra continues to be the mine of archaeological wealth and we notice some important or rather startling discoveries now and then. The inscription discovered at Rabatak near Surkhkotal recording the first regnal year of Kaniṣka is an excellent citation.[39] This not only records the name of some important Kuṣāṇa rulers but also indirectly suggests that Kaniṣka was a co-ruler for some time with Wema Kadphises before being coronated as a full-fledged king.

The products of Gandhāra art which are mostly in the bluish schist stone, some in stucco, a few in metallic terracotta are scattered and deposited in numerous museums and art galleries all over the world. The ivories from Begra, ancient Kapiśā are world famous. These betray the early central Indian and Mathurā sculptural rendendering. We are well aware of the ivory guild of Vidisā through the southern gate of the Sānchi Mahācetīya.[40] Due to uncongenial climatic conditions the Vidiśā products became extinct in the place of their origin but found a good market in Gandhāra and stood well.It is difficult to give an exact figure of specimens of this prolific art style which was at its zenith in the 2nd or 3rd century AD. Despite being somewhat mundane in characteristic and representing somewhat decadent phase of late Greek and Roman features, the Gandhāra art did serve as a forceful vehicle of Buddhist thought which spread in several neighbouring countries.[41] It also influenced the contemporary and later schools of art. The credit of shaping the largest statues of the Buddha also goes to Gandhāra and at Bamiyan the gigantic image one measuring 175′ and other 120′ were world famous.[42]

The Gandhāra region and its art products including the monuments suffered terrible blows at the hands of invaders repeatedly. The fierce attack in the garb of Islam has been the most shocking. The reports are that the Minister of Culture in the Taliban government went to the Kabul Museum with a hammer and himself broke many Buddhist antiquities and also asked the museum staff to do so.[43] It is astonishing that the people of a country resolved to blast their own heritage. This attack on the world civilization was more serious and had far reaching consequences than the destruction of the World Trade Center Towers on September 11 and on the Indian Parliament on 13 December, 2001. This august gathering may also perhaps recommend some guidelines so that the destruction of the world heritage as deliberately executed in Afghanistan is not repeated anywhere in the globe.

NOTES AND REFERENCES

1. Jātaka No. 493.IV.352.
2. C.S. Upasak, *History of Buddhism in Afghanistan*, 1990, p. 17.
3. *Ibid.*
4. *Ṛgveda*, 1.26.7.
5. *Mahābhārata*
6. *Vinayapiṭaka*, Mahāvagga, Nalanda ed., pp. 5-6.
7. *Theragāthā Aṭṭakathā*, Vol. I, pp. 68-70.
8. *Lalitavistara*, Ch.24.
9. G.P. Malalasekara, *Dictionary of Pali Proper Names,* Vol. I, pp. 957, 982-83.
10. R.C. Sharma, *Buddhist of Mathura*, 1984, p. 47.
11. Upasak, *op. cit.,* p. 13.
12. *Ibid.*, p. 15.
13. N. Dutta, *The Buddhist Sects in India*, p. 60.
14. Upasak, *op. cit.*, p. 14.
15. *Dīpavaṁśa*, Chapter VIII, *Mahāvaṁśa*, Chapter XII, *Samantapasadika,* Vol. III, pp. 54 (Nalanda ed.)
16. V.C. Srivastava, *Historical Probings in Afghanistan*, 1997, p. 3.
17. Upasak, *op. cit.*, p. 16.
18. *Aṅguttaranikāya*, Vol. IV, p. 128.
19. *Ibid.*
20. B.N. Mukherjee, *The Rise and Fall of the Kushana Empire*, 1988, p. 26.
21. R.L. Mitra, *Journal of the Asiatic Society of Bengal*, 1870, Pt. I, p. 127.
22. Upasak, *op. cit.*, p. 23.
23. *Epigraphia Indica*, Vol. XXXV, pp. 44-48.
24. *Journal of the Asiatic Society of Bengal*, Vol. XVIII, Pt. I, pp. 492-500.
25. *Atharvaveda*, X.9.76.
26. Upasak, *op. cit.*, p. 81.
27. V.S. Agrawala, *India as Known to Panini.*
28. Upasak, *op. cit.*, p. 181.
29. R.K. Mukherjee, 'Foreign Invasions', *Age of Imperial Unity*, 1960, p. 39.
30. *Ibid.*, pp. 40-41.
31. Lolita Nehru, *Origins of the Gandhāra Style*, 1989, p. 104.
32. P. Banerjee, *The Life of Krishna in Indian Art*, 1978, figs. 1-2.
33. R.C. Agrawal, 'Ūrdhvaretasa Gaṇeśa from Afghanistan', *East and West,* N.S., Vol. XVIII, 1968, pp. 166-68.
34. Sharma, *op.cit.*, p. 143.
35. R.C., Sharma 'Interaction Between Mathura and Gandhara', *National Museum Bulletin*, 7-8, 1993, pp. 7-17.
36. J.M. Rosenfield, *The Dynastic Arts of the Kushans*, 1967, p. 8.
37. N.P. Joshi and R.C. Sharma, *Catalogue of Gandhara Sculptures in the State Museum Lucknow*, 1969, pp. 27-37.

38. S. Konow, *Corpus of Kharoshthi Inscriptions*, Vol. II, Pt. I, p. 161.
39. B.N. Mukherjee, 'The Great Kushana Testament', *Indian Museum Bulletin*, 1995, pp. 15-16.
40. J. Marshall, *Guide to Sanchi*, 2nd ed., p. 52.
41. *2500 Years of Buddhism*, 1956, pp. 65-68.
42. *Ibid*., p. 294.
43. *The Times of India*, 23 November, 2001, p. 8.

2

FIFTY YEARS OF RESEARCH IN GANDHĀRA ART (1947-1997)

SAIFUR RAHMAN DAR

INTRODUCTION

As a result of independence in 1947, the entire ancient territory of Gandhāra became a part of Pakistan. This placed added responsibilities on to the shoulders of scholars of this nascent nation. No doubt, they lost some of the major Gandhāra collections but the whole area of ancient Gandhāra was still with them to traverse, probe and study afresh. In this respect our net contribution during the last 50 years is a good indicator both of our achievements as well as failures. Our own limited contributions have been amply complimented by some foreign expeditions—particularly German, Japanese and Italian and some individual scholars from France, U.K., United States, Italy and Japan. Despite all this, I am constrained to say that our attitude towards planning fresh excavations, at best, remained somewhat lukewarm. Especially, during the first four decades, our further advance of discoveries of Gandhāra art and our attempts at safeguarding what has already been discovered and what was periodically being discovered and even at furthering studies in Gandhāra art has been more or less tardy and sluggish. And, there appears to be a genuine reason for this. With a substantial collection of Gandhāra sculptures already in our collections, and a few foreign missions already in the field, the Department of Archaeology, Government of Pakistan was justified in diverting its meagre resources to explore such areas which for one reason or the other, have remained unattended so far—the Islamic Period Archaeology. But this created a negative affect because the field was practically left to others. The territory of ancient Gandhāra became a den of clandestine diggers and international smugglers of Gandhāra art. This realization came quite late, and the loss is now being compensated as best as it can be through salvage programmes.

FOREIGN EXPEDITIONS

Contributions of foreign expeditions towards understanding of Gandhāra art through fresh excavations cannot be underestimated. Though, in each case, their expeditions are confined to some specific areas and so are their reports and researches, but these have been consistent and substantial.

Italian Mission

The Italian Mission started its activities in Pakistan in 1956 under the leadership of Prof. G. Tucci—the famous Orientalist—under an overall banner of IsMEO (Istituto Med il par Extreme Oriente, Roma), now renamed as IsIAO (Istituto Italiano par l'Africa e Oriente, Roma) under the presidentship of Prof. Gerardo Gnoli. Among all the foreign archaeological missions working in Pakistan, the Italian Mission has been working for the longest in the field with a most diversified team covering all phases from prehistory to Islamic period as well as the fields of ethnology, folklore and crafts. But their first love has always been Buddhist art in Swat. For more than two decades, the director in the field was Dr D. Faccenna who excavated Buddhist sites of Butkara II, Saidu Stūpa and Panr. Lately, Faccenna was replaced by Prof. Murizio Taddei, a renowned scholar of oriental history and art—particularly the art of Gandhāra. It is hoped that under his guidance, the Buddhist studies in Pakistan will get a renewed impetus and new direction.

Although the Italian archaeologists both intensified and extensified their activities in the Swat valley, but their work in Buddhist period and Gandhāra art remained confined to a few sites in the Swat valley such as Butkara (Faccenna 1964a, 1980-81), Saidu Stupa (F. Callieri 1989), Panr (Faccenna *et al.* 1993) and the settlement site of Audigram (Faccenna 1964). The reports of the Italian Mission, though came quite late, provide prestigious additions to our knowledge of Gandhāra art, particularly its early stages of development prior to its maturity during the Kushana period. Among other Italian scholars on Gandhāra art, the contributions made by Prof. M. Taddei are most outstanding. His book *India* (Geneva: 1970) is unique in the sense that for his copious illustrations of Gandhāra section, Prof. Taddei used the freshly excavated material from Swat. It was he, who, at a very early stage, realized that "if there are still so many unsolved problems in the study of Gandhāra art, this probably is due to the absence of any careful analysis of its various cultural components" (Taddei 1970, p. 94). After Taddei, Anna Maria Quagliotti has written several good articles on Gandhāra art. She has offered quite a new interpretations of some of the Buddhist themes well-known through their depictions on Gandhāra reliefs such as Mahakarunika, i.e. figures representing 'pensive' mood (Quagliotti 1989). Among other well-known Italian scholars writing on Gandhāra art can be named Prof. M. Bussagli (1984), Simonetta (1958 and 1978), A. Sontoro (1986), Callieri (1989), G. Verardi (1978), etc.

Japanese Mission

The Japanese Mission, under the banner of Kyoto Scientific Mission to Gandhāra, also started its work in late 1950s under the famous sinologist Prof. Seiichi Mizuno of the Kyoto University. The author of this paper had the honour of working under Prof. Mizuno during 1963-65 at three sites (Chanaka Dheri, Mekha Sanda and Thareli). The team of Prof. Mizuno excavated two stupa sites (Mizuno, 1969, 1978), surveyed one cave (Mizuno 1962) and one enigmatic site of Chanaka Dheri (report not yet published). Prof. Mizuno was succeeded first by Prof. T. Higuchi and then by Prof. Koji Nishikawa—all from Kyoto University. Under Prof. Nishikawa (an architect), the emphasis of the Mission shifted to Buddhist architecture. He spent most of his time on the single site of Ranighat (Nishikawa, 1986, 1988).

As the Italians confined themselves to Swat, so did the Japanese to a single region, i.e. Mardan district, now a division. For Japanese Mission, history and art of Gandhāra always remained their first and the last love. Since 1996, this Mission has been replaced by a new team under Prof. Matsuya Masui, also an architect with their activities diverted to conservation of Gandhāran sites under a UNESCO-Japanese Mission. The team is nowadays busy in carrying out conservation of the site at Ranighat. This itself is a good sign, but it should not have been taken up at the cost of fresh discoveries and new excavations.

We must give credit to the Japanese for being the first to explore Buddhist caves in Gandhāra, i.e. Haibak in Afghanistan and Kashmir Smast in Pakistan (Mizuno 1962). This work has been supplemented only recently by discovery of cave paintings in Swat by Nazir Khan (Khan *et al.*, 1995).

The Japanese Mission was quick to publish their reports. But, despite a brief English summary at the end of each report, the bulk of information being in Japanese, the English-knowing archaeologists in Pakistan and elsewhere could not benefit themselves properly from the valuable information these reports contained.

It is only recently that the monolithic formation and activities of the Japanese Archaeological Mission in Pakistan has been broken as archaeologists from Japan have shown interest in other areas of Pakistan as well. Prof. Sh. Kuwayama had unsuccessfully tried to obtain permission to work in Sindh. However, another team of archaeologists from National Museum, Tokyo has been excavating for sometimes the site of Zar Dheri in the Shinkiari area of District Mansehra. Besides, Madame Haruko Tsuchiya of the Department of Comparative Culture, Sophia University, Tokyo, has been in the field of research along the ancient routes in the Northern Areas of Pakistan since 1991. The specific purpose of Madame Tsuchiya's project was to study that Ancient Route in the Northern Areas of Pakistan which Fa-Hien, a Chinese monk of the fifth century, followed. It was this route which directly connected China, Pakistan and India and transmitted the versatile culture and religion—Buddhism and Buddhist art among others. The sixth fieldwork of Madame Tsuchiya ended in March 1995. She has already explored all the major valleys and sub-valleys of the Gilgit River (Tsuchiya 1997).

German Scholars Open a New Vista on the Karakorum Highway

Prof. Karl Jettmar, from Heidelberg University, in collaboration with Prof. A.H. Dani from Pakistan together with a team of German scholars like Ditte König and Valker Thewalt, opened a new vista of Gandhāra studies. This area has been known since long as an extension of Buddhist art of Gandhāra into Northern Areas of Pakistan, i.e. along the Karakoram Highway on way to Central Asia, China, Korea and finally to Japan. The archaeological evidence, now recorded afresh in Gilgit, Hunza and all along this highway mainly, comprises rock carvings in the form of inscriptions and various Buddhist themes executed by devotees during the short halts at crossings of the rivers while on way to their long sojourn. These rock carvings have been dated back from prehistoric time to modern eras. But, the bulk of these carvings belong to an age (3rd century BC to 8th century AD) when Buddhism was a living force. A proper study of these carvings in conjunction with their dedicatory inscriptions in almost all contemporary languages and scripts, reveal an evolution of Buddhist art which developed in this region and influenced, on the one hand, the Chinese art and, on the other hand, the Buddhist art of Gandhāra (Dani 1981, 1983 and 1985 and Karl Jettmar *et al.* 1989-94). It has been discussed below as to how Chilas region acted as a focal point where the first image of Buddha took its human shape from the form of a *stūpa* in the first century BC. Thus the study of these Buddhist rock carvings and inscriptions added altogether different dimensions to the study of Buddhist art of Gandhāra during the last 15 years (Hauptmann 1997).

British Expeditions

There has not been much contribution towards Gandhāra studies in the form of a regular British expeditions during the last fifty years. In 1958, Sir Mortioer Wheeler conducted excavations at the site of acropolis of Pushkalavati (Greek Peucolāotis) locally called Bala Hisar (High Fort) on the right bank of river Kabul near Charsada. Some of the great archaeologists of future, David Stronac, Raoul Curiel, Dr F.A. Khan, Muhammad Ishtiaq Khan, etc., worked on this site. Wheeler had expected to discover here another Mohenjodaro. However, his two deep trenches on this imposing site revealed the earliest settlement going only as far back as the Bactrian Greeks in the 2nd century BC (Wheeler 1962). A few years after Wheeler, Prof. Raymond Allchin of the Cambridge University started a joint expedition with Prof. A.H. Dani of Peshawar University and excavated at the proper city of Pushkalavati, locally called Shaikhan Dheri on the left bank of river Kabul. The results of this expedition were published by Prof. Dani in 1965. Prof. Allchin never returned to resume his work on any Gandhāran sites, though he did carry out later on explorations in the Potowar area. More recently, Robert Knox of the British Museum, London has been given license to work at the site of Akra near Bunnu jointly with Prof. Farid Khan of Pakistan Heritage Society, Peshawar. Results of the two seasons excavations were published (Khan, Farid, 1998).

FOREIGN CONTRIBUTIONS

German

German contributions towards Gandhāra art are quite old. Names like Christian Lassen (Bonn 1838), C.L. Grotefend (Hannover 1840), Honiberger, Dr A. Leitner, Herman Goetz, etc., are well known with partly or wholly German background. Apart from the contributions made by Karl Jettmar and his colleagues, already mentioned above, the two most important German contributions towards Gandhāra art are by Albert Grünwedel (1901), and Erika Schmitt (1971). Whereas the works of the first one is well-known through his English translation, the Ph.D. dissertation of Erika Schmitt is not adequately known. This thesis published in 1971, in Weisbaden, discusses the important question as to what extent the decorative motifs in Gandhāra art owe their existence to the folk motifs in the regions of Hindukush and Karakorum and how much to the Mediterranean and Indo-Pakistan cultures.

French

Though, after Alfred Foucher, no French archaeologist has ever conducted any field study in Pakistan in the subject of Gandhāra art, but academically they have always remained active in this field directly or indirectly. Indeed they have kept the torch burning as lighted by Foucher. Their basic contribution to this subject has been from the platform of DAFA in Afghanistan. A. Foucher, R. Ghirshman, J. Hacking, D. Schlumberger and J. Barthoux prior to 1947 and, Paul Bernard, G. Fussman, Madellane Hallade, Madame Francine Tissot, H.P. Frankfort, B. Dagens, Le Barre, H. Deydier and Osmund Bopearachchi in post 1947 era, remained preoccupied with the question of 'Hellenism' and its impact on local life in Afghanistan and Gandhāra. Among these Prof. Gerard Fussman and Osmund Bopearachchi have specialized themselves in the linguistic studies of the Kushanas and numismatics of the IndoGreeks respectively. But they have also been casually writing on subject having direct bearings on Gandhāra art. Prof. Fussman, in particular, has remained associated with the fieldwork of German team in the Northern Areas. But, for our purpose, D. Schlurnberger's few studies such as "Descendants non-mediterraneens de l'art grecs" (Schlumberger 1960), "Sir John Marshall and Gandhāra Art" (Schlumberger, 1961) and "Problems of Hellenism in Bactria and India" (Schlumberger, 1961 and 1961a) are very important and interesting essays. Besides, Henri Deydiers book, *Contribution a l'etude de l'art du Gandhāra* (Deydeir 1950) has become a bibliographical source book on Gandhāra art. Like Foucher's *l'art greco-boudhique du Gandhāra*, Madame F.Tissot's book, *Gandhāra* (1985) will remain for long a classic publication on the subject. This monumental work covers such diverse subjects like geography, roads, history, architecture and architectural decoration, dress and headdresses, jewellery and daily life in Gandhāra. Fortunately, she has also published an English summary of her book with a fine set of 289 additional illustrations under the title, *The Art of Gandhāra: Buddhist Monks' Art on the North West Frontier of Pakistan* (Tissot 1986). Similarly, H.P. Frankfort's book, *Los Palettes du Gandhāra* (Frankfort 1979) is an interesting study of Gandhāra toilet trays which appeared almost simultaneously with Dar's more exhaustive study of the same subject (Dar 1979). Besides, Paul Bernard's excavations at Aï Khanum (1967) and Schlumberger's excavation at Surkh Kotal (1961 and 1961b) both in Afghanistan, have helped us a lot in understanding the Hellenistic background and basis of Gandhāra art.

British

Beside three minor British expeditions mentioned above, British contribution towards Gandhāra studies, in the post Independence era, is a significant one. What Sir John Marshall wrote on Gandhāra art between 1947-1960 was actually based on his fieldwork prior to 1934 and that is why I am not dilating on his contributions in this paper. Beside Sir John Marshall, Douglas Barrett and John Irwin as well as F. Raymond Allchin and A.D.H. Bivar (1991) have been writing, on Gandhāran themes. Catalogues of two major Gandhāra collections in two British museums namely the Victoria and Albert Museum, London and the British Museum, have been published by H.C. Ackerman (1975) and Wladimir Zwalf (1996) respectively. Zwalf earlier wrote two books entitled *Shrines of Gandhāra* (1979) and *Buddhism: Art and Faith* (1985). Elizabeth Errington did her Ph.D. Thesis—"The Western Discovery of the Art of Gandhāra and the Finds of Jamalgarhi" from the School of Oriental and African Studies, London in 1987. The emphasis of her studies has always been the search of documents of the 19th century pertaining to the discovery of Gandhāra art be it a site like Tahkal (Errington 1987a), or a sculpture (Athena in Lahore Museum) (Errington 1990) or correction of old record (Errington 1991). Prof. R. Allchin, beside his excavation for one season at Shaikhan Dheri in 1964, also contributed some articles on Shaikhan Dheri and Taxila. His pupil Dr Javaid Hussain of the Karachi University did his Ph.D. from Cambridge on the pottery assemblage from Shaikhan Dheri and has been writing on the same subject. Sir Mortimer Wheeler, beside his excavation at Bala Hisar, Charsada, also contributed a few significant articles in support of his theory of Roman origin of Gandhāra art then strongly being promoted by Benjamin Rowland (Wheeler 1949, 1954 and 1965).

American

Although most of the Gandhāra studies by American scholars pre-date Independence of Pakistan, but the most significant ones post-date 1947. The leader of these studies has been Benjamin Rowland. His Gandhāra studies were actually part of his studies of the Indian art going as far back as 1935 (Rowland 1935) but his articles exclusively addressed to Gandhāra art were written after 1947. After Simpson and Smith, Rowland proved to be the strongest supporter of the Roman and Early Christian influence on Gandhāra art (Rowland 1946, 1949, 1960, 1963 and 1970). He had a good following in the form of Mortimer Wheeler, H. Buchthal (1945), Herman Goetz (1959), Alexander Soper (1949 and 1951) and John M. Rosenfield (1967). However, towards the end of his life and after the discovery of a purely Hellenistic site at Aï Khanum (Schlumberger 1961b) and Paul Bernard (1967), Rowland mellowed his opinion about the Roman and Early Christian (Byzantine) background of the Gandhāra art. After his death, his staunch supporters like Rosenfield, Buchthal, and Soper, drifted to other fields of art history and never reverted to Gandhāra art.

Other American scholars on Gandhāra art are: J.C. Huntington (1980), S.L. Huntington (1985), Carolyn Woodford Schmidt (1990), K.W. Dobbins (1967, 1971 and 1973), M.L. Carter (1968, 1970), and Ingholt (1958) are worthy of note. Among these, the most important of all the books on Gandhāra art from USA is the colossus of Herald Ingholt's *The Gandhāra Art in Pakistan* (1958). Though an excellent work as far as its compendium of photographs of Gandhāra collections in Pakistan is concerned, its historical portion is quite weak and his analysis could never find favour with scholars. Beside, it needs to be read in conjunction with Errington's article (Errington 1991).

Japanese

As Faccenna's failure to publish timely excavations reports was amply compensated by the copious writing of Marizio Taddei, Nishikawa's inaptitude for the same was amply compensated by the writings of a few other scholars from the same country. Prof. Shoshin Kuwayama of Koyoto University, Prof. Masatoshi Konishi of St. Paul University and Dr Katsumi Tanabe of the Institute of Silk Road have contributed a lot towards the understanding of art and architecture as well as history of Gandhāra. Prof. Kuwayama, in particular, had added a new dimension to Gandhāra studies namely the Chinese literature as a background knowledge of history of this region and culture (Kuwayama 1974, 1978, 1982, 1985, 1990, 1992, 1996, 1997). Dr Katsumi Tanabe, on the other hand, added Iranian and Central Asian dimension to the study of Gandhāra art. Another Japanese scholar did a great service by publishing in two volumes a catalogue of Gandhāra sculptures depicting the Buddha's life story and the world of Buddha (Kurita 1988 and 1990) mainly taking his examples from private collections recently acquired in Japan by Japanese museums and private collectors. But, as these Kurita's volumes contain a number of fakes, these must be read in conjunction with Quigliotti 1990.

Indian

For obvious reasons, Indian archaeologists have no chance to work on any Gandhāra site in Pakistan nor did they appear to have availed of any such facility in the neighbouring country of Afghanistan. However, they have sufficient material in their own museums and ample opportunities to study the same material in other countries. They were in a better position to study indigenous literature shedding light on the background of this art. My access to Indian periodical contributions has been quite limited because periodical literature from India is not easily and consistently available in Pakistan. Whatever literature has reached me in Pakistan is in the form of books. A study of this literature reveals that the Indian contribution towards this subject is positive and substantial. In the first instance, N.P. Joshi and R.C. Sharma's *Catalogue of Gandhāra Sculptures in the State Museum, Lucknow* (1969), Suwarcha Paul's *Gandhāra Sculptures in Chandigarh Museum* (1986), and Anasua Sengupta and

Dibakar Das' *Gandhāra Holding in the Indian Museum*, Calcutta (1991) are very useful contributions regarding Gandhāra collections in some of the museums in India. Nilma Sen Gupta's *Cultural History of Kapisa and Gandhāra* (1984) and K. Krishna Murthy's *The Gandhāra Sculptures: A Cultural Survey* (1977) and above all Lolita Nehru's *Origins of the Gandhāran Style* (1989) are admirable studies and cover fields which no Pakistani scholar has so far touched. However, K.M. Varma's *Technique of Gandhāran and Indo-Afghan Stucco Images* (1987) was an outdated study even when it appeared a decade back. Our knowledge of Gandhāra art had advanced much further than revealed in this study.

PAKISTANI EXCAVATIONS AND EXPLORATIONS

At the time of Independence in 1947, Pakistani archaeologists had different priorities than to devote themselves to attend to Gandhāra art. Resources were scarce and there was an extreme dearth of trained personnel in the field of archaeology and art history. Fortunately, two important foreign archaeological missions, Italian and Japanese, offered their services in the field of Gandhāra art. This relaxed the Pakistani archaeologists. They diverted their meagre resources to other such fields where foreign missions were not interested and left the field of Gandhāra studies to foreigners for several decades. It was only after 1963 that Pakistani archaeologists started giving due attention to this field. Fuller attention was paid to it only a decade back. But, by this time, great damage had already been done. Throughout these fifty years, clandestine diggers have been most active on Gandhāra sites and illegal trade in Gandhāra sculptures became lucrative, second only to traffic in white powder.

Departmental Excavations

Though Prof. Dani initiated Gandhāra studies in Pakistan by excavating the site of Shaikhan Dheri (1965) and Chakdara (1968), but on government side the Federal Department of Archaeology, the Alma Mater of all the archaeological disciplines in this country has bitterly failed in its responsibilities towards further expanding or enriching our knowledge of Gandhāra art on scientific lines. Dar was probably the first official who excavated a Buddhist site at Manikyala though for a very brief period (Dar 1970-71). He was followed in 1967 by limited excavation by Mughal at the unique site of Nimogram (Inayatur Rahman 1968) and Pan Dheri near Bakhshali (unpublished). At Nimogram, Mughal was followed by Nazir Khan in 1968. Sharif excavated at Bhir Mound (Sharif 1969), and at Haji Shah Morr (Sharif 1986), whereas Mian Said Qamar excavated for two seasons in 1988 and 1989 at Garh Mauryan (Said Qamar 1990). He excavated a stupa site and the monastery with stucco sculptures and other finds of late Kushanas of 5th and 6th centuries. Dr Ashraf Khan and Said Qamar also jointly excavated some Buddhist sites in Swat (Said Qamar and Ashraf Khan, 1991). More recently, Saeedur Rehman has compiled the reports of reconnaissance work done by some of his officers in Gandhāra (Saeedur Rehman 1996). Mr. Makeen Khan of Swat Museum has excavated in 1996 at a site Asam Koli in Swat. Earlier the same scholars excavated in 1980 at the site of Chinkolai, also in Swat, the reported site of Gandhāra bronzes in the National Museum, Karachi. No fresh"material was, however, found by the excavator. And last of all, M.H. Khokhar has excavated the site of Musa I and III near Attock under the Salvage Programme of Ghazi Barotha Project (Khokhar 1996 and Halim and Khan).

None of these excavations and surveys are the result of a planned programme and prolonged excavations and so are the reports published brief, hurried and sketchy. On all these sites archaeological officers—none, with the exception of one or two, being a scholar of some standing and a specialist in Gandhāra studies were asked to rush and inspect a disturbed site and save whatever has been left by the clandestine diggers. Even recent surveys carried out in ancient Gandhāra and Swat has been done under the title Gandhāra Salvage Project.

Dani's Excavations

The first serious archaelogical digging by a Pakistani scholar was by Dr Dani at the city-site of Shaikhan Dheri at Charsada in 1963 (Dani 1965). This was followed by his excavations at three Gandhāran sites in district Dir, namely Andan Dheri (Dani 1968-69) Chatpat (Dani 1968-69) and Damkot (Rehinan 1968-69). These excavations, for the first time, laid the foundation of a study of Gandhāra sculptures based on stratified chronology. One important element which Dani introduced in his Gandhāra studies was "the living experience" as Dani calls it :

> The changing pattern of the society in Gandhāra has been little understood. Lack of this understanding had led many to view the art from different angles. Cut off from the living forces of a society, an art is no better than a mechanical product of a particular technique worked by a few hired craftsmen. Such an attitude is generally seen in the interpretation of the Gandhāra art by the art historians from America and Europe, who use the classical art of the West as a scale for evaluation. But fortunately, the Gandhāra art has a deeper meaning an undying lesson of living experience that at once beams out from the group of figures who converse to tell the truth of life (Dani 1968, 3).

Fresh Evidence About the Origin of the Buddha Image

Dani also fought, so far the last battle, over the difficult question of making of the first image of Buddha. It was in the 1980s that this long forgotten question was once again taken up by some scholars namely the late Prof. J.E. van Lohuizen-de-Leeuw, A.K. Narain, Susan L. Huntington, John C. Huntington and Joe Cribb on the one hand and Dr A.H. Dani on the other. Writing a little before her death in 1981, Prof. Lohuizen was persuaded to slightly revise her 1949 thesis (Lohuizen-de-Leeuw 1949), on the basis of newly discovered material from Butkara (Swat) and elsewhere in Gandhāra and showed that at least 22 earliest Gandhāra Buddhas, now precisely dated in the late first century BC and early first century AD have their closest relationship with the Mathura Buddha at a time when the classical Kapardan type had not yet completely assumed its fixed canonical form (Lohuizen-de-Leeuw 1981). However, the passion of Mathura precedence of the Buddha origin had been so strong in her mind that she took the Lahore Museum Primitive Buddha in red sandstone as an important piece from Mathura[2] as probably the oldest Buddha image known so far of the early iconic phase at Mathura, with no second example left at the mother-site, i.e. Mathura.

Joe Cribb, a numismatist (1984), dated the first image of Buddha to the reign of Maues in the first century BC either at Mathura or Gandhāra. In another, and his most recent study, Joe Cribb has convincingly shown that long before the first Image of Buddha was born, portrait of the Hindu God Śiva, or a mixture of Śiva, Mithra and some Central Asia and Greek deities appeared on the Greek and Bactrian coins (Cribb 1996). Prof. A.K. Narain, also a numismatist and a Buddhist himself, finally concluded in 1985 that the image of Buddha and Bodhisattva was created during the time of Maues (*c.* 95-97 BC) north of Gandhāra, i.e. in Swat valley and Kashmir (Narain 1985, p. 11).

Susan L. Huntington, in line with her husband Prof. John C. Huntington, does not believe in the iconic or aniconic phases in Buddhist art. According to her, "there is ample evidence to suggest that Buddha images were made in the centuries prior to the Christian era, and perhaps even as early as the lifetime of Śākyamuni Buddha or shortly thereafter" [Susan Huntington, 1985, p. 70, 627 (note 10) and John Huntington 1985].

Dr Dani, the last writer on this subject, for the first time, introduced new elements. On basis of his own researches in Gilgit and along the Karakoram Highway to China, he opines that the Buddha image did originate neither in Gandhāra nor at Mathura. Both these images have developed out of some human prototypes which originated somewhere else. According to him, the real image of Buddha originated out of a *stūpa* shape in Chilas area near Gilgit. The Chilas image of Buddha is actually anthropomorphic, a form given to a stupa, i.e. eyes and nose added to the half dome of the stupa and crossed-legs added to the base (Dani 1987, pp. 40-41). This view of Dani is based on the evidence of a few rock carvings representing stupa in anthropomorphic form clearly identified with inscription, as *Sakamunisa*... of Śākya Muni or *Budhivoto,* i.e. Bodhisattva or even as Hariti. The Buddha image which thus originated and developed in Gilgit, is certainly different from the Gandhāra and Mathura forms. Its meditating pose "left an abiding influence on the subsequent meditating Buddhas carved on the rocks from Swat to Xin-jiang". This Buddha is also different from the Mathura form in which case the headgear and head pose are quite distinctive (Dani 1987, pp. 40-44).

From this Dani concludes: "Both Gandhāra and Mathura forms appear to have human prototypes and not related to *stūpa*" whereas in the same area, i.e. Gilgit, in rock carvings we meet a standing person presenting a bowl to the seated Buddha/Bodhisattva with Kharoṣṭī inscription "*Budhavoto Lavanae Prathataka*" meaning: Lavena established the Bodhisattva. "It is another step forward in the human requirement of a divine concept". Dani in final analysis, suggests that the Gilgit Buddha being unrelated to Gandhāra and Mathura types, needs to be compared with seated figures in the coins of Maues and Kujula Kadphiscs (Dani 1987, p. 41).

What is more important is the soft mood of these discussions. These are no more polemic as these used to be in the past. Instead, these are simply academic, polite and accommodative. It takes into account all types of evidences now available which is more diverse than what Coomaraswamy and Foucher had at their disposal. Such studies help in reaching the more logical conclusions.

More Pakistani Excavations

In Gandhāra region, Dani's work was continued, though somewhat erratically, by some of his students, the most prominent among them being Prof. Fida Ullah Sehrai, Prof. Abdul Rahman, Dr Farooq M. Swati and Prof. Farid Khan. Fida Ullah Sehrai, the former Director, Peshawar Museum, wrote voluminously, but only in popular veins, on various aspects of Gandhāra (Sehrai 1978, 1986). The other three, however, did some more solid work. Rahman during a few last years concentrated his attention on salvaging some of the Gandhāra period sites. His major salvage operations are: Butkara III (Rahman 1992) and Shnaisha Gumbat (Rahman 1993). In early 1960s Rahman also dug some trial trenches at a Buddhist site called Gumbatuna in District Dir about which only a paragraph has been written in his book, *The Last Two Dynasties of the Hindu Shahiyas*, Islamabad: 1979 (p. 279). He also excavated at the Buddhist sites of Khan Mahi and in 1996 the Capital of the Hindu Shahis at Hund. On another part of the Hund, Shah Nagar was also excavated independently in 1996. But none has so far published any report. Prof. Farid Khan, primarily a prehistorian, has also dug for one season at the Buddhist settlement-cum-*stūpa* site of Gangu Dher, also called Aziz Dheri, in District Swabi in 1993. The work on this has continued in 1991, 1995 and 1996 by Zain Wahab and others of Mardan Museum. Some interesting Gandhāra sculptures and reliefs particularly some stair-risers *in situ*, have been discovered from the *stūpa* site of this mound. No report has so far been published. For a brief reference to these excavations and their significance see Kuwayama 1997, pp. 98-99. Currently, Prof. Farid Khan and Robert Knox are busy excavating the extensive settlement site of Akra near Bannu under the joint banner of Pakistan Heritage Society, the Institute of Archaeology, London University and the British Museum, London. Already, there are some interesting results and a long sequence of occupation (900 BC onwards). (For the preliminary report, see Farid Khan 1998). Earlier in 1993, Farid Khan also excavated at the site of Shaikhan Dheri, formerly excavated by Dr Dani. Again, so far no report is available.

Despite its great potentials, as indicated through chance discoveries, the entire Hazara Division on the left bank of the Indus and Chhach area in Attock District has so far failed to attract due attention of our archaeologists. Certain areas of the Hazara Division, particularly along the Gandhāra range and its offshoots between the river Dor and Tarbela Lake has been known since long as having great potentials for the archaeological wealth particularly for the period of Gandhāra art and its precedents. These include: Asokan rock edicts at Mansehra, Scythian gold stag and gold bracelets from Dhamtaur and 81 feet high Zar Dheri *stūpa* as noted by H. Hargreaves in 1922-23, lately discussed by A.D.H. Bivar and now being excavated by a team from Tokyo National Museum. More recently, a silver hoard of 2000 silver coins of Indus-Greek period from Sarai Saleh and Wesa Hoard of 1220 coins in the Chhach region have attracted the attention of the scholars world over (Osmund Bopearachchi and Aman ur Rahman, Pre-Kushana coins in Pakistan, published by IRM Associates (Pvt.) Ltd. Karachi : 1995, pp. 13-14). But it was Mian Said Qamar of the Department of Archaeology and Museums who conducted the first proper excavations in this region in 1988 and 1989. Here he excavated the Buddhist site of Garh Mauryan (the Fort of Mauryans) and excavated a huge Buddhist stupa, part of a monastery and chapels, a number of stucco sculptures and a huge Buddha's head of Kanjur stone—all of late Kushana period of 4th-5th century AD (Said Qamar 1990).

Garh Mauryan is close to Sarai Saleh. It is this area which has now attracted the fuller attention of Prof. Farzand Ali Durrani of the National Heritage Foundation. His initial probing in the Haripur valley were carried out at a mound, off Ranian-Siri Kot road opposite the village Gudwali at a site called Manak Rai Dher (not Pir Manak Rai) in 1993 and 1994. The site, according to a preliminary report of Prof. Durrani, *et al.* (1997) and Shah Nagar and Said Qamar (1928) represents a Sirkap-like city and dates back from 1st century BC to 9th and 10th century AD. A soapstone toilet tray with Dionysian scene carved on it is the most interesting find. In 1994, the Sarai Saleh Hoard of Coins was discovered at the site of Pir Manak Rai, on the bank of River Dor some six km north of Manak Rai Dher. It is this site which has now been selected by Prof. Durrani and Shah Nazar Khan for prolonged excavations. The work was started in March 1997 (F.A. Durrani 1997 and 1997a). This site is currently being excavated by Dr Saifur Rahman, Director of the National Heritage Foundation since October 1998. For the work at Zar Dheri excavation near Shinkiari, a brief mention about this has already been made above.

In Quest of Gandhāra Civilization

The Gandhāra studies have always suffered from one major defect. Majority of the scholars whether before or after 1947 have been studying it as a sculptural art. Dar is probably the only person who for last 30 years has been trying to study this art in the background of the society and civilization which has produced it. Like Foucher, Marshall and several others he too believes that the Greeks marooned in Bactria, Gandhāra and the Punjab had played a much significant role in shaping the constitution of Gandhāra art than the contemporary art of Rome and Byzantine. But, at the same time, he believes in other contemporary influences coming from Central Asia, Iran and mainland India, and even the distant Roman Empire mainly through sea. But the last one is almost negligible. His main studies concentrate on Gandhāra architecture (Dar 1973, 1980, 1983, 1989), numismatics (Dar 1977), toilet trays (Dar 1979, 1980), classical literature (Dar 1983a), east and west cultural contacts (Dar 1984), Gandhāra documentation (Dar 1990, 1992, 1994a), epigraphical evidence and dating of Gandhāra monuments through inscriptions and the art connection between Gandhāra, Mathura and Amaravati (Dar 1991, 1994) and ascertaining parameters of Gandhāra Civilization (Dar 1996), etc. He is the only student of Gandhāra art who has written on this subject in English (Dar 1984), Greek (Dar 1973) and Punjabi (Dar 1977a). He, in particular, has specialized studies of Taxila (Dar 1973, 1977a, 1983, 1984, 1989, 1993, 1998).

Swat Style of Gandhāra Art

Swat valley has always been considered a vital nerve centre of Gandhāra art. Italian scholars have spent almost fourty years in studying various aspects of the archaeological heritage of this beautiful vale. However, more recently, some Pakistani scholars have also ventured to explore and excavate in this area. Fresh studies have started pouring in now (Rahman 1992, 1993, Rehman 1968 and Saeedur Rehman 1996, Said Qamar and Ashraf 1991 and M.F. Swati 1996, 1997 and 1998). Among these scholars Dr Muhammad Faroq Swati has recently (1996) completed his Ph.D. Thesis on "Gandhāra Art in the Swat Valley" from Cambridge University and returned with some new and interesting ideas about the development of Gandhāra art. Briefly, he believes that the Buddhist art orginated in Swat valley and not in Gandhāra proper, that the Buddhist art and not necessarily Buddhism, started in Swat in the second century BC and continued to the ninth century AD (basis for the same is numismatic and not sculptural evidence), that the first image of Buddha was carved and shaped first in Swat than anywhere else, that the so far so-called Gandhāra art, is a misnomer as applied to the Buddhist art which flourished in this region, that it must be divided into different zonal schools, sub-zonal or regional styles of which Gandhāra style is only one and hence be studied under an overall geographical umbrella which he has named Indus-Oxus School of Buddhist Art, etc. and that the Swat valley style or Uddiyana style is the oldest of all (Swati 1997a, pp. 3-4). Actually, as far back as 1985, Prof. Susan L. Huntington in her book (Susan L. Huntington, 1985, pp. 133-134) proposed the term 'Bactro-Gandhāra School of Art' against the term 'Gandhāra Art'. She also advocated for considering the case of various different, distinct and recognizable schools of art at centres like Kapisa, Bactria, Swat and Gandhāra (Huntington 1985, p. 133) in preference to a single school of Gandhāra Art.

It is for the first time that the Swat material has been subjected to chronological studies and there is much that deserves our attention in Dr Swati's hypothesis. However, his emphasis on Swat sector is fraught with some problems especially when Swat sculptures are studied in isolation outside the mainstream of Buddhism and Buddhist art in neighbouring regions—Gandhāra, Taxila, Karakorum, etc. It has long since been acknowledged that Gandhāra is only a term of convenience. Dr Swati himself admits that "Gandhāra had been a region of fluctuating geo-political conditions as well as having a multi-ethnic social fabric (Swati 1997 b). The art which has been associated with the name of Gandhāra was in fact neither wholly Buddhist in spirit, nor entirely confined to the geographical limits of Gandhāra. The cultural boundaries of Gandhāra art have always overlapped their geographical boundaries. In an age when land routes were the only carriers of ideas and art forms, it is not understood as to how Buddhism reached and flourished in Swat without affecting the region through which it traversed before reaching Swat. Notwithstanding Swat's role in spread of Buddhism through its multiple sub-routes as part of major international arteries, but the way in which Buddhist art spread from the plains of Gandhāra, needed a strong political government, solid financial backing and a constant flow of international communities. For such a scenario, the plains of Gandhāra were suited better than the secluded and isolated valleys of Swat. Dr Swati himself admits this when be wrote: "Gandhāra was situated on the crossroad of east and west. The cosmopolitan nature of the region gave, therefore, a special and characteristic impact to its culture" (Swati 1997 b, p. 86). By his own explanation, Swat routes were only an appendix or a bypass of the main Karakorum Highway on the one hand and the Central Asian route through Bajaur, Chitral and Wakhan Pass (Swati 1997d, p. 153) on the other hand.

Another reservation in this respect is that the area of three zonal sub-styles of the 'Swat Style (Jambil sub-valley, the Adinzai and Shamozai sub-valley and Ilam Khwar sub-valley) of Dr Swati's hypothesis applies to the extremely small area of the Swat valley as a whole (Swati 1997a, map at p. 35). Another map (at p. 34) shows Dr Swati's three sub-zones placed next to the areas of greatest concentration of Buddhist sites in that part of Gandhāra on the southern side of the Malakand range. This entire area can be studied as one single unit and not as isolated compartments. No doubt, a study of zonal workshops of Gandhāra art needs to be studied more extensively. In this respect Dr Swati's study is quite admirable. But while serving a much larger community and professing the same faith, how these zonal workshops were interlinked to one another and how each workshop or sub-workshop can show its own chronological development, is difficult to say in the present state of our knowledge. Dr Swati himself has detected different strata of Graeco-Bactrian, Central Asia, Scytho-Parthian, Kuṣāṇa influences in his Swat style of Buddhist art (Swati 1997, pp. 7-15). The same extraneous elements affected contemporaneously the life, ideas and art in the adjoining regions of Swat, i.e. the mainland Gandhāra with a much stronger political urge and administrative drive than in Swat. These extraneous elements not only affected the religious art but the civilization as a whole. Whereas this extended influence is amply listed from excavations at Pushkalavati, Taxila, Begram, Aï Khanum, Takht-i-Sangeen, Surkh Kotal, etc., the similar discoveries in Swat valley are still awaited notwithstanding the excavations at Audigram Bazar site near Saidu Sharif. Another important factor missing in Dr Swati's approach is his total silence about the fresh and ample evidence available along the Karakorum Highway.

CONCLUSIONS

Up-to-date progress of Gandhāra studies in Pakistan during the last fifty years at best is erratic and inconclusive. The contribution of the Department of Archaeology and Museums is certainly not up to the mark. Whatever the net achievements, these have been without a direction and a goal in view. But for the solid contributions of the Italian, Japanese, German fieldworks and studies of the French, British and American archaeologists and art historians, the picture would have been dismal and dark. However, the total picture as it has emerged from the above discussion presents certain bright aspects of Gandhāra studies. In the first instance, instead of a limited group of scholars from three or four countries, scholars from a much wider geographical areas, both individuals and missions, are now busy in studying, researching, writing and publishing about Gandhāra art. Secondly, instead of warring over issues of Greek and Roman background, question of origin of the first image of Buddha or purely Mahāyāna contexts of this art as previously, now much more broader and important issues are being attended to and discussed. For the first time it is now being argued that in the development and spread of this art, the locals have played more important role than the Greeks and Romans. Besides, it is being enquired that neither Mahāyāna Buddhism was the exclusive religion glorified in or through this art nor other sects, cults and religions were totally excluded from its folds. For the first time it has also been widely acknowledged that the cult of Śiva has been universally present throughout Gandhāra territory and its cultural boundaries. Discovery of a huge sculpture from Dargai area representing Umā Maheśvara (now in Sackler Art Gallery, Washington) in typical Gandhāra stone and style has certainly revolutionized our concept of Gandhāra art. Dar's and Frankfort's studies of Gandhāra toilet trays and Dar's studies of Gandhāra architecture, coins and other household objects are good attempts at tracing out the evolution of Gandhāra art, whereas Rehman's studies of Hindu Shahi period archaeology has provided sufficient grounds to trace out continuity of this art after the onslaught of Hun invasion right upto the rise of Hindu Shahiyas. The discussion over the question of making of the first image of Buddha in Gandhāra or Mathura, is no more boisterous and polemic. Instead, it has mellowed down to purely academic discussions with due respect for views from opponent camps.

But still, there are failings in our studies, approaches and even attempts. The foremost one is that the concerned agencies are yet not in full control of potential Gandhāran sites from clandestine diggers. Whatever reconnaissance, survey, exploration and salvage operations have been carried out, have been on the already damaged and plundered sites (see Appendix 'A'). The government is not fully successful in preventing illegally excavated material going out of the country.

The scholars too have failed to study Gandhāra art in the background of Gandhāra civilization as a whole. Their emphasis is still on art and religion but what constituted the total life of the people and the region has failed to attract the attention of the scholars. The reason for the same is insufficient excavations at settlement sites of the period. Taxila still remains the classical example of excavation of a settlement site and still it fails to present a vivid picture of the society contemporary to the Buddhist art which flourished in the Taxila valley or elsewhere in whole of Gandhāra. The contemporary city site of Taxila namely Sirsukh still awaits to be excavated properly, scientifically and extensively. Among other contemporary cities only the site of ancient Pushkalavati (Shaikhan Dheri) has been partially excavated. Extensive excavations at this site are now almost impossible.

The greatest change we observe during this post independence period is a new objective approach towards the study of Gandhāra art. Among new scholars there is neither an obsession for Greek, Roman or classical background of Gandhāra art nor an enthusiasm for condemning it as a non-autochthonous creation. Both these attitudes marred the objectivity of earlier studies. Almost all the works which have so far appeared in post-1947 era, their titles speak about only Gandhāra art and wherever needed in the text they casually refer to the classical aspect of it.

It has now been accepted by all serious scholars that "if there are still so many unsolved problems in the study of Gandhāra art, this probably is due to the absence of any careful analysis of its various cultural components". The local or Pakistani contribution itself in particular, is due for a major reassessment. For this purpose, old studies and reports and material lying in older museums is not of much help. Instead, the archaeological evidence collected from excavations of various sites at Taxila, Shaikhan Dheri, Audigram Bazar, Gogdara and other purely Buddhist sites dug up under more scientific techniques will be of much more help. Dr Dani was the first to emphasize on this aspect of Gandhāra studies. For example, the classical tunic worn by royal ladies needs be studied along with baggy *salwars* and peaked caps (*kullahs*) of Central Asia or an Indian *dhoti*.

Another defect in our past studies is that Gandhāra has been regarded by most as a frontier province of the Indian subcontinent as well of the West. True, but Gandhāra did not lie only on certain frontiers of human civilizations, it also occupies a pivotal position in the movement of population from east, west and north. It had been a veritable homeland as well as holy-land of several people who chose to settle down, merge in the local population and regenerate themselves in the creation of the Gandhāra art and culture. It is this amalgam of several strains of social and cultural life that is represented in this art and only potential research and fresh excavations can disentangle them.

The problem needs to be tackled from two different angles. In the first place the archaeologists should now excavate those settlement sites, towns and villages which once acted as subsistence base for the nearby Buddhist monastic establishments. The settlement sites alone can help us build a reliable framework both for chronological sequence as to when a new ethnic, social, political on linguistic elements penetrated and affected our society and how the mosaic of changing patterns is evolved both in time aspect and space aspect.

As regards 'Greek presence', we have to tackle the problem in an offensive rather than defensive way. In the first instance we will have to explore, locate and then excavate the five Alexandrias which Alexander the Great founded in Pakistan. Search for Menander's Greek city "Sagala, also called Euthydemia", also needs to be searched and investigated. Discovery of a purely Greek city pulsating fully with Greek civilization at Aï Khanum is before us. Why a pure Greek city or a semi-Greek city like Taxila cannot be found here? Only concerted efforts of devoted persons are needed. Sites like Jalalpur Sharif, Mong Rasul, Sodhra, Kotla Mousa Khan, Uch Sharif, Mithan Kot, Sialkot (or some other site nearby), etc., offer promises. Greek levels of a few cities founded by the Indus-Greeks at Taxila and Pushkalavati also need to be reinvestigated at a larger scale than done hitherto.

The 'Western' material recovered from different strata of Greek, Scythian, Parthian and Kuṣāṇa layers of various city sites in Gandhāra and Afghanistan also needs to be reinvestigated and compared with the similar material recovered from intervening countries and reallocated to their historical setting and proper sources—i.e. whether persisting from the earlier generations of Greek settlers or recently imported by way of trade, commerce or mutual exchange as cultural curios, artist's and craftsmen's kit or as a part of household paraphernalia of new immigrants. The material needs to be further sifted out into categories such as to what has reached through land routes and what through sea. Still, what is more important is to study Gandhāra art not simply as a sculptural art or Buddhist art as hitherto done, but as a part of Gandhāra Civilization (Dar 1997). How much Greek or Roman influence is found in sculpture, architecture, numismatics, jewellery, metalware, ceramics, epigraphy, tools and implements, etc.? So far the problem has been tackled mainly from sculptural point of view. Studies from other angles are scarce and scanty. But their results are uniform and consistent, i.e. the Greek influence is persistent and all pervading, continuous and encompasses the entire set up as compared to Roman influence which is sparse, insignificant and disjointed. But still, fresh excavations and more researches both with new objectives in mind, are needed.

NOTES AND REFERENCES

1. Saeedur Rehman has edited and published the survey and brief excavations carried out in Buner (1991-92 & 1992-93), Swat Valley (1992-93), Bajaur Agency (1995), District Nowshehra (1996) and District Swabi (1992) by Dr Muhammad Ashraf Khan and M/s Shabbir Hussain, Muhammad Aqleem, Badshah Sardar, Abdul Nasir, Faizur Rahman, Abdul Azeem, Alia Jawwad, Muhammad Bahadur Khan and Habib Ullah Khan Khattak.
2. The Lahore Museum Primitive seated Buddha (size 120 x 100 x 49 cm) in red sandstone (No. H 671), actually came from the village Ahrwan, 3 miles/5 km from Palwal in District Gurgaon in Punjab, now Haryana. It came to Lahore Museum in July 1883 (see S. No. 389 of the Register I, Register of Additions, 1867-1903, p. 65). It is for the first time that the provenance of this important sculpture is being published.
3. These are : Alexandria Boucephalia and Alexandria Nicaia on the Hydaspes (River Jhelum) (Strabo, XV, 1, 29); Alexandria on the Upper Akesinus (River Chenab) (Arrian's Anabasis, V, 29.3); Alexandria on the confluence of Five Rivers at or near Punjnad and Alexandria Oreita, or Rhambakia or Alexandria Makarene near Makran (Arrian's Anabasis, VI. 29.5 & VI. 23.3). Also see Saifur Rahman Dar, *Taxila and Hellenism*, 2nd edn, Lahore : 1982, p. 5, f.n. 9.

APPENDICES

Appendix – A
PAKISTANI CONTRIBUTION TOWARDS GANDHĀRAN STUDIES AFTER 1947

A. EXCAVATION AND EXPLORATION REPORTS

Dani, A.H., 1965, "Shaikhan Dheri Excavation 1963-64: In Search of the Second City of Pushkalavati", *Ancient Pakistan,* Vol. II, pp. 17-208.

———, 1968-69, "Chakdara Fort and Gandhāra Art", *Ancient Pakistan,* Vol. IV, pp. 1-32.

———, 1968-69a, "Excavations at Andan Dheri", *Ancient Pakistan,* Vol. IV, pp. 33-64.

———, 1968-69b, "Excavations at Chatpat", *Ancient Pakistan,* Vol. IV, pp. 65-102.

———, 1968-69c, "Buddhist Rock Carvings in Dir", *Ancient Pakistan,* Vol. IV, pp. 251-57.

See also Dani under (b) in the following pages :

Dar, Saifur Rahman, 1970-71, "Excavations at Manikyala", *Pakistan Archaeology,* No. 7, pp. 6-22.

Durrani, F.A., 1997a, "Hazara Division: A Cradle of Gandhāra Civilization", *The News,* Lahore. October 19 and 26, 1997.

Durrani, F.A., Mian Said Qamar and Shah Nazar Khan, 1997, "Preliminary Report on Excavations at Manik Rai Dheri Off Panian Sarikot Road", *Athariyat,* Vol. I, pp. 213-26.

Faccenna, D., Ahmad Nabi Khan *et al.*, 1993, PANR (Swat, Pakistan), IsMEO, Rome.

Halim, M.A. and Khan Gulzar Muhammad, 1992, "Ghazi-Gariala Hydropower Project Archaeological Studies", *Pakistan Archaeology,* No. 27, pp. 15-30.

Ihsan Ali, 1994, "Settlement History of Charsada District", *Ancient Pakistan,* Vol. IX, pp. 101-11.

Jawad, Alia, 1994, "A Preliminary Report on the Faunal Remains from Sheikhan Dheri (Scytho-Parthian Period (132 BC - 93 AD)", *Journal of Central Asia,* Vol. XVII, No. 1 and 2, pp. 164-78.

Khan, Farid, 1992, "Recent Discoveries from the North-west Frontier, Pakistan", *South Asian Studies,* Vol. 8, 1992, pp. 67-79.

———, 1997, "Excavations at Akra: A Preliminary Report of 1996-97 Season", *Punjab Journal of Archaeology and History,* (In Press).

———, (ed.), 1998, Akra Excavation, *The Pakistan Heritage Society Newsletter,* No. 1, January, 1998, pp. 1, 5.

Khan, Gulzar Muhammad, see Halim, M.A.

Khan, M.A., 1994, "Historic Rock Carvings in Dir District", *East and West,* Vol. 44, Nos. 2-4, pp. 455-66.

Khan, S.N., 1995, "Marjanai", *Ancient Pakistan,* Vol. XI, pp. 1-74.

Khokhar, Masudul Hasan, 1996, *Archaeological Excavations at Musa I and Musa III.* A Ghazi Barotha Hydropower Project, published by Department of Archaeology and Museums, Lahore.

Rahman, Abdur, 1968-69, "Excavations at Damkot", *Ancient Pakistan* IV, pp. 103-250.

———, 1990, "Butkara III: A Preliminary Report", *South Asian Archaeology,* 1987, Pt. 2, pp. 693-705.

Rahman, Abdur, 1992, "Butkara III: A Preliminary Report", *Ancient Pakistan*, Vol. VII, pp. 152-63.

———, 1993a, "Shnaisha Gumbat: First Preliminary Excavation Report", *Ancient Pakistan*, Vol. VIII, *Professor Ahmed Hasan Dani Felicitation Volume*, Peshawar, pp. 1-124.

———, 1993b, "Recent Developments in Buddhist Archaeology in Pakistan", *South Asian Studies*, Vol. 9.

Rahman, Abdur, and Sardar Muhammad, 1984, "Balo Kile Gumbad (Swat) and Early Mediaeval Architecture of N.W.F.P", *Journal of Central Asian Studies Centre*, Peshawar, No. 15, Winter, pp. 123-46.

Rehman, Inayatur, 1968, "Swat Excavations", *Pakistan Archaeology*, No. 5, Nimogram Site, pp. 123-26.

Saeedur Rehman (ed.), 1996, *Archaeological Reconnaissance in Gandhāra-1996*. The Department of Archaeology, Pakistan, Karachi.

Said Qamar, Mian, "Excavations at Garh Mauryan, Hazara District", *Journal of Central Asia*, Vol. XIII, No. 1, July, 1990, pp. 95-154.

Said Qamar, Mian and Dr Muhammad Ashraf Khan, 1991, "Preliminary Report on the Archaeological Excavations of Buddhist Sites in Swat, NWFP, 1989-90", *Journal of Central Asia*, Vol. XIV, No. 2, pp. 173-234.

Shah Nazar, 1995, "Preliminary Report of Excavations at Marjamai, Kabal, Swat", *Ancient Pakistan*, Vol. XI, pp. 7-25.

Shah Nazar and Said Qamar, 1998, " Pannian Excavation", *Journal of Ancient Civilizations*, Islambad, Vol. XXI, No. 2, December.

Sharif, Muhammad, 1969, "Report on Bhir Mound Excavations", *Pakistan Archaeology*, No. 6, pp. 62-99.

———, 1974-86, "Excavations at Haji Shah Morr", *Pakistan Archaeology*, Nos. 10-22, pp. 36-56.

B. BOOKS, CATALOGUES, GUIDES AND RESEARCH PAPERS

Alam, Humera, 1988, *Gandhāra Sculptures in Lahore Museum*, Lahore Museum Publication, Lahore.

———, 1988a, "Akhnur Terracottas in Lahore Museum", *Lahore Museum Bulletin*, Vol. I, No. 2.

———, 1990, "Lahore Museum Collection of Stucco Sculptures from Rokri", *Lahore Museum Bulletin*, Vol. III, No. 1, pp. 43-54.

———, 1991, "Manila Mukha Jataka: A Pre-natal Story of Buddha Discovered for the First Time", *Lahore Museum Bulletin*, Vol. III, No. 2.

———, 1994, "The Sikri Stupa in Lahore Museum", *Lahore Museum Bulletin*, Vol. VII, No. 1 and 2.

Anonymous, 1956, *Gandhāra Sculptures in the National Museum of Pakistan*, Department of Archaeology in Pakistan, Karachi, Reprinted in 1964.

Dani, A.H., 1968, *Gandhāra Art in Pakistan*, Peshawar University, Peshawar.

———, 1969, "Kushana Civilization in Pakistan", *Journal of Asiatic Society of Pakistan*, Dacca, Vol. XIX, No. 1.

———, 1979, "Buddhists in Sindh as Given in Chachnameh", *Journal of Central Asia*, Vol. II, pp. 25-38.

———, 1983, *Chilas: The City of Nanga Parvat* (Dyamar), Quaid-e-Azam University, Islamabad.

———, (ed.) 1984, *Journal of Central Asia*, Islamabad, particularly refer to two issues—Vol. VII, Nos. 1 and 2, and Vol. VIII, Nos. 1 and 2, July and December 1985, containing several articles devoted to the study of Buddhist history and art of the Karakorum Highway leading to Central Asia in China.

———, 1985, "The Sacred Rock of Hunza" in *Journal of Central Asia*, Vol. VII, Pt. 2, pp. 5-124. (Also reprinted as a booklet).

———, 1986, *The Historic City of Taxila*, UNESCO, Tokyo.

———, 1987, "Origin of the Buddha: The Chilas Evidence", *Journal of Central Asia*, Vol. X, No. 2, pp. 37-50.

———, 1988, *Recent Archaeological Discoveries in Pakistan*. Published by the Centre of East Asian Cultural Studies, UNESCO, Tokyo, chap. 5, Early Historic Period. Discoveries in the Peshawar Valley, pp. 77-92.

Dani, A.H., 1992, *Gandhāran Art in Pakistan*, Department of Films and Publications, Islamabad.

Dar, Saifur Rahman, 1973, *Hellenistic Elements in the Architecture of Taxila* (in Greek), Society of Macedonian Studies, Salonica (Greece).

———, 1977, "Gandhāra Art and the Roman Influence on it: Numismatic Evidence", *Rivista Italiana di Numismatica*, Roma, Italy, pp. 61-89.

———, 1977a, *Taxila : An Ancient City* (in Punjabi), Pakistan Punjabi Adabi Board, Lahore.

———, 1979, "Toilet Trays from Gandhāra", *Journal of Central Asia*, Vol. II, No. 2, pp. 141-84.

———, 1980, "Toilet Trays from Gandhāra and Beginning of Hellenism in Pakistan". Chapter in *Commemorative Volume: Megas Alexanderas - 2300 years After His Death*. Society of Macedonian Studies, Salonica, pp. 49-85.

———, 1980a, "A Fresh Study of Four Unique Temples at Takshasila (Taxila)," *Journal of Central Asia*, Vol. III, No. 1, pp. 91-138.

———, 1983, *Taxila and Hellenism: Architectural Evidence. A New Approach to the Study of Gandhāra Art*. Published by the Author, Lahore.

———, 1983a, "Taxila and the Classical World", *Journal of Central Asia*, Vol. VI, No. 1, pp. 113-39.

———, 1984, *Taxila and the Western World*, Waqar Publications, Lahore.

———, 1985, "Rock-cut Standing Figure at Kargah, Near Gilgit', *Journal of Central Asia*, Vol. VIII, No. 2, pp. 191-212.

———, 1987, "In Search of the Original House of Fasting Buddha" (Urdu), *Fortnightly Deed Shuneed*, Lahore, Vol. 5, No. 4, pp. 31-34.

———, 1989, "Chronology and Typology of Buddhist Monasteries of Gandhāra, *Lahore Museum Bulletin*, Vol. XXI, No. 1, pp. 23-38.

———, 1990, "Criteria and Problems of the Study of Gandhāra Art", *Journal of Central Asia*, Islamabad, Vol. XIII, No. 2, pp. 149-90.

———, 1991, "Kushana Art of Mathura: A Bridge Between Gandhāra and Amaravati", *Lahore Museum Bulletin*, Vol. IV, No. 1.

———, 1992, "Documentation Record of Gandhāra Collection of Lahore Museum", *Lahore Museum Bulletin*, Vol. V, No. 2, pp. 19-44.

———, 1993, "Dating the Monuments of Taxila". A chapter in: *Urban Form and Meaning in South Asia: The Shaping of Cities from Prehistoric to Pre-colonial Times*. Edited by Howard Spodek and Doris Srinivasan. National Gallery of Art, Washington D.C., pp. 109-21.

———, 1994a, "Classical Approaches to the Study of Gandhāra Art", Chap. 2 in *Perceptions of South Asia's Visual Past*, ed. Catherine B. Asher and Thomas R. Metcalf. Published by American Institute of India Studies, New Delhi and Swadharma Swarajaya Sangha, Madras, pp. 37-46.

———, 1997, "In Quest of Gandhāra Civilization", *Lahore Museum Bulletin*, Vol. IX, No. 2, July-December, 1996, pp. 45-50. Paper presented in Panel Debate: "Indus Valley - The Known and the Unknown", organized by the Asian Study Group, Islamabad on 7.3.1997.

———, 1998, *Taxila and the Western World*, Second updated edition with additional coloured illustrations. Library and Information Management Academy, Lahore.

———, 1998a, "Gandhāra Art in Perspective", *Journal of Asian Civilizations*, Vol. XXI, No. 2, Dec., 1998, pp. 71-118.

Dar, Saifur Rahman, *et al.*, 1994, "Kushan Art", in *History of Civilizations of Central Asia*, Vol. II. *The Development of Sedentary and Nomadic Civilizations: 700 B.C. to A.D. 250*. Edited by Janos Harmatta, B.N. Puri and G.F. Etemadi, UNESCO Publication of Paris.

Khan, Ahmed Nabi, 1976 ?, *Buddhist Art and Architecture in Pakistan*, Ministry of Information and Broadcasting, Islamabad, n.d.

Khan, Ahmed Nabi, 1994, *Gandhāra: The Enchanting Land of Buddhist Art and Culture in Pakistan*, Department of Archaeology and Museums, Karachi.

Khan, M. Ashraf, 1993, *Gandhāra Sculptures in the Swat Museum*, published by the author, Saidu Sharif.

Khan, Muhammad Bahadur, 1994, *Gandhāra Stone Sculptures in Taxila Museum*, The Pioneer Publishers, Lahore.

Khan, Muhammad Ishtiaq, 1966, "Mathura Objects in Taxila Museum", *Journal of the Asiatic Society of Pakistan*, Dacca, Vol. XI, No. 1, pp. 41-49.

Khan, Muhammad Ishtiaq, 1978, "Metal Statuetts from Taxila", *Senarat Paranavittana*, Commemorative Volume. Edited by Leelanda Prematillaka *et al.*, Leiden, pp. 122-24.

Khan, Muhammad Wali Ullah, 1965, "Inception of Gandhāra Sculpture", *East and West*, Rome, New Series, Vol. 15, Nos. 1-2, January 1964 - March 1965.

———, 1988, *Gandhāra* (in Urdu), Lok Virsa, Islamabad.

Khan, Nazir Ahmed, 1990, "A New Relief from Gandhāra Depicting the Trojan Horse", *East and West*, Vol. 40, Nos. 1-4, pp. 315-19.

———, 1993, "Rock Engraving from Hatiano Kandao", *Journal of Central Asia*, Vol. VI, No. 2, pp. 59-68.

———, 1994, "Rock Paintings at Nokkono Ghwand (Swat)", in G. Fussman and K. Jettmar (Col.), *Antiquities of Northern* Areas, Vol. 35, Mainz.

———, *et al.*, 1995, "The Recent Discovery of Cave Paintings in Swat: A Preliminary Note", *East and West*, Vol. 45, Nos. 1-4, pp. 333-93.

Namus, M.S., 1958, "The Bodhisattava at Gilgit (A Newly Discovered Buddhist Monument)", *The Museum Journal of Pakistan*, Vol. 12, No. 2, pp. 83-92.

Saeedur Rehman, 1990, "Unique Find of a Gold Ornament from Pattan, Kohistan", *Journal of Central Asia*, Vol. XIII, No. 1, pp. 5-18.

———, 1990a, "Introduction to Gandhāra: Some Fresh Additions to Sculptures in the Possession of the Department of Archaeology, S.R.O., Peshawar", *Journal of Central Asia*, Vol. XIII, No. 1, pp. 47-72.

———, 1990b, "Bodhisattava Image", *Journal of Central Asia*, Vol. XIII, No. 1, pp. 89-94.

Sardar, Badshah, 1995, "Archaeological Panorama of Hazara Division", *Journal of Central Asia*, Vol. XVIII, No. 1, pp. 81-105.

Sardar, Badshah, and Saleemul Haq, 1997, "Gandhāra: A Buddhist School of Art", *Journal of Central Asia*, Vol. XX, No. 1, pp. 151-68.

Said Qamar, Mian, 1976-1986, "Rock Carvings and Inscriptions from Tor-Dherai (District Loralai)", *Pakistan Archaeology*, Nos. 10-22, pp. 168-78.

Sehrai, Fidaullah, 1978, *The Buddha Story in Peshawar Museum*, Peshawar Museum Publications, reprinted in 1982.

———, 1986, *Takht-i-Bahi*, published by the Author, Peshawar.

Shakur, M.A., 1954, *A Guide to the Peshawar Museum*, Peshawar.

———, 1963, *Gandhāra Sculpture in Pakistan*, a SEATO Publication, Bangkok.

Swati, Muhammad Farooq, 1996a, *Gandhāra Art in Swat Valley, Pakistan: A Study Based on the Peshawar University Collection*, Ph.D. Thesis of Cambridge University (unpublished).

———, 1996b, "A Note on the Relief Panels from Chargepate, Dir, Depicting Incidents from the Story of the Stupa of Ramagruma", *The Journal of Humanities and Social Sciences*, Vol. IV, No. l, March, pp. 74-82.

———, 1997a, "Special Features of the Buddhist Art in the Swat Valley", *Athariyat* (Archaeology), Peshawar, Vol. 1, pp. 1-60.

———, 1997b, "Gandhāra and the Exploration of Gandhāra Art of Pakistan", *Athariyat*, Vol. 1, pp. 77-95.

———, 1997c, "Garland Bearer Reliefs from Butkara in Swat", *Athariyat*, Vol. 1, pp. 115-21.

———, 1997d, "Recent Discovery of Buddhist Sites in Swat Valley", *Athariyat*, Vol. I, pp. 151-92.

———, 1997e, "Pre Kushana Reliquaries from Pataka, Swat" *Journal of the Royal Asiatic Society*, 3rd series, Vol. 7, Pt. 2 July, 1997, pp. 249-55.

———, 1998, "The Indus-Oxus School of Buddhist Art", in F.A. Durrani and Ihsan Ali (eds.), *The Glory that was Pakistan: 50 Years of Archaeological Research in Pakistan*, Peshawar, pp. 27-36.

C. EXCAVATION / EXPLORATIONS CARRIED OUT BUT REPORTS AWAITED

(1) In 1967, Dr Saifur Rahman Dar and Gulzar Muhammad Khan, both of the Department of Archaeology and Museums, surveyed some area in District Rawalpindi and identified several

Buddhist sites. They also sunk a deep trench at Manikyala near the main stupa. Only the report of their excavations have so far been published (see Dar, 1970-71).

(2) In 1967, Muhammad Rafique Mughal of the Department of Archaeology, excavated at Nimogram in Swat. The excavations at this site were continued in coming years by Inayatur Rehman and Nazir Ahmad Khan. Only Inayatur Rehman has produced a small report (see Inayatur Rehman)

(3) In 1967, Muhammad Rafique Mughal excavated the site of Pan Dheri, near Bakhshali, Dist. Mardan. The report is still awaited.

(4) In 1993, Prof. Farid Khan of the Directorate of Archaeology, Peshawar, re-excavated the site of Sheikhan Dheri. Only Alia Jawad published a preliminary report on the faunal remains of the Scytho-Parthian period (see Jawad).

(5) In 1993, Prof. Farid Khan of the Directorate of Archaeology, NWFP, Peshawar, excavated at Gangu Dher, also called Aziz Dheri. The report is still awaited. Excavation on this site continued by his successors (Zainul Waheed of the Mardan Museum and others) during 1993, 1994, 1995 and 1996 but reports are still awaited.

(6) In 1966, Dr Abdur Rahman, Peshawar University, dug a trial trench at the site of Gumbatuna, Dir. Only a small paragraph about this excavation appeared in Dr Rahman's book, *Two Hindu Shahiya Dynasties*.

(7) In 1975-77, M/s Abdul Aziz Farooq and Gulzar Muhammad Khan excavated the site of Mian Ali Faqiran, Dist. Sheikhupura. Report is still awaited.

Note [1]:-The contents of Appendix A have been copied from Dar 1998a.
Note [2]:-Contributions in the fields of Aramaic and Kharoshti epigraphy as well in numismatics have been omitted in this paper.

Appendix – B
INDIAN CONTRIBUTION TOWARDS GANDHĀRA STUDIES AFTER 1947

ONLY BOOKS AND CATALOGUES

Bhattacharya, D.C., (ed.), *Gandhāra Sculpture in the Government Museum and Art Gallery*, Chandigarh, 2002.

Das, Sri Dibakar, See Anasua Sengupta (below).

Joshi, N.P. and R.C. Sharma, 1969, *Catalogue of Gandhāra Sculptures in the State Museun, Lucknow*, The State Museum, Lucknow.

Murthy, K. Krishna, 1977, *The Gandhāra Sculptures: A Cultural Survey*, Ajanta Publications, Delhi.

Nehru, Lolita, 1989, *Origins of the Gandhāra Style*, Cambridge University Press, New Delhi.

Paul, Suwarcha, 1986, *Gandhāra Sculptures in Chandigarh Museum*, Chandigarh.

Sengupta, Anasua and Dibakar Das, 1991, *Gandhāra Holding in the Indian Museum: A Handlist*, Indian Museum, Calcutta.

Sen Gupta, Nilima, 1984, *Cultural History of Kapisa and Gandhāra*, Sundeep Prakashan, Delhi.

Sharma, R.C., See N.P. Joshi (above).

Sharma, R.C., (ed.), *Buddhism and Gandhāra Art*, 2004.

Varma, K.M., 1987, *Technique of Gandhāran and Indo-Afghan Stucco Images*, Proddu Santiniketan.

Note : Contributions on Kharoshti epigraphy and numismatic have been omitted in this list as also the articles by scholars like R.C. Sharma and R.C. Agrawala.

BIBLIOGRAPHY

Abu Imam, 1966, *Sir Alexander Cunningham and the Beginning of Indian Archaeology*, Dacca.

Ackermann, H.C., 1975, *Narrative Stone Reliefs from Gandhāra in Victoria and Albert Museum, London*. Rome.

Agrawala, R.C., 1992, "Skanda with Cock and Peacock: A Rare Device in Gandhāra Art", in *Eastern Approaches*, ed. T.S. Maxwell, Delhi, pp. 130-32.

———, 1993a, "Skanda Karttikeya in Gandhāran Art", in *Roopa Lekha*, 62-63, pp. 48-53.

———, 1993b, "Sasthi in Gandhāra Art", *East and West*, Vol. 43, pp. 271-75.

———, 1995, "Skanda-Sasthi in Gandhāran Reliefs-A Review", *East and West*, Vol. 45, No. 1-4, pp. 329-33.

Agrawala, R.C. and Maurizio Taddei, "An Interesting Relief from the Swat Valley", *East and West*, New Series, Vol. 16, Nos. 1-2, March-June, pp. 82-88, figs. 1-5.

Alam, Humera, see Alam in App. 'A'.

Allchin, F.R., 1957, "The Cultural Sequences of Bactrian", *Antiquity*, Vol. XXXI, pp. 131-41.

———, 1968, "Archaeology and the Date of Kanishka : The Taxila Evidence", Papers on the Date of Kanishka, ed. by A.L. Basham, Leiden, pp. 4-34.

———, 1972, "A Cruciform Reliquary from Shaikhan Dheri", *Aspects of Indian Art*, ed. P. Pal, Leiden, pp. 15-26.

Anonymous, 1984, *The Exhibition of Gandhāra Art of Pakistan*, NHK Service Centre Inc., Tokyo.

———, 1992, *Ranigat: A Buddhist Site in Gandhara, Pakistan, Surveyed 1983-1992*. Report of the Kyoto University Scientific Expedition to Gandhāra.

Aviella, Goblet d'Aviella, 1967, Le que I'Inde doit a la Grec: Les Influence Classique dans la civilization de I'Inde. Paris.

Bernard, Paul, 1967, "Aï Khanum on the Oxus: A Hellenistic City in Central Asia", Proceedings, British Academy, LII, pp. 71-95.

Bernard, Paul and Ch. P. Jullien, 1982, "Halteres votives de lutteurs dans le Gandhāra", *Studia Iranica*, tome 11, pp. 33-47, pl. I-IV.

Bivar, A.D.H., 1991, "The Historical Origins of the Art of Gandhāra", *Pakistan Archaeology*, No. 26, Silver Jubilee Number, pp. 61-72.

Bussagli, M., 1984, "L'arte del Gandhāra", Torino.

Callieri, Pierfrancesco, 1989a, *Saidu Sharif I (Swat, Pakistan): The Buddhist Sacred Area, The Monastery*, Rome.

———, 1989b,"Bir-kot-ghwandai : An Early Historic Town in Swat (Pakistan)", *South Asian Archaeology*, 1989, pp. 339-46.

———, 1990, "Excavation at Bir-Kot-Ghwandai, Swat : 1987", *Pakistan Archaeology*, No. 25, pp. 163-92, pl. VII-X.

———, 1997, *Seals and Sealing from the North-west of the Indian Subcontinent and Afghanistan (4th Century B.C. 11th Century A.D.). Local, Indian, Sasanian, Graeco-Persian, Sogdian, Roman*. Instituto Universitario Orientale, Naples: 1997.

Carter, M.L., 1968, "Dionysiac Aspect of Kushana Art", *Arts Orientalis*, Vol. VII, pp. 121-46.

———, 1970, *A Study of Dionysiac Imagery in Kushan Art*, Ph.D. Thesis. Ann Arbor University, Michigan.

Cribb, Joe, 1984, "The Origin of Buddha Image: The Numismatic Evidence", *South Asian Archaeology* 1981, Edited by Bridget Allchin, Cambridge, pp. 231-44.

———, "Shiva Images on Kushan and Kushano- Sasanian Coins", in *Studies in Silk Road Coins and Culture*, Edited by Katsume Tanabe and Joe Cribb. Published by the Institute of Silk Road Studies, Kamakura (Japan), 1997, pp. 11-66 (With excellent bibliography for further reading).

Dani, See under Dani, A.H., in App. 'A'.

Dar, See under Dar., Saifur Rahman, in App. 'A'.

Das, Sri Dibakar, See under App. 'B'

Davidson, J. le Roi, 1955, "Gandhāran Exhibits at Yale and Harvard", *Artibus Asiae*, Vol. XVIII, pp. 77-78.

Dobbins, K. Walton, 1963, "Iconographic Considerations on a Gandhāra Relief in The National Museum of Oriental Art in Rome", *East and West*, New Series, Vol. 14, Nos. 1-2, March-June, pp. 38-55.

———, 1967, A Note on the Hariti Image from Skarah- Dheri, year 399", in *East and West*, New Series, Vol. 17, Nos. 3-4, pp. 268-72.

———, 1968a, "Two Gandhāran Reliquaries", *East and West*, New Series, Vol. 18, Nos. 1-2, March-June, pp. 151-62, figs. 1-11.

———, 1968b, "Gandhāra Buddha Images with Inscribed Dates", *East and West*, New Series, Vol. 18, Nos. 3-4, Sept. - Dec., pp. 281-88, figs. 1-10.

———, 1971, "The Stupa and Vihara of Kanishka I", *The Asiatic Society*, Calcutta.

———, 1973, Gandhāra Art from Stratified Excavations", in *East and West*, New Series, Vol. 23, Nos. 3-4, pp. 279-94.

Errington, Elizabeth, 1987a, *The Western Discovery of the Art of Gandhāra and the Find of Jamal Garhi*, Ph.D. Thesis, School of Oriental and African Studies, University of London.

———, 1987b, Tahkal : The Nineteenth Century Record of Two Lost Gandhāran Sites", *Bulletin of the School of Oriental and African Studies*, London: Vol. L, pt. 3, pp. 301-24.

———, 1990, "Documents Relating to the So-called Athena of the Lahore Museum", *Lahore Museum Bulletin*, Vol. III, No. 1, pp. 19-28.

———, 1991, "Addenda to Ingholt's Gandhāra Art in Pakistan", *Pakistan Archaeology*, No. 26, pp. 48-70.

———, 1993, "In Search of Pa-lu-sha, a City of the Central Gandhāra Plain", *Bulletin of the Asian Institute of Iranian Studies* in Honour of A.D.H. Bivar, Vol. 7, pp. 55-66.

Fabregues, C., 1987, "The Indo-Parthian Beginning of Gandhāra Sculpture", *Bulletin of the Asian Institute*, Vol. 1.

Facenna, Dominico, 1964, *A Guide to the Excavations in Swat (Pakistan), 1956-1962*, Rome.

———, 1964a, *Sculptures from the Sacred Area of Butkara I (Swat), West Pakistan*. Report and Memoirs of IsMEO, Rome, Vol. II-2, Rome 1962, Vol. II-3, Rome 1964.

———, 1974, "Excavations of the Italian Archaeological Mission (IsMeo) in Pakistan: Some Problems of Gandhāra Art and Architecture", in *Central Asia in the Kushan Period. Proceedings of the International Conference*, Dushambe, 2 vols., Moscow.

———, 1980-1981, Butkara I (Swat, Pakistan) 1956-1962, Parts 1-3, Text, Rome: 1980; Part 4, Text, Rome, 1981; Part 5-1, Plates, Rome, 1981.

———, 1993a, "Notes on Decorative Motifs Appearing on a Blanket in a Gandhāra Art Relief" *JCA*, Vol. XVIII, pp. 1-15.

———, 1995, "A Relief in the Lahore Musum Showing a Columned Stupa", *Lahore Museum Bulletin*, Vol. VIII, No. 2, pp. 1-34

Facenna, Dominico, *et al.*, 1993, *PANR (Swat, Pakistan)*, IsMEO, Rome.

Foucher, A., 1963, *The Life of the Buddha*, trans. S.Boas, Wesleyan, Conn.

Frankfort, Henri-Paul, 1979, *Les Palettes du Gandhāra. Diffusion de Boccard*, Paris.

Fussman, Gerard, 1990, "Un masque de Shiva provensnt du Gandhāra", *Revue de la Bibliotheque Nationale*, Automne, pp. 42-47.

———, 1991, "Le MASQUE COURT : Une effigie en laiton de Siva au Gandhāra", *Journal Asiatique*, tome CCLXXIX, Numero 1-2, 1991, pp. 137-174.

Groli, Gherardo, "The Tyche and the Dioscuri in Ancient Sculptures from the Valley of Swat", *East and West*, New Series, Vol. 14, Nos. 1-2, March-June, pp. 1-10, 29-37.

Goetz, Herman, 1959, "Imperial Rome and the Genesis of the Indian Art", *East and West*, New Series, Vol. 10, Nos. 3-4

Grunwedel, Albert, 1901, Buddhist Art of India, London, Indian Reprint : 1965.

Gupta, N.S., see under App. 'B'.

Halim, M.A., see under App. 'A'.

Hallade, M., 1968, *The Gandhāra Style and the Evolution of Buddhist Art*, London.

———, 1968a, *Gandhāra Art of North India and the Graeco- Buddhist Traditions in India, Persia and Central Asia*, Harry N. Abrams Inc. New York.

Hauptmann, Harald, 1997, "Rock Art in the Upper Indus Valley", in *The Indus: Cradle and Crossroads of Civilizations*. Pakistan-German Archaeological Research (Edited by Harald Hauptmann). Published by Embassy of the Federal Republic of Germany, Islamabad, pp. 29-60.

Huntington, J.C., 1980, "A Gandhāran Image of Amitayus Sukhawati", Annali dell Islituto Orientale du Napoli, Vol. 40, Nos. XXX, Naples.

———, 1985, "The Origin" of the Buddha Image : Early Image Traditions and the Concept of the Buddhadar-Sanapunya", in A.K. Narain's (ed.) *Studies in Buddhist Art of South Asia*, New Delhi.

Huntington, Susan L. and John C. Huntington, 1985, *The Art of Ancient India: Buddhist, Hindu, Jain*, New York.

Ingholt, Harald, 1958, *Gandhāran Art in Pakistan*, Pantheon Books, New York.

Jawwad, Alia, See under App. 'A'.

Jettmer, Karl *et al.* (Ed.), 1989-1994, *Antiquities of Northern Pakistan. Reports and Studies*. Mainz. Vol. 1 : 1989, Vol. 2: 1992, and Vol. 3: 1994. *Rock Inscriptions in the Indus Valley*. (Also see copious bibliography of previous works by the members of the Pak-German Expedition in Northern Pakistan at pp. VI-X in Vol. I of this series both by Dr A.H. Dani, Karl Jettmer, G. Fussman and others).

Joshi, N.P., See under App. 'B'

Kempe, D.R.C., 1982, "Nature and Source of the Gandhāra Sculptural Schist", *Journal of Archaeological Science*, London, Vol. 9, pp. 25-28.

Khan, Ahmad Nabi, See under App. 'A'.

Khan, M. Ashraf, See under App. 'A'.

Khan, Muhammad Bahadur, *Ibid.*

Khan, Muhammad Ishtiaq, *Ibid.*

Khan, Muhammad Wali Ullah, *Ibid.*

Khan, Nazir Ahmed, *Ibid.*

Keay, John, 1979, *The Gilgit Game : The Explorers of the Western Himalayas, 1865-95*, London.

Khokhar, Masudul Hasan, See under App. 'A'.

Klimburg-Salter, Deborah and Maurizio Taddei, 1990, "The Ushnisha and the Brahmarandhra: An Aspect of Light Symbolism in Gandaharan Buddha Images", *Aksayanivi*: Essays presented to Dr Debala Mitra in admiration of her scholarly contributions, Edited by Dr Gouriswar Bhattacharya, India Books Centre, Delhi, pp. 73-93, figs. 1-18.

Kurita, Isao, 1988, Gandhāra Art, Vol. I, *The Buddha's Life Story*, Nigensha Publishing Co. Ltd., Tokyo.

———, 1990, Gandhāra Art, Vol. II, *The World of Buddha*, Nigensha Publishing Co. Ltd., Tokyo.

Kuwayama, Shoshin, 1974, etc., *Excavations at Tapa Sikander*, Second Report 1972, Third Report 1974, Fourth Report 1976.

———, 1975, "Khair Khaneh and its Chinese Evidence", *Orient*, Vol. XI, 1975, pp. 93-107.

———, 1978, Notes on the "Introduction of the Square Podium to Taxilan Stupas", *Orient*.

———, 1982, "Kapisi and Gandhāra According to Chinese Buddhist Sources", *Orient*, Vol. XVIII, 1982, pp. 133-39.

———, 1984, "Buddhist Temples in Taxila and Gandhāra: A Historical Review of Monastic Arrangements", in *The Exhibition of Gandhāra Art of Pakistan*. NHK Service Centre Inc., Tokyo, pp. 216-20.

———, 1987, "The Buddha's Bowl in Gandhāra and relevant Problems", *South Asian Archaeology, 1987*, pp. 945-78.

———, 1989, "The Hephthalites in Tokharistan and Northwest India", Reprinted for private circulation from Zibun: Annals of the Institute for Research in Humanities, Kyoto University, pp. 89-134.

———, 1990, The Buddha's Bowl in Gandhāra and Relevant Problems, in M.Taddei (Ed.), *South Asian Archaeology*, 1987, Rome: 964-971.

———, 1992, "The Hepthalites in Tokharistan and Gandhāra", Part I, *Lahore Museum Bulletin*, Vol. V, (1), pp. 1-24, and Pt. II, Lahore Museum Bulletin, Vol. V, No. 2, pp. 1-18.

———, 1996, "Shahji ki Dheri", *Lahore Museum Bulletin*, Vol. IX, 1, pp. 31-58.

———, 1997, *The Main Stūpa of Shah-ji-ki-Dheri: A Chronological Outlook*, Kyoto University, Kyoto,

Lohuizen-de Leeuw, J.E. Van, 1949, The "Scythian" Period, Leiden.
———, 1981, "New Evidence with Regard to the Origin of the Buddha Image", *South Asian Archaeology*, 1979, Edited by Herbert Hartal, Berlin, pp. 377-400.
Marshall, Sir John, 1947, "Greeks and Sakas in India", *Journal of Royal Asiatic Society*, pp. 3-32.
———, 1951, *Taxila*, 3 vols., Cambridge.
———, 1960, *The Buddhist Art of Gandhāra : The Story of the Early Schools, its Birth, Growth and Decline*, Cambridge.
Mizuno, Seiichi, 1969, "Mekha Sanda: Buddhist Monastery in Pakistan", Surveyed in 1962-1967, Kyoto.
———, 1962, *Haibak and Kashmir Smast : Buddhist Cave Temples in Afghanistan and Pakistan*, Kyoto.
Mizuno, Seiichi, and T. Higuchi, 1978, "Thareli : Buddhist Site in Pakistan", Surveyed in 1963-1967, Kyoto, Dohosha.
Mukherjee, B.N., 1993, "The Skarah Dheri Hariti", *National Museum Bulletin*, New Delhi, Nos. 7-8, pp. 3-6.
Murthy, K.K., See under App. 'B'.
Nagar, S.D., 1981, *Gandhāran Sculpture: A Catalogue of Collection in the Museum of Art and Archaeology*, Columbia, Missouri.
Namus, M.S., See under App. 'A'.
Narain, A.K., 1985, "First Image of the Buddha: Ideology and Chronology", in *Studies in Buddhist Art of South Asia*. Ed. by A.K. Narain, New Delhi.
Nehru, Lolita, 1989, *Origins of Gandhāran Styles: A Study of Contributary Influences*, Oxford University Press, New Delhi.
Nishikawa, Koji, 1986, *Gandhāra 1: Rani Ghat : Preliminary Report on the Comprehensive Survey of Gandhāra Buddhist Sites, 1983-84*, by the Kyoto University Scientific Mission to Gandhāra, Kyoto, pp. 69-104.
———, 1988, *Gandhāra 2: Rani Ghat : Preliminary Report on the Comprehensive Survey of Buddhist Sites in Gandhāra, 1986*, by Koyoto University Scientific Mission to Gandhāra, Kyoto, pp. 81-139.
Paul, Suwarcha, See under App. 'B'.
Pugachankova, G.A., 1982, *The Art of Gandhāra* (in Russian with English Summary), Moscow.
Quagliotti, Anna Maria, 1989, "Mahakarunika", *Annali*, Vol. 49, Napoli, pp. 337-70.
———, 1990 "Gandhāra Art, I : A Note on a Recently Published Collection of Photographs", *East and West*, Vol. 40, Nos. 1-4, December, pp. 321-34.
———, 1998, *Buddhapadas : An Essay on the Representation of the Footprints of the Buddha*. Kamakura.
Rahman, Abdur, See under App. 'A'.
Rehman, Inayatur, *Ibid.*
Rhi, Ju-Hyung, 1994, "From Bodhisattva to Buddha: The Beginning of Iconic Representation in Buddhist Art", *Artibus Asiae*, Vol. LIV, No. 3-4, pp. 207-25.
Roberts, Eileen, 1959, "Greek Deities in the Buddhist Art of India", *Oriental Art*, Vol. 3, pp. 114-19.
Rosenfield, John M., 1967, *The Dynastic Arts of the Kushanas*, Berkeley/Los Angeles.
Rowland, Benjamin, 1949, "The Hellenistic Tradition in North Western India", *Art Bulletin*, Vol. XXXI, No. 1, pp. 1-10
———, 1960, *Gandhāra Sculptures from Pakistani Museums*, New York.
———, 1963, "The Evolution of the Buddha Image, New York.
———, 1970, *The Art and Architecture of India*, 1st Ed. Melbourn, London : 1953, Paperback, Harmondsworth.
Roy, Sourindranath, 1951, *The Story of Indian Archaeology*, 1784-1947, Archaeological Survey of India, New Delhi.
Saeedur Rehman, See under App. 'A'.
Said Qamar, Mian, *Ibid.*
Sardar, Badshah, *Ibid.*
Schmidt, Carolyn Woodford, 1990, *Bodhisattva Headdresses and Hairstyles in the Buddhist Art of Gandhāra and Related Regions of Swat and Afghanistan*. Ph.D. Dissertation submitted to the Graduate School of the Ohio State University, Ohio in 1990 (3 vols.).

Schmitt, Erika, 1971, Ornamenti in der Gandharakunst and regenten Volkskunst in Hindukush and Karakorum. Dissertationsreihe des Sudasiens Instituts der Universtat Heidelberg, Weisbaden : 1971.
Sehrai, Fidaullah, See under App. 'A'.
Sengupta, Anasua, See under App. 'B'.
Schlumberger, Daniel, 1960, "Descendants non-mediterraneans de 'Iart grecs', *Syria*, Vol. XXXVII.
———, 1961, "The Excavations at Surkh Kotal and the Problems of Hellenism in Bactria and India", *Proceeding of British Academy*, Vol. XLVII, pp. 77-95.
———, 1961a, "Sir John Marshall and Gandhāra Art", *Antiquity*, Vol. XXXV, pp. 176-80.
———, 1961b, "Problems of Hellenism in Bactria and India", *Proceeding of British Academy*, Vol. XLVII, pp. 55-77.
Shakur, M.A., See under App. 'A'.
Sharif, Muhammad, *Ibid.*
Sharma, R.C., See under App. 'B'.
Sherrier, Julien, 1993, "Siva in Gandhāra", *South Asian Archaeology*, 1991, ed. A.J. Gail and G.J.R. Mevissan, Berlin, pp. 617-24.
Simonetta, A., 1958, "A New Essay on the Indo-Greeks: The Sakas and the Pahlavas", *East and West*, New Series, Vol. 9, pp. 154-83.
———, 1978, "The Chronology of Gondopharean Dynasty", *East and West*, Vol. 28, pp. 1-4.
Snellgrove, David L., *et al.* (ed.), 1978, *The Image of the Buddha*, UNESCO.
Santoro, Arcangela, 1980, "Su tre bassorilievi Gandharici di soggeto non idenificato" (i.e. Three Unidentified Bas-reliefs from Gandhāra), *Revista degli Studi Orientali*, Vol. LIV, fasc. I-II, pp. 97-109 (with English translation).
———, 1986, "Note di iconographia Gandharica: La storia del Buddha e del bue : Idntificazione di due bassorilievi Gandharici", *Annali dell institute Universitario Orientale*, Vol. 46, pp. 35-62, pl. I-V.
Soper, Alexander, 1949, "Aspects of Light Symbolism in Gandhāra Sculpture", *Artibus Asiae*, Vol. XII, pp. 252-83,
———, 1951, "The Roman Style in Gandhāra", *American Journal of Archaeology*, Vol. LV, pp. 301-42.
———, 1965, "A Buddhist Travelling Shrine in an International Style" *East and West*, New Series, Vol. 15, Nos. 3-4, September- December, pp. 211-25.
Taddei, Maurizio, 1968, "Tapa Sardar : First Preliminary Report", *East and West*, Vol. 18, 11-27, 109-24.
———, 1970, Inde, Geneva.
———, 1977, *Monuments of Indian Civilization*, London.
Taddei, Maurizio and G. Verardi, 1978, "Tapa Sardar : Second Preliminary Report", *East and West*, New Series, Vol. 28, Nos. 1-4.
———, 1984, "The Italian Archaeological Mission in Afghanistan, Brief Account at Excavation and Study,1976-1981, Napoli".
Tanabe, Katsumi, 1974, "Kanishka I's Coins with Buddha Image on the Reverse and some references to the Art of Gandhāra" *Orient*, Vol. X, pp. 31-56.
———, 1981, "Iranian Background of the Flaming and Watering Buddha Image in Kushan Period" *Bulletin of the Ancient Orient Museum*, Vol. III , pp. 69-81, pls. IX-X.
Tissot, Francine, 1976, "Remarques iconographiques a propos d'une tete de roi barbare du Gandhāra", *Arts Asiatiques*, tome XXXII, pp. 71-83, figs. 1-21.
———, 1985, *Gandhāra*, in French with English Summary, Paris.
———, 1986, *The Art of Gandhāra. Buddhist Monks' Art, on the North-West Frontier of Pakistan*, Libraries d' Amerique ei d' Orient, Paris.
Tsuchiya, Haruko, 1997, "Field Research Along the Ancient Routes in the Northern Areas of Pakistan (1991-1997)", Paper distributed during the Pak-Japan Colloquium on Gandhāra Art, held in Islamabad (Pakistan), 5th-8th September, 1997.
Tucci, G., 1958, "Preliminary Report on an Archaeological Survey in Swat", *East and West*, Vol. IX.
Varma, K.M., See under App. 'B'.
Verardi, G., See Taddei, Marizio, 1978.

Wheeler, R.E.M., 1949-50, "Romano-Buddhist Art: An Old Problem Restated", *Antiquity* 23, pp. 4-19.
———, 1954, *Rome Beyond Imperial Frontiers*, London.
———, 1962, *Charsada: A Metropolitan of the North-West Frontier*, Oxford.
———, 1965, "Gandhāra Art: A Note on the Present Position", Le Rayonnement des Civilization greque et romaine sur les cultures peripheriques, Congress international d', archaeologique classique 1963, Paris, pp. 555-65.
Zannas, Eliky S., 1972, Two Gandhāra Masterpieces", *CHHAVI, Golden Jubilee* Number of Bharat Kala Bhavan Museum of Banaras Hindu University. Published in March, pp. 309-15, figs. 452-53.
Zwalf, Wladimir, 1979, *The Shrines of Gandhāra*, British Museum Publications, London.
———, 1985, *Buddhism : Art and Faith*, British Museum, London.
———, 1996, *A Catalogue of the Gandhāra Sculpture in the British Musum*, London (2 vols.).

3

PHYSICAL AND HISTORICAL GEOGRAPHY OF GANDHĀRA

T.P. VERMA

NOMENCLATURE

Gandhāra is the name of the country while Gāndhārī is the name of the people who lived in Gandhāra. In the *Ṛgveda* (1.126.7) Gāndhāris are referred to for the good wool of their sheep. The *Atharvaveda* (V.22.14) also refers to Gāndhāris along with Mūjavants, Aṅgas and Magadhas. The *Hiraṇyakeśirs, Śrauta Sūtra* (XVII.6) and the *Āpastamba Śrauta Sūtra* call the people as Gandhāris while the Baudhāyana Śrauta Sūtra (XXI.13) mentions them as Gāndhāris. The tradition records that the name Gandhāra was derived from the name of Druhyu king Gandhāra, the son of Aṅgāra or Aruddha (Pargiter, 1922/1972, 167). I will refer to this episode later.

GEOGRAPHICAL EXTENT

Gandhāra is included among the sixteen *mahājanapadas* of Jambūdvīpa. Gandhāra and Kamboja are mentioned together in the *Aṅguttara Nikāya* of the Pali *Sutta Piṭaka*. These are said to be located in the *Uttarāpatha* or Northern Division. In the 'Aṭṭhakathā' of *Majjhima Nikāya* the Gandhāra *rāṣṭra* is said to be the *pachchantima* or the border *janapada*. The Pāli literature often used Gandhāra with Kassamira as Kāsi-kosala or Aṅga-Magadha are used; *Kasikosale pi Kassamire Gandhāre pi*. Upadhyaya (1991, 373) observes that 'Kassamira is the modern Kashmir and we can take Gandhāra to be the region from Swat river to Jhelam'. Thus, the region of western Punjab and the eastern Afghanistan are included in it. The Peshawar and Rawalpindi districts of Pakistan and Kabul are also included. Bhandarkar (1919, 54) also holds that it included the western Punjab and eastern Afghanistan. According to Cunningham (1924, 48) the following boundaries of Gandhāra may be mentioned: Lamghan and Jalalabad on the west, the hills of Swat and Bunir on the north, the Indus on the east and the hills of Kālabāgh on the south.

It is true that the boundaries of the *janapadas* in ancient India have been shifting from time to time and therefore it is likely that the areas to the east of Indus upto Jhelum also might have included in the Gandhāra. H.C. Ray Chaudhuri (1938, 50) also opines that it lay on both sides of the river Indus. Hiuen Tsang found the country of Gandhāra to be about 1000 *li* from east to west and above 800 *li* north to south. According to him (Watters, *On Yuan Chwang's...*, I, 198-99) the country had luxuriant crops of cereals and a profusion of fruits and flowers; it produced much sugarcane and prepared sugar candy. The climate was warm. The people were faint-hearted and fond of the practical arts (Law, 1967, 88-89). *Rāmāyaṇa* (Gorakhpur, VS 2042, VII.100.10-11) also mentions Gandharva *viṣaya* lying on both sides of the Indus. It again (VII.101.11) says that Bharata, the younger brother of Rāma established Takṣaśilā for his son Takṣa in the *Gandharva deśa* and Puṣkalāvatī for his second son Puṣkala in the Gandhāra *viṣaya*.

Among these Takṣaśilā (Taxila) is situated near Rawalpindi on the east of the Indus while Puṣkalāvatī, identified with Charsadda north of Peshawar is to the west of that river. Thus it can be inferred that the eastern region of the Indus was called *Gandharva deśa* and the western one was Gandhāra in the *Rāmāyaṇa* period. But we cannot go too far with this distinction. However, there is enough archaeological evidence to establish that these were two important cities of Gandhāra and must have served, at different times, the capitals of the region. Monier-Williams (1999, 353) giving the meaning of the word Gandhāra observes: 'Name of a people and of their country (north-east of Peshawar) and giving its name to Kandahara'. But it should be made clear here that Kandahar has nothing to do with Gandhāra except it is a prominent city of the region. Kandahara is a corrupt form of Skandhavara, military camp (probably of the Mauryas) and the spelling of the town still retains its originality.

TRADITION

The tradition claims a hoary antiquity for the Gandhāra. Manu's daughter Ilā was married with Buddha (or Moon) and her son was Pururavas Aila. His son was Āyu and grandson Nahuṣa. The latter's son and successor was Yayāti. Yayāti had five sons and youngest of them Puru succeeded on the main line, later to be called Pauravas. One of them was Druhyu who was given the region west of the Yamunā and north of the Chambal. But the Druhyus could not maintain their territory in Rajputana and the successive campaigns of the Yādava Śaśabindu, the Aikṣvāku Yuvanāśva and Māndhātā and the Śibi compelled them to occupy north-western portion of the Punjab. Māndhātā killed their king Aṅgāra and the Druhyu settlements in the Punjab and west of the Indus came to be known as Gāndhāra after the name of Aṅgāra's successors. Soon the region upto Kabul in Afghanistan came under their sway. Pargiter (1922/72, 144) assigns 21st generation to Aṅgāra after Manu/Ila and Gāndhāra in 23rd. The former was a contemporary of Māndhātā of Ayodhyā and was killed by the latter.

Macdonell *et al.* (1958, 219) quote Zimmel as saying that '...they (Gāndhāris) were settled in Vedic times on the south bank of the Kubhā upto its mouth in the Indus and for some distance down the east side of the Indus itself'. They (*ibid.* 126) also mention that 'a king of Gandhāra' named Nagnajit, is mentioned in the *Aitareya Brāhmaṇa,* who finds place in the list of teachers who handed down the knowledge of the substitute for Soma. In the *Śatapatha Brāhmaṇa* he or some descendant figures are mentioned as giving an opinion on the ritual, which is rejected with the observation that the author was merely a princely person (*rājanya-bandhu*). This king, Nagnajit of Gandhāra, also finds mention in the early Pāli literature as Naggaji, who, in the *Kumbhakāra Jātaka,* is said to be a contemporary of the Videha king Nimi, son of Ikshvāku and King Dummukha (Durmukha) of Pañcāla (Upadhyaya, 373).

The other famous king mentioned in the Pali literature is Pukkusāti. He is said to belong to the race of Pukkus. In the 'Aṭṭhakathā' of the *Dhāti-Vibhaṅga-Sutta* of the *Majjhima Nikāya*, Pukkusāti is said to be a contemporary and friend of the king Bimbisāra. As the story goes on, Bimbisara sent a message to this Gandhāra king through the merchants, who had come to Rajagṛha for trade, about the manifestation of the Buddha. King Pukkusāti became so emotional on hearing about the sermons of the Teacher, that he renounced the world to become a saint and came to Magadha on foot. He stayed in the house of a kumbhakāra named Bhargava where the Buddha also stayed for the night. Both of them talked and at the end of it the saint king could find out that the person with whom he was talking was the Buddha. He gladly accepted this talk as preaching. But alas! He died soon after this being injured by a mad cow (Upadhyaya, 1991, 373-74).

Gandhāra was famous for colourful blankets during the time of the Buddha. In the *Ṛgveda* (I.126.7) also good wool of the sheep of the Gandhāris is referred to. This trade relation continued later also. Merchants used to trade between Gandhāra and Aṅga, Magadha, Kośala and Videha, etc.

The Sarvāstivadī tradition holds that Sthavira Mādhyandina (Pāli Majjhantika) preached Buddhism in Gandhāra and Kashmir during the time of Aśoka. Another Sthavira Dhitika went there during the reign of Menander.

Takṣaśilā was the capital of Gandhāra. It was a great centre of trade and education. Even before the time of the Buddha, Takṣaśilā was famous far and wide for its university. Jatakas informs us that all the three Vedas and eighteen branches of knowledge like archery, medicine, were taught there. Prasenajit, the king of Kosala, Lichchhavi Mahāb and Bandhula Mall was educated at Takṣaśilā. Many Jatakas mention this city as centre for education. *Tittiri Jātaka*, *Bhīmasena Jātaka* and *Rājovāda Jātaka* are among them. *Uddālaka Jātaka* mentions the journey of Takṣaśilā by Uddālaka where he learnt about a famous *ācārya*. *Setaketu Jātaka* also relates the story of Śvetaketu, son of Uddalaka, who went to Takṣaśilā to learn all crafts. It is interesting to note that the Vedic literature also confirms this incident. Uddālaka Āruṇi, in the *Chāndogya Upaniṣad* (6.14) mentions the Gandhāra deśa. The *Śatapatha Brāhmaṇa* (II.4.11) also relates him as journeying in the *Udīcya deśa* (north country). Thus the Vedic and Buddhist, both the traditions mention Gandhāra as an important centre. Pāṇini in his *Aṣṭādhyāyī* (4.3.93) refers Takṣaśilā. In the next *sūtra* word Śālāturiya occurs which means 'born in Śalātura', a name of Pāṇini (Monier Williams, 1899/1999, 1067). This place Śalātura was in Gandhāra. Kauṭilya is also said to be associated with Takṣaśilā.

Takṣaśilā attracted students from all parts of the country. Buddhist literature attests to it. Some Buddhist sthaviras like Kanhadima, Yasadatta and Dhammapala (of Avanti) had their education at Takṣaśilā. The *Tilmuṭṭhi Jātaka* relates the story of a prince of Varanasi who went to this place for education. Similarly, the *Kanha Jātaka* informs us about the son of a Brahmin of Varanasi going for education at Takṣaśilā. The *Nigrodha Jataka* tells us that two sons of a merchant of Rājagṛha were sent to Takṣaśilā for education. Princes from Magadha are also said to have gone there for education. Jīvaka, the famous court physician of King Bimbisāra was a citizen of Magadha and studied at the University of Takṣaśilā. He cured the jaundice of King Pradyota of Avantī being sent by King Bimbisāra.

We have already related the story of the nomenclature of Takṣaśilā by Bharata, brother of Rāma on the name of his son. But Fa Hien narrates another story. The Chinese version of the name Takṣaśilā is Śi-sa-cheng meaning chopping of the head. According to this Chinese traveller, once Bodhisattva cut his head for an animal, hence this name. *Divyāvadāna* also relates the story that once the Buddha born as Chandraprabha, gave away his head here to a Brāhmaṇa. It is believed that the incident of taking out of the eyes of Kunala, the son of Aśoka, by the orders of Queen Tiṣyarakṣita, took place here according to Kuṇālāvadāna of *Divyāvadāna.* This city was conquered by Janamejaya according to *Mahābhārata,* in connection with his *Nāga-yajña.*

As a trade centre Takṣaśilā was connected by trade route with almost all important cities of the country. Pali literature mentions that the *Uttarāpatha* road connected this city with Śrāvastī, Sāketa and Rājagṛha. This route, starting from Rajagṛha used to lead to Nālandā, Pātaliputra, Varanasi, Prayāg-Pratiṣṭhāna, Mathurā to Indraprastha, Sagala and Takṣaśilā.

EPIGRAPHICAL EVIDENCE

Beside these literary references Gandhāra finds mention in several inscriptions also. The epigraphs of the Achaemenian kings like Darius (*c.* 522-486 BC) and Xerxes (*c.* 484-465 BC) mention Gandhāra as their province. Sircar (1965, 3-14) has published these inscriptions. The famous Bisutūn (Behistun) Column Inscription, Persepolis Inscription and Naqsh-i-Rustam Inscription (all of Darius) mention Gandhāra (as Gadara). Similarly, the Persipolis Inscription of Xerxes also mentions this province.

Aśoka in his Fifth Rock Edict (Mansehra version) says that he has appointed *Dharma-yutas* in the bordering provinces like Yavana, Kamboja and Gandhāra. But in his 13th Rock Edict only Yavana and Kamboja are mentioned (Sircar, *ibid.,* 22-23 and 36-37). This means that Gandhāra and Kamboja were adjacent to each other. In the *Assalayana-suttaṇ* of the *Majjhima Nikāya* also the coupling of Kamboja with *yavana* is also seen *(yona-Kambojesu).* Upadhyaya (1991, 378) thinks that this was the Iranian region adjacent to Baluchistan of Pakistan. We have mentioned earlier that coupling of Gandhāra with Kashmir is found in the Pāli literature. This is confirmed by the Nagarjunkonda Inscription of the Ikshvaku king Vīrapuruṣadatta, year 14 (Sircar, *ibid.,* 234-35) where Kāśmīra-Gandhāra are mentioned together.

The above study shows that the region of Gandhāra was included among the sixteen traditional *janapadas* of *Uttarāpatha.* Thus it is implied that the southern Afghanistan including Kabul was in Gandhāra. The Hindu Śahi kings of Kabul were ruling there till the tenth-eleventh century AD. Several items of culture like arts, crafts and sciences like medicine were intensely practised there.

BIBLIOGRAPHY

Ali, S. Muzaffar, *The Geography of the Puranas,* New Delhi, 1966.
Bhandarkar, D.R., 'Lectures on Ancient History of Ancient India', *Carmichael Lectures,* Calcutta, 1919.
Cunningham, A., *The Ancient Geography of India,* ed. S.N. Majumdar, Calcutta, 1924.
Law, Bimala Charan, *Historical Geography of Ancient India,* Paris, 1967.
Macdonell, A.A. and A.B. Keith, *Vedic Index of Names and Subjects,* Vol. 1, Reprint Varanasi, 1958.
Majumdar, R.C., A.D. Pusalker, A.K. Majumdar, 'The History and Culture of the Indian People', Vol. I, *The Vedic Age,* Bombay, 1951/1965.
Monier-Williams, M., *Sanskrit-English Dictionary,* (Reprint 1999), New Delhi, 1899.
Pargiter, F.E., *Ancient Indian Historical Tradition,* Delhi, 1922/1972.
Ray Chaudhury, H.C., *Political History of Ancient India,* 4th edn., Calcutta, 1938.
Sircar, D.C., *Select Inscriptions Bearing on Indian History and Civilization,* Vol. I, Calcutta, 1965.
Upadhyaya, B.S., *Buddhakalina Bharatiya Bhugol* (Hindi), Prayag, 1991.
Watters, T., *On Yuan Chwang's Travels in India,* Delhi, 1961.

4

SOCIETY OF GANDHĀRA REGION
With Special Reference to *Mahābhārata*, *Jātakas* and *Aṣṭādhyāyī*

PRANATI GHOSAL

INTRODUCTION

The early Indian scriptures are stocked with references to Gandhāra region which was known through a number of nomenclatures, viz., Vāhīka, Madra, Sindhu, Sauvīra, Māhiṣaka, Kārkoṭaka, etc. It appears that this vast region was closely associated with India and was treated either as an independent kingdom with several territories or had matrimonial alliances with Indian princes resulting in the close links between the two. Society of this region has been reflected mainly in the *Mahābhārata* (though, by way of reproaching) and to some extent in the *Jātakas*.

PICTURE OF GANDHĀRA REFLECTED IN *MAHĀBHĀRATA*

In the Karṇaparva of *Mahābhārata* we find that after the death of Droṇācārya, Karṇa was requested by Duryodhana to take over the responsibility of Kaurava army as the chief leader and Śalya, the Madra king was appointed as his charioteer. Because of his close relations to Pāṇḍavas, Śalya had no soft feeling for Karṇa. In order to vitiate his valour he denounced Karṇa in most abusive terminology. Karṇa was puzzled to hear Śalya's harsh words and started to repay him with the same coin. Though it was only a reproaching conversation, still it throws ample light on the society of Gandhāra, its geography, inhabitants, their characteristic features and way of life (including food/drink, dress, ornaments, code of conduct, manner, woman folk, etc.).

In order to denounce Śalya and his motherland, Karṇa repeatedly called him *kudeśaja* (born in a sinful country), because purity is lost in that country.[1] In his view not only Gandhāra city but its adjacent places like Madra, Sindhu, Sauvīra all these have been declared as *mlecchadeśa*.[2] V.S. Agrawala[3] in his work has ascertained the geography of this country with reference to Paṇiṇi's *Aṣṭādhyāyī* : 'Gandhāra extended from Kabul valley to Takshaśilā. Two towns of Gandhāra are mentioned here, viz. Takshaśilā, its eastern capital and Pushkalāvatī, the western'. Sometimes it included Kashmira also[4] (Jātaka No. 406). But Karṇa's idea of this territory was far larger and wider. In his view the region which is distant from Himavat, Gaṅgā, Yamunā, Sarasvatī and Kurukṣetra and stands within the orbit of Sindhu and its five tributaries is a sinful country.[5] Therefore, not only Madraka but Sindhu, Sauvīra, Māhiṣaka, Kāraskara and Karkoṭaka all these are covered under the name of Gandhāra region.[6] The whole territory is called *naṣṭadharmā mlecchadeśa.*

People of this country are by nature wicked and untruthful; they maintain their wickedness till the time of their death.[7] They are defiled by ingratitude, theft, drunkenness, harshness of speech, adultery, slaughter of kine and use of other's ornaments.[8] They consider their duty consists in drinking wine, violation of preceptor's bed, absence from house during night for evil purpose, destroying the embryo by miscarriage and robbing other people.[9] They are described to be originated from *piśācas* (8.44.41-42); hence, Brahmā the Creator God condemned these people. Since hoary past lowest grade brahmins live here, noble persons cannot stay here even for a short while.[10]

Even brahmins of this place are corrupt. They are not only ignorant in Vedic scriptures, but they are dullard and void of any type of knowledge.[11] Neither they perform *yajña* nor they can help others in doing so. Gods do not accept any gift from them.[12] All the castes are intermingled here.[13] Regarding means of livelihood they do not practise any fixed mode, but follow any vocation according to their own convenience.[14]

By every means their way of living is indecent. By habit they are promiscuous; they get married within same lineage[15] which is prohibited everywhere. Their contemptuous livelihood is so much well circulated that even *rākṣasas, piśācas* chatter about their evil practice.[16] But the plus point is women of this region are charming and their beauty has been highly praised. They are bulky (*bṛhatī*), of fair complexion (*gaurī*) and have profuse hair. The *Mahābhārata*[17] has thrown some light on their dress and ornaments also. They are dressed in beautiful blankets and deer-skin decorated with shell-bracelets; and paint their eyes and forehead with various salves.

As regards food habit they have no botheration about *bhakṣyā-bhakṣya vidhi* (eatable and non-eatables) as prescribed by śāstras and are habituated to enjoy all the avoidable food-items[18] (e.g. beef, onion, garlic, groats, milk and milk product of any animal). Among these people, use of meat and wine is very frequent. Even ladies are corrupt and shameless and are addicted to wine. Under the craze of liquor they violate code of conduct and behave like wanton.[19]

ITS BACKGROUND

But the picture emerged out of Karṇa's statement must have been partial one and to some extent hyperbolic also. Because Karṇa delivered this statement at the moment of heated exchanges. His purpose was to humiliate Śalya by focussing especially on the drawbacks of his nation. Even if it is taken to be a true report that also had some reasons.

First of all Gandhāra region was geographically so situated that it lay exposed to all sorts of foreign contacts and influences, viz., Persian, Greek, Roman, Śaka and Scythians. From R.C. Majumdar's writings on *Colonial and Cultural Expansion* we find: 'though this region was within political orbit of India still it was subjected to the influence of Persians, Greeks, Parthians, Śakas and Kushanas'. C.S. Upasak[21] in order to justify this situation has stated:

> Gandhāra, one of the largest territory of Afghanistan is situated at its southern border, once which formed a part of Achaemenid empire. Very soon it came under the Mauryan rule who stationed here army personnels to safeguard the border of kingdom. Probably Alexander also stationed here Greek army with a view to combat any revolt from Achaemenids.... And it started to develop as a military regimental head-quarters, not as an administrative centre nor as a metropolis.

On account of its being a military regimental border (since Mauryan period) it witnessed cultural fusion from different sources and traditions. As a result, since long back cultural status of Gandhāra has been a matter of controversy and debate. Besides Indian cultural element, other cultural traditions like Hellenistic, Iranian-Sassanian, Central Asian and Chinese also were operative towards the formation of Gandhāra culture in different degrees. Consequently cultural ethos of Gandhāra territory is neither totally Indian, nor totally Hellenic nor Central Asian nor Chinese nor even wholly semitic. This intermixture of different cultures has been reflected in every aspect of their life, which other people have interpreted as wantonness. That is why inhabitants of this territory could not maintain any type of originality or purity in their life-style.

GANDHĀRA AS A SEAT OF LEARNING

The other factor is, each and every nation and its culture has its own excellence and drawbacks. This is applicable in case of Gandhāra also which had several virtues. Since long back, Gandhāra was well known both as a famous centre of trade and ancient seat of learning.

That Takṣaśilā was one of the most prominent centre of learning and education, has been well reflected in the stories of *Jātaka*. The text throws ample light on the education system of the region. It attracted scholars from different and distant parts of India, viz., Benares (Jā No. 3.252); Rājagir (3.238); Mithilā (4.316); Ujjain (4.392) and Kośala. Names of Asaṅga, Vasubandhu, Jīvaka the famous physician can be mentioned as most prominent students of this University. The fame of Takṣaśilā as a seat of learning was of course due to its teachers. They are described as being well-renowned authorities and specialists in their subjects.[22] The great diplomat Kauṭilya taught here for some time.

As regards tuition fees, richer students paid entire fee in advance, while poorer students rendered their services to the teacher in lieu of fees. They attended their teacher by day and received instruction from him at night.[23] In some cases state scholarships were available for supporting poorer students. Thus, in the *Jātaka*,[24] we come across the story of a poor brahmin boy Jotipāla, who was sent from Benares to Takṣaśilā for the purpose of specializing in the science of archery. Sometimes sons of royal chaplains, at the court of Benares or Rajagir accompanied their respective princes to Takṣaśilā.

Normally tenure of education was fixed for five years. In cases of medical education this course was extended upto seven years.[25] It is interesting to note here that the students were sent to Takṣaśilā to complete their education,[26] which indicates that Takṣaśilā was not a centre of preliminary education but a university, meant for higher and specialized education. Takṣaśilā Mahāvihāra had special faculties of Law, Medicine and Military Science.[27]

Students joined this institute to become well versed in the three Vedas on the one hand and in eighteen *sippas* on the other. According to the *Milindapañho*,[28] any subject other than Vedas comes under the name of *sippa*. It is difficult to identify eighteen *sippas*, referred to in the *Jātakas*. Because the text has not enumerated it. In some passages names of some subjects have been mentioned, but it is not certain whether they would come under so-called eighteen *sippas*. However, the *Milindapañho*[29] has enumerated nineteen *sippas* which were current at that time and taught in the institutes of Takṣaśilā. Among these subjects students could learn any one or more than one according to their choice and convenience.

Apart from Takṣaśilā Mahāvihāra, there were numerous monasteries at the city of Takṣaśilā, Gandhāra and Puṣkarāvatī, which were seen by Hiuen Tsang.[30] From his account we find that these monasteries were flourishing seats of Buddhism where Buddhist Literature, especially Philosophy and Religion were cultivated; where elites like Pārśva, Nārāyaṇa Deva,

Dharmatrāta Manoratha, Vasumitra, Kumāralabdha, etc., were produced and in course of time they enriched Buddhist philosophy with their unparallel expository contributions, viz., *Vibhāṣā Luṇ*, *Abhidharma Kośa Śāstra*, etc.

GANDHĀRA AS A TRADE CENTRE

Besides its educational aspect, Gandhāra was well known as a centre of trade also. The *Aṣṭadhyāyī* of Paṇiṇi, *Mahābhāṣya* and *Kāśikā Vṛtti* have focussed on the details of trade and commerce of this region. Pāṇiṇi's *Aṣṭadhyāyī* while handling *taddhita* suffix throws ample light on traders,[31] currency,[32] trade-routes,[33] barter system,[34] articles of trade,[35] etc.

Dr Prabhu Dayal Agnihotri[36] has stated : '*Aṣṭadhyāyī* and *Mahābhāṣya's* references to the traders' names e.g. *madra vāṇijaḥ*, *Kaśmīravāṇijaḥ*, etc. indicate that Eastern India had mercantile contact with Madra, Kashmir and allied states since the time of Pāṇiṇi and Patañjali'.

Different trade-routes have been mentioned in the *devapathādigaṇa*.[37] Dr V.S. Agrawala[38] has identified the term *uttarapatha* mentioned in *uttara pathenāhṛtaṁ ca* (Pā 5.1.77) with the highway (most probably G.T. Road) running from east India to Gandhāra and thence towards farther west, which was known to the Greeks as Northern Route. On the Indian side this route was linked with Pāṭaliputra and ultimately with the mouth of Ganges. Rawlinson has written about the route: the first thing which struck Megasthenes on entering India was the Royal Road from the frontier Pāṭaliputra down which the envoy must have travelled to the capital. Through this route the traders carried on their business.

The sūtra '*tena krītaṁ*' (5.1.37) points to the practice of sale and purchase of articles for a price fixed among the seller and purchaser. The words like *dviniṣkam*, *dvikārṣāpaṇam*, *śātamānam* prove that articles were named according to the price fixed for them. Existence of various coins, e.g. *paṇa*, *pāda*, *śāṇa*, *kārṣāpaṇa*, etc., inform us about the use of currency as a medium of exchange.[39] At the same time barter system also was conventional, which was called as *apamitya*.[40]

As regards articles of trade, at first blanket,[41] wool and woollen product[42] should be mentioned, because Gandhāra region was famous for its wool since Rgvedic period.[43] Equally popular were its intoxicating drinks especially *kāpiśāyana* (4.2.99), *madya*, *surā*, *gauḍī*, etc. Apart from these linen and linen goods (4.3.158), *vṛhatikā* (a dress reaching upto feet – Pā 5.4.6), *prāvāra* (3.3.54), food-products like molasses, cereals and pulses, vegetables, milk and milk products, garlands, perfumes and musical instruments (3.3.65, 4.3.53-54), etc., are worth-mentioning.

CONCLUSION

Thus a close scrutiny of early texts, particularly the *Mahābhārata* and *Jātakas* sheds light on the social conditions and customs, prevalent in the vast land of Gandhāra in ancient period. It had geographical importance and mercantile significance expanded on the gateway of India, opening to the western society. As a consequence of this, the region was flooded with the cross-cultural currents and developed some sort of mixed society, which was also responsible for the emergence of a mixed school of sculptural art, known as Gandhāra School which had a number of sites yielding thousands of sculptures. It is therefore imperative to study the early society and contemporary social customs while dealing with sculptural art of Gandhāra, as it is well reflected in its products.

NOTES AND REFERENCES

1. *madrakeṣu ca saṁsṛṣṭaṁ śaucaṁ gāndhārakeṣu ca – Mahābhārata* (henceforth MBh) 8.40.30.
2. MBh 8.40.42.
3. V.S. Agrawala, *India as Known to Pāṇini*, II, p. 50.
4. B.C. Law, 'North India in the 6th Century BC', *The Age of Imperial Unity*, I, p. 14.
5. MBh 8.44.6-7; 8.44.31-32; 8.44.45-47.
6. MBh 8.44.43; 8.44.47.
7. MBh 8.40.23-24.
8. *kṛtaghnatā para vittāpahāro madyapānaṁ gurudārāvamardaî /*
   vākpāruṣyaṁ govadho rātricaryā vahirgehaṁ paravastropabhogaî // - MBh 8.45.29.
9. *sīdhoî pānaṁ gurutalpāvamardo bhrūṇahatyā paravittāpahāraî /*
   yesāṁ dharmastān pratināstyadharma āraṭṭān pañcanadān dhigastu // - MBh 8.45.38.
10. MBh 8.45.19-21.
11. MBh 8.44.45.
12. *Ibid., loc.cit.*
13. MBh 8.45.6-7.
14. MBh 8.45.8-9.
15. MBh 8.45.8.
16. MBh 8.44.25-28; 8.45.22-26.
17. MBh 8.40.40; 8.44.16-19.
18. MBh 8.40.27-28; 8.44.21; 8.44.26-29.
19. MBh 8.40.25-27; 8.40.35-39.
20. R.C. Majumdar, 'Colonial and Cultural Expansion', *The Age of Imperial Unity*, XXV, p. 636.
21. C.S. Upasak, *History of Buddhism in Afghanistan*, VIII, p. 173.
22. Jātaka 1.239.
23. Jātaka 2.278.
24. Jātaka 5.127.
25. *Mahāvagga* 8.1.
26. Jātaka 5.162; 5.210.
27. Jātaka 3.171; 4.393; 5.457.
28. *vedā nāma sikkhāni avasesāni sippāni sippaṁnāmāti* – Milinda Pañha 1.8.
29. *Milindapañho* (4.3.16) furnishes a long list of nineteen *sippas*, viz., four Vedas, Itihāsa, Purāṇas, Lexicography, Prosody, Phonology, Verses, Grammar, Etymology, Astrology, Astronomy, six Vedāṅgas, Interpretation of Omens, Dreams and Signs, Prognostication to be drawn from flight of comets, thunder, junction of planets, fall of meteors, earthquake, conflagration, signs of heaven and earth, study of eclipses of Sun and Moon, of Arithmatic, Chemistry, of the interpretation of omens, to be drawn from dogs, deers and rats; Mixture of liquids, sounds and cries of birds.
30. *Account of Hiuen Tsang*, pp. 208-45.
31. Traders: Pā 3.3.52; 6.2.13.
32. Currency: Pā 5.1.10; 5.1.27; 5.1.29; 5.1.34-35.
33. Trade-route: Pā 4.4.21; 5.2.27.
34. Barter System: Pā 4.4.21; 5.2.27.
35. Articles of Trade: Pā 4.1.11; 4.2.22; 4.3.158; 5.4.6; 6.2.44; etc.
36. Prabhudayal Agnihotri, *Patañjali Kālīna Bhārata*, pp. 322-23.
37. *devapathādibhyaśca* – Pā 5.3.100.
38. V.S. Agrawala, *India as Known to Pāṇini*, IV, p. 244.
39. Pā 5.1.10, 5.1.27; 5.1.23; etc.
40. *apamityayācitābhyāṁ kakkanau*—Pā 4.4.21.
41. Pā 4.1.11; 4.2.22; 5.4.6; 6.2.42.
42. Wool: Pā 4.1.11; 4.3-188; etc.
43. Ṛ̣V 1.126.7; cf. AV 5.22.14.

BIBLIOGRAPHY

Agnihotri, Prabhudayal, *Patañjalikālīna Bhārata*, Patna: Bihar Rashtrabhasha Parishad, 1963.

Agrawala, V.S., *India as Known to Pāṇini*, Varanasi: Prithivi Prakashan, 1963.

Cowell, E.B. (ed.), *(The) Jātaka*, trans. Robert Chalmers, 2 vols., Delhi: Low Price Publication, 1993.

Kāṣikā-Vṛtti of Jayāditya Vāmana: Ed with Padamañjarī and Nyāsaṭikā by Dr Srinarayana Mishra, Ratnabharati Series No. 5-10, 6 vols. Varanasi: Ratna Publications, 1985.

Katre, S.M., *Aṣṭādhyāyī of Pāṇini*, 2 vols., Delhi: Motilal Banarsidass, 1989.

Kielhorn, F. (ed.), *(The) Vyākaraṇa Mahābhāṣya of Patañjali*, 2 vols., Poona: BORI, 1985.

Majumdar, R.C., *The Age of Imperial Unity*, History and Culture of Indian People, Vol. II. Bombay: Bharatiya Vidya Bhavan, 1990.

Mookerji, R.K., *Ancient Indian Education*, Delhi: Motilal Banarsidass, 1998.

Shastri, Swami Dwarikadas (ed. & trans.), *Milinda Pañha Pāli*, Bauddha Bharati Series, Varanasi: Bauddha Bharati, 1990, No. 13.

Srivastava, V.C., *Historical Probings in Afghanistan*, Varanasi: Banaras Hindu University, 1997.

Upasak, C.S., *History of Buddhism in Afghanistan*, Varanasi: Central Institute of Higher Tibetan Studies, 1990.

Vaidya, P.L. (ed.), *(The) Mahābhārata* (Karṇaparvan), Poona: BORI, 1954.

5

ISLAMIC GANDHĀRA: HISTORY, SOCIETY AND CULTURE FROM THE EIGHTH CENTURY AD

V.K. SHARMA

The region known as Gandhāra[1] is a later form of the name of the people called Gandhāri in the *Ṛgveda* and *Atharvaveda*.[2] It finds mention in the *Ṛgveda, Atharvaveda*,[3] the Pali texts, *Matsya Purāṇa, Vāyu Purāṇa*, Pāṇini's *Aṣṭādhyāyī*, Darius's inscriptions, Aśoka's Edict V[4] and many other sources.[5] In the *Ṛgveda, Atharvaveda*[6] and the texts belonging to the Archemenian, Hellenistic and Roman periods, it has been mentioned as a region on the north-western frontier of India.[7]

There is no unanimity among the scholars in respect of the extent of the Gandhāra region. The uncertainty regarding its extent has emanated due to two reasons. Firstly, in ancient India, the boundaries of the various kingdoms changed from time to time. Secondly, there is no clear and detailed definition of the term Gandhāra in the various texts available to the researchers prior to the account given by the Chinese traveller Hiuen Tsang in the 7th century AD. Hiuen Tsang's travelogue leaves us in no doubt that the North West Frontier Province of Pakistan formed the core of the kingdom of Gandhāra in his time.[8] But, in the light of the references embodied in numerous texts, the Gandhāra region may be said to have embraced the North West Frontier Province of Pakistan, parts of its Punjab province (west Punjab) and parts of eastern Afghanistan.[9] In other words, the Gandhāra region lay on both sides of the Khyber Pass.[10] It is necessary to give a succinct outline of the history of Gandhāra and its relationship with Afghanistan before we turn to its conquest by the Muslims and the changes it produced in the life of its people.

PRE-ISLAMIC GANDHĀRA

Due to paucity of relevant source-materials it is not possible to give a connected outline of the history of Gandhāra prior to the 6th century BC. Gandhāra was one of the sixteen *mahājanpadas* which existed in India in the 6th century BC[11] and about the middle of this century it was ruled by King Pukkusāti, who was a contemporary of King Bimbisāra of Magadha.[12] Thereafter, for about one thousand years Gandhāra was ruled by the Archemenians, the Greeks, the Mauryas, the Indo-Greeks, the Śakas, the Parthians, the Kuṣāṇas, the Sassanians and the Hūṇas.[12A] After the collapse of the Hūṇa power about the middle of the 6th century AD,[13] Gandhāra passed under the rule of Kapiśā,[14] a Kṣatriya kingdom of Afghanistan,[15] also called Kābul or Kābulistān[16] and ruled by a dynasty called the Turkish Shāhi dynasty.[17] At the time of Hiuen Tsang's visit in the 7th century AD, the kingdom of Gandhāra, whose capital was based at Puruṣapura (Peshawar), was one of the ten vassals of Kapiśā.[18]

Gandhāra was ruled by foreign powers for long. But it did not lose its identity and faithfully stuck to its culture, i.e. the Indian culture.[19]

PRE-ISLAMIC AFGHANISTAN

Afghanistan too remained under foreign rule for long. In the 7th century AD, two Hindu kingdoms—Kapiśā (Kābul or Kābulistān) and Zābul or Zābulistān—flourished in Afghanistan.[20] The kingdom of Kapiśā lay to the south of the Hindukush mountains. It consisted of the valley of the Kābul river and the hilly tracts surrounding it up to the Hindukush mountains.[21] According to Hiuen Tsang, it was a large kingdom and exercised suzerzainty over ten kingdoms including Gandhāra,[22] Lamghān and Jalālābād.[23]

The kingdom of Zābul lay to the south of the kingdom of Kapiśā. Its territory consisted of the upper valley of the Helmand river and a large tract of land to the east and west of this river.[24]

The eastern regions of Afghanistan were Indian in culture and politically too, these were regarded as parts of India.[25] The rest of Afghanistan too, was Indian in culture and fell within the political orbit of India.[26] This conviction was so strong that even as late as the 16th century AD, Abul Fazal, the court historian of Akbar, quoted the old saying that Kābul and Kandhār were the twin gates of India.[27]

THE ARAB CONQUEST OF AFGHANISTAN

In the first half of the 7th century AD, the political scenario in India, Afghanistan, West Asia and Central Asia was characterized by turmoil and expansionism.

Harṣavardhana's death in AD 647 inaugurated an era of political disintegration and confusion in India which, like Germany in the sixteenth century, became a bundle of small and independent warring states.

Hiuen Tsang's travelogue makes it clear that at the time of his visit to India the region lying between the Chinese border and the Hindukush mountains was divided between the Chinese and the Turks.[28]

Afghanistan too was torn by conflict for long and it had culminated in the establishment of the kingdoms of Zābul and Kābul. Kapiśa or Kābul had emerged as a large kingdom and exercised suzerainty over ten kingdoms of the region including the kingdom of Gandhāra.[29]

The political scenario in West Asia was characterized by Arab expansionism. Prophet Muhammad, the founder of Islam, died in AD 632. Islam did not win converts beyond Arabia during his lifetime. But within a century of his death, the Arabs, who were fired with an insatiable missionary and iconoclastic zeal, conquered a large part of Asia, Africa and Europe under the leadership of his successors called the Caliphs.[30] Within twenty years of Prophet Muhammad's death, the Arabs conquered Egypt, Syria, Palestine and Persia.[31] The conquest of Persia (Iran) extended the Arab empire to the borders of Afghanistan and India.

Arab expansionism sought green pastures in India and Afghanistan too. The first recorded Arab invasion of India was directed against the western coastal region in AD 636-37; its objective was plunder and it brought no worthwhile gain to the Arabs.[32] Thereafter, the Arabs invaded

Sindh in AD 643-44. This invasion too ended in smoke.[33]

After these setbacks the Arabs turned to Afghanistan. But Kābul and Zābul too proved tough nuts to crack. The Arab invasions on Kābul and Zābul commenced about the middle of the 7th century AD. These kingdoms heroically fought the Arabs for more than fifty years.[34] The Arabs strained every nerve to subdue Kābul and Zābul, but their persistent efforts brought them no lasting gain.[35] Sindh fell to the Arabs in AD 712. But the conquest of Sindh was merely a passing episode in the history of India and Islam.[36]

Kābul and Zābul fought the Arabs on their own for more than two hundred years.[37] But this long struggle exhausted these kingdoms. The tiny kingdom of Zābul, which had single-handedly fought the Arabs for more than two hundred years, fell to them in AD 870; its king was killed and the people of this kingdom embraced Islam.[38] Kābul too was conquered by the Arabs about the same time.[39] But its conquest did not mean the end of Hindu rule in Afghanistan. It regained independence and formed a part of the Hindu Shāhi kingdom.

FOUNDATION OF HINDU SHĀHI DYNASTY AND ITS STRUGGLE AGAINST THE ARABS AND THE TURKS

We have already stated that the kingdom of Kapiśa or Kābul, which had the kingdom of Gandhāra among its ten vassals, was ruled by a Kṣatriya dynasty called the Turkish Shāhi dynasty for long. Like the kingdom of Zābul it too heroically resisted the Arab invasions for more than two hundred years.[40]

About the middle of the 9th century AD, Kallar, a Brāhmaṇ minister of King Laghutarman of the Turkish Shāhi dynasty, overthrew his master and founded the Hindu Shāhi dynasty.[41] Kallar is identified with Lalliya Shāhi referred to in Kalhaṇa's *Rājataraṅgiṇī*.[42] But in the light of the contents of the Dewai Inscription this identification does not appear to be correct.[42a]

The Hindu Shahi kingdom could not keep Kābul under its control for long. It was captured by the Arabs in AD 870. Therefore, the Hindu Shāhi kingdom transferred its capital to Udbhāṇḍapura[43] or Waihand,[44] a place situated near Attock in Rawalpindi district.[45] But Kābul was not lost to this kingdom for good. It recaptured it from the Arabs. During the reign of King Jayapāla or Jayapāladeva of the Hindu Shāhi dynasty Kābul formed a part of his kingdom.[46]

Jayapāla, who probably ruled from AD 965 to AD 1001,[47] was a powerful king. He ruled over a large kingdom which, roughly speaking, embraced a large part of western Punjab, North West Frontier Province and eastern Afghanistan, including Kābul.[48] The Arab rule in Afghanistan did not last long after the conquest of Kābul and Zābul in AD 870. But the Hindu Shāhi kingdom was not destined to enjoy peace for long. In AD 977, Sabuktigīn, a Turkish adventurer, founded the Yamīnī dynasty at Ghaznī or Ghaznā.[49] The Turkish Yamīnī dynasty is better known as the Ghaznavids.[50] Ghaznī lies to the south-west of Kābul. The foundation of the Yamīnī dynasty at Ghaznī in close proximity to the Hindu Shāhi kingdom, which had its base at Kābul too, posed a serious threat to the security of the latter.

The Turks, who had been converted to Islam by the Arabs, were also imperialists to the backbone. They too were fired with missionary zeal. The foundation of the Yamīnī dynasty at Ghaznī by Sabuktigīn gave a strong foothold to the Turks in Afghanistan. Immediately after his accession in AD 977, Sabuktigīn led frequent military expeditions against the neighbouring Hindu Shāhi kingdom.[51] This was the beginning of a long struggle between the Turkish kingdom of Ghaznī and the Hindu Shāhi kingdom which 'extended from the Chenab river to the Hindukush mountains and included Kābul'.[52]

But in spite of Jayapāla's heroic fight, Sabuktigīn annexed the entire territory of the Hindu Shāhi kingdom lying between Lamghān and Peshawar.[53] Sabuktigīn died in AD 997. Sabuktigīn's son Mahmūd of Ghaznī ascended the throne in AD 998 after defeating his brother Ismail.[54] He had fought against Jayapāla during his father's reign. Mahmūd resumed the war against the Hindu Shāhi kingdom. Jayapāla suffered a crushing defeat in a severe battle fought near Peshawar in AD 1001 and was made a prisoner.[55] He had suffered three defeats at the hands of the Ghaznavids; he could not overpower this humiliation and committed suicide in AD 1001.[56]

Jayapāla was succeeded by his son Ānandapāla. In AD 1008, Mahmūd of Ghaznī led an army against Ānandapāla. A furious battle was fought near Udbhāṇḍapura or Waihand. Ānandapāla was defeated and Mahmūd pursued him upto Nagarkot or Kāṇgrā.[57] The territories of the Hindu Shāhi kingdom lying to the west of the Indus river, including the Udbhāṇḍapura, the capital city, were annexed by the victor.[58]

Ānandapāla made peace with Mahmūd and relationship between the two remained cordial till the former's death in AD 1012. But Mahmūd of Ghaznī resumed aggression against the Hindu Shāhi kingdom after Ānandapāla's death. In AD 1013, Mahmūd marched against Trilochanapāla, son and successor of Ānandapāla, whose capital was at the time located at Nandana in the Salt Range.[59] Trilochanapāla was defeated and Mahmūd of Ghaznī annexed the western and central portions of the Hindu Shāhi kingdom to the kingdom of Ghaznī.[60] Trilochanapāla fought Mahmūd once again. But he was defeated and killed in AD 1021.[61] Mahmūd annexed the remnants of the Hindu Shāhi kingdom.

Trilochanapāla's death in AD 1021 meant the extinction of the Hindu Shāhi kingdom because his son Bhīmapāla who lived up to AD 1026 could not recover the lost territories. The Hindu Shāhi kings were noble persons and great warriors. They fought with the kingdom of Ghaznī for nearly fifty years. The end of the Hindu Shāhi kingdom was mourned by Kalhaṇa and Al Birunī.[62] The extinction of the Hindu Shāhi kingdom proved disastrous for India. It paved the way for the Turkish conquest of northern India in the eleventh and twelfth century AD.[63]

THE ADVENT OF ISLAM IN GANDHĀRA

Islam did not spring to life at once in Gandhāra. The Gandhāra region was Indian to the backbone. The major religions in Gandhāra were Hinduism and Buddhism.[64] Some of its inhabitants were devoted to Jainism and fire-worship too.[65] Most of the pre-Islamic invaders, who had settled in the Gandhāra region, had adopted Indian religions, dress, customs, manners, etc.[66] These ethnic groups had introduced some new trends in the social and cultural life of this region.[67] But Gandhāra did not deviate from its inherent Indian character.

Buddhism, which spread to the Gandhāra region during the reign of Aśoka, proved to be a great unifying factor. It created religious unity in Gandhāra. It also created an unbreakable bond between Gandhāra and the rest of India. This bond was materially strengthened by the Buddhist art of Gandhāra. The Buddhist art of Central Asia, China, Japan, Indo-China and Indonesia owes a lot to the Buddhist art of Gandhāra.[68]

But a break with the past was in the offing. Initially, the Indian society of Gandhāra totally rejected Islam. But its tide could not be checked for long. Pathi Dharaṇī Deva, the king of Kābul, suffered a crushing defeat at the hands of the Arabs in AD 815-16 and embraced Islam.[69] Probably his conversion encouraged the gradual conversion of this region to Islam.[70] The inhabitants of the kingdom of Zābul embraced Islam after their king was killed in an encounter with the Arabs in AD 870.[71] Sabuktigīn introduced Islam in the territory that lies between Lamghān and Peshawar.[72] Sukhapāla, a grandson of Jayapāla, was forcibly converted to Islam by Mahmūd of Ghaznī.[72a]

According to Al Birunī, the armies of Ghaznī carried fire and sword in Gandhāra. The persecution of Gandhāra caused irreparable damage to Indian religions in this region. The ruins of cities, temples, monasteries, etc., bear mute witness to these acts of vandalism.[73]

After its conquest by the Ghaznavids, Gandhāra has mostly remained under Muslim rule. Gradually, an overwhelming majority of its population embraced Islam. Presently, the territories comprising the ancient Gandhāra form parts of Afghanistan and Pakistan. The bulk of its population belongs to the Pathān, Pakhtūn or Pashtūn ethnic group. This ethnic group is divided into many tribes. The religion of these tribes is Islam. The language of this region is Pashto. This language has many dialects. Many words in Pashto are derivations from Sanskrit. The popular male dress of this region, which appears to be a modification of the Kuṣāṇa dress, consists of a long shirt, a salwār, a turban or a typically roundish cap popular among the Muslims. The female dress also consists of a long kurtā and a salwār. Many females wear the burqa too. The Pakhtūn male dress, sometimes called the Pathān suit, is very popular.

The diet of the people consists mainly of nān, eggs, meat preparations, sweets, vegetables and tea. Much water has flown down the rivers since the conquest of Gandhāra by the Ghaznavids. The Gandhāra region is now an Islamic land.

NOTES AND REFERENCES

1. It is also known as Gandhāra. See A.A. Macdonell and A.B. Keith, *Vedic Index of Names and Subjects*, Vol. I, London, 1912, pp. 218-19.
2. *Ibid.*
3. *Ibid.*
4. B.C. Law, *Historical Geography of Ancient India*, Paris, p. 76.
5. T.P. Verma, 'Physical and Historical Geography of Gāndhāra', paper presented at the International Seminar on Buddhism and Gandhāra Art, Varanasi, pp. 1 ff.
6. *Vedic Index*, Vol. I, *op.cit.*, pp. 218-19.
7. *Gandhāran Art in Pakistan*, New York, 1957, p. 13.
8. *Ibid.*, p. 13; Thomas Watters, *On Yuan Chwang's Travels in India*, Vol. I, London, 1904, pp. 198ff.
9. T.P. Verma, *op.cit.*, pp. 1 ff.
10. *Ibid.*
11. B.C. Law, *op.cit.*, p. 76; B.K. Kaul Deambi, *History and Culture of Ancient Gandhāra and Western Himalayas*, New Delhi, 1985, p. 9.
12. Rhys Davids, *Buddhist India*, Calcutta, 1950, p. 21.

12a. B.K. Kaul Deambi, *op.cit.*, pp. 10-12; *Gandhāran Art in Pakistan*, *op.cit.*, pp. 16-17.

13. B.K. Kaul Deambi, *op.cit.*, p. 12; *The Struggle for Empire*, ed. R.C. Majumdar and A.D. Pusalker, Bombay, 1957, Foreword, XI.
14. B.K. Kaul Deambi, *op.cit.*, p. 12.
15. Samuel Beal, *Buddhist Records of the Western World*, Popular edition, London, p. 54.
16. *The Classical Age*, ed. R.C. Majumdar and A.D. Pusalker, Bombay, 1954, p. 164.
17. *The Age of Imperial Kannauj*, ed. R.C. Majumdar and A.D. Pusalker, Bombay, 1955, p. 111; B.K. Kaul Deambi, *op.cit.*, p. 12.
18. Samuel Beal, *op.cit.*, pp. 97-98.
19. Nilima Sen Gupta, *Cultural History of Kapisa and Gandhara*, Delhi, 1984, pp. 71-88; *Gandhāran Art in Pakistan*, *op.cit.*, p. 17.

20. *The Classical Age, op. cit.*, p. 164.
21. *Ibid.*
22. *Ibid.*, p. 164; Samuel Beal, *op.cit.*, pp. 54-55.
23. *Ibid.*, p. 164.
24. *Ibid.*
25. *The Age of Imperial Unity*, ed. R.C. Majumdar and A.D. Pusalker, Bombay, 1951, p. 635.
26. *Ibid.*
27. *Ain-i-Akbari,* Vol. II, Jarret and Sarkar edition, Calcutta, 1949, pp. 408-09.
28. Thomas Watters, *op.cit.*, pp. 39-115; Nilima Sen Gupta, *op.cit.*, p. 27.
29. Samuel Beal, *op.cit.*, pp. 54-5; Thomas Watters, *op.cit.*, p. 199.
30. *The Cambridge History of India*, Vol. III, ed. W. Haig, Delhi, 1958, p. 1.
31. Ishwari Prasad, *History of Medieval India*, Allahabad, 1928, p. 47.
32. *Ibid.*
33. *Ibid.*, p. 48; *The Classical Age, op.cit.*, p. 168.
34. *The Classical Age, op.cit.*, p. 168.
35. *Ibid.*
36. *The Cambridge History of India, op.cit.*, p. 1; *The Struggle for Empire., op.cit.*, Foreword, xi.
37. *The Age of Imperial Kannauj, op.*cit., pp. 111-25.
38. *Ibid.*, p. 125.
39. *Ibid.*
40. *Ibid.*, pp. 111-25.
41. *Ibid.*, p. 111; B.K. Kaul Deambi, *op.cit.*, p. 12.
42. *Ibid.*, p. 111; *ibid.*, p. 13.
42a. B.K. Kaul Deambi, *op.cit.*, p. 13.
43. *The Age of Imperial Kannauj, op.cit.*, p. 111; A.L. Srivastava, *The Sultanate of Delhi*, Agra, 1953, p. 35.
44. A.L. Srivastava, *op.cit.*, p. 35.
45. *The Age of Imperial Kannauj, op.cit.*, p. 111.
46. *The Cambridge History of India, op.cit.*, p. 11; A.L. Srivastava, *op.cit.*, p. 42.
47. B.K. Kaul, *op.cit.*, p. 18.
48. *The Age of Imperial Kannauj, op.cit.*, p. 113; *The Cambridge History of India, op.cit.*, p. 11; A.L. Srivastava, *op.cit.*, p. 42.
49. *The Struggle for Empire, op.cit.*, pp. 2-3.
50. *Ibid.*, pp. 2-3; *The Cambridge History of India, op.cit.*, p. 9.
51. Elliot and Dowson, *History of India as Told by its Historians*, Vol. II, Aligarh, 1952, pp. 18-19.
52. A.L. Srivastava. *op.cit.*, p. 42.
53. Elliot and Dowson, *op.cit.*, pp. 18ff.; *The Struggle for Empire, op.cit.*, p. 5.
54. *The Struggle for Empire, op.cit.*, p. 5; A.L. Srivastava, *Bhārat kā Itihāsa*, Agra, 1980, p. 9.
55. Ishwari Prasad, *op.cit.*, p. 70.
56. *Ibid.*, pp. 70-1; *The Struggle for Empire, op.cit.*, pp. 6-7.
57. *Ibid.*, pp. 72-4; *Ibid.*, p. 9.
58. *Ibid.*, pp. 72-4; *Ibid.*, p. 10.
59. *The Struggle for Empire*, p. 11.
60. *Ibid.*, p. 12.
61. *Ibid.*, p. 17; B.K. Kaul, *op.cit.*, p. 19.
62. *Ibid.*, p. 17.
63. *The Age of Imperial Kannauj, op.cit.*, p. 113; A.L. Srivastava, *Bhārat... op.cit.*, p. 14; *The Struggle for Empire, op.cit.*, p. 22.
64. Nilima Sen Gupta, *op.cit.*, p. 88; B.K. Kaul Deambi, *op.cit.*, p. 78.
65. *Ibid.*, p. 88.
66. *Ibid.*, p. 71.
67. *Ibid.*
68. *Gandhāran Art in Pakistan, op.*cit., p. 17.

69. Nilima Sen Gupta, *op.cit.*, p. 39.
70. *Ibid.*, p. 88.
71. *The Age of Imperial Kannauj*, *op.cit.*, p. 125.
72. *The Struggle for Empire*, *op.cit.*, p. 5.
72a. A.L. Srivastava, *Bhārat... op.cit.*, p. 12.
73. Nilima Sen Gupta, *op.cit.*, p. 137.

6

ISLAM AND ICONOCLASM

KRANTI KUMAR

Geography has played a major role in the history of Arabia, both as homeland of Arabs and cradle of Islam. This huge quadrilateral-shaped region is divided into two almost clear-cut divisions. The south and part of west is surrounded by sea and is rain-fed. With only one river in south all the movement of men and material was land-based. The rest of the region is arid and inhabited by nomadic tribes generally on the move from oases to oases.

> The peninsula, thus is a land of strident contrasts which contains in its frontiers the two extremes, side by side, as in the case of the fertile south, blessed with soil and climate ... and the adjacent area to the northeast, a veritable hell on earth known as Empty Quarter, the arid area and the most extensive body of continuous sand in the whole world (TCH)*.

This area was dominated by domestication of camels by bedouins and date palms. Their life was a constant struggle for existence, hence war was a natural institution waged by tribes for survival in the clan to which the bedouins belonged. The bedouins of the deserts and the sedentarized nomads of the oases were the two main group in the arid area of the north. Their language was Aribyya (Arabic) with its various dialects.

The topography of the south-western portion of the peninsula was inhabited by Sabeans of four areas. Their language was Sabean which was not Arabic, nor, Sabeans were of Arabic descent. Those of the arid areas of the north, the Arabs lived mostly in north, both as nomads of the steppe and as sedentaries in the ring caravan cities (CHI-4)—while the semetic south with developed civilization was prosperous and because of the international sea-traffic and land-traffic dominated the Arab peninsula. They were governed by *Mukarribs* (priest-kings) with a powerful chief called 'qual'. But the interface allowed migration on both sides to some extent 'Religion was an important fact in the history of the south' (TCHI-7). 'There was a close relationship between the deity and the man in south' (TCHI-9). The economic history is noteworthy in the development of Arabian peninsula. Of the luxury articles frank incense and myrrh and spices, etc. from Indian Ocean area were profitable trade items. Marib was

* For abbreviations, please see Bibliographical References in the end.

the centre of trade routes through north region also. The affluent society had internecine wars also on economic grounds. At this time the famous Arabian horses came into picture which greatly changed the political history of the peninsula after AD 300. Christianity, Judaism and Zoroastrian ideas soon percolated. Theirs was a business culture, their ideal was materialistic, relentlessly pursued towards the acquisition of wealth. There was, therefore, impermanence, except in their elegant and graceful scroll *musand*. This existence had its fall with the mission of Muhammad and the rise of Islam. Before this, however, the peninsula had developed in three zones of influences or orbits. The Persian, the Roman and the Sabean-Armenian influence was in north. Their clear manifestation was the adoption of its script as that of classical Arabic. Their influences lasted for three centuries till the rise of Islam. Changes were taking place and Mecca developed due to its sheltered western route. The literary changes developed a sort of common bond in the form of *al-arabiyya*, giving north a clear identity and awareness. Mecca slowly developed not only as a caravan station but also as a holy city. Founder or Querish dynasty (AD 500) contributed to development of religious life which was unmistakably of polytheism and idolatory, which included the three goddesses Al-Lat, Al-Uzza and Manat, the daughters of Allah. Nearly a century later was born Muhammad (c. AD 570) who changed the face of not only Arabia but also of the whole world. The common literary idiom perfected by the poets of pre-Islamic Arabia proved to be indispensable to Muhammad as Qur'anic revelations which took it as a model and which became a sacred, well understood and universal language of Islam through the Qur'an.

Till AD 624 Islam had many things in common with Jews and Christians. They prayed with their face towards Jerusalem. Abraham's role at this time became a decisive factor. 'Muslims treated him neither as a Jews nor as a Christian, as he stood for pure monotheism'. The Qur'an therefore claimed that it was restoring the pure monotheism of Abraham which had been corrupted in various ways, not clearly specified, by Jews and Christians. On 11th February AD 624, an event is said to have taken place which symbolized the Muslim's break with the Jews. Muhammad was conducting prayers at Salina clan's place of worship facing Jerusalem, as was customary and this was itself a mark of Muhammad's desire to be accepted by Jews. As they prayed, however, he received revelation bidding him to take Mecca as his *qwibla*, that is, face in the direction of Mecca and he and those praying turned around. This break with Jews meant that from this time onward no attempt was made to win them by acceptance of Jewish practices. On the contrary Islam was developed as a separate religion, superior to Judaism and Christianity and specially connected with the Arabs and Mecca. What appears as a religious decision, probably also had political aspects. Mecca's rich business community had not taken side of Muhammad. The battles of Badr and Uhud took place which made Muhammad's Medinese group stronger. Razias (attack on caravan) became more common and lucrative. Even in the month of Ramadan, Muhammad allowed an attack on a caravan, resulting of course in bloodshed which was justified by the saying that a smaller sin is better to cover a bigger sin. For the next two decades or so treaties, alignments and consolidation of Islamic forces took place side by side with killing; violence, bloodshed became an integral part of Islamic expansion. However, not everything went smoothly for *Pax Islamica*, 'as war of apostasy' (Ridda) shows.

The last two and a half years of Muhammad's life were thus occupied in dealing with the problems created by his successes. In March AD 632, he led the Great Pilgrimage or Haj to Mecca and thereby incorporated in Islam pre-Islamic ceremonies. In June AD 632 the Prophet breathed his last. It is said that a revelation which he revealed on his death bed was not recorded as people close to him felt that he was in delirium. What it was is not known. Muhammad's achievements during his lifetime itself was enormous in forging a strong religion based on political unit but the effects continue till date. He had the great gift of a seer *par excellence*, a gift of great charm in the handling of men and understanding their value to the cause. The rapid Arab expansion and the growth of Islamic culture would not have existed but for the unique combination of gifts in Muhammad himself.

Naturally, after his death the people who founded schools of thought, as also some heretics, also came into that picture. It took almost a century and half for Islam to get established. However, despite stricture upon 'innovators', methods were employed which were not within the spirit of the Qur'an. Land belonging to Christian churches were appropriated and possessions distributed among military chiefs (THL-126). Historians record that Sultan Chakmak once grew angry with Christians and ordered a number of their churches to be destroyed. The series of massacres and plundering which have marked Muslim rule over Christians had always some occasion which was not merely difference of belief. (THL-126).

'There are some peculiarities of Islam which are closely connected with its history (THL-4)'. Firstly, a man must join Islam as a member and then only he can learn what his obligations are. While many religions enjoy some sort of knowledge of religion before a neophyte can join the order, it is not permitted in Islam and if after joining he perverts, he forfeits his right to live. And it follows from this principle that martyrdom in Islam is different from, say that in Christianity. The Christian dies for his faith professing it, but not resisting it. A Muslim martyr is the man who dies for his faith on the battlefield, more often in endeavouring to force it upon others, than defending his ownself. His sacred book does not permit him to confess, which may result in torment or death. Moral worthiness is secondary. All the past sins are washed off when he joins creed.

It follows, then, that Islam had to be preached with sword. They must pay homage to revelation first and then can examine any evidence, but then the evidence hardly matters. Muhammad argued for thirteen years and made converts by the unit or the decade; he drew the sword and won them by hundreds and thousands. Twenty years of fighting effected more than a thousand years of pleadings and arguing would effect. But just as the argument of reason is apt to be weakened if the sword be behind it, so the argument of the sword is not strengthened by the fact that the other form of reasoning has been tried in vain. Hence the periods of inquiry and probation are not desirable.

Islam started as a secret society and for sustenance it needed accretion of loyal members. Thus when Qur'an was compiled, they knew that some parts did abrogate others but no change was effected (Surah XXIX. 46-49 confirms this).

Probably there were more copies of Qur'an during compilation, but they were destroyed except the final version which we have today. To accept Islam simply meant to promise obedience to the Prophet and the revelations. (Based on THL 8-19). The Qur'an eulogizes itself but rarely quotes itself, the only exception being the story of Abraham (Surah XIX 48 and others). It also states what is lawful and what is not.

At this stage we must carefully understand the meaning of two words which have guided the destiny of Islam since beginning.

(1) Jihad – 'Striving', 'exertion', usually translated as holy war against infidels; also the effort directed towards overcoming one's inner passions and imperfections of the soul (more specifically called *Jihad-al-nafs*).

(2) Sharia – The will of Allah, as expressed in the Qur'an and the Sunnah of Prophet, the sacred law of Islam. (AITI, pp. 283, 287).

Islam grew in a melting pot of paganism, Jewish and Christian traditions in Mecca/ Medina in the 7th century AD but established a totally clear identity of its religious principles which has grown to such an extent that it is the third largest religion followed in the world after Christianity and Buddhism.

The followers of Islam are called Muslims. The word Islam or correctly Al-Islam means, 'The surrender'—i.e. man's surrender to God's will and purpose. (Pickthal translation of the meaning of Glorious Qur'an—Surah II, p.32 fn.). While Prof. Waines in his book *An Introduction to Islam* translates it as 'the willing and active recognition of and submission to the command of the One, Allah' (p. 3). Needless to say that both these authors are scholars of Arabic language and teachers of Islam in famous institutions. To understand Islam one must study the environs before its advent. Dr Holt, Professor of Arab History in University of London, has this to say (Introduction, p. xi):

> Primarily, of course, Islam is like Christianity a religion, the faith of Islam has, again like Christianity, been a great synthesizing agent. From its earliest days it displayed features of kinship with the earlier monotheisms of Judaism and Christianity...it was compelled to maintain and define its autonomy against older and more developed faiths.... It met the challenge of Greek philosophy. The first three centuries of Islam, like the first three centuries of Christianity were critical for establishing the norms of belief, practice and tradition. It did not stop here. The external frontier of Islam has continued to move until our own day. For most part this movement has been one of expansion—into Central Asia, Indian Subcontinent and South-east Asia and into trans Saharan Africa. There have been retreats also.
>
> But besides this external frontier, which has largely been the creation of conquering armies there has also been throughout Islamic history an internal frontier—the invisible line of division between Muslim and non-Muslim'. This has brought both permanent and transient changes based on local effects. The Islamic *Ummah* or community of believers, organized power for mutual support in the maintenance of faith.
>
> Two of the principal institutions of Islam, Sharia and Jihad, the Holy Law and Holy War, are expression of the concern of its conservative and militant aspects respectively—aspects moreover which are not wholly distinct since the Holy war is fought in defence of the Holy law against its external and internal enemies.
>
> Like Christianity, Islam is a monotheism with an historical founder and a sacred book, although its theology in regard to both differs. There is a perceptible difference in the criteria of membership of the Community; whereas in Christianity acceptance of the Catholic creeds has been the basic criterion, in Islam creedal theology has been of less relative importance, adherence to the Holy Law is the characteristic manifestation of faith and hence orthopraxy rather than orthodoxy has been the usual token of membership. Another difference is that Islam has no equivalent to the Christian Sacraments, (although certain practices, notably the fast Ramadan and the Pilgrimage, appear to have an unacknowledged quasi sacramental character) and no priesthood, although the 'Ulemā' (the religious scholars and the leaders of Sufi orders have played an analogous part). The absence of Sacradotal hierarchy or of any conciliar system to define the faith, has made Islam more tolerant of variations of belief than Christianity. It is also true to say that since Islam is both a religious and a political community the distinction between religious and political dissent is not clearcut.
>
> The early historians (of Islam) were primarily religious scholars. The traditions which they recorded were in part 'Tradition' in the technical Islamic sense i.e. Hadith, the memorials of the alleged acts and sayings of the Prophet, as transmitted by a chain of informants. There was no formal distinction between the historical Hadith and the main body of Traditions—they in deed had in fact legal and social purposes. There is also the problem of knowing what is veritable record of Muhammad's activities and how much is of subsequent and extraneous origins, assimilated in this form into Islam (*ibid.*).

Recent ethnographic survey has found about 300 ethnic and linguistic group of people following Islam. Considering the ethnic, linguistic and geographical diversity of this vast group it may not be proper to speak of Muslim world in singular. This, worldwide forms the 'Ummah' (in Arabic), which in the modern world, indicates a trans-national and cross-cultural loyalty shared by Muslims everywhere. This loyalty is based on the possession of a scripture which they hold to be the very words of Allah revealed through his messenger, Prophet Muhammad, for the guidance of his people and mankind. In this sense 'Ummah' forms one community. But when you go further and analyse it you may find the manner in which Qur'an has been related. There is a persistent pluralism of views and customs throughout the history. One jurist may read the scripture to find a meaning which will be different from that of a mystic. In this sense religion is a happening and provides complex religious culture.

Dr Margoliuth, professor of Arabic in the University of Oxford in his 'Hibbert Lectures' (1913) in the University of London has delved deeply in this psyche of Islam from which it will be possible to understand many events in correct perspective.

In Surah-1-of Qur'an is Al-Fatiha lat (the opening) which is treated as the essence of Qur'an. It is recited as an essential part in all worships, public or private by all Muslims. No agreement or solemn contract is valid without this. It was introduced probably in the tenth year before Hijrah, because by that time regular congregational prayers were offered by small groups of Muslims in Mecca. In that year, as the result of insult and attack by the idolators, the Prophet arranged for the services, which had till then been held out of doors, to take place in a private house (Marmaduke, *Qur'an*, p. 31).

THE OPENING

Revealed at Mecca

In the name of Allah, the Beneficent, the Merciful.

1. Praise be to Allah. Lord of the worlds.
2. The Beneficient, the Merciful.
3. Owner of the day of the judgement.
4. Thee (alone) we worship, thee (alone) we ask for help.
5. Show us the straight path.
6. The path of those whom Thou hast favoured.
7. Not (the path) of those who earn Thine anger nor of those who go astray.

This essence of Qur'an negates the Vedic saying एकं सद् विप्रा बहुधा वदन्ति (*ṚV I.164.46*) and denies the right of all other religions, the validity including Judaism and Christianity, to provide the reasoned approach towards worship of their religious rites, *et al*. This very prayer divides the world into two simple groups, those who are Believers and those who are not, i.e. all other religions and groups.

It is interesting to study the development of the word Allah. Mecca, where Prophet Muhammad was born in a Querish family, had Jews on one side, Christian on another side and the rest of the population was what is termed as pagan. Mostly Arabic tribes, who consistently fought each other for their clans supremacy. Arabic poets of these periods have mirrored the religious and moral values then existing.

Among them was Zubair who flourished in the last days of paganism before the emergence of Islam. His cautionary words in a famous ode are highly revealing. It reads:

Do not conceal from
Allah whatever is in

Your breasts hoping it
May be hidden. Allah
Knows whatever is
concealed.

Zubair was reflecting upon the attempts of conciliators to terminate an eruption of bloodshed. These conflicts known as 'The Day of Arabs' was a warning to each to honour the agreement in good faith, for the inevitable consequence of deception would be the punishment of the betrayer.

The poets reference to Allah contradicted neither the pagan values nor the pessimistic ethos. Human life and artefacts were treated as inconstant destroyed by time. Yet certain natural phenomena resisted its destructive force like mountains, sky, etc. This was the beginning of the abstract notion of eternity. This was beyond *dahr* (Time) and embraced the idea of a single, unique eternal entity.

It was the god in whose name Zubair's younger contemporary, the Prophet Muhammad, would address his first revelation to his kinfolk and probably a secret society group. The poets perception of Allah was of the Prophet's. The two were alike in name but not in substance. It was the Prophet's message which would displace the pagan conception of Allah providing dramatic departure from the cultural religious norms of his day and marking a new era on the religious map of the Middle-East.

In pagan eyes 'Allah' was the 'High God'; neither the sole object of worship nor indeed the sole existent god, he was only above other tribal divinities. Thus in matters of daily concerns Allah occupied a particular place, but alongside other gods in the Arabic pantheon. In case of immanent danger the pagan responded not by acknowledging Allah's mercy but by reverting to worship of familiar graven images of tribal cults.

Tradition records that the city of Mecca was an important place of Pagan worship. Allah was lord of the central shrine, a cube like structure called Kabah. He was said to have three daughters, called Al-Lat and Al-Uzzah, both astral deities and Al-Manat, a goddess of fate. In or around Kabah the representations of more than 300 gods were housed. One of them, the greatest was called Hubal, a bulk of red agarte in the form of a man whose right hand was broken but was replaced by one of gold. The guardians of shrines were drawn from Muhammad's clan of Querish. Other shrines also existed elsewhere but they were not important. There were portable gods also. Veneration of ancestors in some cases led to their elevation to deities. The afterlife held neither special terror nor concern for the Arabs then. Only tribal laws were upheld and ostracisation turned the person into a non-being.

There is historical evidence about discontent with such a concept. Before Muhammad *Hanifs* also had begun to seek religious alternative, to the problem of idol-worship. Ibn Ishaq, describes the *Hanifs* dismissal of the idols as objects which could 'neither hear nor see, nor hurt, nor help'. The word *Hanif* occurs several times in Qur'an but no definite or clear meaning is available. However, it is significantly associated with the Prophet Ibrahim (Abraham) who resembles Muhammad most in the scripture (2.124, 10, 153). Both suffered a lot in their belief for omnipotent God, a belief which resulted finally in their bringing down the helpless idols worshipped by their peoples. Muhammad's mission was thus to restore *Hanifite* faith. He is treated as the first Muslim, i.e. one who submitted himself to the act of belief in one God to the exclusion of others. The Qur'anic command (10.105) conveyed through Muhammad states 'set your face steadfastly towards the true faith as a *Hanif* and be not among others who ascribe divinity to others besides Allah' (25.3). The conclusion was simple, the threat to the Meccan way of life was the replacement of Sunnah of their forefathers with the Sunnah of Allah (48.23). According to Ibn Ishaq, coercion inducement of wealth, power and prestige failed to deter Muhammad. His message was simple 'Exalted be my Lord. I am but a mortal, a messenger of God' (17.93). Very soon, the power of Allah, the One omnipotent God made changes and the idols seemed to offer no real protection to society. Over two decades of wars turned most of these pagans into believers of one God. When Muhammad died, Abu Bakr admonished, 'If any one worships Muhammad, Muhammad is dead, if anyone worships Allah. He is alive'. After Muhammad's death these revelations were collected and set forth in the form of today's Qur'an.

We now come to the word 'Icon'. Its dictionary meaning is a figure, image, a portrait, carved painted, etc., but not sculpture. Iconoclasm means breaking of images and opposition to image-worship or an idea. In this sense Islam has been an iconoclasm religion right from the days of poet Zubayr, Prophet Abraham and Prophet Muhammad. Today there are obviously no images of that period in Mecca Only the Kabah exists. Destruction started both in thought and physically right at that time. But very surprisingly there is no mention of the breaking of idols in the Qur'an. In various Surahs both of Mecca and Medina reference have been made against idolaters. Some of these are seen in the Appendix attached. The general impression is of exclusion and inferior status of the idolators and their sufferings in afterlife.

The revelation of Qur'an was not in Arabic language but in a 'divine language' which was revealed by Prophet for the benefit of the general masses (S.XLIII.2, XLIV.58).

At this juncture there emerged an aspect of more general world view against Kafirs (ungrateful disbeliever, 2.257) which ways 'Allah is the protector of the believers; He brings them out of the darkness into light. And the unbelievers whose protectors are the idols, that bring them forth from the light into darkness deep, those are the inhabitants of Fire, therein dwelling forever'. By the eighth year of Hijrah (AD 630) the Muslim occupation of Mecca was complete. Ibn Ishaq describes the end of pagan Mecca, marked by the destruction of the idols of Kabah, on which occasion Muhammad recited the Qur'anic verse—'The truth has come and falsehood has passed away' (S.17.82). Two years later Prophet Muhammad passed away addressing the community in his final public address the words that 'all Muslims are brothers and there should not be any fighting between themselves'. It is also clear that there is no wholesale rejection of pagan moral ideals. Generosity, courage, loyalty, veracity and patience were assimilated but under the covering guidance and command of Allah.

Initially Islam was Mecca-Medina centric. The expansion due to conquests brought problems not acknowledged earlier. Because Qur'an cannot be described as a compendium of laws, not surprisingly traditions developed as a support structure. It had two components, the substance (*matn*) and the chain of transmitters (*isnad*).

Kitab-ul-Muwatta (AD 795) contain many of the traditions. There is also 'hadith quids' which was revealed by Allah but was not a part of the scripture.

This brought about the broad group of learned persons of Qur'an collectively known as 'Ulemā' who were responsible for reproduction and dissemination of religious knowledge. They were followed by clerics who guided the believers in day-to-day life and the third group was that of the believing masses. This religious hierarchy stands even today. This resulted later in conflict (*fitnah*). The first major schism was of Sunni's and Shias. A third and smaller group emerged as Kharijites, or as some say, the Fundamentalists.

A question which normally arises is why such differences arose. It is accepted that Surahs are not in any sequential order of time and principles. Thus a later Surah may not be in consonance with the previous one. The accepted principle in Islam is to accept that the later one is correct as the later revelation corrected the earlier one. Some say there is some error also in commentaries. The tradition was that the scripture/books would be copied and then get duly certified. Hariri, the author of the work which perhaps comes second to Qur'an in popularity, informs us that he would have introduced a correction had it not been that by that time he had certified 700 copies. Of course, the error is not known (THL-H8).

The Hibbert Lecturer gives another example. To many of the Surahs letters of alphabet are prefixed, like ALM, TSM, T.S. HMASQ etc. It has been explained as follows by Dr Margoliuth:

A.L.M.	:	That is the writing those there is no mistaking it, for, those are the letters of wise writing.
T.S.M.	:	Those are the letters of perspicuous writing.
T.S.	:	Those are the letters of the reading and a perspicuous writing.
HMASQ	:	Thus doth God (Allah) reveal unto thee as unto thy predecessors.

With the help of the sword the Muslim victories grew in area but posed the problem of how to treat the subject of those areas. The Ulemās decided that as Muslims only were to follow Muslim way of life, the non-Muslim subjects were to be treated 'Dhimmi', or protected person. It included Jews, Christians, Zoroastrians, Samaritan and even idol-worshippers and fire worshippers. They were guaranteed safety of a person's life, property and religious practices on payment of Jizayah.

Gradual development of jurisprudence took place and four schools became prominent. The Baghdad School died early. The Hanafi school remained strong in Iraq, Syria, Afghanistan and India. The Maliki school went westward to Egypt, north Africa and central and west Africa and the Iberian peninsula. The Shafi school developed in Cairo. It exists in Egypt, part of Arabia, east Africa, Central Asia and part of coastal India. The Hānabalis had a slow start and remained in Baghdad and Damascus and later it was adopted as official religious school (of Wahabis) in Saudi Arabia. (The Taliban regime adopted the Wahabi School). Then came the turmoil created by Kharjities and the Musijites.

Later development was of Sufi Path. A divine saying (*Hadith qudsi*) is 'I am with my servant when he thinks of Me'. Another is 'My servant does not cease drawing near Me with devotions of his free will until I love him I am the hearing with which he hears, the sight with which he sees, the hand with which he works which he grasps and the foot with which he walks'. This devotional attitude brought a tremendous amount of tolerance.

During the last hundred years and particularly in past fifty years a lot of research has taken place both by Muslim scholars and western scholars of Europe and USA. They take support from the available subsidiary material of that period. There are two groups, the 'hawks' banks and the 'doves'. Some of them have challenged that Qur'an was not Mecca-Medina centric but was developed in the northern Arabia. There is also a view that Aristotalian ideas find place in Qur'an. However, these are not accepted by bulk of the scholars. As far as Hadith is concerned there is a general agreement of its being not authentic, if not in whole, atleast in bulk of it.

The secular concept of statehood went against Islamic theology and reformers like Sir Syed Ahmed Khan (1850) in India and in Egypt voices arose to adjust other system of governance with Islamic ideas. There is no mention of idol-breaking as a divine order either in the Qur'an or in any other writing even till today. Yes, iconoclastic ideas have constantly perturbed everybody.

Every religion has a psyche as a whole which provides the general framework in which the adherents are to function. This, however, may or may not always be the same for the individual follower. He follows it to a great extent on his perception. Ajit Singh (The Speaking Trees Series in *The Times of India*) in his article calls this as their brand of religion. They can kill, maim, set ablaze, destroy, demolish without causing a ripple in their conscience for the sake of their so-called religion. It becomes a subterfuge. Before we discuss iconoclasm, we see, as said earlier, Islam utilized the edge of sword as a means for finding adherents. The political history of Islam, the magnificent growth after the Prophet, whether caliphate, Mamluks of Egypt, the great Ottoman empire, the incursion in Russian areas upto Mangolia, the torching of Moscow, the battle of Cyprus in which 350 ships and 19,000 men were destroyed, were based on this psyche.

Their Islamization of Persia and penetration in India all point to this factor. The victors had enough justification to destroy not only idols but all that was ever of some religious value for the unbelievers. Because according to Islam these unbelievers were already destined for hell-fire. Michael Cook has struck a proper judicious saying: 'The bottom line in the study of early Islamic tradition may well be that anyone can wriggle out of anything' (Princeton pps.).

For centuries Bamiyan and sculpture in Kabul museums were not un-Islamic. One fine day the ruling Ulema said, they were un-Islamic and they were destroyed knowing very well that like burning of the library of Alexandria, humankinds' property was being destroyed with no chance of their reconstruction ever. The damage was not to material only but to human thought, effort and the grandeur of the creativity of art and knowledge.

The experiences of the Prophet's life the constant bloodshed which marked his career at Medinah, seem to have impressed his followers with a profound belief in the value of bloodshed as opening the gates of Paradise. Among the many pathetic stories which Tabari has preserved is that of the Penitents, inhabitants of Kufah who had invited the Prophet's grandson Husain to come and be their sovereign but owing to the vigorous measures of the governor of Kufah, left Husain in the lurch, who was presently surrounded by the Umayyad troops at Karbela, where he and many members of his family met their deaths. The death of Husain has been to a large portion of the Moslem world the analogue of the Crucifixion: the culminating crime of the whole world, too horrible to mention, yet always to be kept in mind. When these Penitents became conscious of the offence which they had committed, they decided that they must not appear before their Creator without having taken steps to atone for it; they must take the life of those by whose hands Husain had fallen. When they had taken this resolution, there was already a considerable reaction against the Umayyads, for indeed the slaughter of the Prophet's household was eminently calculated to produce on; the authorities in Kufah promised the Penitents their aid and support, merely desiring that this endeavour to avenge Husain should be undertaken with caution and prudence: only the Penitents declined. It appeared that their desire was far more to lose their own lives in the pursuit of their aim than to compass that aim, an avenue to Paradise was opened to them and they hastened to take it (THL. 55/56).

History has always justified such initial reaction but the interface later on proves that the initial reaction was not correct. Yet the violence and destruction of images and temples and churches satisfied the individual's psyche, but not of the religion (5.ix.6.S-II, 190, 5-IX.7).

Appendix

RELEVANT REFERENCES FROM THE QUR'AN

(1) Neither those disbeliever among the people of the scriptures nor the idolaters love that there should be sent down unto you any good thing from your Lord. But Allah chooseth for his mercy whom He will and Allah is of infinite bounty. (Surah-II, 105)

(2) Fight in the way of Allah against those who fight against you, but begin not hostilities. Lo! Allah loveth nor aggressors. (S-II, 190)

(3) And slay them wherever ye find them and drive them out of the places whence they drove you out, for persecution is worse than slaughter. And fight not with them at the Inviolable Place of Worship until they first attack you there, but if they attack you there, then slay them. Such is the reward of disbelievers. (S-II, 191)

(4) Allah is the Protecting Friend of those who believe. He bringeth them out of darkness into light. As for those who disbelieve, their patrons are false deities. They bring them out of light into darkness. Such are rightful owners of the Fire. They will abide therein. (S-II, 257)

(5) There is no compulsion in religion. The right direction is henceforth distinct from error. And he who rejeceth false deities and believeth in Allah hath grasped a firm handhold which will never break. Allah is Hearer. Knower. (S-II, 256)

(6) Abraham was not a Jew, nor yet a Christian; but he was an upright man who had surrendered (to Allah) and he was not of the idolaters. (S-III, 67)

(7) Is one who followeth the pleasure of Allah as one who hath earned condemnation from Allah, whose habitation is the Fire, a hapless journey's end? (S-III, 162)

(8) O ye who believe! Take not the Jews and Christians for friends. They are friends one to another. He among you who taketh them for friends is (one) of them Lo! Allah guideth not wrongdoing folk. (S-V, 51)

(9) And if anyone of the idolaters seeketh thy protection (O Muhammad), then protect him so that he may hear the word of Allah and afterwards convey him to his place of safety. That is because they are a folk who know not. (S-IX, 6).

(10) How can there be a treaty with Allah and with His messenger for the idolaters save those with whom ye made a treaty at the inviolable Place of Worship? So long as they are true to you, be true to them. Lo! Allah loveth those who keep their duty. (S-IX,7)

(11) It is not for the idolaters to tend Allah's sanctuaries, bearing witness against themselves of disbelief. As for such, their works are vain and in the Fire they will abide. (S-IX, 17).

(12) Those who disbelieve, theirs will be an awful doom; and those who believe and do good works, theirs will be forgiveness and a great reward (S-XXXX, 7).

(13) And those who put a way false gods lest they should worship them and turn to Allah in repentance, for them there are glad tidings. Therefore give good tidings (O Muhammad) to my bondmen. (S-XXXIX, 17)

(14) He hath ordain for you that religion which He commended unto Noah and that which we inspire in thee (Muhammad) and that which we commended unto Abraham and Moses and Jesus, saying; Establish the religion and be not divided therein/ Dreadful for the idolaters is that unto which thou callest them. Allah chooseth for Himself whom. He will and guideth unto Himself him who turneth (toward Him). (S-XLII, 13)

(15) That He may bring the believing men and the believing women into Gardens underneath which rivers flow, wherein they will abide and may remit from them their evil deeds. That, in the sight of Allah, is the supreme triumph. (S-XLVIII, 5)

(16) And may punish the hypocritical men and the hypocritical women and the idolatrous men and the idolatrous women who think an evil thought concerning Allah. For them is the evil turn of fortune and Allah is worth against them and hath cursed them and hath made ready for them hell, a hapless journey's end. (S-XLVII, 6)

(These revelations are taken from *The Meaning of the Glorious Koran*. An explanatory translation by Mohammad Marmaduke Pickthal, published by Mentor Books).

REFERENCE

1. *The Meaning of the Glorious Koran (Qur'an)* (An explanatory translation), by Mohammad Markaduke Pickthal, published by Mentor Books by an arrangement with George Allen & Unwin Ltd.
2. *The Early Development of Mohammadanism* (THL) (Hibbert Lectures II Series — May-1 June 1913), Dr D.S. Margoliuth, D. Litt., London: William and Norgate, (1914).
3. *An Introduction to Islam* (AITI), Prof. David Waines, Cambridge University Press, 1995.
4. *The Cambridge History of Islam* (1970) (TCHI), Editors Prof. P.M. Holt, Prof. Ann K.S. Lambton, Prof. Bernard Levis. Cambridge University Press.
5. *The Cambridge History of South-East Asia* (Vol. II) From Early Times to *c.* 1800 (TCHSA) Editor: Prof. Nichilas Tarling, Cambridge University Press (1922). Prof. J.G. DeCasparis, Institute Kern, Leiden; Prof. I.W. Mobbet, Monash University, Australia.
6. '*Samanvaya*', January 2001 issue, published by Maitri Bhavan, Varanasi.
7. एकं सद् विप्रा बहुधा बदन्ति
   ('The Truth' is explained by Learned People in different ways.)

7

ISLAM AND ICONS

AMAR SINGH

On 26 February 2001, Afghanistan's Taliban government declared statues as insulting to Islam and ordered destruction of all the icons including the 175 feet high, world's tallest standing Buddha, located in Bamiyan, 150 km west of Kabul and on 1 March 2001, the destruction and demolition of all the statues started, which shocked the world. Moved by this act of Taliban, Jñāna-Pravāha, Centre for Cultural Studies, Varanasi, resolved to organize an 'International Seminar on Buddhism and Gandhāra Art with Special Reference to Afghanistan' in November 2001, to discuss many related issues including 'Islam and Iconoclasm'. The purpose of this paper is to investigate:

(i) How far does Islam approve acts like icon worship or iconoclasm, and
(ii) What is the stand of Islam regarding these matters.

Before the advent of Mohammed and Islam, during the late 6th and early 7th centuries AD, the land of Arabia, where Mohammad was born, was the centre of commercial activity, which increased besides luxurious habits of Arabians and specially Meccans who were addicted to drinking, gambling and music. The people were superstitious and cruel and practice of female infanticide was common. Fathers buried alive their infant daughters. Human sacrifices were also frequent. All the tribes of Mecca at this time were practising idolatry. The mode of worship of these idols was mainly phallic. Animals, plants and trees, the horse, the camel, the palm tree, pieces of rock, stones and spirits were also the principal objects of adoration. Each tribe had its specific idols and particular temples. Besides, special idols located in the temples, each family had household penates.[1]

Kābā in Mecca, the holiest and most sacred temple of the Arabs, housed three hundred and sixty idols, one for each day, round the great god Hobal.[2] Its fame as a holy shrine extended far back into antiquity because within the compound of the Kābā was a Black Stone which is supposed to have fallen from the heaven with Adam, when he was expelled from paradise.[3] Here the tribes came year after year to touch or kiss this Black Rock and to be blessed. Pilgrims from all over Arabia visited Mecca since time immemorial and this city had become not only a centre of religious associations, but also a place of commercial activity due to its position on the highway.[4]

Mohammed, the Prophet of Islam was born in the family of famous Querish tribe of Mecca in about AD 570. Upto the age of forty he lived in Mecca engaged in trade and business. Then a day came when he began to hear voices and messages of God through archangel Gabriel and started announcing them. The basic tenets which Mohammed preached were simple. He said, God was one, unseen and all powerful.[5] There is no god whatsoever but Alla:la ilaha illa-l-lah.[6]

Mohammed's basic conception of God was that of an absolute transcendent power—the creator, omniscient and omnipotent. Nothing materialistic or worldly can be associated with God. The Qur'an says, 'God pardons everything except associating aught with him.[7] He created the heavens and the earth with the truth, highly exalted be He above what they associate (with him).[8] ... And what He has created in the earth of varied hues; most surely there are signs to people of understanding.[9] ... And Allah knows what you conceal and what you do openly. And those (the idols) whom they call on besides Allah have not created anything, but are themselves created. They are dead and not living.[10] Yet some men take idols beside God and love them as with the love due to God.'

From the above passages of Qur'an it is clear that there was no place for icons or icon-worship in Islam. Thus, Islam was a revolt against the idolatry and superstitions of the Arabs. It was a struggle between the old faith and the new faith which sought to overthrow of the idols and the establishment of the worship of the one God.

Mohammed appealed publicly to the people to abandon their idolatry. For three long years he tried quietly to abolish it but could not succeed due to various reasons:

(1) Polytheism was deeply rooted among the tribal society of Meccans.
(2) The ancient cult offered attractions which the new faith did not possesses.
(3) The Querish had vested interests in the old system of worship and their prestige was involved in its maintenance.
(4) The priests attached to temples received rich offerings from the devotees.
(5) The prestige of the Kābā stood unparallel among all. The custody of this temple was a great honour among the tribes.
(6) The Querish tribe, who looked after the Kābā, were not alarmed by the preachings of the Prophet because their economy, power but their prestige were in danger as they were the real custodians of the idols whom Mohammed threatened with destruction.

So the Meccans decided to stop Mohammed from preaching against their religion. They accordingly formed an organized system to persecute him. The hostile Querish stopped him from offering prayers at Kābā and tried to harass him by various ways. Mohammed thought of migrating to some other place and finally decided to leave for Medina, the town of Yathrib with all his disciples. At Medina the number of his followers increased tremendously. There were several attacks by the idolaters of Mecca and their allies, for which Mohammed was compelled to organize his followers in self-defence. Many of the battles in which he and his followers engaged were forced upon them by their enemies who never succeeded in their mission. At last towards the end of the seventh year of the Hegira, Mohammed and his followers decided to perform the traditional pilgrimage to the Kābā. On the first visit they only performed the rituals as usual and ignored the idols kept in the Kābā giving the impression that they would respect its sanctity and the prestige of Kābā was safe under Islam. There was no danger to trade and commerce of Mecca as well. Thereupon the Querish and their allies violated the terms of peace concluded at Hudaibia. The Prophet immediately marched for Kābā again with ten thousand followers against idolaters and conquered Mecca peacefully almost unopposed. A general amnesty was extended to the people as they accepted Islam. The idols kept in the Kābā and in all their temples or in the private houses of the city were cast out and destroyed as these icons were now irrelevant for them.[11]

Unfortunately, for us and the world, this was used or rather misused as a precedent by third and fourth generation Muslims to feed their imperial ambitions and expand their empires by terrorising people of other faiths by declaring it as an essential part of the creed of Mohammed. Little did they realize that this every act counters the spirit of Islam and the infunctions of the Holy Qur'an which explicitly says: There is no compulsion in religion.[12]

NOTES AND REFERENCES

1. Ameer Ali, *The Spirit of Islam*, Introduction, LXIV-LXVII, Delhi : B.I. Publications, 1978,
2. *Ibid.*, LXIV.
3. Robert Goldston, *The Sword of the Prophet*, New York : 1981, p. 17.
4. *Ibid.*
5. Ameer Ali, *op. cit.*, pp. 8-10; Robert Goldston, *op. cit.*, pp. 27-34.
6. Surah, VII, 158.
7. Ameer Ali, *op. cit.*, p. 166.
8. Surah, XVI.3.
9. Surah, XVI.13.
10. Surah, XVI, 19-21.
11. Ameer Ali, *op. cit.*, pp. 22-100; Robert Goldston, *op. cit.*, pp. 36-49.
12. Surah II, 256.

8

MATHURĀ AND GANDHĀRA : THE TWO GREAT STYLES

R.C. Sharma

Mathurā and Gandhāra—the two great schools of early sculptural art—originated, flourished and also disintegrated almost simultaneously. Both began in the middle of the 1st century BC, had their blooming phase under the patronage of the early Kuṣāṇa kings from the last quarter of the 1st century AD to the 3rd century AD and both suffered heavily and almost finished as effective art styles due to fierce attacks of the Hūṇas and other forces from 5th to 7th century AD.

While qualitatively Mathurā continued to ascend till the end, the Gandhāra idiom lost its glamour just after the fall of the mighty Kuṣāṇa rule in the 3rd century AD. Gandhāra seems to have based itself mainly on the royal patronage, hence it became difficult for the ateliers to sustain after the political turmoil. On the other hand, the Mathurā School was mainly supported by the society itself particularly the wealthy merchants, officers of high rank and monks and devotees. Thus even after the disintegration of the Kuṣāṇa rule the artists continued their work. Of course, the export of products decreased due to less demand from distant quarters in the post-Kuṣāṇa epoch but this loss was well compensated by the improvement of quality[1] and we have several outstanding specimens of the Brahmanical, Buddhist and Jaina pantheons in the Gupta period. Inspired from its counterpart of Mathurā, Gandhāra tried to recover in the late 4th and 5th century and a large number of fine works came out of the workshops both in stone and stucco.

The Mathurā studios were unconcerned with the creed or sect[2] but the Gandhāra sculptors had great fascination for the Buddhist theme and the other deities are seen only casually.[3] The Mathurā School used the locally available stone, i.e. the spotted red sandstone but the Gandhāra artists first chose the local variety of stone, i.e. the schist or slate stone and subsequently switched over to an easier medium of stucco.

The Mathurā School was concentrated in a small region with headquarter in the city itself. Sometimes the services of well-known artists were commissioned outside also, although they preferred to work at their ateliers. On the other hand the Gandhāra School was spread over a large region and had different offshoots. Consequently, despite some variations, the

Mathurā art style is compact and integrated while the Gandhāra School had various regional peculiarities. At the same time the Mathurā School even after bearing and absorbing several alien trends looks uniform in exposition but the Gandhāra style presents somewhat a complex picture with Hellenistic, Roman, Iranian, Bactrian and Indian influence.[4] Sometimes, one trend is overdominating and in other cases it is obscurely mixed.

A good number of Mathurā sculptures bears the year and specified date of consecration and it has been possible to frame a reasonably correct chronology of Mathurā art.[5] But surprisingly, despite their close association with the west, Gandhāra artists did not bother to record the dates and so far only eight dated Gandhāra sculptures are known to us and three of these are in the collection of the Indian Museum, Calcutta.[6] All these factors have led to the uncertainty of dating of the Gandhāra art.

Both Gandhāra and Mathurā regions were included in the Kuṣāṇa empire. One important western metropolis was Puruṣapur (Peshawar) which was also known for sometime as Kaniṣkapur after the name of the great king. The metropolis of the vast kingdom in east was Mathurā.[7] It was but natural that the two great styles developing contemporaneously in different regions came in close contacts with the fast changing political and social movements. The doors of such intermixing were already open and we have the references of Gandhāra region and its people in the Vedic and epic literature.[8] The great grammarian Pāṇini of the 6th-5th century BC belonged to this country.[9]

We, therefore, find the cultural and political links already established with Gandhāra and this intermixing is not confined to the Kuṣāṇa period. Such glimpses are testified by some early archaeological finds also. But here we are concerned with the interaction of the two schools of art and this seems to have begun towards the end of the 1st century AD or beginning of the 2nd century AD.

Since the Buddhist pantheon was common and popular in both the schools, we shall mainly deal with this aspect to analyse the process of interaction. There has been a great deal of debate on the basic issue of the origin of the Buddha image and the scholars are divided into two camps, one favouring Mathurā and the other siding with Gandhāra.[10] There are strong arguments in favour of each and the present author has discussed this problem in detail elsewhere.[11] But the fundamental point is that the essential requirements of the Buddha figure either in Gandhāra or Mathurā have no significance in the Greek, Roman, Iranian or Bacterian art traditions which have a direct bearing on the Gandhāra School. The *nāsāgradṛṣṭi, dhyāna, padmāsana, siṁhāsana, ūrṇā, uṣṇīṣa,* celestials showering flowers, flywhisk bearers, etc., are associated with a *yogin* or *cakravartin* in Indian traditions.[12] As such Gandhāra must have been on the receiving end for the evolution of the Buddha image and the only place which could contribute to this great event was the eastern metropolis Mathurā which had long religious, spiritual, philosophical, literary and artistic background even before the inception of the Gandhāra School of art. For canonical interdiction, Mathurā Buddha figures were sometimes recorded as Bodhisattva,[13] but the Gandhāra School did not have such compulsion.

The early seated Buddha/Bodhisattva images of Mathurā carved till the end of the reign of Kaniṣka do not bear any Gandhāra impact. Their salient features are[14] high relief, nimbus with scalloped border, back slab with foliage of the bodhi tree, celestials on the upper back slab with flowers, two flanking acolytes with flywhisk, top hair of the Buddha shaped like the snail shell, right hand raised in *abhaya*, left hand resting on the left thigh or knee, shaven head, *ūrṇā* between the eyebrows, almond-shaped wide open eyes, small earlobes, slightly smiling expression on the face, left shoulder covered with garment and thick pleat on the upper arm, legs crossing each other in *padmāsana*, soles of feet marked with auspicious motifs, lower garment covering only half legs, frill of this cloth falling on the seat, deep navel, prominent chest, rather stiff posture, corpulent effect of *yakṣa*, seat fabricated as an altar with ridges, lions supporting the seat, or an object of worship devotees or donors. The famous image from Katrā (Mathurā Museum No. A1) can be cited as the best example of this group.

The early standing Buddha/Bodhisattva figures are noted for the following characteristics:[15] the left hand held akimbo resting on the waist, lower garment reaching below the knee with its hem on the left hand, the waist terminating into a double knot with two fillets hanging on the thigh, the thin cloth with transparent effect, a bunch of flowers or knot of hair or a lion between the two legs. The colossal statue of the Bodhisattva of year 3 of Kaniṣka installed at Sarnath is an important representative of this group.

These statues represent the pure indigenous rendering and no Gandhāra impact is noticed. It is quite likely that the Gandhāra School was in its infancy and it took some time to establish itself and to impress others. After about three decades, the Buddha figures seem to experience some novelties which were somewhat unfamiliar to the native traditions. These as seen in the National Museum, New Delhi, statue no. L 55.25 are: One attendant holds a thunderbolt in the right hand (*Vajrapāṇi*), he wears a short pant (*udīcyaveśa*), he also wears buckled scarf around the neck, the turban has criss-cross motif. Beside the drapery and neck ornament, his physiognomy looks non-Indian. The presiding deity does not convey a feeling of natural peace as reflected in the case of earlier icons. The legs suggest rather upward trend which makes the figure somewhat uneasy. Additional thick pleats on the left shoulder is also a new feature. This has concealed the transparent effect of garment and a beginning is made to provide somewhat thick cloth. We are well aware of the fact that the region of Gandhāra was known for fine quality of woollen blanket.[16]

The image unearthed at Ahichchatra is dated in the year 32 (AD 110) which falls in the early reign of Huviṣka, the successor of Kaniṣka I. This seems to be the first Mathurā product clearly bespeaking the first stage of romance with its counterpart Gandhāra. Prof. Van Lohuizen thought that the affair began in the year 51 with the statuette from Anyor (Mathurā Museum No. A.65).[17] She observes, 'During the reign of Huviṣka, however, there is a great revolution in the style of Mathurā. This change is caused by a strong influx from Gandhāra probably due to the fact that the art of this country had by this time risen to such a height that its products passed the borders and drew the attention of sculptors from other parts of India. The result of this can clearly be seen for instance in the Buddha images at Mathurā'.[18]

While the assessment of Prof. Lohuizen is justified, we feel that this influence has different stages and she seems to have missed the development due to the paucity of materials available to her. The second stage is marked by the following peculiarities: the drapery covers both the shoulder, the feet of presiding deity are covered with garment, the broad pleats after covering the feet fall in a semicircular fashion, the left hand is now raised up for holding the hem of the drapery and it is almost parallel to the right hand held in *abhaya*, the left elbow does not rest on the knee and the upper garment forms a semicircular 'V' shaped pattern round the neck.[19] The representative specimens are, a) headless seated figure in the Lucknow Museum (No. B.14) and b) standing figure in the Mathurā Museum (No. A.4). While no dated sculpture of this stage has been acquired, it may be concluded that the phase had a brief spell of about twenty years between the dated figures from Ahichchatra of year 32 (AD 110) and from Anyor of the year 51 (AD 129).

The third stage of development is marked by the furtherance of the Gandhāra impact which displays these trends: the garment is coarse with thick pleats and a rib effect, but somewhat transparent effect is retained; a triangular shape is formed on both sides at the shoulders by wearing of the robe; the right hand which in earlier statues was in profile now becomes frontal; snail shell fashion of hair is replaced by the rows of notches of semicircular scratches: the *dhyāna mudrā* appears for the first time; the lions on the pedestal give a frontal appearance and are often standing and the flanking acolytes generally disappear.[20]

The Buddha figure from Anyor dated in the year 51 (AD 129) of the Mathurā Museum (A.65) is the best citation in this category.

The fourth stage of contact of Mathurā with Gandhāra is noticed in the culmination of a free adoption of the Gandhāra traits in Mathurā with these additions: the drapery becomes more stiff and thick with broader folds, the rib effect is replaced by the shutter effect, a control or master pleat is formed at the elbow from where the lower pleat is seen covered by the upper one, a 'V' shaped scarf seems to have been added around the neck, the folds suspending from the left shoulder are gathered to the right aise and the frill of the garment on the pedestal takes the shape of the cushion.[21]

The best examples are, a) Buddha from Govindnagar (Mathurā Museum No. 76.69) and b) Buddha in the Lucknow Museum (B.5).

Subsequently, the Mathurā products show somewhat different features, viz., the shutter drapery becomes fan shaped on the right side, the 'V' shaped space below the neck is roundish and cushion of *kuśa* grass covers the pedestal. A yellowish figure of the Buddha from Śrāvastī (Lucknow Museum No. 66.183) and lower part of the Buddha image dated in the year 93 (AD 171 Mathurā Museum No. 76.1) are notable specimens.[22]

The harmony in relations between schools of Mathurā and Gandhāra continued for about three generations and then started a feeling of disgust and repulsion for the dominating alien features. In the last quarter of the 2nd century AD, fashion reappears. The drapery becomes relaxed and light, giving away the rib or shutter treatment. Snail shell of hair, *uṣnīṣa*, bare feet and *padmāsana* also return. The recycling of the indigenous trends gained further momentum with the decline of the Kuṣāṇa power. The Buddha image from Govindnagar now in the possession of the Archaeological Survey of India is a beautiful specimen announcing the retreat of the Gandhāra idiom. There are several other statues with the Mathurā Museum which bespeak the same phenomenon (Mathurā Museum No. 42.2919, 76.33, 76.21, 76.18 and 46.3231).[23]

There are some dated Mathurā Buddha figures with Gandhāra impact but these do not comfortably fit in our frame of chronology. These have been discussed by scholars like Van Lohuizen, J.M. Rosenfield, B.N. Mukherjee and G.S. Gai with different options and explanations. I have scrutinized their theories elsewhere[24] and offered my suggestions and possibilities to solve such controversy of date and style and it is not proposed to furnish such details here.

The post-Kuṣāṇa phase of the Mathurā School continued the process of reverting to the original form with these changes: rejection of Gandhāra influence, resurgence of transparent drapery but retaining the fold, also experimenting the foldless drapery, serene expression on face, horizontal shaping of eyes, tendency of elongation of earlobes, curly hair, slim body, clear and elaborate carving of halo and concentration of refinement in carving.[25] Some of the notable examples of this phase of transition (between the 3rd and 4th century AD) are standing Buddha of the year 230 in the Lucknow Museum (B.10), statue from Govindnagar with foldless robe (Mathurā Museum No. 76.26) and the Seated Buddha from Bodh Gaya dated in the year 64 (Indian Museum, Calcutta).

Beside the Buddhist images, the Gandhāra influence is noticed in the Brahmanical sculptures where the Scythians in *udīcyaveśa* are seen worshiping the *Śivaliṅga*,[26] Sūrya clad in the same fashion,[27] attendant of Kubera, Bachas or Silenus in drinking scenes.[28] Herakles and Nemean lion, sculpture showing Keśibadha (Mathurā Museum No. 58.4476).

The *Tīrthaṅkara* images do not furnish elaborate evidence as they are nude but the carving of pedestals, position of lions and some devotees bear unmistakable Gandhāra influence.[29] Drinking goblets as depicted at Mathurā and Sanghol is a Gandhāra item.

The other area of Gandhāra influence on Mathurā is the royal portraiture. Life size or heroic size statues of Vima Kadphises, Kaniṣka and Caṣṭana or Maṣṭana were recovered from the mound of Õkrī or Iṭokrī at Māṭ about 122 km to north of Mathurā city. The word seems to have derived from Tukhāra and became synonym of a foreigner, particularly the Kuṣāṇas. Ir has been mentioned as *Devakula* in the inscriptions, probably for the fact that the Kuṣāṇa kings used the epithet of *Devaputra* and the place where their statues were installed was called as *Devakula*. Scholars like S.K. Saraswati opine that these portraits may not be the products of Mathurā art being strikingly overwhelmed by the alien trends.[30] This is of course a debatable issue and we have the earliest tradition of *Devakula* or *ālekhyagṛha*.[31] Resembling the so-called European sitting posture as seen in the case of Vima Kadphises, we have earlier inscribed image of *Yakṣī* Lāyāva from Naglā Jhīngā, Mathurā Museum No. 72.5 datable to the 2nd century BC. Similarly, about the lion throne we were reminded of the Cakravartins who are supposed to sit on *siṁhāsana* and the *Śākyasiṁha* Buddha who belonged to the royal family was also provided with the lion throne as his seat in the Buddha images. Thus, every element is not alien, of course this impact is conspicuous on garments, shoes with embroidery work and weapons worn or held. It may be conjectured that the Māṭ royal portraits were the outcome of the joint venture of Mathurā and Gandhāra sculptors who were probably also associated with the carving of other *Devakula* images at Surkh Kotal near Kapiśā and Balkh in the greater Gandhāra region.

The Mathurā sculptures unearthed in 1985 at Sanghol in Ludhiana district of Punjab do reflect several Gandhāra traits in dress, wavy hair style of the Buddha, pseudo-Corinthian pilasters, etc. It has, therefore, been suggested that it was a meeting place of Gandhāra and Mathurā Schools.[32]

The Mathurā School also influenced the Gandhāra sculptures. Although the workshops of Mathurā were localized in small region yet the products were in great demand in distant quarters of the Indian subcontinent and these were taken to the Gandhāra region as well,[33] *Jātaka* narrations, curly hair, lotus seat, drapery covering only one shoulders, *abhaya* pose, monks with *dhoti* and shawl, ladies wearing *sārī*, lion throne, railing pattern, *śalabhañjikā, brāhmaṇa* ascetics wearing sacred thread (*yajñopavīta*), several auspicious motifs of symbols, particularly lotus, wheel and *triratna*, half or full lion used as supports for doorjamb, etc., elephants, peacocks, *garuḍa* with human ears and earrings, lady with parrot perched on shoulder, four or five rectangles of diminishing size arranged one over the other (*pañcapaṭṭika*), lotus creeper, wheel on palm, etc.,[34] are these features which are noticed on numerous sculptures hailing from different sites but it is not possible to form a convincing chronology to discuss them in sequence.

On the other hand, the large number of ivory objects recovered from Kapiśā (Begram) bear an unmistakable imprint of Mathurā sculptures.[35] The ivory specimens could not withstand the adverse climatic conditions at Mathurā but remained intact in the emporia at Kapiśā. We come across the well-established ivory trade guild from the Sanchi Gateway epigraphic record.[36] It appears that the beautifully carved light objects of ivory were taken away from Mathurā as souvenirs by the visitors coming from western region. When these became very popular, the emporia of Kapiśā started selling them. Kapiśā was famous for excellent wines and Kauṭilya has also recorded this fact in his *Arthaśāstra*.[37] We, therefore, have some drinking scenes in the Mathurā sculptures.

A Sūrya temple was exposed at Khair Khaneh about 20 km to north of Kabul. Datable to the 4th century AD, the deity sits in the squatting pose with his attendants *Daṇḍa* and *Piṅgala*. He is drawn in a chariot of *Aruṇa* without legs.[38] This image is to be compared with the earlier Sūrya images of the Kuṣāṇa period from Mathurā. There is a good deal of similarity in the architecture of Khair Khaneh and the *Śiva* temple of Bhūmarā in Madhya Pradesh.

The stucco sculptures in the ancient palace at Termez on the north bank of the Oxus River bear the figures of *kāmalatā* and *mithunas*[39] which seem to have been derived from the Indian concept of *kalpalatā, kalpavṛkṣa* and the source must have been the early Mathurā sculptures.

In the hall of fortress at Gyaur Kalā in the vicinity of Khwaresm are seen the pillar bases and identified as *kumbhakas*[40] recovered from the Huviṣka monastery.

Stone images of Devī—Śrī, Lakṣmī and Bhū have been found in the Gandhāra region.[41] But these are subsequently supersuaded by the cult of Hārītī which became very popular. Similarly, among the male deities Brahmā, Indra, Śiva, Sūrya, Candra and Kārttikeya, occasionally seen in the sculptural renderings in Gandhāra,[42] must have been inspired by the Mathurā School where the plethora of early divinities outbroke. The square tablets excavated at Taxila and termed as *āyāgapaṭṭa* by Marshall[43] and toilet trays by Lohuizen[44] must have been derived from the Mathurā *ayāgapaṭṭas*. A deity standing on *makara* on the entrance of a shrine at Jaulian had to be identified as Gaṅgā.[45]

While the origin of the Buddha Image was discussed unconclusively several times, the scholars generally accepted the view that the Buddhist pantheon developed in Gandhāra. But now we have an excellent pedestal inscription from Govindnagar, Mathurā dated in the 26th year and also recording the name of Huviṣka (i.e. his first regnal year) that an image of Amitābha Buddha was consecrated. The new evidence shatters the earlier non-Indian or Gandhāran origin of the Buddhist pantheon and we may safely conclude that this also emerged at Mathurā and later fructified in the land of Gandhāra.[46]

The Gandhāra impact on Mathurā has been studied in detail but due justice has not yet been done to the Mathurā School influencing the Gandhāra style. The reason seems that Mathurā being more compact, localized and accessible did not pose these difficulties as faced in studying the Gandhāra remains produced in vast region in different places under various influences and now scattered in numerous places under diverse control. Political and geographical factors have also been responsible for non-fulfilment of the task. Let us hope he hindrances will be overcome and a better picture of interactions will emerge.

NOTES AND REFERENCES

1. B.N. Mukherjee, *Mathurā and its Society*, Calcutta, 1981, p. 133.
2. M. Hallade, *The Gandhara Style and the Evolution of Buddhist Art*, London, 1968, p. 75.
3. *Ibid.*
4. *Ibid.*, pp. 42-43; W. Zwalf, *The Shrines of Gandhara*, British Museum, London, 1979, pp. 27-31.
5. V.S. Agrawala, *Indian Art*, Varanasi, 1965, p. 271.
6. R.C. Sharma, *Introduction to the Gandhāra Holding in Indian Museum* (A handlist), prepared by A. Sengupta and D. Das, Calcutta, 1990.
7. B.N. Mukherjee, *op. cit.*, Calcutta, 1981, p. 117.

8. V.S. Agrawala, *op.cit.*, p. 261.
9. *Ibid.*
10. R.C. Sharma, *Buddhist Art of Mathurā*, Delhi, 1984, p. 149.
11. *Ibid.*, pp. 150-67.
12. *Ibid.*, p. 168; V.S. Agrawala, *op.cit.*, p. 271.
13. R.C. Sharma, *op.cit.*, p. 173.
14. *Ibid.*, pp. 176-78.
15. *Ibid.*, pp. 182-83.
16. *Ṛgveda*, I.126.7.
17. Van Lohuizen, *The Scythian Period*, Leiden, 1949, pp. 181-88.
18. *Ibid.*, pp. 180-81.
19. R.C. Sharma, *op.cit.*, p. 195.
20. *Ibid.*, p. 197.
21. *Ibid.*, pp. 199-200.
22. *Ibid.*, pp. 203-05.
23. *Ibid.*, pp. 206-07.
24. *Ibid.*, pp. 208-10.
25. *Ibid.*, p. 215.
26. Govt. Museum, Mathurā, Acc. No. 2661.
27. R.C. Sharma, *Mathurā Museum and Art*, Mathurā, 1976, p. 52.
28. N.P. Joshi, *Mathurā kī Mūrti Kalā*, Mathurā, 1965, pl. 46.
29. J.E. Van Lohuizen de Leeuw, *The Scythian Period*, Leiden, 1949, pp. 220-22.
30. S.K. Saraswati, *A Survey of Indian Sculpture*, 1975, p. 69.
31. *Raghuvaṁśa*, 14.15
32. S.P. Gupta, 'Sanghol: The Meeting Place of Works of Art of Gandhāra and Mathurā Schools' in *Investigating Indian Art*, ed. by M Yaldiz, Berlin, 1987, p. 102.
33. R.C. Sharma, *op. cit.*, p. 128; Van, Lohuizen-de Leeuw, J.E., 'Gandhara and Mathura : Their Cultural Relationship', in *Aspects of Indian Culture*, ed. by P. Pal, Leiden, 1972, p. 39.
34. N.P. Joshi and R.C. Sharma, *Catalogue of Gandhāra Sculptures in State Museum*, Lucknow, 1969, pp. 28-36.
35. V.S. Agrawala, *op.cit.*, p. 266.
36. G. Būhler, 'Votive Inscriptions from Sanchi', *Epigraphic Indica*, 11 (1892) p. 92.
37. V.S. Agrawala, *op.cit.*, p. 266-67.
38. *Ibid.*, p. 267; M. Hallade, *op.cit.*, p. 158.
39. V.S. Agrawala, *op.cit.*, p. 269.
40. *Ibid.*, p. 270.
41. J.E. Van Lohuizen de Leeuw, 'Gandhāra and Mathurā : Their Cultural Relationship' in *Aspects of Indian Culture*, ed. by P. Pal, Leiden, 1972, p. 39; Marshall, J., *Taxila*, Vol. III, pl. 211, Nos. 3 & 4.
42. *Ibid.*, pp. 40-41; Taddei, 'Non-Buddhist Deities in Gandhāra Art—Some New Evidence' in *Investigating Indian Art*, ed. by M. Yaldiz, Berlin 1987, pp. 349-62.
43. J. Marshall, *Taxila*, Vol. II, p. 452; Vol. III, pl. 134, No. 56.
44. J.E. Van Lohuizen de Leeuw, 'Gandhāra and Mathurā : Their Cultural Relationship' in *Aspects of Indian Culture*, p. 31.
45. *Ibid.*, p. 42.
46. R.C. Sharma, *op. cit.*, 1984, pp. 168, 231-32.

9

CENTRAL ASIA : BUDDHISM AND GANDHĀRA ART

C. WILLEMEN

The north-western Indian cultural area did not wait for the Muslim conquest to develop a rich culture. The north-western area comprises the regions called Bactria, Gandhāra (and Uḍyāna), Kāśmīra. Much of the cultural life there has been destroyed but is preserved in Chinese sources. Buddhism and Indian culture (astronomy, healing techniques, etc.) went to China from Gandhāra and Bactria. Before Kumārajīva, i.e. the 1st century AD, Gandhāran culture and Buddhism influenced China. In Chinese this area is known as Jibin. Most scholars interpret this word as a phonetic rendering of a Prākṛta place name. However, the official history of the Han Dynasty (200 BC – AD 220) informs us that the Chinese appreciated a cloth, called 'ji', coming from across the Karakorum. The second part, bin, means 'foreigner, guest'. So, Jibin may just be an appellation used by Chinese for those foreigners with their famous 'ji' – cloth. The area originally seems to have been Uḍyāna, gradually including Gandhāra and Bactria. Kāśmīra was included around AD 200 and rapidly became its main area, so much so that modern authors often equate Jibin with Kaśmīra. Very important in the cultural history of the north-western area, i.e. Bactria and Gandhāra, is the 1st century BC. In that period the *Abhidharmahṛdaya* and the *Aṣṭagrantha* were written, in *Gandhāri* and *Kharoṣṭī*. The *Aṣṭasāhasrikā Prajñāpāramitā* was written, in that same area, as is shown by *Prakrit* in the text. The Chinese translation calls this text *Yogācāraprajñāsūtra*. The main philosophical school was Sarvāstivāda, but at the same time a reaction against it was there, saying that nothing exists and emphasizing *prajñā*, not *vijñāna*. Also in that same period the Dharmaguptakas were active. They had a *Bodhisattvapiṭaka*. Could it be that they separated from the Sarvāstivādins as a result of a devotional movement, believing in saviours, Bodhisattvas?

Around AD 200, a Sarvāstivāda 'orthodoxy' was established with an *Abhidharmapiṭaka* in Kaśmīra, the new cultural centre, writing Sanskrit and Brāhmī. In the south Nāgārjuna organized Mādhyamika. Āndhra was Mahāsāṁghika country, as opposed to the north-west. Could it be that *śunyatā* and *prajñā* has a Mahāsāṁghika link, also in the north-west? Anyway, early Buddhism in China (2nd, 3rd, 4th centuries) originated in the north-west, west of Kāśmīra and along the southern silk-road.

Also painting and sculptures travelled the same way. During the 2nd half of the 2nd century the Chinese were confronted with the measurements of Buddhist figures (Śākyamuni, Maitreya). This led to the inclusion of rules 5 and possibly also 6 in the Chinese 6 rules of painting. The oldest transmitted text of these 6 rules dates from the early 6th century, but the rules probably date back to the early 3rd century, i.e. a time of Gandhāran influence in eastern Asia. Rule 5 says: Locate (i.e. on silk, paper, a wall) according to plan. The wording is taken from architecture. Rule 5 is inspired by *śilpavidyā*. Could there be a link with the Dharmaguptakas in China? We know that their influence was not limited to the *vinaya*. Belief in Bodhisattvas was peculiar to the Dharmaguptakas, who professed themselves to be *śrāvakayāna*. One should look at the cultural developments in the north-west, forgetting about *mahāyāna*-schools. *Śūnyatā* and *prajñā* were there (Mahāsāṁghika?) and also the belief in Bodhisattvas (Dharmaguptaka?), long before the word Mahāyāna appeared.

Many questions must be studied further, but we should acknowledge that there are questions and we should be willing to eventually revise our textbook-opinions.

10

GREATER GANDHĀRAN ART Vs. GANDHĀRA ART
A Summary

S.P. GUPTA

Gandhāra as a satrary of the Ahaemenian empire was, in all probability, confined to Kabul Valley, Peshawar Valley and Swat Valley of Afghano-Pak territories of the present-day political boundaries of the north-west Indian subcontinent. Today it is the name of a district in Pakistan. However, we are adding a new concept that of Greater Gandhāra which extends from the Oxus basin to Taxila. The areas involved are: (i) The Oxus Basin in Bactria, comprising of southern Uzbekistan and northern Afghanistan, broadly north of Hindukush mountains, (ii) The Kabul Basin, from the upper reaches till it meets the Indus and beyond including Peshawar and Swat highlands and (iii) Taxila Valley. Here three things happened. One, the Mauryas moved into the Taxila Valley and Aśoka established the Dharmarājikā *stūpa* complex. Second, the Greeks established a temple at Ai-Khanum on the Oxus. Third, the local rulers of Bactria established a palace complex at Khalchayan in Uzbekistan. The roots of the Greater Gandhāran art, therefore, lie buried in all the three events of history since all of them left behind rich legacies in the field of art and architecture which, in the course of time, intermingled and created a new style in the 1st and 2nd centuries of the Common Era (CE) when the Kuṣāṇas came to the scene. It kept on developing through the 7th century. This 1000 years of the history of art and architecture of Greater Gandhāra could hardly be either monolithic or static in style. This realization has led us to evolve a new scheme of periodication characterized by a new scheme of schools of Greater Gandhāran art and architecture.

GREATER GANDHĀRAN ART

The Formative Period

3rd – 2nd century BC
Juxtaposition of the Greek, Bactrian and Mauryan art and architecture. But north (Oxus Valley) and south (Kabul Valley) remain separate entities.

The Early Period

1st century BC – 1st century AD.
Śaka and Parthian art and architecture enter into the scene and the Kuṣāṇas make their presence felt from Kujula Kadphises times through Kaniṣka's time. Marginal interaction between north and south Afghanistan. Introduction of the 'Kuṣāṇa Style'.

The Mature Period

2nd and 3rd centuries AD.
Gandhāra art and architecture takes a definitive shape during the time of the Kuṣāṇas in the Late-Kaniṣka period. Development of the Kuṣāṇa Style.

The Flowering Period

4th-5th century AD.
The Gandhāra art and architecture assumes a new style which was developing in India, called the 'Gupta Style'. It pervaded the entire Greater Gandhāra and crossed the Afghan boundaries to reach Syr Darya in Uzbekistan and Tarim basin in Xianjiang province of China.

The Late Period

7th century AD.
The Gandhāra art and architecture witnesses a marked decline due to the unstable socio-political conditions created by the invasions generated by the Sassanian kings. Monasteries are found deserted by the Chinese pilgrims.

The Period of Expansion

8th century AD.
While the Gandhāra art and architecture had declined in the Kabul and Oxus valleys, the Gandhāra art started expanding in the Far East, China, Korea and Japan.

Sites which played the major role in the growth and development of the Greater Gandhāran art and architecture:

(1) Khalchayan
(2) Ai-Khanoum
(3) Surkh Kotal
(4) Taxila
(5) Butkara
(6) Saidu Sharif
(7) Thareli
(8) Bimran

SCHOOL OF GREATER GANDHĀRAN ART

1. Asiatic Greco-Roman School of Greater Gandhāran Art and Architecture: Beginning in the 4th century BC.

2. Bactrian or Oxus School of Greater Gandhāran Art and Architecture: Beginning in the 3rd century BC.
3. Taxila School of Greater Gandhāran Art and Architecture: Beginning in the 3rd century BC.
4. Swat School of Greater Gandhāran Art and Architecture: Beginning in the 1st century BC.
5. Kabul School of Greater Gandhāran Art and Architecture: Beginning in the 1st century BC.
6. Kuṣāṇa School of Greater Gandhāran Art and Architecture: Beginning around the middle of the 1st century AD.
7. Gupta School of Greater Gandhāran Art and Architecture: Beginning in the 4th century AD.
8. Post-Gupta Schools of Greater Gandhāran Art and Architecture: Beginning in the 6th century AD.

11

RECENTLY EXCAVATED SITES IN UḌYĀNA AND GANDHĀRA

FARID KHAN

The three Buddhist sites (Butkara III and Shnaisha in Uḍyāna and Gangudher in Gandhāra) have one thing in common that these were investigated scientifically and the sculptures were found in a secure context. The finds recovered from these sites had a clear stratigraphic position and are also associated with structures. Most of the finds have reliable numismatic evidences. Except Shnaisha which was disturbed by illegal digging, the other two sites were intact and undisturbed. The excavation of these sites throw a new light on the different aspects of Gandhāra art.

BUTKARA III

It is a sacred area site near to the town of Saidu Sharif in Swat, NWFP, Pakistan. The site was excavated in Nov-Dec. 1982 and May-Oct. 1985, by the Department of Archaeology, University of Peshawar under the field directorship of Dr Abdur Rehman. The site was intact and no signs of disturbance was found because it was buried under more than 20 ft. thick deposit of hill detritus. The excavated area measures 54 x 46 m. The site is divided into area A and B.

Area A

Area A is situated to the east of the Nari Khawar (ephemeral stream) was the main focus of the excavation. The exposed structure can be conveniently divided into two main groups: those (1) in the underground chambers and (2) in the open court. The shrines in the underground chambers have been named as A, B, C, D, E and F. In the open court ten *stūpas* having square bases have been exposed and the tallest being 2 m high. The sizes of the *stūpa* vary from 1.5 to 3.33 m a side. No drum of these *stūpa* have survived.

The Shrines

Underground chambers are shrines of this kind is the first known example in Uḍyāna and Gandhāra. Each shrine consists of a porch and an inner chamber floor is unpaned. The floor is raised from level of the court. The front side on each shrine is open. One of the shrine have a corbelled vault and two are *vihāras* with a domical roof.

Inner chamber consists of a square room almost 4 m a side with a roof cut of the underside of a dome. One metre wide entrance is provided to the shrines. *Stūpas* in chambers are all circular in plan, well preserved upto the level of *harmikā*. The tallest of these is 3.20 m from floor level. *Stūpas* were plastered showing traces of blue and red colours. One *stūpa* yielded 42 sculptures. Umbrellas found in the shrines were three in numbers. The *harmikā* were made of square blocks of solid stone. In one late example different parts of *harmikā* were prepared separately and then joined together. Some of the *stūpas* yielded one or two relic caskets.

Phases

Four structural phases have been recognized. Phase II and III are associated with the coins of Soter Megas and Vāsudeva respectively. Phase I is represented by shrine B, C, D and inner chamber A. Early diaper masonry, pre-Soter Megas phase *stūpas* 1, 3, 4, 7, 8, 9 and 10 (all in open court), porch of shrine A and *vihāras*. A workshop for making sculptures has been found associated with coins of Soter Megas.

Phase III : This phase is represented by *stūpas* 2, 5, 6 (all in open court) and shrine E together with clay sculptures in the hall adjacent to the workshop. Masonry purely late diaper and partly ashler.

Total sculptures discovered were 188. Among them 19 are free standing human figure and the rest are rectangular panels of green phyllite. Shrine C produced mostly relief of garland bearer.

Area B

Area B has a monestic cells which were partly excavated. It is worth mentioning to note that two Bodhisattva figures have been found.

SHNAISHA GUMBAT

It is a huge Buddhist establishment comprising of a sacred area and a monastery. It was first excavated by the Department of Archaeology and Museums, Govt. of Pakistan, for a short period in 1989 under the field directorship of Nazir Ahmad.

The Dept. of Archaeology, University of Peshawar undertook the excavation in June, 1990. The excavation was directed by Dr Abdur Rehman. The excavation continued for seven months. These investigations were of a preliminary nature. Shnaisha Gumbat is situated some 6 km south of Saidu in Swat. The site got its name from small hamlet of Gugar houses called Shnaisha. Aural Stein visited Shnaisha site in 1926. The site of Shnaisha has been robbed by illegal diggers and a huge debris spreading over an area of 15 m has been left. A 15 m long section was cut from top to the paved floor of the *stūpa*.

During the excavation of different trenches capitals were found on top of the plinth of the main *stūpa*.

Stratigraphy

The coin of Huviṣka was found in the foundation trench of the main *stūpa.*

Periodization

The stratigraphy suggest three main building periods above the pre-*stūpa* level.

Pre-*Stūpa* Level

Stratigraphically it is pre-main *stūpa* associated with NBP and grey burnished shreds suggests a data earlier than Kuṣāṇa period.

Period I

The main *stūpa* and the monastery wall belong to this period. A kind of Soter Megas was found on the paved floor associated with *stūpa* II. But keeping in view the large-scale disturbance in the strata even this peace of evidence should be treated cautiously. But two Huviṣka coins were found in a secure and reliable context—1 each in association with the foundation wall of the main *stūpa* and the monastery steps. Fine diaper masonry is also associated with this period.

Period II

Cells 1 and 2 belong to this period having poor diaper masonry. The floor level to the east of cell 1 has risen by 1 m.

Period III

A wall having poor diaper masonry resting on layer 7 have been exposed, the precise dating of which cannot be determined. This phase is not well defined due to the limited excavation.

Structural Remains

(1) The main *stūpa*, the monastery wall, flight of steps – Period 1
(2) Three votive *stūpas* bearing nos. 1-3 – Period 1
(3) The tank – Period 1
(4) Two cells bearing nos. 1 and 2 – Period 2
(5) Foundation wall – a late period structure – Period 3

The Main *Stūpa*

It has an elevation of 17 m. It is square in plan, 23 m a side and consists of a tall square podium / platform with an imposing flight of steps ascending of the middle of the north side. It has a projected plinth 1.4 m in height. A pavement of flags having occasional circular post-polls run all around the *stūpa*. The core of the *stūpa* is composed of heavy limestone blocks laid in regular coerces with small pebbles and mud filling in interstices. It has a diaper masonry. Moulding and plasters made of locally available limestone, the whole *stūpa* was originally having a thick lime plaster. The top of the plinth was used in Period 2 as a platform for placing sculptures both in stone and stucco. The lower tier of the drum was the highly embellished by panel relief found in debris on top of the podium, i.e. second circumambulation path. No sculpture associated with the drum was found *in situ*. A number of stair risers were found during the first excavation.

Votive *Stūpas*—Nos. 1-3

Three votive *stūpas* have been discovered.

Cells 1-2

These cells meant for images belong to period 2. In cell no. 1 nothing has been found inside. Cell no. 2 measures internally 1.97 x 5 x 1.90 m has a rough type of masonry. The most important find in the cell no. 2 is a standing image in stone. This image has been interpreted by the excavator as Śiva Mahādeva. But others consider it may represent a yogi Bodhisattva.

Sculptures

379 sculptures were found comprising mainly of panel reliefs, large size independent reliefs, capitals and cornice reliefs. Only 183 were in good state of preservation, others were in a very bad shape. Soapstone used for capitals greenish schist or phyllite for other sculptures. Stucco is rarely used. Nine stone capitals belong to period 1.

It is interesting to observe that the site of Shnaisha has produced large numbers of Bodhisattva figures.

GANGUDHER EXCAVATION

Gangudher also known as Azia Dheri situated 45 km from Mardan is a settlement site also having a sacred area. It is connected with two passes Daran and Sher Darra leading to Bunner.

The site is bounded by Chorakai Hills to the north and east. Numerous other archaeological mounds around Gangudher show that it was not situated in isolation. But these mounds have been completely robbed of their antiquities. The site of Ranighat now being explored by the Japanese mission can be seen from Gangudher.

Objectives of the Excavation

(1) It was the only well preserved site which could be expected to yield scientific results if properly excavated. Excavation of this site may help resolving some of the chronological problems of the history of Gandhāra and perhaps also of Gandhāra Art.

(2) The site was facing a human hazard and likely to be disturbed, demanding immediate action on the part of the Directorate of Archaeology and Museums, Govt. of NWFP. The illegal diggings had already started. The timely action was needed to save the site from further disturbance.

Only a limited area of the site was brought under excavation during the first season of work in 1993. The results are highly encouraging. Five main periods were recognized. From top to bottom these are:

Period I – Mughal
Period II – Hindu Shahi
Period III – Late Kushan/Khusano Sessanian
Period IV – Early Kushan
Period V – Scythian

This sequence is confirmed not only by architectural remains but also by very clear numismatic evidence. The earliest occupation level goes to he time of Azes the II as indicated by his coins.

Above this level were found coins of the early Kuṣāṇas including those of Vima Kadphises, Kaniṣka, Huviṣka and Vāsudeva I.

An important discovery in the levels above the early Kuṣāṇas was that of the sacred area comprising a large *stūpa,* some votive *stūpas* and a few shrines.

To the north of the large *stūpa* was found a row of monastic cells. Numismatic evidence shows that these structures belong to the Kuṣāṇo-Sassanian period. Of the total number of 885 coins, most of the coins were found at Kuṣāṇo-Sassanian level. This included a hoard of 521 coins. The main *stūpa* except for the stair and platform was found in a much ruined condition. The dome has totally disappeared. The main *stūpa* shows two phases.

Phase 1 shows the original *stūpa* roughly square in form coated with thick layer of lime plaster, showing remnants of red colour here and there. And on the west side is a flight of steps decorated with stair risers found *in situ.* The steps were eleven in number, but only five of them had stair risers panels. It is interesting to note that almost all the stair risers reliefs were found associated with coins of the Kuṣāṇo-Sassanians. Some of the coins were found at the back of the stair riser reliefs at the time when the panels were removed by us from their original places. This chance evidence which seems to be very rare in Buddhist archaeology can provide reliable and firm date for these panels. The rest of the sculptures including images of Buddha and Bodhisattva and few other reliefs were found in the debris in the same general contest. After some time the worship at the *stūpa* was neglected for unknown reasons so that a thick layer of debris accumulated alround and covered the three lower most steps. This debris was never cleared away. The second time when the *stūpa* again became the focus of worship, the top of debris was used as a second floor level. All the stucco remains, some of them still *in situ* on the drum, belong to this 11 phase of reconstruction. After this the *stūpa* probably continued to be worshipped till about the time of the Hindu Shahi. No coins of the Huns period came to light. Nor is there any sign of disturbance attributable to the post little Kuṣāṇa period.

Results Achieved from this First Season

(1) This limited excavation has provided us with general sequence with clear cut chronological subdivisions. It is not complete in all details but the gaps may be filled up through further investigations and excavation at this site.

(2) Some of the stair risers show Hellenistic features in a late context that is the Kuṣāṇo-Sassanian. This may emphasize the need to modify the previously held views that Hellenistic features in Gandhāra art belong to its earliest phase.

(3) This provide us with a sure basis for comparative study of undated Gandhāra art specimens now lying in numerous museums almost all over the world.

12

EXCAVATION AT AMBARAN AND AKHNUR TERRACOTTAS

B.R. MANI

Srinagar Circle of the Archaeological Survey of India under the direction of the author as Superintending Archaeologist has carried out excavations (Fig. 1) for two seasons (1999-2000 and 2000-2001) at the hamlet called Pambarwan at Ambaran, Lat. 30° 54' N and Long. 74° 46' E near Akhnur about 28 km north-west of Jammu on the right bank of river Chenab (ancient Asiknī or Candrabhāgā, Greek Akesines). The site is significant for earlier yields of beautiful and artistic Buddhist terracotta heads which were identified and studied as belonging to a separate school of art by Charles Fabri, but not correctly dated by him. These terracotta heads are preserved in a number of museums throughout the world including the British Museum (London), Victoria and Albert Museum (London), Ashmolean Museum (Oxford), National Museum (New Delhi), State Museum and Art Gallery (Chandigarh), Dogra Art Museum (Jammu) and Central Museum (Lahore).

In order to know the association and stratigraphic position of the famous Akhnur terracotta heads with the Buddhist monastic establishment at Ambaran and to study the lay out and planning of the site, believed to be the only early Buddhist site in the Jammu region, excavations were carried out in 42 quadrants of 16 squares, each square measuring 10 x 5 x 10 m (Fig. 2). Excavations were taken up from January 2000 to June 2000 in the first season[2] and December 2000 to May 2001 in the second season. The ancient site at Ambaran is spread in an area of about 500 m in east-west direction on the right bank of the river terraces of Chenab in between two rivulets which come down the hill and join the river. The site is about 100 m in width from north to south. On either side of the river there are middle Pleistocene boulder conglomerate deposits over which there are loose boulders and pebbles mixed with sand, silt and clay belonging to the late Pleistocene period which is the natural soil below the cultural deposits. Thickness of the cultural deposits vary according to the original contours of the site and in square ZA1, quadrant 4 it was found to be 2.90 m thick over the natural soil.

Burnt brick structures of various phases were encountered in almost all of the trenches which were found damaged mainly due to three reasons: repeated floods in Chenab,

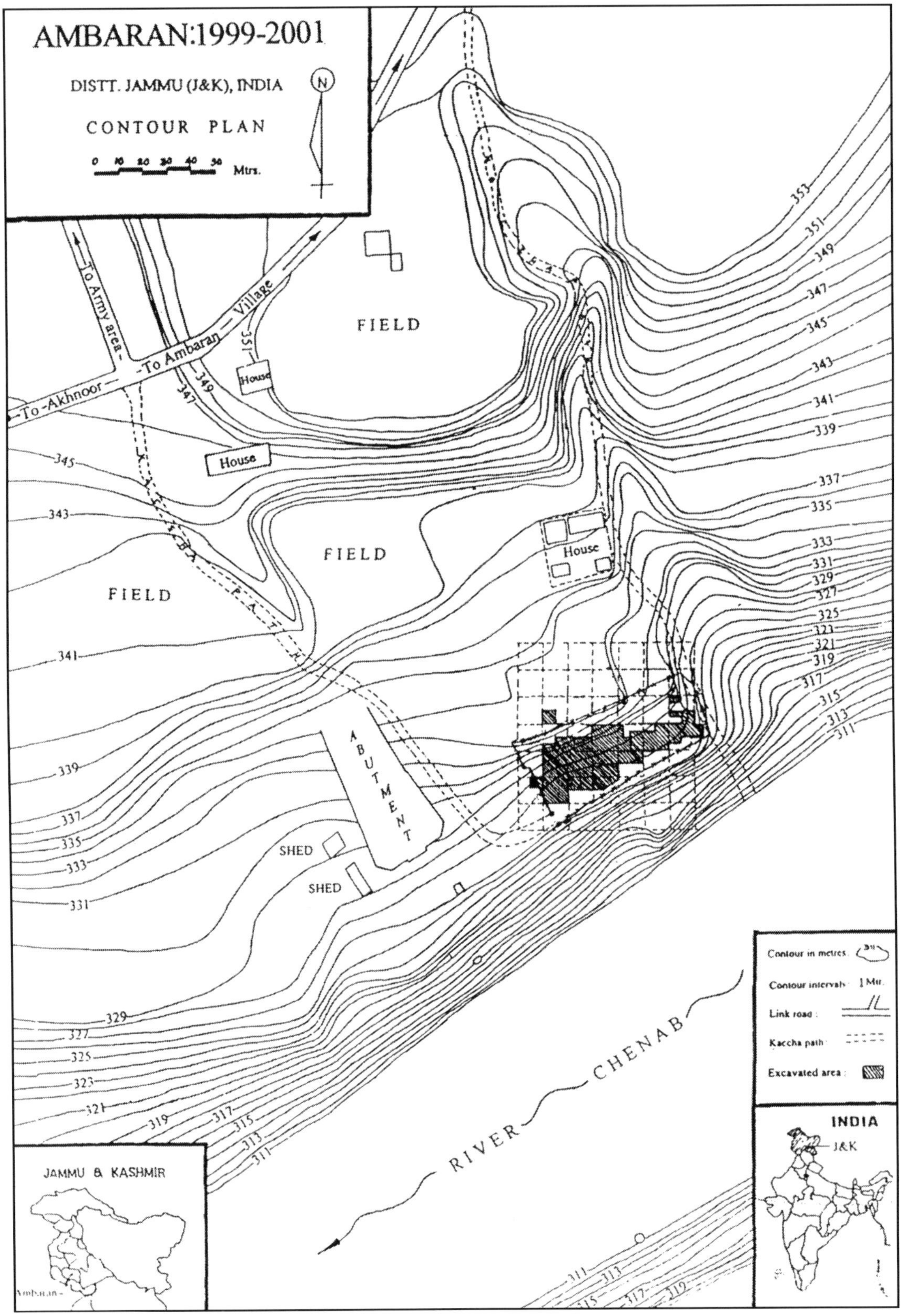

Fig. 1. Ambaran : 1999-2001— Dist. Jammu (J&K), India

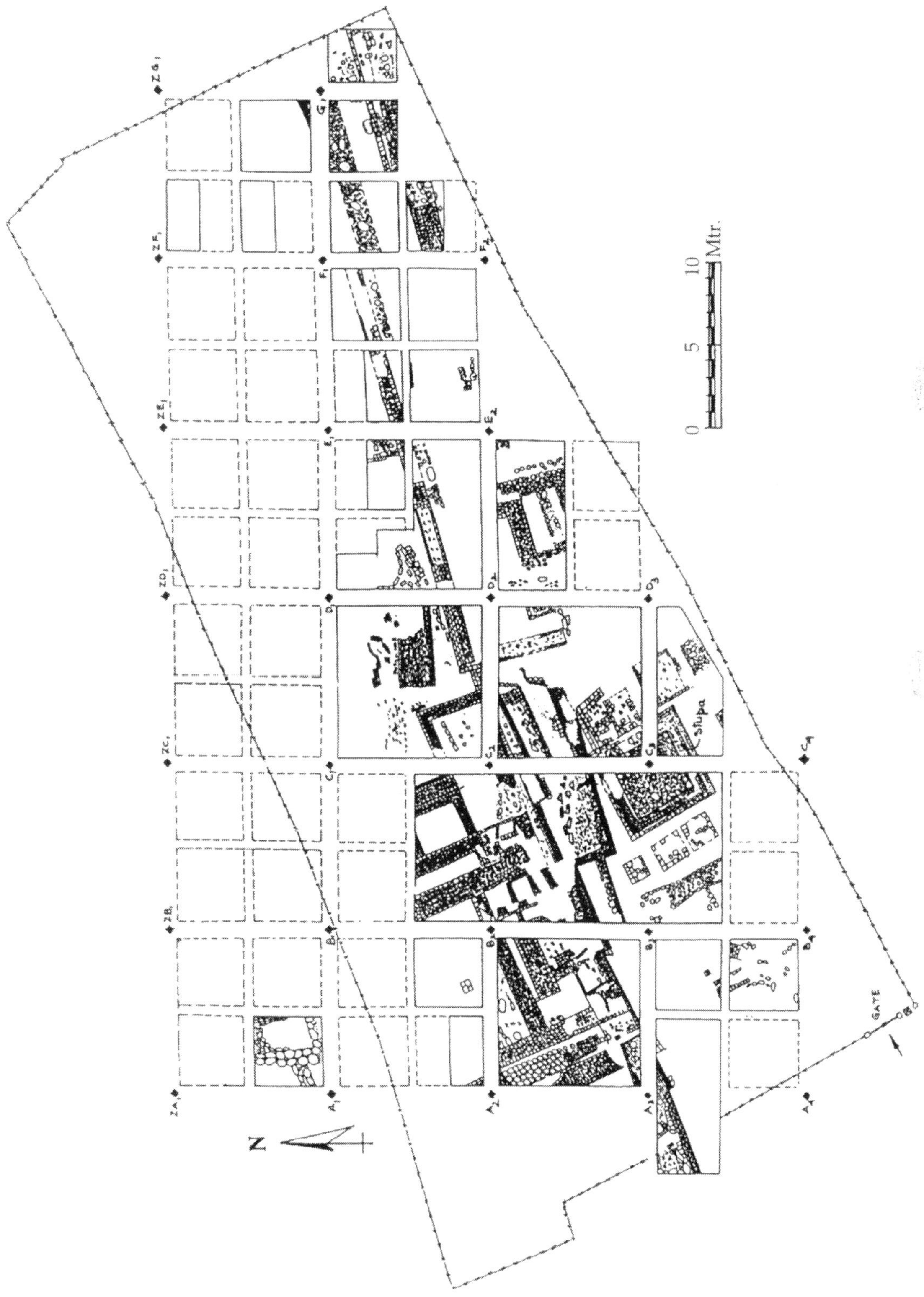

Fig. 2. Ambaran : 1999-2001— Key Plan of Structures

cultivation and unauthorized digging operations in the area in the past. The site seems to have been abandoned sometimes around 7th century AD, mainly due to flash floods in the river and decline of Buddhism in the area. Brahmanical sculptures of Kashmir style belonging to the following centuries have been reported from Ambaran-Akhnur area and are preserved in Dogra Art Museum at Jammu.

A preliminary study of the site revealed the cultural sequence of following periods:

Period I	:	Pre-Kuṣāṇa Period (*c.* 2nd-1st century BC.)
Period II	:	Kuṣāṇa Period (*c.* 1st to 3d century AD)
Period III	:	Post-Kuṣāṇa (Gupta) Period (*c.* 4th-5th century AD)
Period IV	:	Post-Gupta Period (*c.* 6th-7th century AD)

PERIOD I

No structural remains of Period I were found. A separate horizon of the period was noticed in square ZA.1, qd. 4 over the natural soil. The thin deposit contained grey ware sherds of bowls and red ware vases (Fig. 3). The deposit was also noticed in sq. C3, qd. 1 below the foundation of the *stūpa*.

PERIOD II

Buddhist monastic establishment was founded at the site in Period II. A *stūpa* votive *stūpas* and walls of a monastery and another long structure were exposed which are all built of burnt brick masonry with bricks usually measuring 36 to 38 x 5 x 24 x 5 x 6 to 7 cm. After partially exposing two squarish structures in quadrants 3 and 4 of square B2 during the first season, it was inferred that they may be bases of *stūpas*. The same was confirmed during the second season when the larger of the two structures was found to be a base of a 6 x 6 m *stūpa* and smaller one being a votive *stūpa* measuring approximately 1.50 x 1.50 m. Besides, two more 2 x 2 m square bases of votive *stūpas* were exposed on the western side of the main *stūpa* towards south of the former votive *stūpa*. Parallel to the three votive *stūpas* was located an elongated stone paved foundation over which more votive *stūpas* must have existed earlier as such structures have large stone pebble foundation. Belonging to the same period were remains of three more votive *stūpas* towards south of the main *stūpa*. The original enclosure brick wall of the monastery was exposed up to a length of 32 m running parallel to the main *stūpa* towards its north which had undergone additions and alterations during the following periods. Another brick wall having a thickness of 1.05 m belonging to an elongated structure of this period was exposed upto a length of 25 m to the east of the enclosure wall of the monastery in almost the same alignment.

The main *stūpa* is described separately, however towards the closing time of second season's work, remains of another large *stūpa* were located in quadrant 2 and 4 of square F1 and quadrant 1 of square G1 which belong to the same period having typical Kuṣāṇa bricks. The measurements suggest that the square base of this *stūpa* was 10 x 5 x 10 m which requires to be exposed in future excavations. Construction of this *stūpa* is in the same manner as of 6 x 6 m square *stūpa* having apron and brick veneer work encasing the core which is made of pebbles mixed with earth. Remains of another possible *stūpa* were noticed during first season in square C1 where a large tapering structure with its fallen superstructure was noticed. The red ware of the period comprised bowls, basins, vases, sprinklers, lids including ink pot type of lids, lamps and spouted pots. The important antiquities of the period include

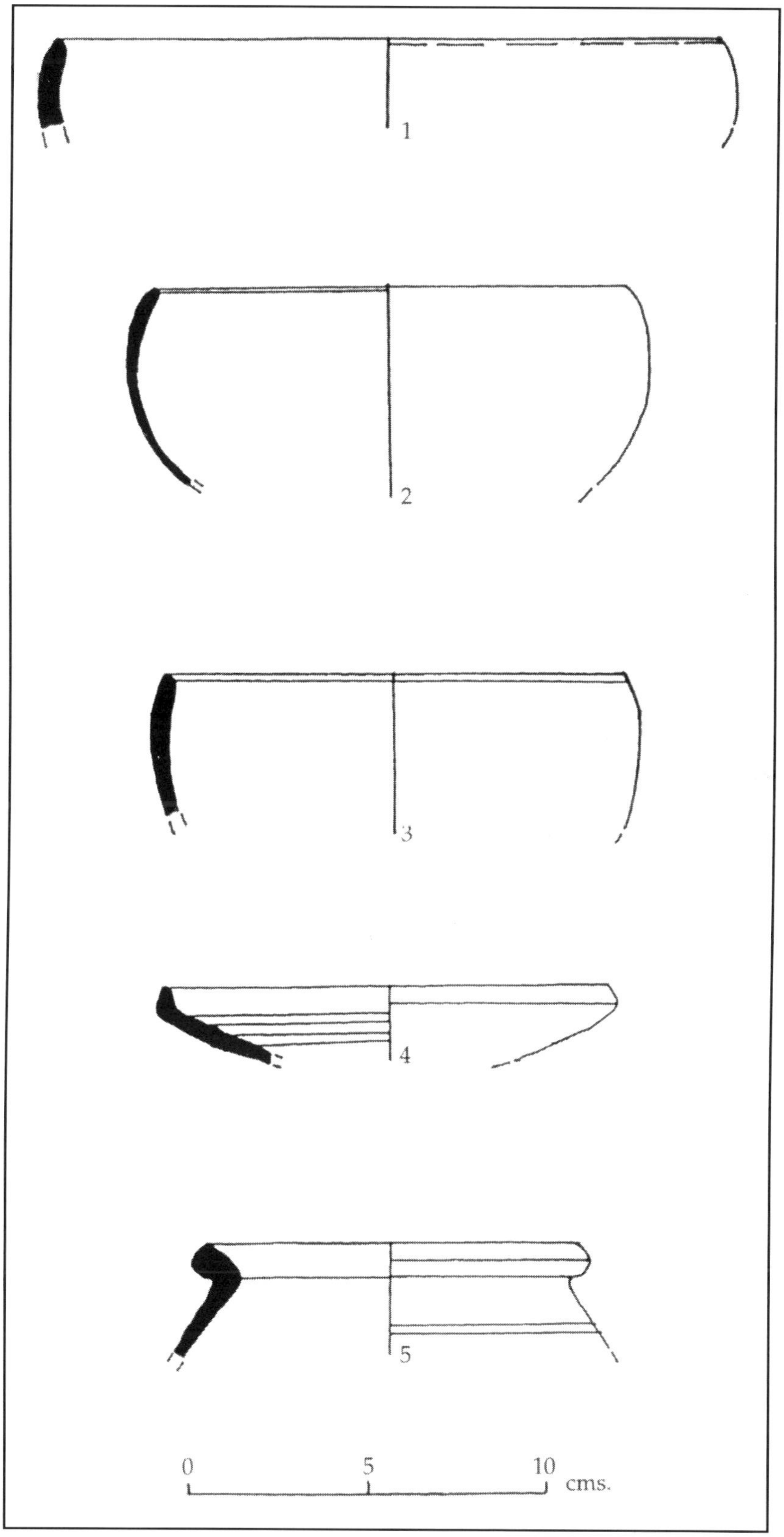

Fig. 3. Ambaran : 1999-2001, Period-I

the reliquary[3] and its contents with associated objects found along with it in the main *stūpa* which are described elsewhere ahead into details owing to its exceptional significance.

PERIOD III

Two distinct structural phases of Period III were noticed, the first having structures with bricks measuring 27 x 22 x 7 cm in general and the second phase with bricks and brick bats of earlier structures reused, mostly in strengthening the walls which most likely suffered damages due to flash floods in the river. Remains of an entrance of some important complex was found in sq. A2 where there was a concentration of terracotta figurines and their fragments which were all used for decorating the wall, probably the façade of the gate of the monastery. A stone pitched pathway leading towards north and flanked by brick walls was noticed. It seems that the entrance was blocked or narrowed during the next phase by putting a wall at the southern end of the pathway, parallel to it at the gate.

Terracotta heads, occasionally showing profile of the face along with other fragments of torso, ornaments and drapery bearing marks of reinforcement have been found which were meant to stick to the plaster of the wall. Extensions of walls of the structures of Period III were traced in squares B1 and B2. It was noticed that structures of the first phase were given extra support and also repaired at different stages during the second phase and even afterwards when they were damaged due to floods. The wall abutting the gate was traced in eastern direction in qd. 3 of sq. A2, qds. 3 and 4 of sq. B2 and qds. 1, 2 and 4 of sq. C2. It was observed that its tapering nature and projections were meant to save the structure from floods which were added to the original construction during the Period III in two phases. Towards west of the gate, the wall in the same alignment was traced in qd. 4 of A2, qd. 1 of A3 and qd. 2 of XA3 and was found still continuing. A maximum of 31 courses of bricks were found in it in qd. 4 of sq. B2 of which the lower 21 courses belong to phase I and the top 10 courses to a later phase when it was repaired. The lower courses slightly project after three courses each giving the tapering nature to the wall and consist of full bricks while the top ten courses do not follow the same principle and were outcome of the repairs taken up in the second phase when bricks and brickbats were utilized to maintain the height of the structure in a haphazard manner. A few decorated bricks were also found reused in this repair work in the top courses.

A rectangular structure with its walls having the width of 0.70 m was exposed towards west of the large structure of period II. From the floor of the rectangular structure chunks of lime plaster were found lying upside down which suggest that they are the remains of the fallen stucco ceiling which was painted with red strips. Its northern wall was found damaged due to unauthorized digging probably by antiquity hunters in the past. Overlying the levels of Period III burning activity was also noticed in the sealing layers at some spots which is quite distinct in the northern section of square C1, but it would be too premature to relate it to the invasion and destruction of the site by the Huṇas as no other evidence is available in this regard. Some reed impressions were also found on clay lumps.

A 2 x 2 m square base of a votive *stūpa* along with evidence of its circular superstructure was found in quadrant 2 of square C2 which belongs to the Period III. A rectangular brick platform with associated finds of iron slag in considerable quantity along with iron objects and clay pipes located in square E1, quadrants 3 and 4 and square F1, quadrant 4 suggests the evidence of an ironsmith's workshop in this period which was most probably attached to the monastic establishment.

PERIOD IV

The large complex which is seemingly a monastery, partly survived during the Period IV when additions and alterations were made in its original structure and repairs were also carried out. Due to cultivation and unmindful diggings at the site, the structures of this period, which were nearer to the surface suffered heavy damages and walls with only one or two courses of brick bats could be found. A square structure which is probably base of a brick pillar was seen in qd. 4 of sq. A1 besides supporting walls and partitions in structures made during this period. The maximum deposit of the period was observed in qd. 1 of sq. A2 consisting of four layers with a distinct layer of brick-debris of some structure. A blurred coin possibly a Huṇa issue was found near the pillar in this level.

Pottery of Periods II to IV (Figs. 4 and 5) does not have much difference in shapes, except that in the last period rims of bowls became sharp and straight which were thick and slightly incurved during the earlier two periods. Important shapes are basins, bowls, sprinklers, vases, lids, lamps, keep with hole in the base, handled cup, spouts including one with a grotesque animal head and storage jars. Stamped designs have also been found on a few sherds. Amongst the pot lugs an interesting piece bears head of a lion.

Among important antiquities, a large number of decorative terracotta figurines mentioned earlier including one having the left profile of a princely looking male head, a broken terracotta mould showing the bust of a lady wearing a beaded hair ornament with a boss at the centre, ear pendants, necklace and armlets, two small terracotta grotesque heads, terracotta moulds of leaves and ornaments, terracotta, skin, rubber, beads and gamesmen, iron nails, hooks and rings, a few copper objects, a glass and a stone bead, part of a small stone sculpture in Gupta style showing a male attendant holding some object in his right raised hand and the left resting on his thigh and other minor antiquities have been found. An interesting broken terracotta tablet mould bears on its different faces negative impressions of a pendant, fruits and leaves, a bird sitting on a twig having fruit and leaf and a squatting figure of a monkey. Twelve circular copper coins were found during excavations of which two require cleaning, one is blurred, eight belong to the Kuṣāṇa rulers Soter Megas, Kaniṣka and Huviṣka and one to perhaps Toramāṇa, the Huṇa ruler.

THE TERRACOTTA HEADS

The Akhnur terracotta heads from the site of Ambaran have found their way to different museums throughout the world in the past. They mainly have Buddha, Bodhisattvas, male and female worshippers, princely figures, ascetics, philosophers, children, animals like horse, lion and elephant, decorative features including ornaments, floral and other designs, body parts including fingers, palms, feet, torso, drapery and female breasts, plasters dividing panels and such other features. They no doubt represent stories from the life of Lord Buddha, such as the dream of Queen Māyā, the Great Renunciation of Prince Siddhārtha and other favourite scenes.

Charles Fabri was the first to locate the findspot of these Akhnur terracotta heads at Pambarwan (Ambaran) when in 1938 he visited the site twice in September and October in the company of Ram Chand Anant Ram Saraf of Akhnur town who had earlier taken some beautiful terracotta heads from the site to Lahore and supplied them to the Central Museum, Lahore.[4] Fabri's visit to the site was the outcome of his investigative work started in 1936 after joining the Museum and coming across the beautiful terracotta heads. During these two years before coming to Akhnur he also made visits to Baramulla, Ushkur (Ushkar), Harwan

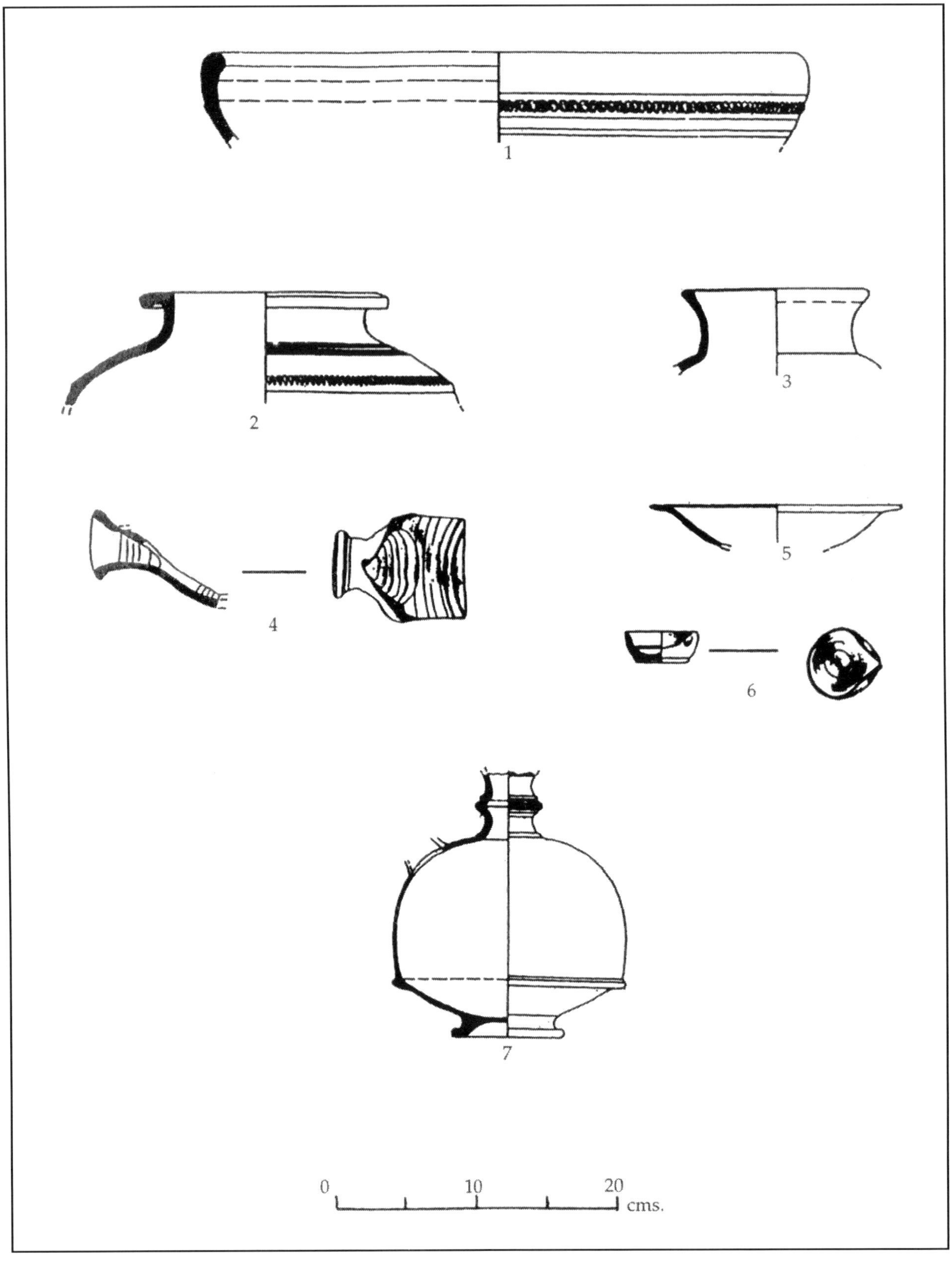

Fig. 4. Ambaran : 1999-2001, Period-II

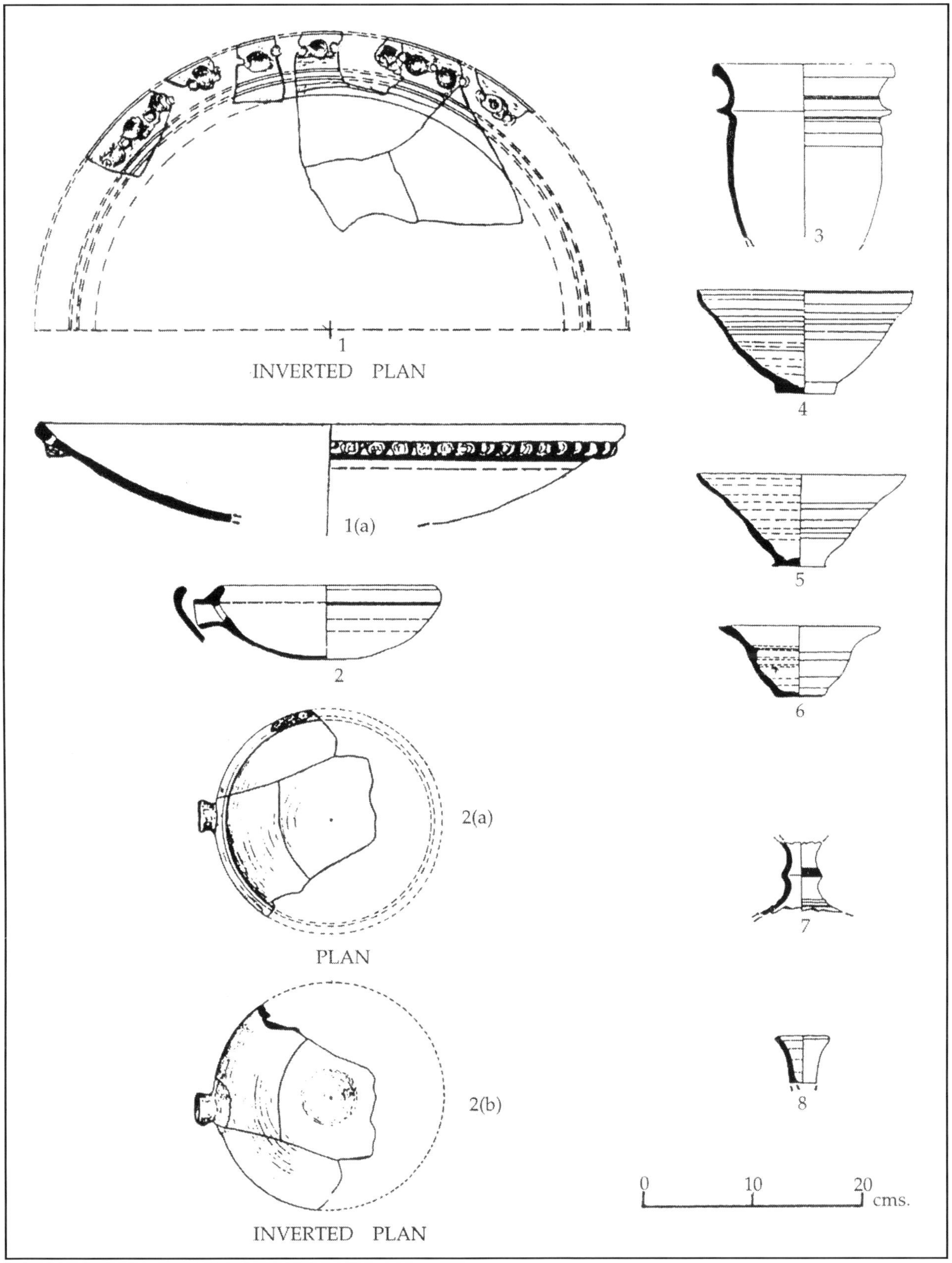

Fig. 5. Ambaran : 1999-2001, Period-III

and Srinagar and inspired by the Ushkur terracottas of similar style, he excavated a few trenches at Ushkur.

Charles Fabri, after visiting the site of Pambarwan at Ambaran, called 'the cemetery of what was once the finest school of sculpture of this country'.[5] Writing further about the distinct art style of Akhnur, Ushkur and Harwan terracottas, he mentions

> other schools of sculpture no doubt have their merits, but the Kashmir terracotta school, with all its baroque love for striking elements must be given first place when it comes to charm. No school of sculpture in Indian art history can be compared with it in this respect; some of the faces can be described as adorable in their delineation of feminine delicacy; and in that respect this school can hold its head high among any other schools of sculpture in any country.[6]

It may be mentioned here that walls in the monastery of Kuṣāṇa period at Jaulian located near the Kuṣāṇa city site of Taxila were decorated with similar narrative panels which suffered destruction during Hūṇa invasion towards the latter half of the 5th century AD. Fabri has correctly described the functional use of these terracottas at Ambaran when he writes

> As in Taxila, as at Harwan, as at Ushkar, the monastery once possessed a mighty stone wall, upon which was displayed to all comers a magnificent large terracotta relievo, many times life-sized probably as high as thirty five or forty feet. Badly fired, the burnt clay relievo slowly crumbled down when the Buddhist site was deserted; and the heavy heads were the first to roll from the necks. Excavations would yield now nothing but a few more fragments; for these fields, like those of Ushkar monastery, have been cultivated, may be for centuries.
>
> Year after year, when the plough wends its wearied way among the pebble-strewn earth, a few fragments turn up, only to be thrown away by the farmer, or given to the children to play with.[7]

He seems to be wrong in two assertions above—firstly in a haste he seems to have thought the stone wall at Ambaran as the enclosure wall of the monastery. During present excavations it was found that terracotta were decorated over brick enclosure wall. Secondly, Fabri was not very enthusiastic about the excavations as mentioned above, but during the course of present excavations not only terracotta fragments of such types were found but remains of *stūpas*, votive *stūpas*, monastery and above all, reliquary in the main *stūpa* were discovered.

Fabri notices strong baroque mannerism in the art of these terracotta heads and on artistic grounds supported by his unintelligible theories regarding antiquity of similar findings at Harwan and Ushkur (Huviṣkapura) dates the terracottas around AD 700.

The sites at Ushkur, Harwan and Ambaran (Akhnur) are all located outside the area of Gandhāra and therefore the artistic representations on the figures from these sites may not be typical Greco-Roman or Hellenistic, but undoubtedly they are influenced at a great extent by the Gandhāra art as it is evident from their technical execution and style. These sites are located in the area, which remained under the rule of Indo-Greek kings before their occupation by the Kuṣāṇas. Thus, on artistic grounds, separating the art of these sites from Gandhāra art by Charles Fabri cannot be totally accepted. Gandhāra School of Art vanished after the invasion of Hūṇas around AD 500 and therefore, the date of these terracottas as AD 700 seems impossible.

Fabri seems to have deliberately tried to refute the findings of R.C. Kak at Harwan where the artistic activity has been dated to about AD 300 or belonging to the late phase of the Kuṣāṇa period. Although he mentions that Daya Ram Sahni and R.C. Kak have placed the Harwan fragments in the Kuṣāṇa period.[8] Fabri's idea of placing the Akhnur terracottas around AD 700 originated from his excavations at Ushkur where within a quadrangle a stone structure called the temple was partly exposed and trial trenches by Fabri yielded terracotta fragments in 1937. Ushkur represents the city site of Hushkapura (Huviṣkapura) which was founded by the Kuṣāṇa king Huviṣka[9] in the 2nd century AD.

In fact, the so-called temple is a *stūpa* and it is quite evident that its structure belongs to the 8th century AD and is the same as mentioned by Kalhaṇa in his *Rājataraṅgiṇī* as constructed by Lalitāditya Muktāpīḍa.[10] Fabri has ignored that it is definitely built over an older structure, perhaps belonging to the time of the Kuṣāṇas, stone blocks of which were seen after removal of silt and some of the loose ones lying on ground near the *stūpa*. In a recent study of the art of Kashmir, Pran Gopal Paul has compared the terracotta heads of Ushkur and Akhnur with those of Taxila and beyond including Fondukistan and has refuted the dating of Fabri suggesting 6th century as more convincing date on artistic grounds. While he has rightly identified the residual Hellenism of Gandhāra art infused by a few Gupta elements in these terracottas, his dating is mainly based on the idea that sculptors of Akhnur and Ushkur had copied the tradition of Taxila, Fondukistan or Madhyadeśa. Writing about Akhnur terracottas, he mentions

> The geographical position of Akhnur in a buffer zone, between Gandhāran and Gupta spheres of influence, largely determined the style of its sculpture. Out of a combination of elements of the two major artistic traditions, viz. the 4th to 5th century stucco and terracotta art of Taxila and the sculptures of contemporary Madhyadeśa, the idiom of this school evolved. Its tendency towards naturalism or rather realism is derived from Gandhāra and its serenity and grace from Gupta aesthetics.[11]

He further emphasizes that 'of the two contending sources Gupta elements are far outweighed by Taxilan traits in Akhnur'.[12]

Taxilan prototypes, in general, belong to the period from 2nd to 4th centuries AD and it is evident from Sir John Marshall's extensive excavation that Taxila was caught up in a political turmoil in the middle of the 5th century when the monasteries and other edifices were completely destroyed during Hūṇa invasion. Thus considering the Taxilan influence on Akhnur, Paul's dating of 6th century cannot be relied upon as Taxila must have influenced Akhnur quite earlier as it is also evident from the style of construction of the Kuṣāṇa *stūpa* exposed in the present excavations and discovery of reliquary and its contents which are all akin to the Taxilan evidence. The region of Jammu and Kashmir also came under the rule of the turbulent Saivite Hūṇas who were opposed to Buddhism, a fact which also suggests the upper age limit of the particular school at Akhnur or Ushkur in the middle of the 5th century AD.

As per Allahabad Pillar Inscription, Samudragupta[13] seems to have already forced the later Kuṣāṇa kings—*Daivaputra śāhi śāhānuśāhi* to enter into alliance with him in the first half of the 4th century, a fact which is also proved by numismatic evidence of coins of Gaḍahra, a later Kuṣāṇa king of Gandhāra who started mentioning the name of the mighty Gupta emperor on his coins in place of that of Shāpur II (AD 309-379), the Sassanian emperor who seems to have had overpowered the Kuṣāṇa king earlier as it is also evident from a passage in the Narrative History of the Roman Officer Ammianus Marcellinus which states that Kuṣāṇas were in conflict with Shāpur II.[14] The territory of Madra (Madradeśa) which roughly corresponds to ancient Śākala or modern Sialkot and the surrounding regions between the Rāvī and Cenāb rivers[15] were subjugated by Samudragupta who mentions in the Allahabad Pillar Inscription that his formidable rule was propitiated with the payment of all tributes, execution of orders and visits (to his court) for obeisance by such frontier rulers as those including Madrakas.[16] With the adoption of Buddhism by Milinda or Menander, the Indo-Greek ruler of Śākala (Sagala), the area had already come under Buddhist influence. It is, therefore, easier to understand that the political influence of the Guptas in the 4th century increased further cultural impacts of art of Madhyadeśa on artistic activities in the border areas and further beyond in the north-west region. Thus in the light of political events and on stylistic grounds Akhnur Buddhist terracottas can be dated to the second half of the 4th century AD which is further confirmed by the stratigraphical evidence of the excavations conducted at Ambaran (Akhnur) recently. The excavations have also made it clear that the site came into prominence in the early Kuṣāṇa period and thus it must have enjoyed the cultural links with the centres of Gandhāran art for a long period due to its proximity with Gandhāra region. New impetus of Gupta classicism helped Akhnur artists in evolving a fresh mixed style in the 4th century AD which was seemingly followed by the artists at Ushkur and Harwan.

A large number of terracotta human fingers, palms, hands, legs, ears, torso parts including those of lady figures with breasts covered with chiton like cloth and nipples shown with four dots which are quite similar to one published by Charles Fabri, parts of bodies and drapery of Buddha or female devotees, decorative ornaments having floral and other designs, a fly whisk, a headless female deity and one full and some fragmentary relief heads of devotees with open eyelids and elaborate hairdress and ornaments were found in the present excavations. Upper part of a Buddha head with urea and left profile of a princely figure deserves special mention. Some of the fingers belong to life size images while most of them might have been from smaller ones. Shapes of the fingers suggest different postures intended for expression. These terracottas must have embellished the walls of the monastery in the first phase of Period III. Pieces of terracotta plasters that once divided and decorated panels of the great relievo, which were earlier noticed by Charles Fabri,[17] were found during excavations.

THE *STŪPA* AND RELIQUARY

Remains of a structure with squarish plan were noticed in quadrant 3 of square B2 during the first season and its squarish nature was confirmed through a control pit in quadrant 2 of square B3 towards the close of the season and it was presumed that this structure may be part of a square base of a votive *stūpa* with its extant maximum 14 courses of brick work with concave and convex sided moulded bricks besides plain ones at regular intervals. It was also noticed that the structure belongs to the Kuṣāṇa period. Further excavations during the second season brought to light the complete plan (Fig. 6) of the structure which was found to be 6 x 5 x 6 m square base of a *stūpa*, not votice one as it later yielded relic casket with charred bones, suggesting its conception as a *Śārīrika stūpa*. The measurement includes 0.30 m wide apron of *stūpa* all around, over which was constructed the brick veneer of the square base of the *stūpa* in such a manner that it encases the core of the *stūpa* comprising pebbles mixed with mud as in the case of some Taxilan *stūpas*. The extant maximum height of the *stūpa* is 1.10 m on its north and upto the height of 0.65 m mouldings were made, over which plain brick work continued (Fig. 7). The brick veneer of the *stūpa* base is 0.60 m in thickness. The core has both small and medium-sized pebbles. Decorated bricks having bands of dentil brackets and other decorated bricks of the drum and the *harmikā* of the *stūpa*, a red sandstone *yaśṭi* and a few pieces of the wedge-shaped thin bricks suggesting their use in the *chatrāvalī* were found from the structural debris overlying the *stūpa* remains. A conjectural view (Fig. 8) of the *stūpa* based on these data and evidence of Taxilan prototypes suggest that the *stūpa* must have been nearly 9 m in height. A rectangular brick paved platform was found associated with the *stūpa* on its eastern side over which some lamps were found amongst pottery, suggesting the use of the platform for worship purpose.

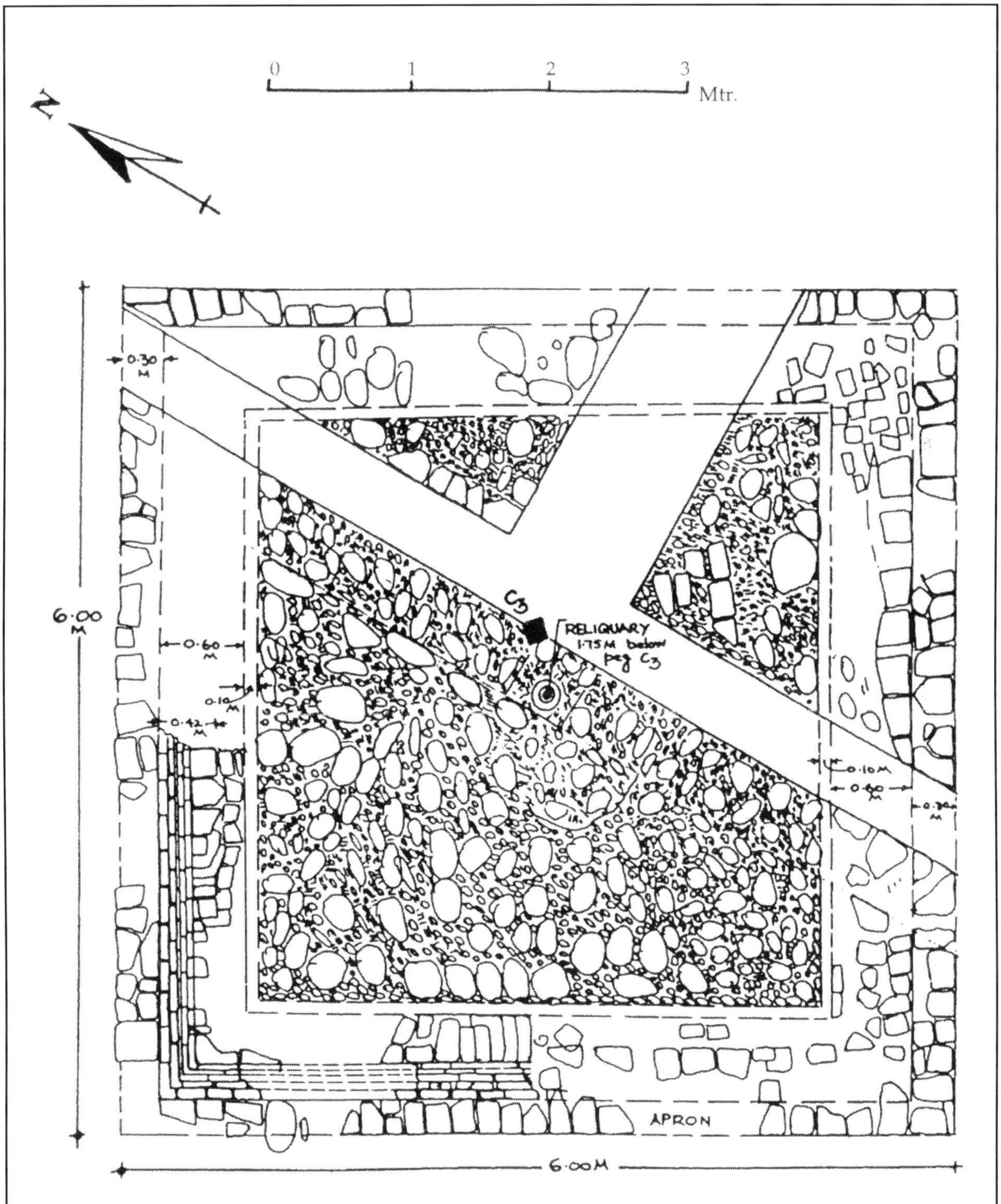

Fig. 6. Ambaran: 1999-2001, Plan of *Stūpa*

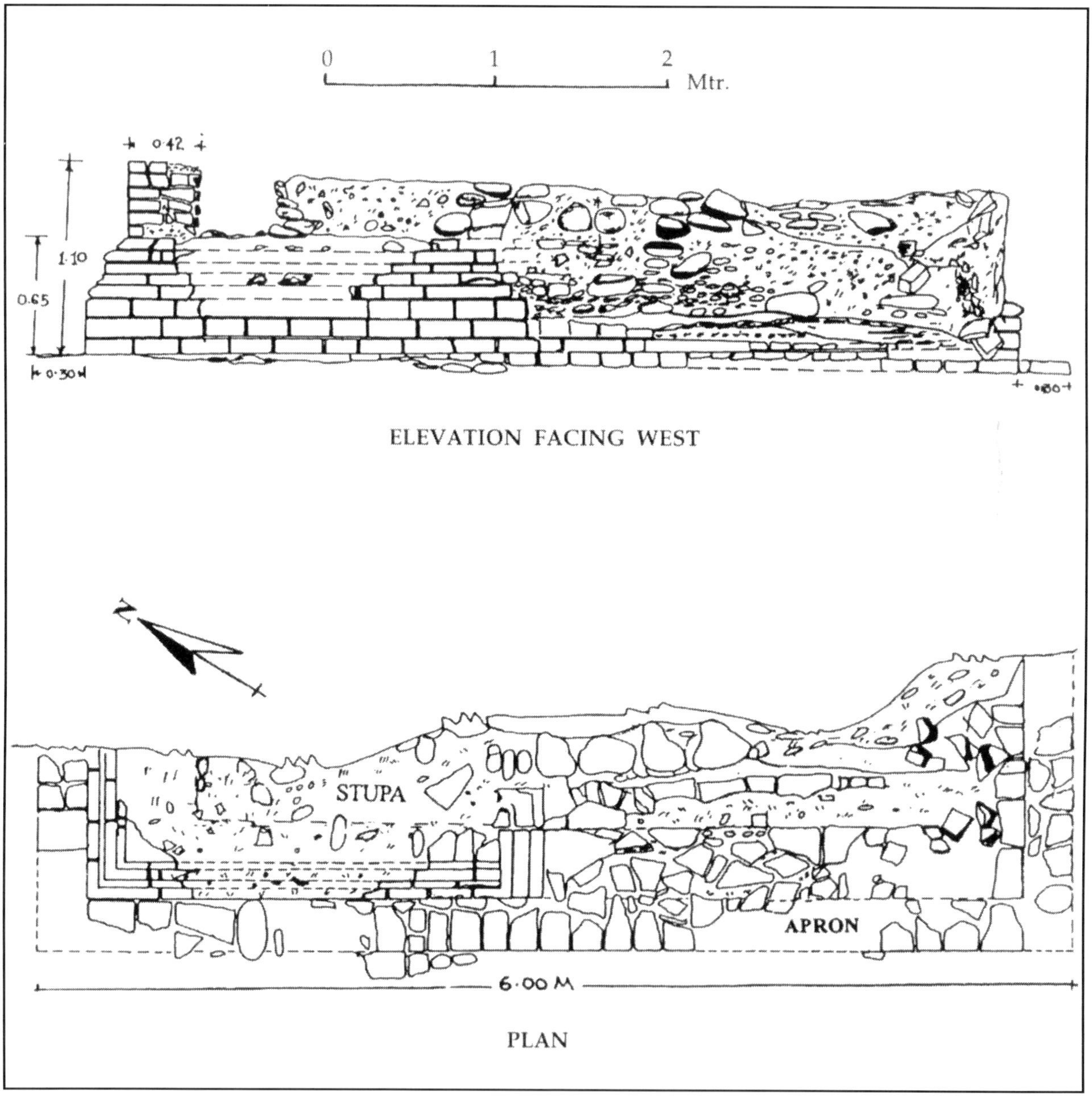

Fig. 7. Ambaran : 1999-2001, *Stūpa*

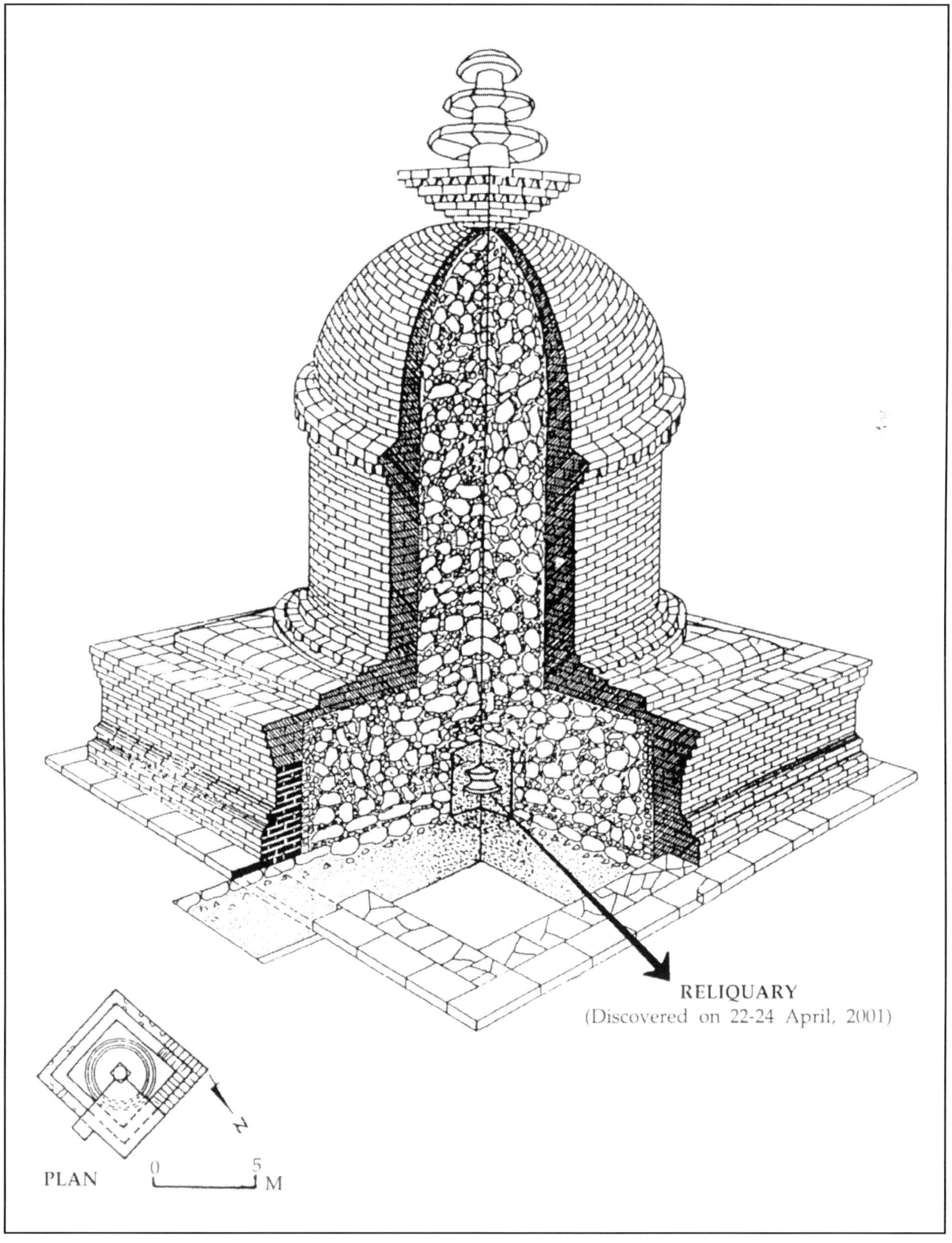

Fig. 8. Ambaran : 1999-2001, *Stūpa* (Conjectural View)

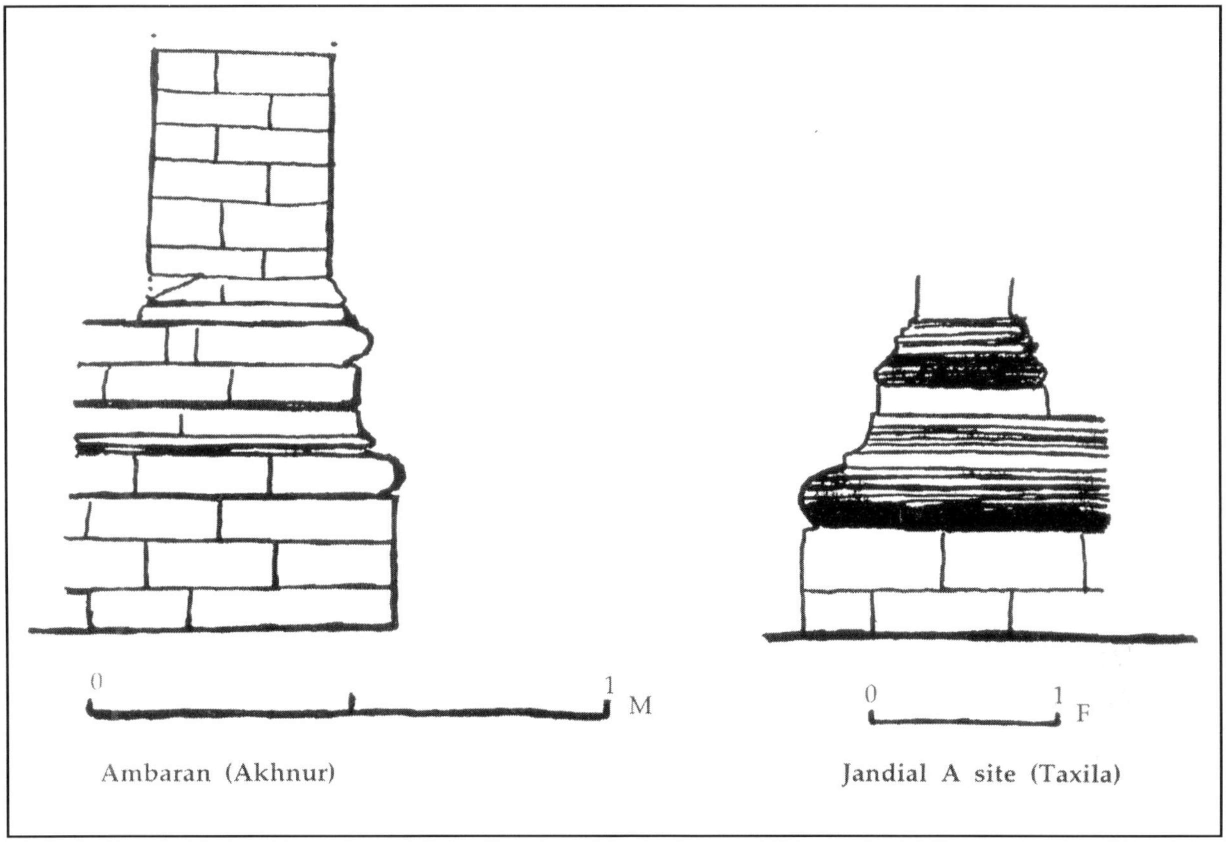

Fig. 9. Elevation of *Stūpas*

Stūpas belonging to the Śaka-Parthian and Kusāṇa periods in Taxila including those at Dharmarājika, Kalwan and Jandial monastic establishments depict similar constructional pattern visible in their elevation and plan. Decorative mouldings at the *stūpa* bases at Ambaran and Jandial (a site)[18] are remarkably similar (Fig. 9). Another common feature between these Taxilan *stūpas* and the *stūpa* at Ambaran is in their core which is constructed of pebbles closely compacted with earth or pebbles set in mud.[19] An interesting point to be taken care of in these Taxilan *stūpas* is that they contain relic chambers and reliquaries and caskets have been found in a number of them. The *stūpa* J2 at Dharmarājikā belonging to the 1st century AD has yielded a casket being a flat pyxis of grey schist which contained a small box of silver and had a small box of gold in it which contained some minute fragments of bone and also some beads in the casket.[20] The *stūpa* shrine A1 at Kalwan had in its relic chamber a casket of schist covered with gold-leaf containing another spherical casket covered with gold-leaf and twelve rosettes of thin gold sheet, fragments of bone, different beads and other objects including copperplate inscription of year 134 of Azes engraved in Kharoṣṭī.[21] Sir John Marshall believed that in the 4th and 5th centuries it was usual to construct the relic chamber of large *stūpas* high up in their dome instead of low down in their foundations and that is why the main *stūpa* at Bhamala site belonging to 5th-6th century AD did not reveal any relic chamber around its base or in its foundation.[22]

Inspired by the above Taxilan evidence, the author was sure to get some relic casket in the *stūpa* base at Ambaran. For this purpose the one metre baulk running north to south was retained and the one metre baulk running between pegs B3 and C3 was removed as the central point of the square base of the *stūpa* was measured and located a few centimetres south-west of the peg C3. All the precautions were taken to minimize the damage to the *stūpa* and the main operation was taken up on 22 April 2001 and as its northern brick veneer was already damaged during ancient period due to water flow towards it from the north, a 0.50 m strip of the core of the *stūpa* was removed to horizontally approach the centre. Simultaneously, a part of the north-south baulk in its west having 1.0 m in length in north-south orientation with 0.50 m thickness on either side of the peg C3 was removed layer by layer so as to reach vertically up to the foundation level of the *stūpa*.

It was around 1130 hours on the same day when the pick-axe lifted a small chunk of earth along with an orange carnelian bead. The excitement increased and soon a copper object was noticed. The sections (Fig. 10) of the trench were trimmed and photographed and three-dimensional recording was completed. Further scraping brought out several pieces of copper. The main copper object was removed which was found to be a heavily encrusted reliquary with its broken lid, part of which was already attached with the body of the reliquary and the copper pieces found in the scraping were identified to be the remaining pieces of the lid which were scattered around the reliquary which was possibly crushed due to natural factors and earth pressure. As the lid was already found broken, soil was seen set inside the reliquary in which some thin circular gold sheets were visible. The reliquary was found to be 2.4 cm high with its diameter being 5.6 cm.

The contents of the reliquary were slowly and carefully taken out which comprised—

(1) 30 circular thin sheets of gold with their diameter approximately between 1.2 cm to 1.4 cm.
(2) 2 circular rimmed thin sheets of silver, possibly to keep gold sheets having the diameter of 2.1 cm.
(3) About 150 micro-beads of pearl.
(4) 12 cylindrical coral beads.
(5) 2 metallic micro-beads.
(6) Oval shaped silver casket in two equal parts, but having their diameter 2.5 cm and 2.3 cm respectively so as to fit in with each other. Some liquid seems to have been applied over their edges and heated to fix the two parts together which was opened by the author.
(7) A circular gold casket, again in two equal parts with their diameter 1.5 cm and 1.4 cm respectively was found already open inside the silver casket along with small pieces of charred bone and probably a minute part of tooth. Originally, it was also closed after applying some liquid and heating the round edges.

Some small bone pieces were found in the same level from the spot just outside the reliquary. As already stated, a carnelian bead was found there. The excavation work was suspended on 23 April being non-field day and the next day when it was started again the following objects were found from the same spot after scraping the earth :

(8) 4 full and 6 broken circular thin sheets of gold as found in the reliquary making their total number to be 34 full and 6 broken parts.
(9) 1 bead of amethyst.
(10) 3 encrusted copper coins, two of which are possibly Kuṣāṇa issues which require chemical cleaning for their decipherment.

The above objects are definitely parts of the contents of the reliquary which were scattered

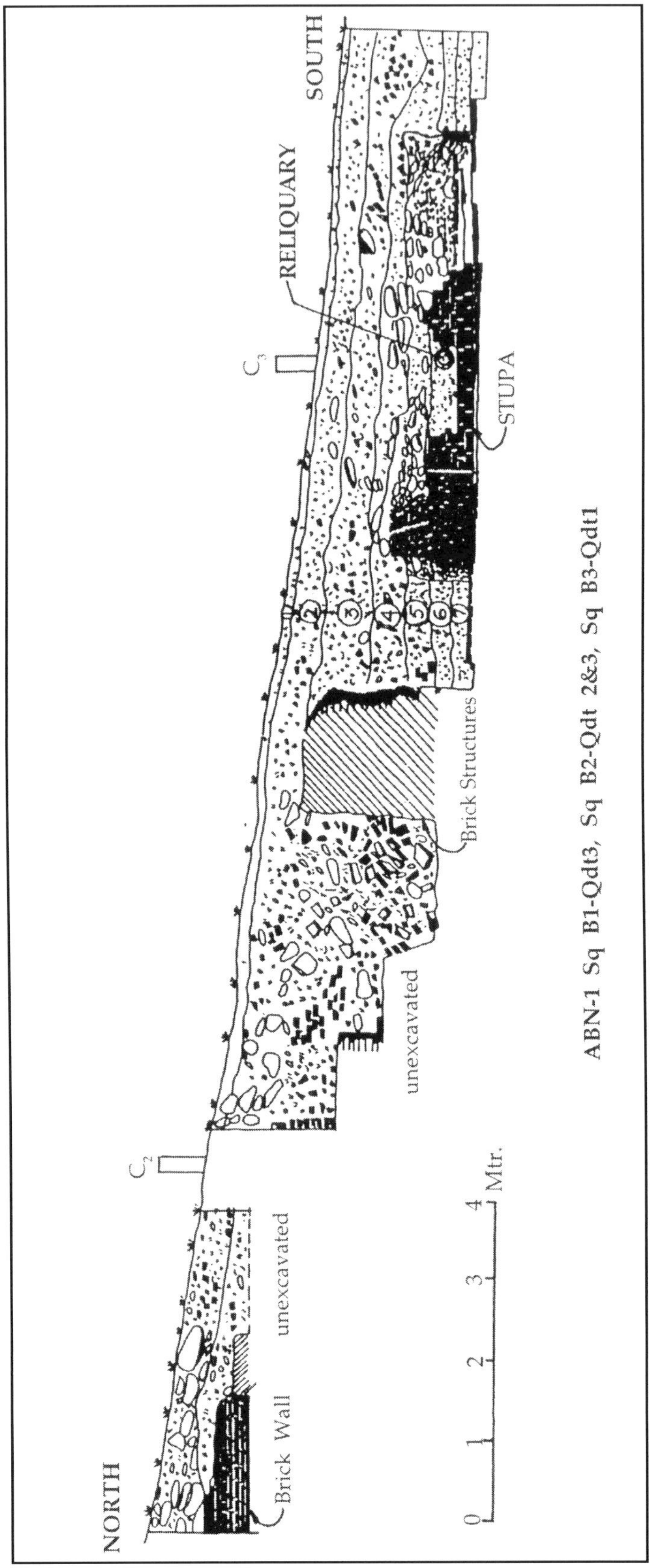

Fig. 10. Ambaran : 1999-2001, Section Facing West

at the spot when its lid was crushed and gave way much earlier.

The discovery of these relics has opened a new chapter in the study of history and culture of the region as it is for the first time that in the province of Jammu and Kashmir such significant Buddhist remains have been found. Identification of the great personality whose relics were enshrined in the *stūpa* still remains a matter of discussion in the absence of a definite proof. In this context, the following passage[23] from the *Mahāparinibbānasutta* is relevant in which Lord Buddha himself informed Ānanda that four personalities are eligible over whose corporeal remains *stūpas* are constructed. They being Tathāgata Buddha himself, Pratyeka Sambuddha, Buddha's Śrāvaka or disciple and the Rājā Chakravarti or an emperor—

'Chattārome Ānanda ! Thūpāraha. Katame Chattāro?
(1) *Tathāgato arahaṁ Sammāsambuddho thūpāraho.*
(2) *Pachchekasambuddho thūpāraho.*
(3) *Tathāgatassa sāvako thūpāraho.*
(4) *Rāja chakkavatti thūpāraho' (136).*

Association of the relics found at Ambaran with a Pratyeka Sambuddha or with a Śrāvaka of Buddha may not be possible in this region on the borderlands of the Madhyadeśa. Marshall[24] has cited W.W. Tarn in stating that according to Plutarch after the death of Menander, the cities raised *stūpas* over his ashes. The ritual was in origin reserved for such category of great men as he was thought to be a Buddhist emperor—Chakravartin. He was the ruler of Madra country with Śākala or Sialkot as his capital, which is quite near Akhnur on the other side of the border. But he seems to have died around *c.* 150 BC and thus his date seems to be at least two centuries earlier than the construction of the *stūpa* at the present site. Under these circumstances, it seems quite reasonable that the relics of Lord Buddha himself might have been enshrined in the *stūpa* at Ambaran with full dignity and honour as per the practice of the Kuṣāṇa times as noticed elsewhere, particularly in Gandhāra region.

ACKNOWLEDGEMENTS

I am grateful to the Director-General, Archaeological Survey of India for according permission to take up the excavations. I sincerely acknowledge the hard work of my team which included P.C. Chowdhary, A.K. Khanna (first season), V.C. Sharma (second season), M.K. Joshi, P.L. Meena, Gulzar Singh, B.S. Jamwal, Raghbir Singh, R.K. Kaul, Arunji Siddha, V.K. Koul, A.K. Kaul, S.K. Bhat—all from Srinagar Circle of the Archaeological Survey of India and Sunil Kumar Jha. Exceptionally important Buddhist remains were brought to light by the team at Ambaran at the time when unmindful fanatic destruction of heritage took place in Bamiyan and other places in Afghanistan. I am also thankful to Major General (Retd.) S.C. Kashyap, Major General A.S. Bahia, GOC, 10th Division and other army officers stationed at Akhnur who regularly visited the excavations and provided all possible help to the team and the camp.

NOTES AND REFERENCES

1. Charles Fabri, 1939, 'Buddhist Baroque in Kashmir', *Asia*, October 1939; Five popular articles under the title 'Buddhist Masterpieces', I to V, *Kashmir* (Government of India, Publications Division, Ministry of Information & Broadcasting in 1951); 'Akhnur Terracottas', *Marg*, Vol. VIII, No. 2, Bombay, March 1955, pp. 53-64.

2. B.R. Mani, 2000, 'Excavation at Ambaran, Jammu & Kashmir, India, 1999-2000 and Dating of the Akhnur Buddhist Terracotta Heads', *Newsletter*, Circle of Inner Asian Art, SOAS, Issue 12, London, December, 2000, pp. 3-10; 'Excavations at Ambaran 1999-2000 and Dating of Akhnur Buddhist Terracotta Heads', *Pragdhara*, No. 11, 2000-2001, Lucknow, 2001.
3. B.R. Mani, 2001, 'New Finds at Akhnur, Jammu & Kashmir, India', *Newsletter*, Circle of Inner Asian Art, SOAS, Issue 13, London, June 2001, pp. 24-25.
4. Charles Fabri, 1951, *op.cit.*, 'Buddhist Masterpieces-V', *Kashmir*, pp. 559-61.
5. *Ibid.*, p. 559.
6. *Ibid.*, p. 561.
7. *Ibid.*, p. 560.
8. Charles Fabri, *op.cit.*, 1955, p. 53; *Annual Report, Archaeological Survey of India*, 1915-16, p. 62, note; Ram Chandra Kak, *Ancient Monuments of Kashmir*, London, 1933.
9. M.A. Stein, (tr.) 1979, *Kalhana's Rajatarangini*, I, 168, Vol. I, reprinted Delhi, pp. 30-31.
10. *Op.cit.*, Rajatarangini, IV, 188.
11. Pran Gopal Paul, 1986, *Early Sculpture of Kashmir*, Leiden, p. 80.
12. *Ibid.*, p. 92.
13. *Corpus Inscriptionum Indicarum*, Vol. III, Inscriptions of the Early Gupta Kings, Archaeological Survey of India, New Delhi, 1981, pp. 213, 217-18.
14. B.R. Mani, 2000, 'Excavations at Kanispur: 1998-99 (district Baramulla, Kashmir)', *Pragdhara*, No. 10, 1999-2000, Lucknow, p. 7.
15. B.C. Law, 1984. *Historical Geography of Ancient India*, First Indian edition, New Delhi, p. 105.
16. *Corpus Inscriptionum Indicarum*, Vol. III, *op.cit.*
17. Charles Fabri, 1951, *op.cit.*, p. 560.
18. J. Marshall, 1975. *Taxila*, Vol. III (reprinted), pl. 90.
19. *Op.cit.*, Vol. I, pp. 327, 355.
20. *Ibid.*, pp. 244-45.
21. *Ibid.*, p. 327.
22. *Ibid.*, p. 392.
23. *Mahaparinibbanasuttam*, edited and translated into Hindi by Bhikshu Dharamarakshita, Banaras, Samvat 2015, p. 146.
24. J. Marshall, *op.cit.*, Vol. I, p. 33, Fn. 5 and p. 34.

13

THE ORIGIN OF BUDDHA IMAGE
Some Reflection on the Problem

PUSHPA TIWARI

There are very few issues as controversial as the origin of Buddha Image. The debate is restricted only to the origin of 'first surviving ones' carved in stone and discovered from Gandhāra and Mathurā. In the 19th and early 20th century, the main propounders of the theories of Greek and Indian origin were Foucher (1917) and Coomaraswamy (1972, Ind. Ed.), respectively. Since then many important discoveries have come to light but instead of solving the problem they have renewed the debate on the issue of origin, particularly by Lohuizen (1949) and R.C. Sharma (1984).

There are three theories in this regard: (1) the theory of Greek/foreign origin at Gandhāra on the model of Greek God Apollo or Roman kings; (2) the theory of Mathurā origin on the model of standing *yakṣas* and earliest seated Jina type; (3) the theory of simultaneous origin of Gandhāra and Mathurā type in their respective art styles.

Earlier the debate was confined to the chronology of Kuṣāṇa period in general and to the date of Kaniṣka in particular. But now the debate is more on pre-Kaniṣka origin than on the association of Kaniṣka. Let us examine them one by one.

Gandhāra Buddhas: Earlier the debate on the Gandhāra origin of the Buddha image was based on the following evidences:

(1) 'Bodo' type coin of Kaniṣka – standing Buddha with halo and heavy dress.
(2) Kaniṣka reliquary – seated Buddha with Brahmā and Indra on either side. Some scholars identified the name Kaniṣka with the II and III in the series. But recently B.N. Mukherjee has described it as a reliquary of year 1 of King Kaniṣka I.
(3) Bimran reliquary – depiction of standing Buddha and dated on the basis of Azes I, II coins in the late 1st century BC which is a point of contention among scholars who think that the reliquary must have been buried at a later date, with the early coins. So the debate on the chronology of this reliquary fluctuates between a range of 1st BC – AD 1st century.
(4) There are very few dated specimens of Gandhāran art. Among them following are the Buddha images –

(a) Standing Buddha from Loriya Tangai which gives year 318 in an unspecified era.
(b) Hastnagar standing Buddha in the year 384 of an unknown era.
(c) Mamano Dheri Buddha in the year 89 of an unknown era.
(d) Sahari Bahalol Buddha in the year 399.
(e) The seated Buddha in the year 5 of an unknown era (S.A.A., 1979, p. 129).

From Skarah Dheri a statue of Hārīti has been discovered which gives a date in year 399 of an unknown era. The identification of these dates in a particular era is a controversial issue. Foucher, Bachhofer, Vogel, Soper, Rowland, Mukerjee, Rosenfield, Ghirshman and several other scholars have expressed their views on the date of Kaniṣka and identification of era/s in which the above dates along with Mathurā series of dates from 2-98 are given: Seleucid era (312 BC), Mauryan era (321 BC), Śaka era (150 BC), Kuṣāṇa era (129 BC), Vikrama era (58 BC), Kaniṣka era (AD 78) have been suggested by these scholars. The range of difference is well beyond three and a half century. Now generally there seems a consensus among scholars regarding the date of Kaniṣka's accession and the beginning of his era is supposed to be in AD 78.

In the post-independent studies the debate on the Gandhāra origin of the Buddha image is centred around the new discoveries from Gandhāra region, particularly from Swat in the excavation of Butkara I, II and III. These excavations prove that this region was an important, flourishing site and centre of Buddhism and Buddhist art at least since the Śaka-Parthian period. Butkara I and III images are supposed to be the earliest depiction of the Buddha in human form and they betray strong Parthian and early Indian influences (Nehru, 1989; Lohuizen, 1981; Huntington, 1993). The most important point is that some of the images portraying the Buddha in *ekāṁsika saṁghāṭi* like Mathurā art idiom. The date of Swat reliefs and images is based on the series of associations like a coin of Azes I, comparison of art style of the earliest phase with that of Taxila's earliest reliefs and association of the sculptures with some *in situ* evidences. Earlier they were placed in 1st century BC and later these Buddha images were placed in early decades of 1st century AD (Nehru, 1989). Lohuizen was of the view that Gandhāra was imitating Mathurā even before the canonical form of the Buddha image was established at Mathurā (Lohuizen, 1981; Nehru, 1989). Notwithstanding the heated argument in favour of the priority of either of these two art-schools, the importance of these discoveries lies in the fact that they suggest the pre-Kushan origin of the Buddha image. Here references must be made to the discovery of Chilas which lies on Karakoram Highway beyond the Shangla pass. Chilas is a small town situated in a unique high altitude desert which extends all the way into Tibet. The surrounding has hundreds of rock carvings some dating back to prehistoric times. Buddhist rock carvings have been found mainly following the old routes of trade and pilgrimage along the Indus, Gilgit and the Hunza River. In the area of Chilas a tremendous concentration of Buddhist carvings and inscriptions has been discovered which are yet to be properly documented. Inscriptions are in Indian scripts—Kharoṣṭī, Brāhmī, proto-Śāradā and some of them are in Bactrian, Tibetan, Chinese and even in Hebrew characters.

The importance of Chilas lies in the fact that carvings display a vast variety of Buddhist iconology and the development of architectural forms and designs, especially that of *stūpas*. According to Volker Thewalt (1985, p. 779) the oldest representation of *stūpas* very closely resemble the types in Central India, particularly in Sanchi and Bharhut. Chilas I represents Vyāghrijātaka. Rock carvings of the most archaic *stūpa*-type have been discovered in Chilas II and Chilas III.

Besides the representations of *stūpas* and decorative designs many carvings have been discovered depicting the Buddha himself and several Bodhisattvas (Jettmar, 1980; Dani, 1983).

Jātaka stories are also very common. In the site known as Thalpan Bridge the Buddha is displayed in both *ekāṁsika* and *ubhayāṁsika saṁghāṭi*. It is interesting to note that figures of the Buddha and Bodhisattvas have been found nearly exclusively in the sites of Chilas I, Thalpan Bridge with a few exceptions at Thor-Nord, Chilas II and Shatial. The process of documentation, classification and fixing the chronology of these rock carvings is still going on. Stylistic and epigraphic, petroglyphic evidences may be crucial in fixing the date of these Buddhist carvings. At the moment we can only say that these discoveries bear concrete evidence and testimony to the fact that Buddhism went via silk route to Central Asia and China much earlier than it is supposed by various scholars. Many of these elaborate rock carvings are attributed to highly skilled craftsmen who received their artistic training in the great monasteries of Gandhāra, while other crude imitations would have been executed by travelling laymen or the inhabitants of the neighbouring villages. As some of the carvings are very close in their resemblance with Bharhut and Sanchi style, we can say that at least the antiquity of these carvings go back to 2nd-1st century BC in context of Buddhist art. This has a direct bearing on the issue of origin of the Buddha image in Gandhāra region. The depiction of *ekāṁsika saṁghāṭi* like Butkara I, III and other Swat series depiction is also connected with the fact that Mathurā Buddha type iconography was already established.

Mathurā Buddhas: Mathurā has a hoary past going back to prehistoric period. In literary tradition it is described as one of the populous and rich cities of India which was a flourishing centre of Brahmanism, Buddhism and Jainism (Sharma, 1984). Mathurā has yielded several sculptures giving a series of date from year 2-98 in an unknown era. As the origin of the Buddha image from Maholi, etc. Bodhisattva, images were carved on the model of standing *yakṣa* images. They wear a lower garment fastened by a belt and portray *ekāṁsika saṁghāṭi*, *abhaya mudrā*, shaven head, bunch of is also intimately connected with the question of priority of Gandhāra and Mathurā schools, therefore before we begin it is imperative to know the theories on the identification and explanation of the series of dates from year 2-98. They are—

(1) The theory of omitted hundreds suggested by Lohuizen who thinks that the low number dates suggest the dates of 2nd century of Kuṣāṇa era where the 100 was omitted, i.e. for 115 only 15 is given and hundred is dropped (Lohuizen 1949);
(2) Rosenfield has suggested that a second Kuṣāṇa era was employed at some point after the year 98 of the Kaniṣka era;
(3) Most of other scholars take these as representing a single century of Kaniṣka Era (Rosenfield, 1967).

The point of contention is also on the issue exactly when these eras or era began. Now the argument generally range between AD 78 to 120 (R.C. Sharma, 1984, pp. 29-30).

Earlier the origin of the Buddha image was discussed in the light of those standing figures which were carved and erected in the years 2 and 3 of Kaniṣka and are described as 'Bodhisattvas' in the inscription on their pedestals (Sharma, 1984). Several uninscribed images of this standing type of Buddha are available from Maholi, etc. These 'Bodhisattva' images were carved on the model of standing *yakṣa* images. They wear a lower garment fastened by a belt and portray *ekāṁsika saṁghāṭi*, *abhaya mudrā*, shaven head, bunch of flowers or a lion between legs. All of them are life-size images. Seated Buddha type are found from Katra, Anyor, Ahichhatra etc. They are *Kapardin* type, wear *ekāṁsika saṁghāṭi* and depict nimbus behind the head. As the paper aims to analyse the question of the origin of Buddha image, therefore I would not enter into detailed iconographic description of these images. Earlier they were supposed to be the earliest depiction of the Buddha in human form.

In post-independent phase, Lohuizen and R.C. Sharma have tried to prove pre-Kaniṣka origin of the Buddha image. Lohuizen describes the depiction of a seated figure on an architrave as the earliest Buddha image. R.C. Sharma has identified erstwhile erroneously described Jina image on a piece of architecture as the first evidence of the image of Buddha (Sharma, 1984). It is important to note that Lohuizen and Sharma date the depiction on architrave in 1st century BC, but Nehru dates that piece in 1st century AD and that also at the end of it (Nehru, 1989).

Lohuizen and Sharma both have argued that the earliest seated Buddha type were modelled after the seated Jina figure depicted on Jaina *āyāgapaṭṭa*. On the basis of these evidences they have suggested not only the pre-Kaniṣka origin of the Buddha image, but also the priority of Mathurā over Gandhāra. Sharma thinks that Gandhāra influence infiltrates Mathurā in the time of Huviṣka whereas Lohuizen accepts it after Huviṣka. Lohuizen has described the art of Mathurā during the Kuṣāṇa time in three phases—(1) *Kapardin* type of Buddha, (2) Buddha image undergoing Gandhāra influence, (3) re-nationalized Buddha type on the basis of her analysis of hair, dress, seat of these images (Lohuizen, 1949). Sharma has divided these Buddha images into seven broad categories on the basis of dress, hair, *mudrā* and art style (Sharma, 1984).

Recently, J.C. Huntington has suggested that the Buddha images were not carved only at Mathurā or Gandhāra. According to him,

> In spite of paucity, there is artistic proof that Buddha images were made at an early date. One notable work of art that has been totally ignored by scholars since it was published by Alexander Cunningham in the 19th century is a small plaque that was found at Sāṅkāsy, that bears the remains of what appears to be a representation of a seated Buddha.

(Huntington 1993; Cunningham, ASR II 1880, reprint Varanasi, 1968; Pl. 9, Fig. 2). On stylistic ground he dates this plaque in early 2nd or late 3rd century BC. According to him a Chinese urn or jar with a date equivalent to 36 BC portrays a seated Buddha (Huntington, 1993) and on the basis of this evidence he suggests that an Indian image-making tradition has already been well-established before it went to China with an established canonical form.

The above description clearly suggests that now the debate on the origin of Buddha image is centred more on pre-Kaniṣka origin than during the period of Kaniṣka's rule. But the question of priority still persists. The priority of Gandhāra School is now being supported by the so-called Swat series of sculptures particularly from Butkara I and now also from Butkara III as well as Chilas carvings. Indian origin of the Buddha image is suggested on the basis of several sculptures from Mathurā and now rediscovered Sāṅkāsa plaque by Huntington.

In this regard I wish to draw the attention of scholars to two facts—(1) there is no explicit tradition of prohibition against image-making / worship in Pāli literature as was earlier suggested by various scholars; (2) we will have to accept the existence of an original Buddhist before it was divided in Hīnayāna and Mahāyāna. The concepts of *Kāya* system particularly *rūpakāya* and *dharmakāya* are very much present in early Buddhism which paved the way for the morphological development of the idea of Buddha and this development both in textual, oral and visual traditions of perishable material preceded the established visual transformation of the idea in stone. Therefore the debate on the origin of the Buddha image should take into account the development of the idea of Buddha as contained in the textual tradition not only of India but of China and Sri Lanka as well. We can conclude by stating that the origin of the idea is purely Indian. Visual manifestation and priority of both the schools will always remain a point of contention though in recent times it has somewhat diffused and now the scholars talk about the pre-Kuṣāṇa origin in time and besides Gandhāra and Mathurā, several other centres in space. It should not be forgotten that to those who had created Gandhāra Buddha type, were neither altogether foreigners and nor to them the idea of the Buddha would have seemed 'misrepresented' as was construed by Coomaraswamy. We can only say that the ideal of Buddhahood is a unitary form with the scope of plural expression.

NOTES AND REFERENCES

1. A.K. Coomaraswamy, 1972, (Ind. ed.), *The Origin of the Buddha Image.*
2. A.H. Dani, 1983, *Chilas—The City of Nanga Parvat (Dyamar).*
3. A. Foucher, 1917, *The Beginnings of Buddhist Art and Other Essays.*
4. S.L. Huntington and J.C. Huntington, 1993 (ed.), *The Art of Ancient Times.*
5. J.E. van Lohuizen, 1949, *The Scythian Period* (1981), 'New Evidence with Regard to the Origin of the Buddha Image' in S.A.A. 1979, Ed. H. Härtel, pp. 377-80.
6. Lohita Nehru, 1989, *Origin of the Gandhāran Style.*
7. John M. Rosenfield, 1967, *The Dynastic Arts of the Kushanas.*
8. R.C. Sharma, 1984, *Buddhist Art of Mathura.*
9. Volker Thewalt Verlag, 'Rock Carvings and Inscriptions Along the Indus' in S.A.A. 1985, pp. 779-800.

14

DĪPAṄKARA JĀTAKA IN GANDHĀRA ART
Indian Museum Collection

ANASUA DAS

The collection of Gandhāra art in the Indian Museum, Kolkata, started as early as 1833-34 when a circular schist stone sculpture excavated at a site near Kabul, Afghanistan, was presented to the Asiatic Society of Bengal by Dr J.G. Gerard and subsequently deposited in the Indian Museum.[1] The collection was further enriched in 1876 by the objects acquired through the explorations of General A. Cunningham in and around the British occupied district of Yusufzai during 1848 and 1872-73. The area is stated to have been inhabited by a clan of the Afghans known as Yusufzai or the 'sons of Joseph'.[2] The principal sites yielding Gandhāra sculptures in this area were Sahri-Bahlol, Takht-i-Bahi, Kharkai and Jamalgarhi. Among early presentations mention may be made of several stucco heads collected from the vicinity of Peshawar, probably coming from the Shahji-ki-dheri *stūpa* excavated by the Archaeological Survey of India.[3] A good number of these were acquired through H.H. Cole's[4] excavations in the ruined monasteries of Koi Tangi and Nathu in the Sanghao Valley. Some of the objects were made available to the Museum by A.D. Caddy,[5] originally recorded from a site at Loriyan Tangai on the northern slopes of the Shahkot Pass in the Swat Valley. A few specimens were also received as permanent loan from the Archaeological Survey of India during 1922-23,[6] mostly from the excavated sites around Taxila, Shahri-Bahlol, Charsadda and Takht-i-Bahi.

Most interestingly out of the eight definitely dated images, belonging to this school of sculptural art, found so far in the world, three are in the possession of the Indian Museum. They are the figure of a Maitreya (dated to AD 134), a standing Buddha (datable to *c.* AD 148) and a slab showing Buddha, Bodhisattva and other figures (dated to *c.* AD 230).[7] The other sculptures acquired represent free-standing Buddha-Bodhisattva figures as well as reliefs showing them in different pose and postures, several architectural fragments containing floral, animal, vegetal, geometric motifs as also figures of Atlas, garland-bearers, few brahmanical divinities, besides a large number of reliefs showing in life scenes of Gautama the Buddha and stories from his previous births—the *Jātakas*.

In this article I would like to present few such reliefs depicting the *Dīpaṅkara Jātaka*. The

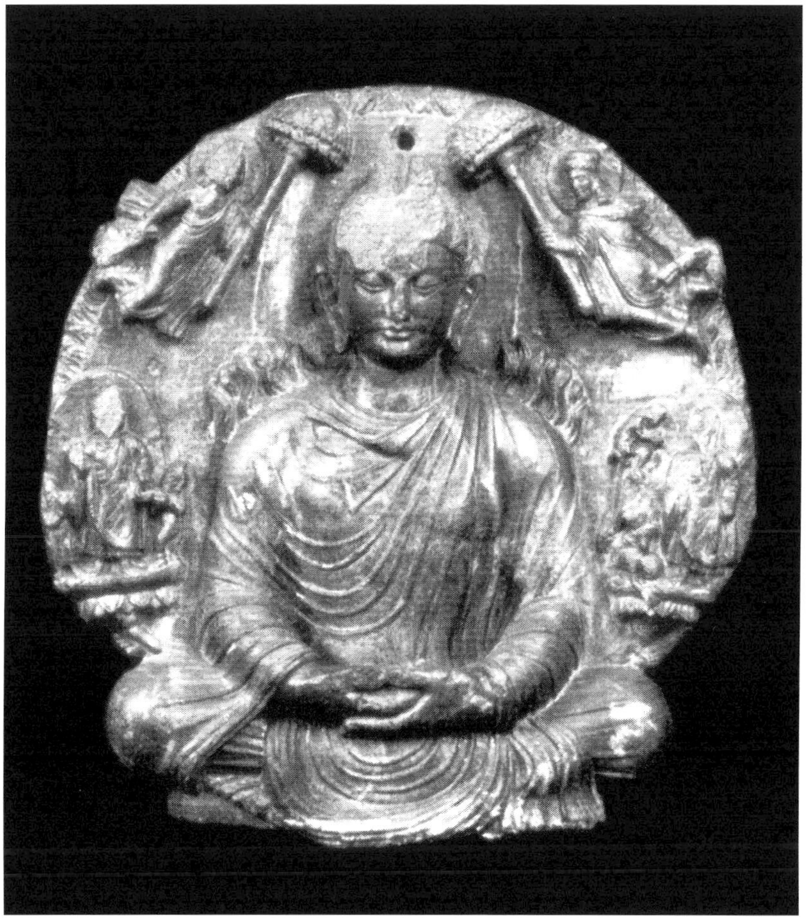

Pl. 1. Buddha Śākyamuni at Śrāvastī

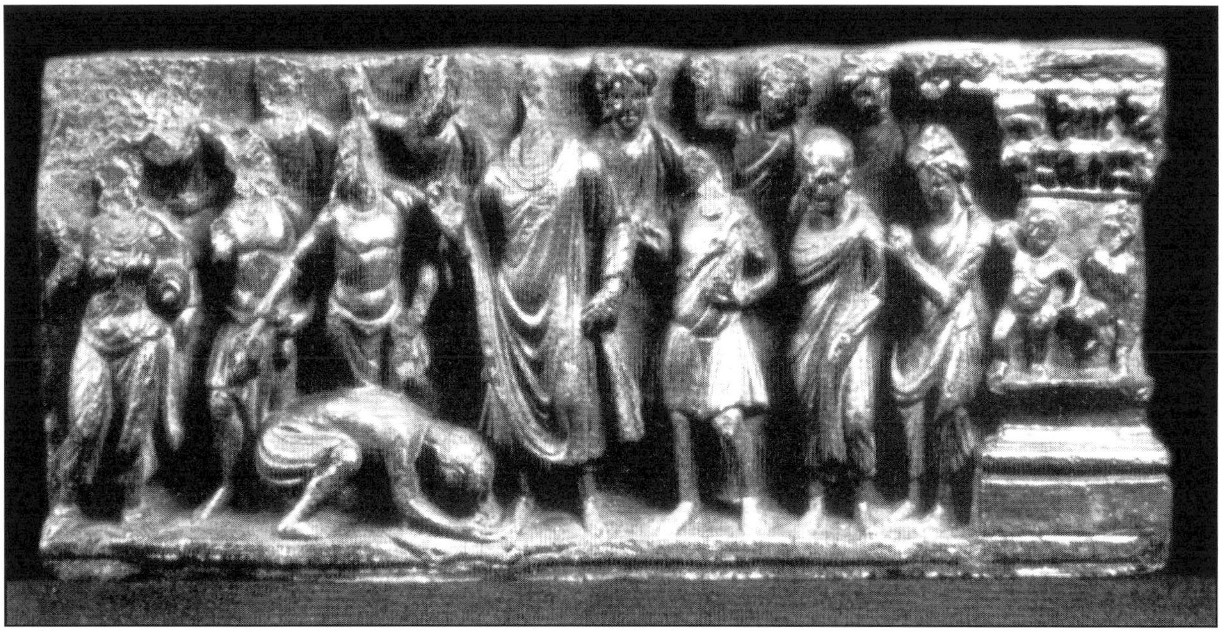

Pl. 2. Indo-Corinthian pilaster showing two westlers on the shaft

story of Dīpaṅkara, which has reference to the penultimate existence of Śākyamuni Buddha appears to have been a very popular theme for the narrative art of the period. The Indian Museum, Kolkata possesses as many as nine such reliefs from places like Kabul, Jamalgarhi, Loriyan Tangai, Yusufzai and some other sites in the Swat Valley.

It will not be out of place to mention here that the story of *Dīpaṅkara Jātaka*, where the Master is stated to have born as a Brahmin versed in the Vedas, is related both in the Pāli and Sanskrit texts. The Pāli version, however, has no reference to a girl[8] and her lotuses, two of the chief elements of the story as depicted in sculpture and as preserved in the Sanskrit version contained in the *Divyāvadāna* and the *Mahāvastu*.

Without going into minute details of the story described in different texts, we may sum up the episode in the following manner. The hero of the Jātaka appears to be Sumati (according to the *Divyāvadāna*, Sumedha of the Pāli texts and Megha in the *Mahāvastu*). A king named Vāsava, on the conclusion of his twelve years' sacrifice, offered five 'great gifts' (namely, a golden staff, a water pot, a bed decorated with gold and jewels, five hundred Kārṣāpaṇas and a bride bedecked with ornaments) to Sumati, who possessed the highest proficiency in the Vedas. Sumati accepted the first four, but not the bride. The girl herself struck with the personal charms of Sumati requested him to accept her as a bride, but with no effect. She then, sore at heart, proceeded to the city of Dīpāvatī, dedicated herself to the service of the god and having taken off all the ornaments from her person, made them over to a gardener, who in turn agreed to supply her daily a number of blue lotuses for worship.

Meanwhile Sumati, advised by a foreteller, came to the same city to meet Dīpaṅkara, the Buddha, who was expected to visit there shortly on a royal invitation.[9] Sumati reached Dīpāvatī on the day of Dīpaṅkara's visit and found that elaborate arrangements were being made for his reception. On the same day the girl went to the gardener for her daily share of flowers, but found that all the flowers of the locality had already been collected by the king's men and sent for the worship of Dīpaṅkara. At that moment miraculously seven lotuses blossomed in the gardener's tank. The girl had these plucked and put them into her water jar, so that no one can notice them. Sumati requested the girl to part with the flowers by accepting five hundred coins as the price. But she refused his offer and later when learnt, that like herself he also wanted the flowers for the worship of Dīpaṅkara, she relented and agreed to part with five only, retaining two for herself, but on one condition. She insisted that Sumati must, at the time of offering the flowers to the Buddha, cherish a desire to have her in every future birth as his wife. Sumati had to agree and they came out to the road where a huge crowd had assembled to get a glimpse of Dīpaṅkara and the couple were not able to get near him. By his supernatural power the Buddha perceived this and caused a heavy shower of rain to disperse the crowd. Thus Sumati got an opportunity to come near him and at once threw the lotuses at him. The flowers instead of dropping on the ground remained steadfast in the air, forming a wheel like canopy. The girl also threw her flowers and these likewise remained fixed near the Buddha's ears. The road had now become full of mud because of the heavy shower, but Sumati forthwith spread his long hair in front of Dīpaṅkara to enable him to pass. Dīpaṅkara placed his feet upon it and walked over[10] predicting that in time Sumati would be born as the Buddha Śākyamuni for the benefit of mankind. As soon as this prediction was uttered Sumati soared up in the heaven and in this position was seen by the people.

Let us now have a glimpse of the delineation of the story on Gandhāran reliefs as preserved in the Indian Museum. Our first relief (Acc. No. K1/A23220, acquired by Gerard as stated earlier) is a circular schist stone specimen showing in the main the incident of the

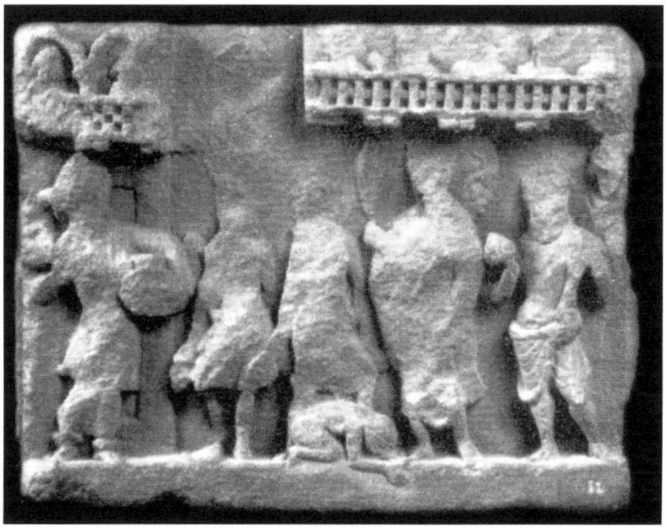

Pl. 3. A fragment from the base of stūpa from Loriyan Tangai

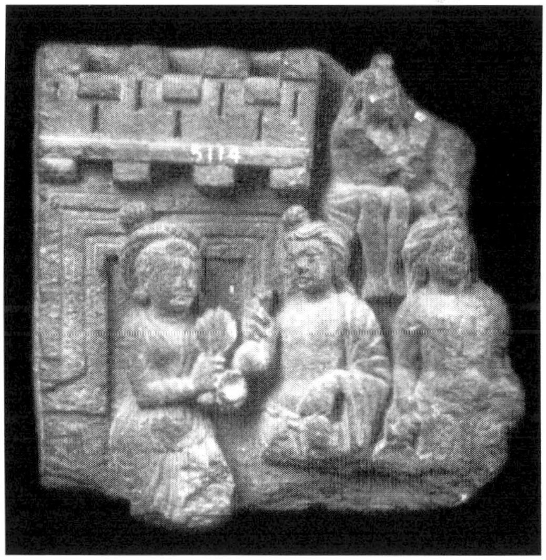

Pl. 4. Relief from Loriyan Tangai showing the lady who sold flowers to Sumati

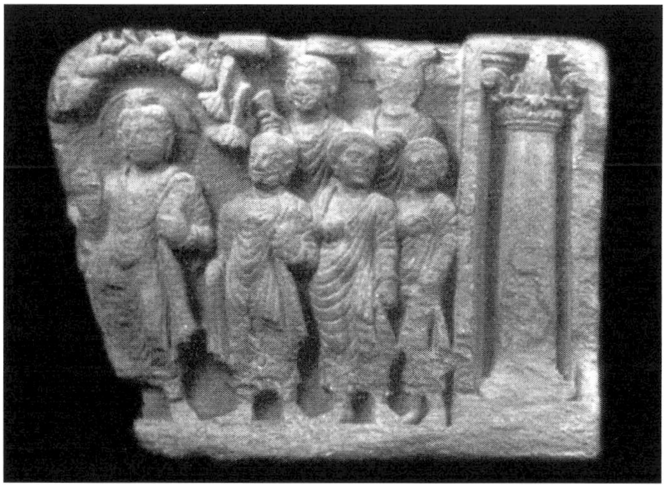

Pl. 5. Buddha in association with Vajrapāṇi and four monkish figures

miracles shown by the Buddha Śākyamuni at Śrāvastī (Pl. 1). He is seated in meditation on a lotus. From his shoulders, as also from the edge of the halo, fire is represented as emanating. From his two sides spring up two lotuses on which two separate scenes are being shown. To his left Sumati, the ascetic is seen making obeisance to Dīpaṅkara. He is shown twice: first, throwing flowers at the Buddha and then soaring up in the sky. The other sprouting lotus depicts the episode when a child put dust into the bowl of the Buddha who made a prophecy that the child will be born as Aśoka, the great.[11] From Jamalgarhi site (Acc No. G174/A23246) we have a slab[12] showing only the *Dīpaṅkara Jātaka*. At the extreme left corner a lady (probably the would be wife of Sumati) stands with flowers in her right hand and a water vessel under the left arm. Sumati is shown twice. Once in the act of throwing flowers and then kneeling before the Buddha and spreading his long hair on which the first Buddha Dīpaṅkara could walk. Behind the defaced Buddha stands Vajrapāṇi along with several other figures. The story terminates with an Indo-Corinthian pilaster showing two wrestlers on the shaft (Pl. 2).

The next is a fragment (Pl. 3) from the base of a *stūpa* (Acc. No. 5125) from Loriyan Tangai. Here also the story commences from the left where the lady is standing before the city-gate with a water vessel held by the left hand and flowers by the right. The defaced figure of Sumati is seen in the act of purchasing flowers from her. He is again shown next in the attitude of throwing flowers at Dīpaṅkara approaching towards him in association with Vajrapāṇi and a monkish figure (shown upto bust). Sumati is shown for the third time in a kneeling position with his hair stretched towards the feet of the Buddha. The scene is being witnessed by several figures from the upper balconies.

From the same site, i.e. Loriyan Tangai, we have four more reliefs. Of these[13] Acc. No. 5114 (broken into two parts, lower left panel seems to have been missing). The left fragment (Pl. 4) shows the lady selling the flowers to Sumati holding a purse in his right hand and a water vessel in his left. He is shown next in the act of throwing flowers to the Buddha and again is shown seated in the air. The other fragment (Pl. 5) shows the Buddha in association with Vajrapāṇi and four monkish figures. The Buddha is standing in *abhaya* posture under a semicircular canopy formed by the stalked flower thrown by Sumati whose prostrate figure is no more. An Indo-Corinthian pilaster inside a niche is at the extreme left.

Another slab[14] (Acc. No. 5087/A23247) appears to be a fragment from the drum of a *stūpa*. Here Sumati with the coin purse is asking for the flowers from the lady with a strong physique, who at the extreme left is standing in front of a doorway with flower and the pitcher (Pl. 6). Sumati is again shown above in the act of tossing flowers which make a circle around the head of the haloed Buddha standing in *abhaya*. Vajrapāṇi stands behind. Sumati is shown for the third time kneeling at the Buddha's feet with his hair spread to avoid mud. The scene terminates with a simple pilaster.

The third relief (Acc. No. 5379) shows in a similar fashion the lady standing in front of the gateway with flower in her right hand (Pl. 7). The long-haired Sumati is purchasing flowers from her. He is again shown throwing the flower at the Buddha standing in *abhaya*. Vajrapāṇi is seen behind the Buddha. It is to be noted that the kneeling figure of Sumati is absent here.

The next is a fragment (Pl. 8) from a horizontal frieze (Acc. No. 5116/A 23456) illustrating the same episode. The female figure under the doorway has a flower and bargains with Sumati who is again seen throwing the flower and then kneeling before the standing Buddha and spreads his long hair. Vajrapāṇi and other attendants are seen in the extreme right.

On the left is part of another story where a male attendant sits with a spear under a

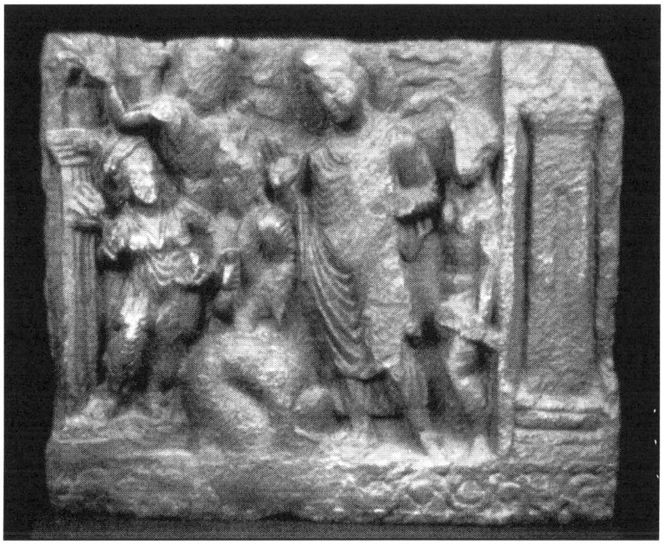

Pl. 6. A fragment from the drum of a *stūpa* showing Sumati

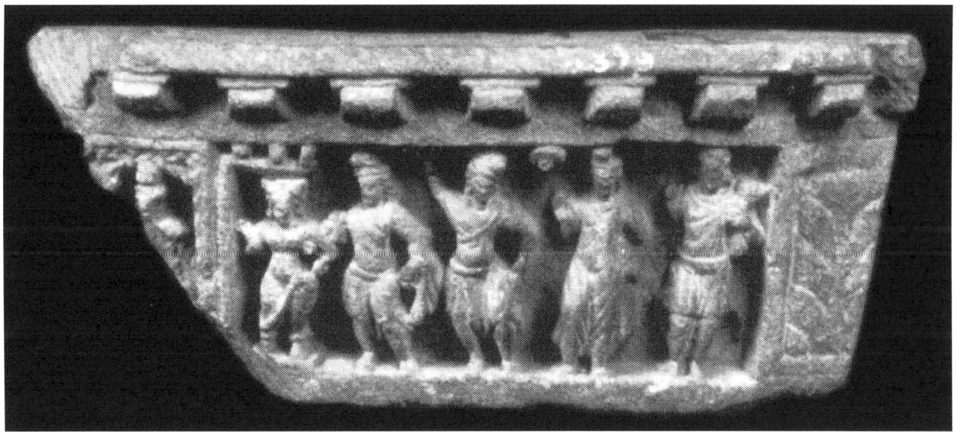

Pl. 7. Long-haired Sumati purchasing flowers from a lady

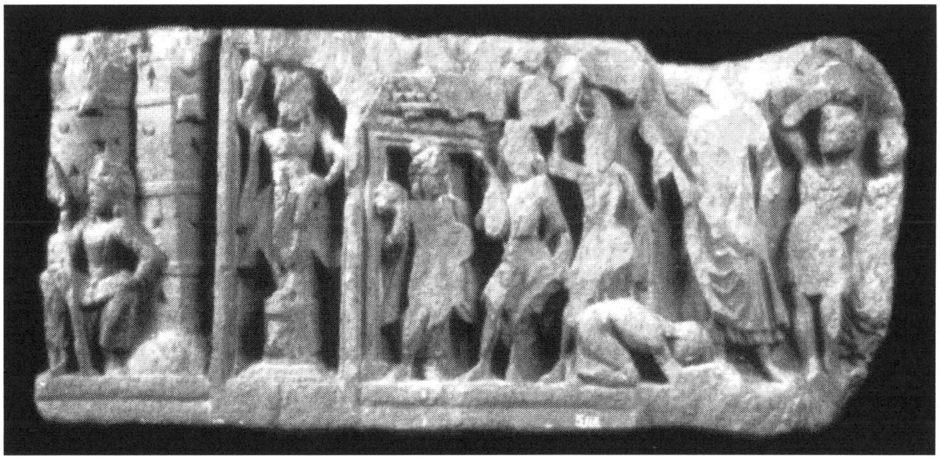

Pl. 8. A fragment from a horizontal frieze showing Sumati standing & then kneeling before Buddha

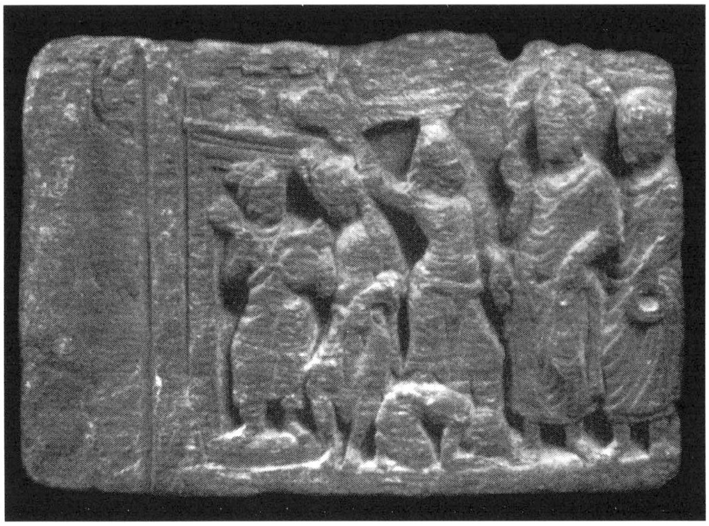

Pl. 9. Sumati purchasing flowers from the lady under the gateway

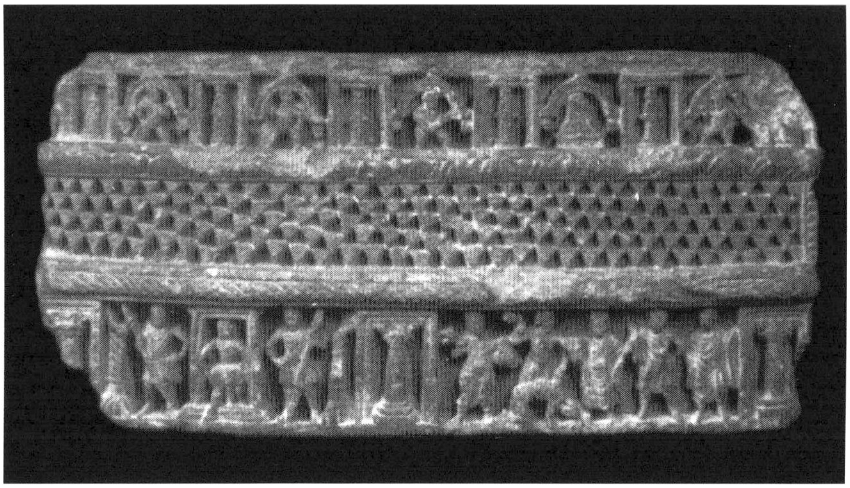

Pl. 10. Framed Indo-Persepolitan pilasters demarkating five arches with suspending flowers

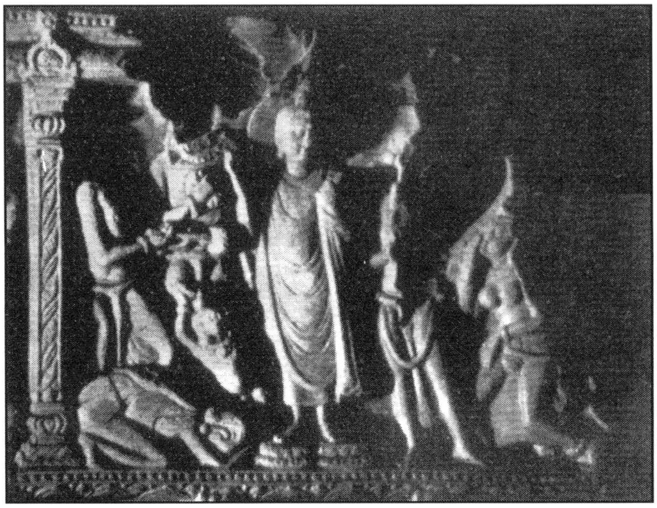

Pl. 11. Figures paying homage to the standing Buddha

building bearing incised marks and projecting moulding. He may be identified as Pañcikā. The frieze, when complete, must have depicted the guarding of urn which contained relics of the Buddha.

Between the two scenes is seen a high niche occupied by a lady on a high stool and carrying flowers in her upraised hand and the left arm held akimbo. If this female forms a part of the first scene then she probably represents the flower-seller.

A much weathered unnumbered slab (Pl. 9) shows the lady under the gateway with a pitcher in her left hand and probably flowers in the right. Sumati with matted hair is standing in the act of convincing the lady for purchasing flowers from her. He is again shown once as throwing flowers and then kneeling down at the feet of the Buddha spreading his hair under the right foot of the Master. The flowery halo of the Buddha in *abhaya mudrā* presupposes the miraculous happening of the flowers in the form of a garland. A shaven-headed monk with begging bowl is standing behind the Buddha.

The last fragment (Acc. No. 2438) from the drum of a *stūpa* (found from Yusufzai proper) is divided into three tiers by two carved mouldings (Pl. 10). The uppermost tier shows framed Indo-Persepolitan pilasters demarcating five arches with suspending flowers. Of these four arches contain miniature male figures in profile. The other shows most probably the funeral pyre.

The central tier is carved with latticed-window design. The lowermost panel illustrates the episode of *Dīpaṅkara Jātaka* with Sumati throwing the flowers at the Buddha and kneeling at his feet. The lady, holding the pitcher and flower is standing behind Sumati. Vajrapāṇi and another monkish figure is standing behind the Buddha.

It is interesting to see that the British Museum has as many as five reliefs depicting the same story, out of the fourteen *Jātaka* illustrations in their collection of Gandhāra reliefs, which mark the immense popularity of the said *Jātaka* during the period of concerned artistic activities. We have the same story illustrated in the Gandhāra collection of Chandigarh Museum, National Museum, New Delhi and other museums as well. But depiction of this *Jātaka* is rarely to be found among the narrative panels of earlier period and sites of the Indian subcontinent. Reliefs showing this theme, however, are found at Mathurā and in the Andhra country, particularly from Nāgārjunakoṇḍā, where the impact of contemporary art of Gandhāra is clearly discernible.[17]

A highly eroded relief (Pl. 11) of this site shows how deeply the art form as well as iconography were influenced by the tradition of Gandhāra, exuding an unmistakable dramatic quality where the figures are arrested at the moment of dramatic action of paying homage either standing erect or kneeling down. The long robe covering both the shoulders of the standing Buddha suggests the influence of Hellenistic art.

Question naturally arises at this point what was the reason behind this popularity? Few interesting points may be raised at this stage:

(1) Was it because of the fact that the story establishes Gautama as destined to be born as the Buddha already in his previous birth?

(2) The city of Dīpāvatī mentioned in the texts could have been in the area around the Yusufzai district, the region of Gandhāra being known in Indian history as early as the period of the Vedas.[18]

(3) If we accept that the Kuṣāṇa artists, whether in Gandhāra or in Mathurā wanted to present the Master anthropomorphically they selected most of his previous birth story, where he could be represented in his human form.

(4) Another interesting point is that there grew up a great interest among the artists of the period to show their interest in storytelling, the craftsmen trying to bring the stories closer and closer to actualities of everyday life and nature. In the reliefs of other early sites of, this period nature seems to recede completely at the background and men and women play prominent roles in the narrative panels.

(5) The *praṇidhāna* aspect as referred to in the *Divyavadāna*, meaning 'prayer for the future birth' may have played a prominent part in the socio-religious life of the region or period.

NOTES AND REFERENCES

1. *Journal of Asiatic Society of Bengal*, Vol. III, pp. 362, 552 and pl. XXVI, fig. 1.
2. Anderson, *A Catalogue and Handbook of Archaeological Collection in the Indian Museum*, Part I, p. 198.
3. *Proceedings of Asiatic Society of Bengal*, 1870, p. 217.
4. Second Report of the *Curator of the Asiatic Monuments in India for the Year* 1882-83, Appendix I, pp. CXIV, ff. and plates.
5. Block, *Supplementary Catalogue of the Archaeological Collection of the Indian Museum*, pp. 4ff.
6. N.G. Majumdar, *Guide to the Sculpture in the Indian Museum*, p. 3.
7. cf. A. Sengupta and D. Das, *Gandhara—A Handlist*, Appendix by Prof. B.N. Mukherjee.
8. cf. Chinese version of *Abhiniṣkramaṇa sūtra*, translated by Samuel Beal, 1875.
9. According to the *Mahāvastu* version Dīpaṅkara Buddha was born as the son of a king named Acimat and after retaining Buddhahood he started for the city of Dīpāvatī, where his father was ruling.
10. The *Mahāvastu* enumerates that Sumati (or Megha) forthwith set aside his *kamaṇḍalu*, knelt down and began to brush the Buddha's feet with his locks of hair.
11. Incidentally we may point out that association of the episode of offering of dust and the *Dīpaṅkara Jātaka* is not very rare. M. Taddei, noting the frequent association of the two stories, quotes a Chinese account of a missionary from the north-west of the subcontinent, who painted with his own hand 'a figure of Rājula and the scene of the scholary youth spreading his hair...'. He has also suggested that the well-established parallelism between a Buddha and a *Cakravartin* could account for associating stories of a *praṇidhāna* directed to each end. Referred to by W. Zwalf, *Catalogue of the Gandhara Sculptures in the British Museum*, Vol. I, p. 197, fn. 13.
12. N.G. Majumdar, *op.cit*, No. 1, p. 33.
13. *Ibid.*, No. 3, p. 34.
14. *Ibid.*, No. 4, p. 34.
15. *Ibid.*, No. 2, p. 34.
16. cf. W. Zwalf, *op.cit.*, London, 1994.
17. Amita Ray, *Life and Art of Early Andhradesha*, p. 170.
18. Mentioning Kubha or Kabul, Suvastu or Swat River, Gandhārī and the people like Drahyu and the Paktha of what is now the frontier region and perhaps eastern Afghanistan.

15

BODHISATTVA-CULT IN AFGHANISTAN
A Critical Review

V.C. Srivastava

The Bodhisattva-cult in Afghanistan appears to have been concentrated around three Bodhisattvas—Siddhārtha, Maitreya and Vajrapāṇi of initially Hinayanist tradition as is attested by the evidences of art and foreign accounts.[1] Most of the art-examples whether images, heads or paintings from Afghanistan are of either Siddhārtha or Maitreya or Vajrapāṇi. Some prominent examples of them may be briefly cited here in order to confirm the hypothesis.

One schist sculpture from Shotorak (2nd-3rd century AD)[2] has a triad of the Bodhisattva Śākyamuni standing in *abhaya mudrā* in the middle in princely dress flanked by two Bodhisattvas—Maitreya in the right holding a vase and another Bodhisattva on the left. Two worshippers—a layman and a monk are found on the right and the left of the Bodhisattvas, respectively. It is in the Gandhāran style which became the model for Bodhisattvas of the Mahāyāna tradition. Another schist sculpture from Shotorak[3] depicts a Bodhisattva—probably Siddhārtha or Maitreya flanked by two indistinct figures sitting in European style and is in *dharmacakra mudrā*. The other Shotorak sculpture[4] known as Dīpaṅkara-Jātaka Buddha has a Bodhisattva-Siddhārtha on the left side of Dīpaṅkara Buddha. On the lower side of the stele is the Bodhisattva Maitreya seated between figures making offerings in *dharmacakra mudrā*. Some scholars[5] suggest that it may be Siddhārtha. Yet another schist sculpture from Shotorak[6] is that of seated Maitreya having *abhaya mudrā* with Brahmā and Indra. Maitreya has vase in the left hand and *abhaya mudrā* in the right hand. The next schist sculpture from Shotorak[7] has Buddha in *dharmacakra mudrā* which has been termed by Foucher[8] as Maitreya. It has two Bodhisattvas—the right one has some vase like object in his right hand and as such may be regarded as Maitreya. We have Siddhārtha Bodhisattva in another schist sculpture from Shotorak[9] where Siddhārtha is shown in astute penance. Another schist sculpture[10] from Shotorak has two parts—in the lower Buddha is shown seated in *abhaya mudrā* along with worshippers while in the upper part we have Maitreya with right hand in *abhaya mudrā* and *kamaṇḍalu* in the left along with worshippers. There is a headless Maitreya from Shotorak[11] which has *kamaṇḍalu* in the left hand and figure of Siddhārtha[12] in the lower side. An interesting figure is found in the *Parinirvāṇa* Buddha schist sculpture from Shotorak.[13] We have Maitreya in the upper panel of the image of Buddha venerated by the three Kāśyapas from Shotorak.[14]

There is no representation of any other Bodhisattva except Siddhārtha, Maitreya and Vajrapāṇi at Shotorak.

Many stucco heads from Hadda have been associated with Maitreya because they have the *stūpa* in their *mukuṭa*.[15] A few bust images of stucco from Hadda have been reported which have been identified as Vajrapāṇi because they possess *vajra* in their left hand.[16] Stucco stele from Hadda have representation of Vajrapāṇi having *vajra* in his right hand.[17] A clay image from Hadda (Tepe Shotur) has broken figure of Buddha and a smaller image of Vajrapāṇi in typical Greek style of Heracles.[18] A schist image of Buddha with Vajrapāṇi to his left has been reported from Tepe Kalan[19] (Hadda). Two schist bas-reliefs from Hadda depict the scene of *Dīpaṅkara Jātaka* with Buddha standing along with worshippers, etc., and Vajrapāṇi bearded and having *vajra* (indistinct).[20] One schist bas-relief depicts the *mahābhiniṣkramaṇa* of Buddha who is sitting on a horse with Vajrapāṇi in the extreme right.[21] Here Buddha may be regarded as Siddhārtha. A few other schist bas-relief depict Vajrapāṇi along with the main theme of Buddha.[22] Some Vajrapāṇi images have been made in the style of Apollo.[23] Many schist bas-reliefs from Hadda have Maitreya having vase in hand.[24] It is to be noted that Vajrapāṇi and Maitreya and some times Siddhārtha are the only Bodhisattvas which have found a place in the art of Hadda. We have no evidence of any other Bodhisattva from Hadda so far.

Paitava has given us a schist bas-relief in which we find Maitreya having vase in the left hand and the right hand is in *varada mudrā*.[25] He is flanked by donors on both sides. In another schist bas-relief[26] from Paitava we have Maitreya in lower panel with vase in the left hand and *varada mudrā* in the right hand. In the main upper portion we have Buddha seated in *dhyāna* having flames coming out of the shoulders. Both these belong to the Kuṣāṇa period.

Tepe Ahingaran (Qunduz) has given us four images of Maitreya[27]—one headless with small vase in the left and *abhaya mudrā* in the right hand, three similar Maitreyas in the lower part while the upper part contains *Mahābhiniṣkramaṇa* Buddha. Two representations of Siddhārtha[28]—one leaving Yaśodharā and the other leaving Kapilāvastu (*Mahābhiniṣkramaṇa*) have been reported from Baghlan (Kuṣāṇa period). Lalma Bodhisattva heads and busts cannot be identified as they have no speciality.[29] Basawal (Ning-rahar) has given us many Buddhist heads but it is difficult to identify them. Mizuno[29a] finds similarity in the hairstyle of one of such heads and that of Maitreya from Hadda. The cave having 38 metre-image of Buddha from Bamiyan has given us many Buddhist heads but they cannot be identified in our present state of knowledge. The 53 metre Buddha image of Bamiyan has been interpreted as Maitreya and 38 metre image as Śākyamuni in the light of the statement of Hiuen Tsang.[30] The heads of Bodhisattvas from Fondukistan (7th century AD) cannot be identified in our present state of knowledge. Gulbahar (Parwan) has given us a fragmentary schist relief of Maitreya[31] of the Kuṣāṇa period.

While no definite information can be gleaned from the evidence of images from Bamiyan and Fondukistan about the type of Bodhisattva prevalent there, the wall paintings from these places testify to the popularity of Maitreya. We have representation of Maitreya on the ceiling paintings in the cave of 38 metre Buddha.[32] Another Maitreya is found painted in the niche in the east of 38 metre Buddha image.[33] Some other wall paintings in the 38 metre cave complex have Maitreya as in group E and I.[34] The 53 metre Buddha cave complex have Maitreya with his *cacti* in the wall paintings.[35] Maitreya is seated in ease and hand is in *dharmacakra mudrā* or *vitarka mudrā*. Bamiyan, group K, cave 4 wall painting (5-6th century AD) has a beautiful Bodhisattva representing Bodhisattva Maitreya[36] with a rich diadem on his head and a vase in the left hand. He is in the centre of radiate circles all containing figures of Buddha which appears to be the classical design for a *maṇḍala*. At Kakrak also we have most probably a representation of Bodhisattva Maitreya in the middle of a circle[37] (*maṇḍala*). Maitreya is found in the painting at Fondukistan[38] (Niche E. 7th century AD). He appears with a nimbus and a halo, holding a vase in the left hand and a blue flower (*nāgakesara*) in his right. Thus the painting of Afghanistan also bears witness to the popularity of Maitreya.

In Central Asia, Bodhisattvas of the Mahāyāna school such as Avalokiteśvara, Kṣitigarbha, Samanatabhadra, Mañjuśrī and Mahāsthānaprāpta became quite popular as is attested by art and literature[39] but Maitreya continued to be popular in Central Asia in spite of the rise of new saviour gods of the Mahāyāna pantheon. We find Maitreya at Kara Shahr in painting on wood[40] (6-7th century AD). He is wearing princely dress and is seated with his feet cross-legged beneath a horse-shoe arcature. With his right hand he is making the gesture of argument (*Vitarka mudrā*). From Balawaste[41] wall painting also we find Maitreya seated in European fashion, his feet together resting on a lotus in front of him (6th-7th century AD). In embroidery from Qoco[42] (9th-10th century AD, Turfan region) we have probably Maitreya in crossed feet aspect and the gesture of the hands folded on his chest recalls that of Shotorak and the Chinese Buddhist sculpture in the Wei period.[43] The tradition of Maitreya in his Tuṣita heaven is more popular in Central Asia as is evident from the depiction of the Pure-Land of Maitreya in the Tuṣita heaven where the Bodhisattva awaits the moment of his rebirth. In Afghanistan we have a depiction of Tuṣita heaven as Shotorak.[44] Maitreya bearing a figure of Śākyamuni enthroned in his headgear, is seated under the tree with *nāgakesara* surrounded by Bodhisattvas in the cave of *apsarās* at Kumtura (7th century AD).[45] Maitreya is represented enthroned in the Tuṣita heaven, sitting cross-legged in the midst of a gathering in a palace in Kyzyl, Mayahohle III wall painting (7th century AD).[46]

In the Khadalik wall paintings (7th century AD)[47] we have two Bodhisattvas with a vase both standing on a lotus on two sides of Buddha. The Bodhisattva in the right with a vase and something like a flower in the other hand may be identified as Maitreya. The world of Maitreya (Tuṣita heaven) is a popular theme in Dunhuang such as in the cave no. 25 (Yulin Grottoes, 9th century AD).[48] The popularity of Maitreya in Central Asia may be gauged from the fact that Hiuen Tsang still wished to be reborn in the Tuṣita heaven in spite of the rivalry between Maitreya's heaven and Amitabha's Pure-Land and the resultant controversies in the Turfan region. Texts from Khotan also assign a very important place to Maitreya.[49] We have evidence of a Maitreya temple having been built by the royal family in Turfan in the 5th century AD.[50] Many more evidences including inscriptional as shown by Lotika Lahiri[50a] may be cited from Central Asia for the popularity of Maitreya even after and side by side the Bodhisattvas of the Mahāyāna cult.

Vajrapāṇi also remained popular in Central Asia along with the Bodhisattvas of the Mahāyāna cult as is evident from representations of Vajrapāṇi in wall paintings at Kyzyl (peaceful aspect)., Bazeklik (material aspect) and again at Kyzyl (AD 650) (Herakles) and in wood-carving from Subashi (5th-6th century AD).[51] In short, it may be surmised that Maitreya and Vajrapāṇi remained popular in Central Asia even after the spread of the cult of Mahāyāna with its various Bodhisattva saviours like Avalokiteśvara, Samantabhadra, Kṣitigarbha, Manjūśrī, etc.

Maitreya—the Buddha of the future and Śākyamuni seem to be associated with each other as the saviour-god throughout the pilgrim-routes right from Afghanistan to China and this is evident from their association in the numerous Hīnayāna monasteries from Afghanistan to China as Shotorak, Bamiyan, Fondukistan (Afghanistan) and Yun-kang, Long Men (China).[52]

Vajrapāṇi—the Bodhisattva of both vehicles represents the hypostasis of Indra. The *vajra*—the thunderbolt which is his characteristic *āyudha* represents the force, the indestructible truth which came to be represented in the art of Afghanistan and Central Asia as in Buddha's haloes in Rawak, Dandan Kiliq, Juca (with points), with three prongs in Turfan region in Tantric *maṇḍalas*.[53] With force with him he became the faithful assistant and protective genius of Buddha Śākyamuni. His faun-like ears show his *yakṣa* aspect and as such he became in Mahāyāna pantheon next to the leading protectors of law. Two types—peaceful youth type and atheletic Heracles warrior type existed. Both types persisted in Hīnayānist monasteries in the Tarim basin for some time but soon after the latter type prevailed with more and more Tantric features in Turfan region.[54] It appears that Vajrapāṇi as the protector *par excellence* and faithful ally of Buddha became intimately associated with Maitreya.

The popularity of Siddhārtha, Maitreya and Vajrapāṇi in Afghanistan and Central Asia is to be traced in certain common element in all these three gods which actually associated them with each other. Since there is definite evidence for Afghanistan and Central Asia that Hīnayāna and Mahāyāna both were existing side by side in these regions[55] and no exclusive area can be marked for either tradition, the explanation cannot be limited to regional affiliation of Hīnayāna and Mahāyāna, or in doctrinal differences.[56] These Bodhisattvas with monumentality cannot be explained in terms of the rise of Mahāyāna doctrine as these deities are found before the official rise of Mahāyānism as well as they are initially in the tradition of the *Mahāsāṁghika-lokottaravādin* sect of Hīnayāna tradition in Afghanistan. The secret for the rise and popularity of the cult of Maitreya which associated Siddhārtha and Vajrapāṇi with itself because all of them played the role of deliverance of the worshipper from the *saṁsāra* lies in the role of a saviour-god *par excellence*. The saviour-concept is quite universal in the Mahāyāna Bodhisattva ideal but it appears that it came to Afghanistan from the West in the wake of Mithraism and it was this saviour aspect which led to the development of the cult of Maitreya and all developments from Hīnayāna to Mahāyāna and then to Vajrayāna it continued its successful journey in Afghanistan, Central Asia and further east.

The development of an intensive cult of Maitreya along with Siddhārtha and Vajrapāṇi in Afghanistan and throughout the pilgrim-route from Afghanistan to China through Central Asia may be understood in terms of socio-religious crisis[57] that Afghanistan and beyond had been facing. Broadly speaking, there had been a crisis within Buddhism itself—the crisis of Hīnayāna versus Mahāyāna. It has been attested by Fa-Hien, Sung Yun, Hiuen Tsang and Korean traveller Hui Chao that both the Hīnayāna and the Mahāyāna were existing side by side in Afghanistan.[58] The presence of *stūpas* and scenes from the life of Buddha show that the Hīnayāna was prevalent there. The Hīnayāna with its ideal of the *Arhat* and orthodox and rigid attitude was getting detached from the laymen and the masses while the Mahāyāna with its charitable and altruistic mass-oriented ideal of Bodhisattva was getting popularity and had been gaining ground among the laymen and the masses in a few centuries earlier and later than the Christian era. It is well known that within the Hīnayāna sect itself there had been controversies between the orthodox and liberal cults like *Sarvāstivādins* and *Mahāsāṁghikas*.[59] The Lion capital inscription of Mathurā of the time of Soḍāṣa[60] refers to the rivalry between these two subsects and points out that the headquarters of the *Sarvāstivādins* was at Nagarhāra in Jalalabad. It notices the fact of a dialectian, the *Sarvāstivādin* monk Budhila from Nagar to teach the foremost *Mahāsāṁghikas* the truth. The Kalwan copperplate inscription[61] and Taxila casket inscription[62] indicate the prevalence of Sarvāstivādins school in Afghanistan and north-west India. The Wardhak inscription of the year 51 of Huviṣka[63] proves the existence of *Mahāsāṁghikas* in Afghanistan. There are references to several monks from

Kabul who went to China for translating Buddhist texts which shows that Afghanistan had a sound base of different schools of Buddhism.[64] The *Mahāsāṁghikas* and specially the *Lokottaravādins* believed in the ideal of Bodhisattva and the superhuman aspect of Buddha and it was from this that the way for the Mahāyāna was paved for its official recognition in the time of Kaniṣka.[65] Thus it is indicated that Hīnayāna was facing a challenge within itself as well as without with Mahāyāna and probably it was in response to this social crisis that the concept of the saviour-god like Maitreya, Śākyamuni and Vajrapāṇi was given an accentuated importance in Afghanistan and Central Asia which had the need for a religion of saviour-god who could protect the laymen, the merchants and the masses from the risks of trade and commerce and life as such.

Buddhism faced another challenge from outside in early centuries of the Christian era. This had been the challenge of Mithraism. Iranian religions as such believed in a future saviour.[66] Mithraism believed in a god of protection and Mithra became the prime saviour-god. Mithra was the god of the sun, the mediator, the god of oath, of king and soldiers and of war also. His cult had been very popular in Iran in few centuries before and after the Christian era. It posed a challenge to other religions on account of its popularity among the soldiers, aristocracy as well as among the masses.[67] He was the god of justice and contract.[68] It became popular outside Iran also and posed a challenge to Christianity in the Roman empire. It also became popular in north-west India.[69] Hellenistic religions also emphasized the saviour aspect and saviour gods replaced the priests for salvation. There had been fights and tensions between Mithraism and other cults including Buddhism in the East and West[70] both. There are evidences to the effect that elements of Mithraic-sun cult are absorbed in Buddhist art of Afghanistan and Central Asia. A few examples from Afghanistan and Central Asia may illustrate this point. The Hīnayāna shrines in Afghanistan and the Tarim basin retain traces of the importance attached to cosmic divinities—the sun and the moon and there is impact of Mithraism on these representations.[71] This appears to have been due to the impact of the Near and Middle East religions. Foucher's statement[72] is revealing—'The trade of translator of sacred texts and of peddler or maker of images was practiced in the 2nd and 3rd centuries mainly by Bactrians and Sogdians'.

The coins[73] reveal that the sun and moon cults occupied important position along with the Buddhist religion before during and after the Kuṣāṇa period. There is solar symbolism in figures of Buddha at Hadda, Rawak, Tumsuq, etc. The ceiling of 38 metre Buddha contains a number of cosmic divinities. Such themes have been repeated in the Kuca region by the Hīnayānists. In Bamiyan the divinity in armour is depicted in typical northerner's dress as in the case of Mithra. Besides two wives on the chariot we have figures of the warrior fashion of Mithra.

> So this representation contains an entire cosmic symbolism which seems to have combined all the various aspects of the Persian and Vedic astral solar, lunar deities—Mithra, Sūrya and Candra in accordance with the great cult-image of Buddha, Lord of the universe.[74]

In Fondukistan, we find the figures of Sūrya-Candra dressed as Scytho-Parthian warriors. In the shrines of Kuca such zenithal strips are found. This also contains symbolism of the flight of the soul from the Candra to the Sun and ultimately to Tuṣita.[75] In short, it may be surmised that Buddhism-Hīnayāna and Mahāyāna both have taken over the cosmic symbolism of Mithraism and local cults of Bactrians and Sogdians also. The evolution of a future saviour in Maitreya was also inspired by the Mithraic tradition of a future saviour. Maitreya has taken elements of Iran also. Zenithal strips are found at Kyzyl, Kiris-simism, Dunhuang, etc.[76] There is similarity in the name of Mithra and Maitreya.

Afghanistan as well as Central Assia had their prosperity through trade and commerce and they did need a saviour for the protection of traders, missionaries and laymen on the trade-routes spread throughout from Afghanistan, Central Asia to China. There had been a social demand for such protection on the way and Buddhism which had been specially associated with the traders and commercial men gave a response to this demand by emphasizing the saviour aspect in their gods like Maitreya, Siddhārtha and Vajrapāṇi. It has rightly been pointed out that 'undoubtedly the view that the Buddha or the Bodhisattva was beyond the passage of time gained ground because of a profound social crisis affecting in particular the merchant class which from its beginning had supported heterodox religious movements, first of all, Buddhism itself'.[77] Kosambi[78] also has pointed out that the monasteries on the borderlands had supported commerce and trade. The following statement of Śāntideva in *Bodhicaryāvatāra* shows the association of Bodhisattvas with the travellers: *Anāthamahaṁ Dātaî Sārthvāhaśca Yātrīnām...* The episode of Maitrakanyaka from Kyzyl wall painting[79] also shows that Maitreya in particular had been a great help to a merchant. He assumes the form of a young merchant and delivers a damned soul from his torment.

The monumentality of Bodhisattva representations in Afghanistan and Central Asia may be taken to be a product of the political ideology of the Kuṣāṇa who were influenced by the Roman tradition of representing the divinized kings as big and monumental. It is well known that Mithraism and political ideology came to be identified wherein the king became the saviour and this aspect could be represented by depicting Buddha and Bodhisattvas on a colossal scale in the mature phase of Gandhāran art.[80] This monumental aspect may be seen in meditating Buddha with flames issuing out from his shoulders from Paitava[81] and Dīpaṅkara Jātaka Buddha from Shotorak[82] with flames again coming out from his shoulders. The luminosity in them connect them with supreme divinity and kingship.[83] The monumental Buddhist images from Bamiyan, Fondukistan, Kakrak and many big figures in Central Asia show the popularity of big images which was meant to show the supernatural, superhuman aspect of these images and the inspiration for this appears to have come from the monumental effigies of Roman and Kuṣāṇa kings. It became a religious tradition to build a colossal statue of Maitreya at the border of every new country which had been won over by Buddhism.[84] Fa-Hien and Hiuen Tsang saw one such image (30 feet high in golden sandal wood) of Maitreya at Darel in the upper Indus. The tradition of building big images continued throughout the rock-monasteries from Bamiyan and beyond (for example the great recumbent Buddha at Adjina Tepe in Tajikistan) as far as China in Kyzyl, Kumtura and Kirish.[85] Besides the existing big Buddha images at Bamiyan, Hiuen Tsang has seen 1000 feet Buddha *nirvāṇa* image, which could not be traced so far.

Besides these mundane factors for the popularity of Maitreya, there appears to have been a philosophical factor also for its popularity. Maitreya helps and guides the faithful and refreshes and delivers the souls of the *pretas* and allows them to be reborn in his own paradise as Bodhisattvas the last stage before they escape from the cycle of rebirths and reach Buddhahood.[86] This role as psycopomp which was due to Iranian influence (Mithra-cult) appears to have been another factor for the popularity of Maitreya in Afghanistan and Central Asia and beyond.

Beyond Afghanistan other Bodhisattvas of Mahāyāna tradition also became popular but it must be remembered that features of Maitreya came to be incorporated by such Bodhisattvas and only then they could become popular along with Maitreya and Vajrapāṇi. Avalokiteśvara delives like Maitreya the soul from perils. He has a full-blown flower and a vase like Maitreya. Kṣitigarbha also assumed the role of a psycopomp like Maitreya as the conductor of souls whom he helps to steer away from the path of evil. This is simply a revival of one of the aspects of Maitreya. He appears to have figured in Maitreya's suite as an attendant. He appears to have been a creation of Central Asia and his popularity was assured only when he revives the psycopomp role of Maitreya.[87]

To conclude, the singular popularity of Maitreya-cult in Afghanistan and beyond may be considered as a product of Hīnayanist responses to two-fold challenges—of Mithraism with a popular saviour-god and of *Mahāsāṁghika* Mahāyānist altruistist philosophy of Bodhisattva in the early centuries of the Christian era. In the second place, the Maitreya cult became intensively popular because it provided a satisfying response to social crisis prevailing in the region due to political destabilization in the wake of ethnic movements at that time. Traders, missionaries and laymen in the routes from Afghanistan to China needed and got a god of their necessity and choice in Maitreya. The impact of royal ideology and divine kingship with saviour element in it as prevalent in the Kuṣāṇa empire under the Iranian and Roman influences also made his cult popular. Lastly, but more fundamentally , Maitreya-cult provided a response of philosophical type in the sense that it promised final deliverance of the soul from *saṁsāra*. Thus the popularizing of Maitreya-cult may be situated against historical backdrop of contemporary social and religio-philosophical demands of the region.

NOTES AND REFERENCES

1. S. Gaulier, R. Jera-Bezard and M. Maillord, *Buddhism in Afghanistan and Central Asia*, Leiden, 1976, 11-12. J. Rai in his Ph.D. Thesis (unpublished, Banaras Hindu University, 1990) entitled *'Prācīna Afghanistan main Bodhisattva: Eka Viśleṣaṇa* (in Hindi) has also come to this conclusion.
2. J. Meunie, Shotorak, *Memoires de la Delegation Archaeologique Francaise en Afghanistan* (*MDAFA*), Vol. 10, Paris, 1942, p. xxxiii, fig. 72.
3. S. Gaulier *et al., op.cit.*, figs. 54, 26.
4. *Ibid.*, figs. 22, 20.
5. *Ibid.*
6. Meunie, *op.cit.*, pl. III, fig. 45.
7. *Ibid.*, pl. xiv, fig. 48.
8. A. Foucher, *L'art Greco-boudhique de Gandhara*, Vol. II, p. 234.
9. Meunie, *op.cit.*, pl. xvi, fig. 53.
10. *Ibid.*, pl. xix, fig. 62.
11. *Ibid.*, pl. xxiv, fig. 73.
12. *Ibid.*, pl. xxiv, fig. 74.
13. *Ibid.*, pl. xxii, fig. 68.
14. *Ibid.*, pl. xix, fig. 62. Cf. P.L. Snellgrove, *The Image of Buddha*, New Delhi, 1978, pls. 139, 189.
15. J. Barthoux, Les Foulles de Hadda, Figures et figurines, *MDAFA*, Vol. 6, Paris, 1830, pls. 30B, 31, 32, 51d, 71b, 71.
16. *Ibid.*, pls. 79f., 97c, B. Rowland, *Art in Afghanistan, Object from the Kabul Museum*, pl. 124, London, 1971, p. 83.
17. Barthoux, *op.cit.*, pl. 40a, S. Gaulier, *op.cit.*, pl. 40a, S. Gaulier, *op.cit.*, p. 72.
18. Barthoux, *op.cit.* pl. 33, P.L. Snellgrove, *op.cit.*, pls. 132, 180.
19. *Ibid.*, pl. 40b.
20. B. Dagens, *et al.*, Monuments Pre-Islamiques d' Afghanistan, *MDAFA*, 19, Paris, 1964, pls. 1, 2.
21. *Ibid.*, pl. 3.
22. *Ibid.*, pls. 4, 7.
23. *Ibid.*, pl. 9.
24. *Ibid.*, pls. 14, 17.

25. B. Rowland, *Art in Afghanistan*, pl. 108.
26. P.L. Snellgrove, *op.cit.*, pl. 134, p. 186.
27. S. Mizuno, *Haibak and Kashmir Smast*, pls. 125, 122, 123, 124, 106-07.
28. S. Mizuno, *Basawal and Jalalabad*, Kabul, pls. 20-22, 109.
29. S. Mizuno (ed.), *Durman Tepe and Lalma*, 1971, pls. 40-44, 112.
29a. S. Mizuno (ed.), *Basawal and Jalalabad*, Kabul, 109.
30. B. Rowland, *The Wall Paintings of India, Central Asia and Ceylon*, p. 69, fn. 1, Cf. Beal, *op.cit.*, pp. 50, 51.
31. T.N. Ram Chandran and Y.D. Sharma, *Archaeological Reconnassance in Afghanistan: Preliminary Report of the Indian Archaeological Delegation*, 1956, Mizuno, *op.cit.*, 1971.
32. B. Rowland, "The Wall Paintings of India, Central Asia and Ceylon", *Marg*, 24, pls. 8, 38.
33. A. Godard, *et al.*, Les Antiquitis Boudkhiques de Bamiyan, *MDAFA*, 2, Paris, 1928, pl. xxvia.
34. Rowland, *op.cit.*, pls. 10, 11, 63-65. *Marg*, 24, No. 2, pls. 10, 37.
35. Rowland, *op.cit.*, pl. 13, *Marg*, 24, No. 2, pls. 13, 39.
36. S. Gaulier, *et al.*, *op.cit.*, I, 35, 37.
37. J. Hackin and J. Carl, Nouvelles recherches archaeologiques a Bamiyan, *MDAFA*, 3, Paris, fig. 71, pl. 11, fig. 63H.
38. J. Hackin, J. Carl and J. Manuie, "Diverses Researches Archaeologiqus en Afghanistan", *MDAFA*, 3, Paris, 1933, pls. 196, 198, 149; P.L. Snellgrove, *op.cit.*, fig. 149, p. 199.
39. S. Gaulier, *et al.*, *op.cit.*, pp. 12-15, figs. 60-66, 67-69, 70-71.
40. *Serindia*, pl. c. xxiv.
41. S. Gaulier, *op.cit.*, fig. 59.
42. *Ibid.*, fig. 58.
43. *Ibid.*
44. *Ibid.*, fig. 84.
45. *Ibid.*, fig. 42.
46. *Ibid.*, fig. 46.
47. *Ibid.*, fig. 53.
48. *Mogao Grotto – Dunhuang*, New Delhi, 1991, fig. 40.
49. Quoted by S. Gaulier, *op.cit.*, p. 12.
50. B.N. Puri, *Buddhism in Central Asia*, 1987, p. 129.
51. A. Mittal and Agrawal (ed), New Delhi, 1992.
52. S. Gaulier, *op.cit.*, figs. 73-76.
53. *Ibid.*, 12.
54. *Ibid.*, figs. 72-76.
55. *Ibid.*, 15.
56. B.N. Puri, *op.cit.*, 129-130. Chinese pilgrims attest to the coexistence of the Hīnayāna and the Mahāyāna though disputations between them used to occur.
57. P.L. Snellgrove, *op.cit.*, p. 184.
58. B.N. Puri, *op.cit.*, pp. 129-130.
59. S. Beal, *Life of Hiuen-tsiang*. London, 1911, 39 refers to controversy between Hiuen Tsang and a Mahāyāna scholar in Kucha. He denounced the Yogaśāstras heretical to the great indignation of the Chinese pilgrim because he accepted it as its importance was revealed by Maitreya to Asaṅga.
60. *Corpus Inscriptionum Indicarum*, II (i), pls. 30 ff.
61. *Journal of the Royal Asiatic Society*, 1932, p. 949.
62. B.N. Puri, *India Under the Kushanas*, pls. 141 ff. Puri in *Buddhism in Central Asia*, 1987, p. 103, writes 'Sarvāstvādins were facing the stiff opposition of the Mahāsāmghikas'.
63. B.N. Puri, *op.cit.*, p. 103.
64. *Ibid.*
65. G.C. Pande, *Bauddha Dharma ke Vikāsa kā Itihāsa*, p. 313.
66. *Encyclopaedia Britannica*, Vol. 24, p. 86.
67. Frank Cumont, *The Mysteries of Mithra.*

68. *Encyclopaedia Britannica,* Vol. B, 196. Alberuni, *India,* tr. Sachau, Vol. I, London, 1988, p. 21 refers to the imposition of Magism in Balkh and banishment of Buddhism from there.
69. See V.C. Srivastava, *Sun Worship in Ancient India,* Allahabad, 1972.
70. *Encyclopaedia Britannica,* Vol. 18, p. 925.
71. S. Gaulier, *op.cit.,* pp. 34-36.
72. A. Foucher, *L'Art Grecobouddhique des Gandhara,* Vol. II, Paris, p. 644.
73. V.C. Srivastava, *Sun-worship in Ancient India,* Allahabad, 1972.
74. S. Gaulier, *op.cit.,* p. 35.
75. *Ibid.,* p. 35.
76. S. Gaulier, *op.cit.,* II, figs. 89-91.
77. P.L. Snellgrove, *op.cit.,* p. 184.
78. D.D. Kosambi, *The Culture and Civilization of Ancient India,* Delhi, 1981, p. 182.
79. S. Gaulier, *op.cit.,* figs. 26, 21.
80. See J.M., Rosenfield, *Dynastic Arts of the Kushanas,* Berkeley, Los Angeles, 1976, pp. 200-01.
81. P.L. Snellgrove, *op.cit.,* pl. 136, p. 186.
82. *Ibid.,* pl. 137, p. 187.
83. On this aspect see A.C. Soper, *Artibus Asiae,* Vol. 12, 1949, pp. 252-83, 314-30, Vol. 13, 1950, pp. 63-85; M. Bussagli, *Revista dell 'Institute Nationale d' Archaeologia e Storia dell Arte,* 5-6 (1956-57), pp. 198-205. M. Taddei, *Gururājamanjarikā. Studi in onore di Guseppe Tucci,* 2, Naples, 1074, 435-49.
84. Quoted by Gaulier, *op.cit.,* p. 12.
85. *Ibid.,* p. 12.
86. *Ibid.*
87. *Ibid.,* pp. 13-14, fig. 67. Such role has been assigned to him in the *Vajrasamādhi sūtra* and the *Mahāvaipulya Daśacakrasūtra,* quoted by Gaulier, *op.cit.,* p. 14.

16

FIRST SERMON RELIEF IN MATHURĀ AND GANDHĀRA

USHA RANI TIWARI

The representation from the life events of Buddha was a favourite subject at all the important Buddhist centres of art. The abundant and varied sculptural production of Mathurā and Gandhāra Schools comprise several bas-reliefs showing the life events of Gautama Buddha. In the present paper I have touched upon some representational differences and mutual influences in respect of the first sermon reliefs of Kuṣāṇa period from Mathurā[1] and Gandhāra.[2] As one of the four principal events from the life of Buddha, the first sermon became a very favourite theme to the sculptors of both the Kuṣāṇa schools of Mathurā and Gandhāra. However, subsequently during the Gupta period this event became all the more important particularly at Sarnath, apparently because it was the holy place of the first sermon of the Buddha.

After attaining the supreme knowledge, Buddha gave first sermon to his five disciples and set in motion the wheel of law (*dhamma cakra*) at Sarnath. This was indeed the key event when Buddha comes back in the midst of people to benefit them with his tremendous spiritual experience and insight about various aspects of life and its miseries streamlining the goal of life. The event is mentioned in many Buddhist texts but indeed with varied narration. The event is technically described in all the versions of Buddhist texts as *Dhammacakrapavattana*.[3]

Mathurā and Gandhāra both were important schools of Kuṣāṇa art. No doubt that the Kuṣāṇas stimulated trade and other contact mechanism between the far flung regions of their empire. As a result both the centres started exerting strong influence on one another.

It is interesting and noteworthy that Mathurā was a stronghold of indigeneous Indian sculptures while Gandhāra developed a distinctive[4] style in which Hellenistic elements in particular played a major role. Besides their varied nature it is obvious that these centres had continuous process of mutual borrowing.

In sculptural representation of the event of first sermon of Buddha at both the centres, the scene is depicted in two different ways: one being symbolic or an iconic and other being anthropomorphic. It may again be subdivided into two types, according to their respective style of format: (a) in the form of horizontal relief and (b) in vertical composition with scenes being one above the other. In anthropomorphic representations two types are found. First the event is represented in narration style showing generally the four major events of his life also. Second it is shown in the form of single incident image to make it an icon.[5]

Regarding symbolic carving of the first sermon at Mathurā in early examples, it may be noted that only the wheel on throne is depicted without any other details like the depiction of deer and *bhikṣus* (monks) which are carved commonly in Gandhara examples. Now the question at this juncture arises as to whether the wheel in Mathurā examples was to indicate the first sermon or the presence of Lord Buddha only? Apparently at Gandhāra the wheel with two deer and monks make it clear that the wheel signifies the first sermon. The deer however, indicate precisely the place where this specific event did take place. This is how the artists visualized the accurate rendering of this auspicious event and accordingly carved it on the reliefs found from Gandhāra. Here in the symbolic representation[7] of the episode the Buddha is indeed physically absent. Five monks[8] are seated on their seats around the *triratna* which is placed on another small wheel having petal flowers instead of spokes. Most significant point in this context is that the top ends of the *triratna* are surmounted by the three wheels representing respectively *Dhamma, Buddha* and *Saṅgha*, the three essentials of Buddhism. The *triratna* was frequently depicted in symbolic and anthropomorphic representations in such examples of art. Such examples with *triratna* also reveal the philosophical aspects of the event.[9] Another striking feature of the Gandhāra representation is the plain pedestal. Two badly defaced figures of deer facing in opposite direction are carved on either side of the lower wheel.

Another relief (now in Bharat Kala Bhavan, Varanasi) of this group is particularly significant because of this event being carved in a peculiar and totally different manner.[10] On a rectangular pedestal which is devoid of any carving, a Persipolitan pillar is also shown on which there is carved a wheel in the centre with rosette design. Two poles are mounted on the pedestal on either side of main pillar bearing garlands. The unique feature of the relief is two other wheels flanking on either side of the central wheel and being supported by the bracket figures.[11] This type of depiction reminds us of the tradition of *Śālabhañjikā* figures from Sanchi and Mathurā. The four monks on this relief are shown in adoration poses.[12]

In Gandhāra relief we sometimes find only a *triratna* being worshipped by a seated devotee with folded hands. Other details like the depiction of deer and *bhikṣus* which was a regular feature in Gandhāra art are somehow missing here. Although there is nothing to indicate the first sermon, yet Ingholt[13] has identified it with the first sermon incident. If we relate the symbolic rendering of wheel at Mathurā, as already discussed earlier, with the event of first sermon then the depiction of *triratna* even without any other details, in case of Gandhāra may also be taken to indicate the same event.

Regarding the anthropomorphic representation we shall now take up the second type showing only the Buddha figure. This single incident image is distinguished by both a unique format and iconography. This is indeed a very original way of representing the turning of the wheel of law. In one singular example from Mathurā, the Buddha is seen as keeping his right hand on the wheel to suggest his turning of the wheel having thirteen spokes. The wheel however, rests upon the pillar instead of a *triratna*, as frequently met with at Gandhāra. In fact this type of representation form an icon. We have also noticed that this type of depiction never ties up with Gandhāra reliefs where we find such depictions in elaborated manner. In case of Gandhāra reliefs, Buddha is seen seated cross-legged on high throne beneath the branches of a *pīpal* tree. Buddha is shown turning thirteen spoked wheel supported by a *triratna* with his right hand. The striking feature is the presence of a second wheel which has spokes made of petals. In Gandhāra relief we also find the depiction of Vajrapāṇi just above the wheel. The inclusion of Vajrapāṇi in such reliefs from Mathurā was never found which clearly suggests that the sculptors of Mathurā had a tradition with its own root. It may, however, be noted that figure of Vajrapāṇi at Mathurā is found in some other scenes during the Kuṣāṇa period.

As regards the first type of anthropomorphic form wherein the first sermon episode is carved in the midst of other four principal events from the life of the Buddha, it is interesting to note that the examples are commonly found both at Mathurā and Gandhāra with certain representational variations in composition. We shall now make brief observations on the points of comparative features and peculiarities of Gandhāra and Mathurā Schools in respect of the anthropomorphic renderings of the scene of the Buddha's preaching in the midst of other four major events.

(1) All the reliefs of Mathurā and Gandhāra form the part of door jambs, pillars and *stūpa* etc. In case of Gandhāra they are generally carved in a rectangular plaque fixed around the plinth and drum of *stūpa*.

(2) In Mathurā almost all the depictions are identical and do not reveal any process of change or elaboration as found in Gandhāra.

(3) There was a tendency at Mathurā to depict the story in abbreviated composition while in case of Gandhāra we find the vent in somewhat elaborate manner. Gandhāra relief shows the cluster of figures around Buddha like Brahmā, Indra[14] and several other divinities which are said to have assembled around the Buddha as referred to in the *Lalitavistara*[15] in the *Nidānakathā*[16] and in the *Buddhacarita*.[17] In the rendering of the host of divinities the artists did not miss even the minute details in respect of the main event.

(4) At Gandhāra the Buddha is always seated under a tree while at Mathurā usually a halo is carved behind his head.

(5) Regarding the *mudrā*, the event distinctly may be put into two groups. In one group Buddha is shown giving a turn to the *dhammacakra* by his right hand while in other group he is seated in *abhaya mudrā* . In some of the examples from Gandhāra we find even the preaching *mudrā*. It has to be remembered that preaching *mudrā*[18] has been used for the first sermon as well as for the miracle of Śrāvastī. Thus preaching *mudrā* as an iconographic distinction was not regularly adopted for the first sermon only, though they were fully aware of it.

(6) The pedestal at Mathurā is plain and devoid of any depiction while at Gandhāra we have some figural depictions related to the event.

(7) Buddha usually wears the *ubhayāṁśika saṅghāṭī*, while in one case at Mathurā he also wears *ekaṁśika saṅghāṭī*.

(8) The treatment of *dhammacakra* is almost the same at both the places which is placed on short pillar. It is carved in frontality in most of the examples but sometimes it is kept even in profile.

(9) It has been noticed that it was not always necessary to depict *bhikṣus* on other side.[18] Instead the figures of two, three and even four[20] *bhikṣus* are carved arbitrarily. The variation in the number of *bhikṣus* tempt us to recall some such literary references like that of the *Nidānakathā* and the *Buddhacarita* wherein it is stated that Buddha preached only one *bhikṣu* in a day and thus he took five days for five *bhikṣus*. Such depiction may indicate the sense of continuity of preaching of the Buddha for several days.

(10) Not only the number of *bhikṣus* vary but they are engaged also in various actions and attitudes, suggestive of adoration and *dhyāna*. Sometimes, they are looking attentively towards the Buddha, but occasionally on the same relief they are carved in mixture of *dhyāna mudrā* and adoration pose. In Mathurā they are always shown seated on ground. But in one example they are seated even on a low pedestal like that of Gandhāra.

The above study thus throws light on the style and iconographic developments of both the schools in respect of the rendering of the Buddha's preaching in Kuṣāṇa art. The aniconoc and anthropomorphic renderings began and progressed simultaneously at Gandhāra, while at Mathurā aniconic representation precede the anthropomorphic forms. The main aim of the artists at both the places was possibly to accommodate all the details in more or less given space but in a lucid composition.

NOTES AND REFERENCES

1. Most of the examples are housed in Government Museum, Mathurā, Acc. No. H-1, H-7, H-9, 261, 46.17, 4740, N.2. Some of the examples are housed in State Museum, Lucknow, Acc. No. B.208 and 46.123.
2. Examples of Gandhāra School housed in famous museum of India and abroad also.
3. The *Nidānakathā*, pp. 207-08. The *Buddhacariha*, pp. 171-89, The *Mahāvastu*, Vol. 3, pp. xxxi, *The Lalitavistara*, pp. 341-68, The *Divyāvadāna*, p. 393. T.W. Rhys David (translated), The *Dhammacakrapavattana sutta* (Oxford 1881), *The Sacred Book of the East*, Vol. 10, pp. 146-55.
4. Though there was a reciprocity between the two schools. But they vary in their nature so the sculptors of Mathurā were not as readily and easily accepted Gandhāra flavour. On the other hand, Gandhāra in its term from Mathura had no difficulty to assimilate its cultural pattern— by J.E. Van, Lohuizen-De-Leeuw in 'Gandhāra and Mathurā: Their Cultural Relationship', *Aspects of Indian Art*, Ed. by P. Pal.
5. We find regularly the depiction of this event in the form of an icon at Sarnath during the Gupta period. Indeed the event occurred at Sarnath itself so the artists of Sarnāth were deeply concern with this event. Moreover, they were genious enough to introduce new features with variation in order to break monotony. For an illustration see figs. 46-49. *Sculptures of Mathurā and Sarnath— A Comparative Study*, New Delhi, 1998, by Usha Rani Tiwari.
6. For an illustration, see fig. 9 of *Mathura Sculptures*, by N.P. Joshi.
7. As this relief belongs to the late Kuṣāṇa period clearly indicate that Hīnayāna and Mahāyāna both the traditions were prevalent simultaneously at one place.
8. For the same type of illustration see, fig. 15 in *Catalogue of Gandhāra Sculptures in State Museum*, Lucknow, 1969, by N.P. Joshi and R.C. Sharma.
9. The *triratna* presumably symbolizing the fact that the first sermon consisted of the three fundamental percepts of Buddhism, (i) Four noble truths, (ii) Eight fold path, (iii) Middle way as told in *Dhammacakrapavattana Sutta.*
10. Published as fig. 5 in *Gandhāra Sculptures in Bharat Kala Bhavan*, Varanasi, 1999, by Shashi Asthana and B. Jha.
11. These bracket figures has close resemblance with the *Śālabhañjikā* figure of Chausā who also supports a Jaina wheel on their head.
12. See footnote no. 8.
13. Fig. 78, *Gandhāra Art in Pakistan*, New York, 1957, by H. Ingholt.
14. Sometimes only Indra and Brahmā are carved on either side of the Buddha as we find in plate XLIIIa, in *Narrative Stone Relief from Gandhāra* in the Victoria and Albert Museum, London, by Ackermann, Hanschirstoph, 1975.

15. The *Lalitvistara*, chapter 26, pp. 300-02.
16. The *Nidānakathā*, p. 82.
17. The *Buddhacarita*, 15.118.
18. In fact the artists of Sarnath school evolved preaching *mudrā* as an iconographic distinction and set a model for the other contemporary and subsequent schools.
19. Fig. 115, *Buddhist Art of Mathurā*, Delhi, 1984, by R.C. Sharma.
20. This is published as fig. 65 in *Kalā*, Vol. V, 1998-99.

17

IMAGES OF BUDDHA AND GANDHĀRAN INFLUENCES

I.K. SARMA

The image of Buddha is due to manifestation of bhakti. Buddha was no longer a teacher or even a superman, but a deity. The claims of the schools of the north-west, commonly known as Gandhāra and Mathurā as the first iconographer of Buddha is still controversial. Available evidence pointed out a simultaneous appearance of images in both these regions[1] during the time of Kaniṣka. Based on the Indian conception of a great man (*mahā-puruṣa*) with his distinctive marks (*lakṣaṇa*), the image of the Master is created in their own way relying on certain art traditions and techniques.

SPREAD OF BUDDHISM: DEVELOPMENTS IN THE ORDER

After the death of the Great Master, Buddhism got divided into two broad schools, the Hīnayāna and Mahāyāna. The Hīnayāna school mainly relied on the preachings of Buddha in their original form while Mahāyāna school made the human Buddha a Śākyamuni, an eternally supreme deity. Thus in Buddhism, Man became god and as a result of the subsequent developments several cults like Mantrayāna and Tantrayāna grew up paving way for several extreme cults linked to the Goddesses.

Buddhism crossed the borders of India right from early Mauryan times and the earliest recipients seem to be Sri Lankans. The recent excavations conducted by the Anurādhāpura Citadel Archaeological Project (ACAP), resulted in the discovery of NBP Ware, silver Punch Marked Coins (PMC) from the excavations at Anurādhāpura Citadel and Gedige *caityas*.[2] A consistent run of C-14 dates from the excavations suggest that the earliest settlements can be dated to 600-450 BC. Based on these new evidences, F.R. Allchin pointed out that some of the major settlements in the South, no less than Sri Lanka, may have been the products of pre-Mauryan Gangetic colonialism; while others may be found to have been the products of Mauryan imperial and administrative expansion.

Coming to some direct evidences, the Brāhmī inscriptions of the time of Śrī Māṭharīputra Vīrapuruṣadatta, the second Ikṣvāku king (dated to 14th regnal year corresponding to AD 286) are the foremost.[3] The *Theravādins* from Tāmraparṇidvīpa (Śrī Laṅkā), greatly influenced the

Saṁghas at Śrīparvata and converted to the faith those who belonged to Kāshmira-Gāndhāra-Chīna-Chilata-Tośali-Avarānta-Vaṅga-Vanavāsa-Yavana-Damila-Pālura and Tāmra parṇidvīpa. These countries are also mentioned in the *Mahāvaṁśa* among other territories which had been converted to Buddhism after the Third Council. The mention of China, besides Śrī Laṅkā and other places, in this record is of seminal importance.[4]

The debate over when and where the first images of the Buddha emerged still remains. Image making was known by the end of the 3rd century BC itself as the figural style[5] emerged among the *yakṣa-yakṣiṇī* figures at Bharhut, Sanchi and Amarāvatī *stūpas*. Devotional worship to Buddha in the manner of bhakti cult, the great teacher was transformed into a supreme god Svamatasya Devasya,[6] lord of one's religion. The earliest Buddha images are those that bear dates in the reign of Kaniṣka, for example, the red sandstone images from Kauśāmbi dated in the 2nd regnal year of Kaniṣka; the Sarnath Bodhisattva dated in the 3rd year of Kaniṣka.[7] 'The priority of the claims of the North-west, commonly known as Gandhāra and Mathurā as the first iconographers of Buddha is still controversial'.[8] Graceful and luminous figures appeared in Āndhra too during this period. From the middle of 2nd century AD, the image of Buddha became popular and he is regarded as a *mahāpuruṣa* whose body was radiant with 32-marks[9] (*dvā trimśat mahāpuruṣa lakṣaṇam*). The image of Buddha gained supremacy and installed in separate *caitya gṛhas*. The images were not merely installed but consecrated[10] (*pratiṣṭhā*). Bronze images about 2 ft. high from Amarāvatī and Buddham served as *utsava vigragas*[11] or for worship of individuals in the houses. The ivory carvings of Begram from the western end of the Kuṣāṇa empire are closely reminiscent of the sculptures (limestone) found in the eastern and western borders of the Sātavāhana empire.[12]

BUDDHA IMAGES IN AND OUTSIDE INDIA

The life-size stone images of Buddhas of Amarāvatī and Nāgārjunakoṇḍā dated to the middle of 2nd and 3rd centuries AD came to be regarded as standard icons. The typical *uttarāsaṅga* (over-garment on the left shoulder) and in *varada mudrā*, the pre-pleated cloth, typical *uṣnīṣa* either plain combed hair (early ones), or in snail-shell curls reached along the sea route to Sri Lanka and other South-East Asian countries.

Buddhas, both standing and in seated posture, have been found sumptuously all over Far-East. Iconography dominated everywhere. Buddhas are multiplied (*Buddha sahasra).* The rock-cut caves of Longmen (Guyang dated AD 494), the Lotus cave (North Wei period AD 521-523, Ten Thousand Buddha Caves, AD 680) are littered with Buddha images of nearly a lakh, ranging in size from 17.4 metres height to about 2 cm. The cave paintings in Dunhuang[13] (nos. 329 and 472) of the Sui period, *c.* AD 581-618 depict the miracle of Śrāvastī. It is virtually a pictorial litany of Buddhas exactly paralleled to those in Ajanta Cave No. 11 of the same period.[14] The biggest monolithic sculpture in the world is a sandstone Buddha, 75 metres high at Lungshan West of Louyang (Henan).[15] Next in height is the Watpole (Indonesia), Buddha in wood, 70 metres high. The tallest colossal wooden statue, a seated one, measuring 33 metre high in Central Cave No. 96 at Dunhuang; the second biggest also from Dunhuang is 26 metres high (Cave 130) dated AD 726. Largest reclining Buddha image is 15 metres long (wooden one), is again from Dunhuang Cave No. 158 (AD 780). In Yunkang grottos of weathered sandstone (AD 460-494), the largest Buddha is 17 metres high and the smallest is just 2 cm. The Longmen seated Vairocana Buddha measured 17.14 metres high (AD 675). The Vairocana Buddha of Todaji (Nara) is 16 metres high made of copper and gold coated, dated AD 746.

In later periods, the Mahāyāna Buddhism transformed itself into Vajrayāna (a name for tāntric Buddhism), also known as *Sahajayāna* and *Kālacakrayāna*. The main focus was eastern and south-eastern India. The elementary pantheon of a few Bodhisattvas and Tārā was developed into an elaborate one with Ādi Buddha and Dhyānī Buddhas. According to the Buddhist tradition, Bodhisattva went through five-hundred births—as bird, beast and man for ultimate goal of Buddhahood. An inscription in a cave temple at Mahābalipuram dated 7th century AD, Buddha is cited as 9th *Avatāra* in place of Kṛṣṇa.[16] In Jayadeva's *Aṣṭapadi* of the *Gīta Govinda* (12th century AD), Buddha is regarded as the 9th incarnation of Viṣṇu.

ANDHRA ART OBJECTS IN OTHER COUNTRIES: TRADE CONTACTS

In a pioneering study and meticulous documentation of the '*Buddhist Sculptures in Śrīlaṅkā*, Dr Ulrich Von Schroeder (Hong Kong, 1990) has listed up with measurements several limestone sculptures, both round and in relief, from the Śrī Laṅkān sites. The chapters in the work clearly go with a heading 'Imported Sculptures from Early Amaravati School' and 'Imported Sculptures from late Amarāvatī (Nāgārjunakoṇḍā) and so on. It is therefore clear that the artist guilds in Amarāvatī-Nāgārjunakoṇḍā were engaged in the large-scale supply of Buddhist sculptures, as also brahmanical to Sri Lanka and other South Asian countries.

Religious ideology was a potent force providing cohesion and identity to trading communities and it was perhaps through these channels that the early Buddhist/Brahmanical images found their way into South-East Asia and Sri Lanka.[17] At Sempaga in Celebes, a bronze image of Buddha of the Amarāvatī School[18] was found. The earliest sculptures from Dong-Duong, Dong Tuk (Siam), exhibit Amarāvatī style.[19] A bronze Buddha from south Djember and Sikendeng on the west coast of Celebes and the colossal statue at Bukit are all in characteristic Amarāvatī style. It is quite likely that these images were brought from Andhra centres by the colonists. The transport of the large stone Buddha of Palembang must have been more difficult. It is the oldest relic from Amarāvatī in the archipelago. Sea route voyages connected Indian ports of the South with Indonesia.[20]

BAMIYAN BUDDHAS: THEIR DESTRUCTION

The irrepairable vandalism caused by the Talibans to the shrines of Bamiyan Buddhas in Afghanistan concerns the mankind as a whole. We would place below the great archaeological and artefactual importance of the site, deeply regretting at the fate met by these world treasures of Buddhist art.

Bamiyan in Afghanistan is situated 250 km from Kabul on the north-west. Its ancient name was the great Bamikan. Two large Buddhas were carved during 3rd-4th century AD[21], the small one earlier than the bigger one. The rock in which the Buddhist shrines were carved is tertiary conglomerate which lacks compactness and weathered due to cold and arid condition.

Big Buddha at Bamiyan

An earlier earthquake damaged the images and two wide cracks developed across the façade of the rock. The lower part of the right leg upto the knee and waist level of the left leg were broken due to the vandalism. However, the big Buddha measured 55 metres high, the chunks of the rock were precariously holding the damaged body.[22]

The conservation works carried out by the Archaeological Survey of India during the year 1975-77 have helped to restore the images to past glory. The damaged parts of the image were fitted, the knee portions strengthened by rock-bolting and grouting. The stucco work in the shrines was cleared of soot, dirt and dust and preserved. All the shrines around the principal niche at the ground level were repaired: on the drapery of the image of Buddha was brought to light very neatly the folds and pigment of bright red paintings over the dress.

The Small Buddha

It measured 38 m high, sheltered within a vaulted niche. The image has been carved out of rock, on the three sides in the manner of *alto-relievo*, the wavy folds of the garment painted in bronze. The heavy porportion of the body, the shematic drapery and the posture of standing with the right hand in *abhaya mudrā* recall Gandhian style. Though damaged the image inspired an overwhelming reverence.

The ceiling of the niche and walls were decorated with paintings depicting human figures and ornamental features. Most important is the depiction of the Sun god above the head of Buddha, a rare feature which elevated the Buddha as a universal king—Cakravartin.[23] Such rare figures are no more existing now due to the cruel acts of religious fanatics who held control of Afghanistan.

NOTES AND REFERENCES

1. D. Mitra, *Buddhist Monuments,* 1971, Calcutta, p. 13.
2. F.R. Allchin, 'Pattern of City Formation in Early Historic South Asia', *South Asian Studies*, Vol. 7 (1991), pp. 168-69. Also Robin Coningham, 'Anurādhāpura Citadel Archaeological Project. Preliminary Report of the Second Season of Śrī Laṅkān British Excavations at Salagahawatta, June-Aug, 1990', *South Asian Studies*, Vol. 7, pp. 167-74. F.R. Allchin, 'City and State Formation in Early Historic South Asia', *South Asian Studies*, Vol. 5, 1989, pp. 12-13. Rolin Connigham, 'Śrī Laṅkā Rewritten', *Minerva*, Vol. 6, No. 2 (Britain, March-April, 1995), pp. 27-33.
3. JP.H. Vogel, 'Prākrit Inscriptions from a Buddhist Site at Nagarjunakonda', *Epigraphia Indica*, Vol. XX, pp. 7, 22.
4. Akira Hirakawa, *The Rise of Mahāyāna Buddhism and its Relationship to the Worship of the Stūpa, Memoirs of the Tonyo Bunko,* Vol. 22, 1963, Tokyo.
5. Robert E. Fisher, *Buddhist Art and Architecture,* 1993, London, pp. 42-44.
6. *Epigraphia Indica*, Vol. XX, pp. 23-24.
7. V.S. Agrawal, 'Origin of the Buddha Image', *Śatābda Kaumudi*, Central Museum, 1964, Nagpur, p. 30.
8. D. Mitra, *op.cit.*, pp. 13, 23.
9. V.S. Agrawal, *op.cit.*, pp. 31-32.
10. *Epigraphia Indica*, Vol. XXX, pp. 12-13.
11. *MAR*, 1907-08, p. 2 and *Indian Antiquary*, Vol. I, p. 153.
12. P.V. Bapat (ed.), *2500 Years of Buddhism,*1976 Publications Division, New Delhi, pp. 255-257.
13. I.K. Sarma, 'Ancient Port Towns of South-East India: Their Role in the Spread of Buddhist Art and Religion to China and Japan', G. Kuppuram and K. Kumudamani (ed.), *Researches in Indian History Archaeology and Religion*, Prof. Upendra Thakur Felicitation Volume, Vol. II, 1990, New Delhi, pp. 551, 558.
14. J. Auboyer, *Buddha—A Pictorial History of His Life and Legacy,* 1983, New Delhi, pp. 54-56 and iii.
15. I.K. Sarma, *Buddhist Monuments of China and South-East India* 1985, New Delhi, pp. 73-78.

16. I.K. Sarma, 'Archaeological Evidences Pertaining to Buddhism in Tamilnadu', *Śrī Ratna Chandrikā*, 1993, New Delhi, pp. 65-77.
17. I.K. Sarma, in S.R. Rao (ed.), *An Integrated Approach to Marine Archaeology*, 1997), Goa, pp. 95-101.
18. M.C. Subhadra Diskul, 'The Lord Buddha Protected by Nāga', *SPAFA Digest*, Vol. XI, No. 3, 1990, Bangkok, pp. 3-6, fig. 6.
19. H.P. Ray and Jean Francois (ed.), *Tradition and Archaeology: Early Maritime Contacts in the Indian Ocean*, 1996, (New Delhi, pp. 65-67, 119, 135, 144.
20. K.A. Nilakantha Sastri, *South Indian Influences on the Far East*, 1945, Madras, p. 119.
21. *Indian Archaeology: A Review*, 1974-75, p. 118.
22. *IAR*, 1975-76, p. 128, pl. 4-LXXX; *IAR*, 176-77, p. 131, pl. XCII.
23. R. Sen Gupta, *The Buddha in Afghanistan*, 1978, New Delhi, Ministry of External Affairs, p. 9.

18

BRAHMANICAL SCULPTURES IN THE GANDHĀRA ART

N.P. Joshi

The term Gandhāra as used in ancient Indian classics denotes the territory roughly covered by modern regions of Peshawar, Swat (ancient Uḍḍīyāna) and Bunar in the north, tract of land upto Indus in the east and adjacent regions including Taxila in the south-west. Majority of the sculptures datable to the early centuries of the Christian era hailing from Gandhāra represent the Buddhist themes, but traces of coexisting Brahmanism too are seen in shape of some images. Though the number of the brahmanical sculptures is much lesser than those belonging to the Buddhist faith, these are no less interesting and show that the deities like Śiva, Skanda, Durgā, etc., also commanded worship. On the basis of some epigraphical and numismatic evidence it can be said that even the Vaiṣṇava deities like Vāsudeva and Balarāma were also known to the people. In the present paper we shall be mainly confining ourselves to the sculptural evidence only.

ŚIVA

The numismatic data regarding different forms of Śiva on the Kuṣāṇa coins has been discussed elsewhere.[1] Contemporary images of Śiva in stone from the Gandhāra region are very few. Till now we know of only four following figures:

The Rome Figure[2]

This figure of three faced and four-handed Śiva has been reported from a private collection in Rome. The central one is a human face with moustaches and the third eye on the forehead. The hair form a thick knot above. The two lateral faces have animal features. The one to the right is that of a lion, while the other on left is of an antelope. Śiva carries rosary, trident, discus and small water vessel in his hands clockwise. A part of his upper garment rolls on his left shoulder and the lower garment reaches the knees. The erected phallus (*ūrdhvaliṅga*) appears concealed. The pose of the right hand with rosary, but at the same time pointing to his own self, as if inviting the devotees deserves notice.

The Berlin Figure[3]

This sculpture in relief is very much similar to the above with slight difference in hair arrangement and pose of the right hand, which is injured, but certainly it did not touch the chest. Among the attributes the trident in the upraised extra right hand and the water jar in the suspended normal left are extant. The lateral faces, namely that of a lion and antelope, horizontal third eye, erect phallus, upper garment partly covering the left shoulder and knee reaching lower garment are common features. On the other hand unlike the Rome figure, the god in this case puts on no ornaments in neck or wrists, but his sacred thread (*upavīta*) has been prominently shown. The image is broken almost below the knees.

The central face with moustaches is seen in both the cases, which may be taken as a special Gandhāra feature, as in this school we come across figures of Bodhisattva and the Buddha too with moustaches.[4]

Śiva Emanating from the Central Bodhisattva Figure in the Peshawar Museum[5]

A Bodhisattva is seen seated in meditation and from his body emanate six figures—three are seen on right and three on left—all different from one another. Among the group on left side the middle one is Śiva, who is unfortunately headless but is ithyphallic carrying a trident in his right hand and the water vase is in his lower left. Discussing this and other figures in the group Teddei refers to the *Saddharma-puṇḍarīka*, which informs that Bodhisattva Gadgadeśvara preaches this *Dharmaparyāya* under many shapes he assumes like Brahmā, Indra, Śiva, etc.[6] That is how appearance of Śiva and Skanda too, as we shall shortly see, is well justified.

The fourth figure, a Gandhāra panel in the collection of Julian Sherrier depicts Śiva-Pārvatī and Skanda-aṣṭhī in a line.[7] Śiva, as described by Agrawala stands with his organ erect and Pārvatī with a long handled mirror in her left hand.

Something More About the Animal Faces

Three faced and four-armed Śiva is seen, according to Härtel[8] on a gold coin issued by Huviṣka. The scholar holds that the face on the right side seems to be that of a lion, while the one on the other side cannot be identified. We would like to suggest that the two animal faces in our sculptures may be for his terrific (*ugra, aghora*) form and the antelope for his benign (*saumya*) form. It may further be noted with interest that in the four-faced (*caturmukha*) *liṅgas* the *aghora* face occupies the right (*dakṣiṇa*) side, while on left the female face (*strī mukha*) is to be seen. It may also be recalled that the beautiful eyes of a young damsel are always compared with those of an antelope or deer (*mṛgākṣī, hariṇākṣī*).

Comparison of Gandhāra and Mathurā Śiva

A comparative study of Śiva figures in the Gandhāra and Mathurā Schools flourishing contemporarily reveals the following points:

(1) The Gandhāra Śiva is somewhat rough and crude representing his 'Rudra' aspect; while in Mathurā he is much more sophisticated and benign answering to his Sadāśiva form.
(2) In Gandhāra he is multi-armed and multi-faced, sometimes with animal faces on the two sides. His central face, the human one, bears moustaches. All these features are absent at Mathurā.

(3) Śiva's main weapon, the trident, is conspicuously absent at Mathurā.
(4) The Gandhāra sculptures rarely show Śiva's consort Umā or Pārvatī with him, while at Mathurā she is often to be seen by his left.
(5) His mount, the bull Nandi, is seen at both the places, but the lion, which sometimes appears at Mathurā, is absent in Gandhāra.

SKANDA OR KĀRTTIKEYA

This god, always of tender age, has been described as the elder son of Śiva, commander-in-chief of the gods (*deva-senāpati*) and fatal enemy of the demon Tāraka. In early centuries of Christian era he commanded worship in Mathurā regions and had reached Gāndhāra also, where he more appears as a warrior. Till now we know of seven figures of Skanda in the Gandhāra art as detailed below:

(1) The Taxila figure[9] about 8 inches in height standing with a spear in his right hand and a cock in the left. He wears long boots in his feet.
(2) The figure in the British Museum, London[10] is similar, but devoid of shoes. Skanda's armour, halo and a sword tucked near the waist are clear. He puts on a turban.
(3) Almost similar to the above there is a figure in the Museum at Rome,[11] but here instead of the *dhoti*, tight fitting trousers have been used.
(4) A small figure in the Museum at Vadodara, Gujarat (No. Baroda Ac. 2.194, A.R. 100) shows the god with crested headgear and armour on body. Besides his spear in hand he has a bow in his neck and the sheath of arrows on his back. The cock is absent.
(5) The Berlin Museum of Indian art also has a fine image of Skanda (MIK. 5811). In this case besides the head gear, armour, halo, spear and cock two additional features are noteworthy. One is a bell tied to his spear seen near his left shoulder; another is appearance of a peacock, which with its turned head looks towards a devotee seated in adoring attitude.
(6) Skanda as emanating from the Bodhisattva figure in the Peshawar Museum.[12] We have already referred to this figure of Bodhisattva in connection with Śiva. The central figure in the group of divinities on the right side of the seated Bodhisattva is well-armoured baloed Skanda with a spear and a bird obviously the cock.
(7) **Skanda with Ṣaṣṭhī** : We shall discuss this type in details under Ṣaṣṭhī.
(8) **Skanda with flames** : The Victoria and Albert Museum in London houses a miniature figure of Skanda[13] with *dhoti* and a spear and cock in his right and left hands. It differs from other Gandhāra images and is more akin to the Mathurā prototype. He puts on a short loin cloth and a small *uttarīya*, but no turban, armour or boots. At the same time an additional notable feature is the rising flames of fire seen in the halo behind his neck. These clearly go to establish his close relations with Agni, the fire-god, which have been often spoken of in the Purāṇas.

Weapons, Mount

A spear or *śakti* is favourite weapon of Skanda sometimes seen with a bell tied to it; and the peacock is his mount. Similarly a cock is his significant attribute seen in the Gandhāra sculptures. It will therefore be worthwhile to see what literature speaks about them.

The *Mahābhārata*[14] informs that the bell Vaijayanta by name was presented to Skanda by Indra. Similarly, his spear with upraised tip (*udagra śakti*) came to him from Viṣṇu[15] and

Tvaṣṭā gave him the cock, a toy capable of assuming different shapes at will (*kāmarūpī krīḍanaka*).[16] As per *Mārkaṇḍeya Purāṇa*[17] Skanda's spear was one of the weapons, which were made by Viśvakarmā from the Sun's heat. All these presentations were made by respective gods on the occasion of Skanda's anointation as commander-in-chief.

Comparison of Gandhāra and Mathurā Skanda

We know of no less than twenty figures of Kuṣāṇa Skanda from Mathurā, the number in the Gandhāra art is much lesser. However a comparative study of the two reveal the following points:

(1) The Gandhāra School preferred depiction of Skanda as commander of the army well equipped with weapons like spear, sword, bow and arrow and armour on his body. The Victoria and Albert Museum figure (No. VIII) is however an exception, but it is of late date also. At Mathurā though with a spear he is literally seen as Kumāra, a young boy with tender features.
(2) The cock is pretty common in Gandhāra, but it is rare in Mathurā.
(3) The Gandhāra images are much smaller in size.
(4) In Gandhāra Skanda is seen alone or with ṣaṣṭhī in very limited cases, but at Mathurā besides being alone, he is often seen with the group of the Mothers (Mātṛkās), or when with ṣaṣṭhī he often accompanies his brother Viśākha.
(5) Mathurā Skanda puts on no boots.

Skanda with Ṣaṣṭhī

The goddess Ṣaṣṭhī, closely associated with child welfare, or even otherwise, has been described as Skanda's wife in the *Mahābhārata*[18] and sister in the *Kāśyapa-saṁhitā*,[19] which also makes mention of her brother Viśākha. In the Kuṣāṇa art at Mathurā this goddess is either six headed, or is seen with five female figures emerging from her body.[20] In the Gandhāra art till now we are in know of only two depictions of Skanda with Ṣaṣṭhī. One is a wing of portable diptyche in the Cleveland Museum of Art. [21] It is a small piece datable to *c.* 2nd century AD in the upper field of which Skanda has been shown seated on a high seat with a spear and cock in his hands. On his right appears six handed Ṣaṣṭhī similarly squatting on a high seat carrying a lotus in the right hand a purse in the left. The other example is to be seen[22] in the collection of Julian Snerrier, to which reference has already been made. In this case Skanda stands holding a very long spear in right hand and the cock in the left. In between his two legs appears a peacock facing front. Next to him stands six headed ṣaṣṭhī putting on typical Gandhāran dress with a lotus in her right hand. It is significant to note that the *Mahābhārata*[23] equates Devasenā, the wife of Skanda with Ṣaṣṭhī, Lakṣmī and others. It is well-known that a lotus goes on a symbol of Lakṣmī.

In the Mathurā art Skanda has often been sided by Ṣaṣṭhī and his brother Viśākha, but in the Gandhāra cases under reference Viśākha or anybody else has been dropped. Of course he is to be seen on some coins of Huviṣka with Kumāra and Mahāsena.[23a]

THE GODDESS WITH LION

Teddei has noticed two very interesting sculptures of a female divinity seated in European fashion on a high seat. One such figure is in the Fujii-Yārnikan Museum, Kyoto[24] and the other is perhaps in the Lahore Museum.[25] In both the cases the deity holds a bowl in her right hand; but the Kyoto figure in her left hand carries a severed head of a ram, while the Lahore figure is said to be holding 'a horned animal's head'. Appearance of a lion in the composition is another noteworthy feature. According to Taddei in the Kyoto figure a lion's head protrudes from the deity's right temple, but in the accompanying photograph this is not clear. The Lahore figure, on the other hand, has two poorly modelled lions (or lionesses?) seated on their hind legs beside the goddess looking up at her.

The bowl, perhaps a wine-cup, severed animal head—clearly a ram in one case—and the lion can apparently be interpreted as links with Durgā, who rides a lion, holds a wine cup and in whose worship animal sacrifice plays a prominent role.

Prevalence of the Śakti cult in the Gandhāra and Baluchistan regions is well supported by some literary evidence also, which is being summarized below.

(1) One of the groups of Vedic people was called Paṇi. The Paṇis were traders, who according to one scholar Krishna Tapanlal Jetley, lived in Baluchistan[26] and as per *Bhāgavata Purāṇa*,[27] Vṛṣalarāj, a Paṇi ruler, was a devotee of Bhadrakālī and had tried to please her with a human sacrifice. Bhadrakālī, as we know, is a form of Durgā.
(2) Among the follower deities of Pārvatī, the *Mahābhārata*[28] makes mention of Gauri, Gāndhārī and other four. The *Jaina-Kalpasūtra*[29] also mentions Gauri-Gandhārāī.
(3) The *Kālikā Purāṇa*[30] describes Uḍḍiyāna-pīṭha (Swat) as sacred to Kātyāyanī, another form of Durgā.

In this connection attention may be invited to a post-Gandhāran stele, which is in highly injured position housed in the Swat Museum at Sai-du-sharif.[31] This stele depicts an eight-handed female divinity, which has got great similarity with *aṣṭabhujā* Durgā, but in this case instead of the buffalo (*mahiṣa*) a caprid is being killed. Now this stele is said to be hailing from a place named Guligram. Could it be ancient Gaurīgrāma, sacred to the goddess Gaurī in Gandhāra?

It can be rightly pointed out that by 2nd century AD, Ambā, alias Umā (consort of Śiva) had become known as 'giver of fortune' and another goddess Nanā on lion too had imbibed some similar iconographic features.[32]

Thus the sculptural, numismatic and literary evidence together go to show that from early centuries of Christian era down to the medieval times—say upto *c.* 9th century (end of the Shāhī rule) worship of Śiva, Durgā and Gaṇeśa [now we do not know about the fate of the two Gaṇeśa images (Mahāvināyaka) in Kabul] did flourish in the Gandhāra and surrounding regions.

CANDRA

Depiction of Sūrya and Candra often go together. We do not know of any Gandhāra Sūrya in stone, though he can be well noticed on the Kaniṣka casket from Sahji-ki-ḍehrī, Peshawar[33] flanking the effigy of King Kaniṣka on right side. Here the figures of Sūrya and Candra are only half length. The Gandhāra representation of Candra in stone is preserved in the Indian Museum, Kolkata (IMC. G. 58) seated in a chariot drawn by four horses.[34] The figure has been taken as that of Sūrya, but prominent crescent behind his head and the style of sitting clearly show that the god depicted is Candra. Contemporary illustration of Candra in horse drawn chariot along with similar Sūrya can be seen in the Kuṣāṇa image of Nṛ-varāha in the Mathurā Museum (GMM. 65.15). Candra seated in chariot drawn by ten horses had come to be canonized by the time of the *Viṣṇudharmottara Purāṇa*.[35]

BRAHMANICAL DEITIES IN BUDDHIST GARB

Indra, Brahmā and Madana or Kāmadeva as Māra are some other Brahmanical deities seen in the Gandhāra sculptures in relation to the Buddhist themes. Brahmā appears as an ordinary Brāhmaṇa, while Indra is there in the royal dress with high crown on his head. His mount, the elephant can also be seen in some cases.

VAISNAVISM

Though no image of Viṣṇu has yet been reported from the Gandhāra region, existence of Vaiṣṇavism in the land can be well traced from the epigraphical and numismatic sources. Some coins of Agathocles from Aikhonum in Afganistan depict Vāsudeva Kṛṣṇa and Saṅkarṣaṇa or Balarāma with shoes in typical dress.[36] The names of the two deities as Baladeva and Vāsudeva appear in some Kharoṣṭī inscriptions from Gilgit, which have been deciphered by Dr A.H. Dani.[37] One gold coin of the Kuṣāṇa king Vāsudeva depicts four armed Viṣṇu carrying a club, wheel, conch and purse or rosary.[38] Discussion of these deities in details is certainly beyond our present scope.

NOTES AND REFERENCES

1. N.P. Joshi, 1984, 'Early Forms of Śiva', *Discourses on Śiva*, Ed. N.W. Meister, Bombay, pp. 47-61.
2. Herbert Härtel, 1985, 'A Śiva Relief from Gandhāra', *South Asian Archaeology*, Scandinavian Institute of Asian Studies, Occasional Papers 4, Ed. Karen Frifelt and Per Sorensen, fig. 2, p. 392.
3. See No. 2 above, fig. 4, pp. 393 ff.
4. Sarala D. Nagar, *Gandhāran Sculptures* (Museum of Art and Archaeology, University of Missouri-Columbia, 1981, illustration on pp. 7, 29, 35.
5. M. Taddei, 'Non-Buddhist Deities in Gandhāran Art—Some New Evidence', *Investigating Indian Art*, Ed. Marianney Yaldiz and W. Lobo, Berlin, 1987, fig. 1, pp. 349 ff.
6. *Ibid.*, p. 355.
7. R.C. Agrawala, 'Skanda-Āṣṭhī Couple in Gandhāran Art', *Prāgdhārā*, Lucknow, No. 5 (1994-95), pp. 147ff.; Sherrier Julian, 'Śiva in Gandhāra', *South Indian Archaeology*, 1991, Ed. A.J. Gail and G.J.R. Mevisoen 1993, Berlin, pp. 617-24, pls. 48.1-4.
8. See No. 2 above, fig. 5, pp. 395-96.
9. R.C. Agrawala, 1968, 'Gandhāra Skanda with Flames', *East & West*, N.S., Vol. 18, Nos. 1-2, Rome, p. 163.
10. P.K. Agrawala, 1967, *Skanda Kārttikeya*, Varanasi, pl. XIXa, pp. 84, 101; No. 9 above, p. 164.
11. See No. 9 above, p. 164.
12. See No. 5 above, p. 352.
13. See No. 9 above.
14. *Mahābhārata*, Vana., 231.18-19, p. 610 (Gita Press Ed.).
15. *Padma Purāṇa*, *Sṛṣṭi.*, 46.149-57, p. 460 (Mor Ed.0).
16. G. Rao, *Elements of Hindu Iconography*, II.2, pp. 430ff.
17. N.P. Joshi, *Mātṛkās, Mothers in Kuṣāṇa Art*, New Delhi, 1986, p. 66; *Mahābhārata.*, Vana., 229.45-52, pp. 1603ff. (Gita Press).
8. N.P. Joshi, *Mātṛkās*; p. 66; *Kāśyapa-saṁhita*, Cikitsā., Bālagraha., pp. 99-100.
19. N.P. Joshi, *Mātṛkās*, figs. 39, 40, 41, 42, 43.
20. R.C. Agrawala, 1993, 'Āṣṭhī in Gandhāran Art', *East & West*, Vol. 43, Nos. 1-4, pp. 271-75.
21. See No. 7 above, p. 148.

22. *Mahābhārata.*, Vana. 229.50-52, p. 1604 (Gita Press).
22a. J.N. Banerjea, 1985, *The Development of Hindu Iconography*, pl. X.7, p. 145.
23. See No. 5 above, figs. 9, 10, p. 357.
24. See No. 5 above, fig. 13, p. 358.
25. कृष्ण टोणलाल जेतली, पणयो व्यलोचस्थानञ्च, *Bhārata Itihāsa Samśodhaka Maṇḍala Traimāsika*, Pune, Varṣa 43, saṅka 1-4, pp. 1-6.
26. *Bhāgavata* V.9.12-15 : वृषलपतिः भद्रकाल्यै पुरुषपशुमालभतापत्यकामः – V.9.12; वृषलराजपणिः पुरूषपशोर सृगासवेन देवीं भद्रकालीं यक्षमाणः — V.9.16.
27. *Mahābhārata.* Vana., 231.49, p. 1612 (Gita Press Ed.)
28. बृहत्कल्पसूत्र, सगरिकोपाश्रय 2508, p. 709.
29. *Kālikā Purāṇa*, 1.18, 5.42, 5.50, Vaṅgavāsī Ed., p.79.
30. See No. 5 above, fig. 13, p. 359.
31. B.N. Mukherjee, 1969, *Nanā on Lion*, Calcutta p. 17.
32. Prudence R. Myer, 1966, 'Again the Kaniṣka Casket', *The Art Bulletin*, XLVIII, fig. 1, pp. 396-403.
33. J.N. Banerjea, 1985, *The Development of Hindu Iconography*, pl. XXVIII.3.
34 *Viṣṇudharmottara Purāṇa*, III.68.4, folio 343.
35. R.C. Agawala, 'Early Vaiṣṇava Icons from Rajasthan', *Vaiṣṇavism in Indian Art and Culture*, Ed. Ratan Parimoo, 1987, New Delhi, p. 329, Plate 20.
36. *Ibid.*, p. 330
37. This coin under reference was sent to the Department of Coins and Seals in the British Museum, London by some coin collector in Japan. Joe Cribb had examined it and had presented a paper entitled 'Images of Indian Deities on North-West Indian Coins in the pre-Gupta period' with a photograph and plaster cast of the coin in the Berlin Seminar on 4-5th May 1986. The two were seen on this occasion by the author along with R.C. Agrawala and Herbert Härlet.

19

SVASTIKA: THE GANDHĀRAN ENIGMA

PREETY A. TRIVEDI

Symbols defined by some as signs which are semantically non-arbitrary[1] or as objects used to represent something abstract, have been a part of human development right from the inceptive stages of human civilization. Humans have an extraordinary trait of creating and using symbols to express their ideas, beliefs and emotions. Every civilization, the world over, displays a plenitude of symbols which marks its material culture. Some symbols remained typical to a perticular civilization, whereas some symbols migrated to and were adopted and extensively used by other civilizations too.

Amongst the most popular of such archaic symbols, is the *Svastika*, which found its way into every country and was used for a variety of reasons. Many scholars have done researches on thus omnipresent symbol; one of the oldest amongst these is Wilson's 1894 work on the history of the *Svastika*. It is a symbol, which has been used in far-off places of the world for a variety of reasons and is also made in a variety of ways. Considered to be one of the oldest symbols associated with human culture, it is used extensively even in modern times. It has been associated with many religions of the world and is said to symbolize fire, movement of the earth, stages of life, the sun or even sometimes, the appearance of comets in the sky has been depicted in the shape of a *Svastika* in certain ancient paintings (found from China). In Hindu scriptures, the *Svastika* simply means something 'conducive to well-being' (*kuśal-kṣema-kalyāṇa-ho*). For the Jain faith, it is the sign of the Seventh Tīrthaṅkar and the Buddhists probably consider it to mean four possible rebirths; (1) animal, (2) plant, (3) hell or earth, (4) spirit world. It is also extensively found in Mesopotamian seals. Tablets and seals found from Indus Valley culture sites, ranging from Afghanistan in the west to Bengal and Bihar in the east, display the right-handed as-well as the left-handed *Svastika*, i.e. 卐 or 卍. During the later period, however, the right-handed *Svastika* prevailed upon the left-handed one, called the *Sauvastika* in India. The Scandinavinas used left-handed symbol as a sign of Thor's hammer. In Christian and Byzantine art, it was known as the Gammadial cross or cross-*Svastika* is frequently seen on doors of houses, offices, etc., on account books religious places, etc. The *Svastika* is sometimes used for political purposes like the 'haken kreuz', placed obliquely within a circle, was adopted by Hitler as a symbol of the Nazi Party. The Gnostics have formed their own symbol, the Gnostika, based on the *Svastika*, incorporating basic symbols of the Hindus, Buddhists, Jews, Christians, etc., into its shape (see Fig. 1).

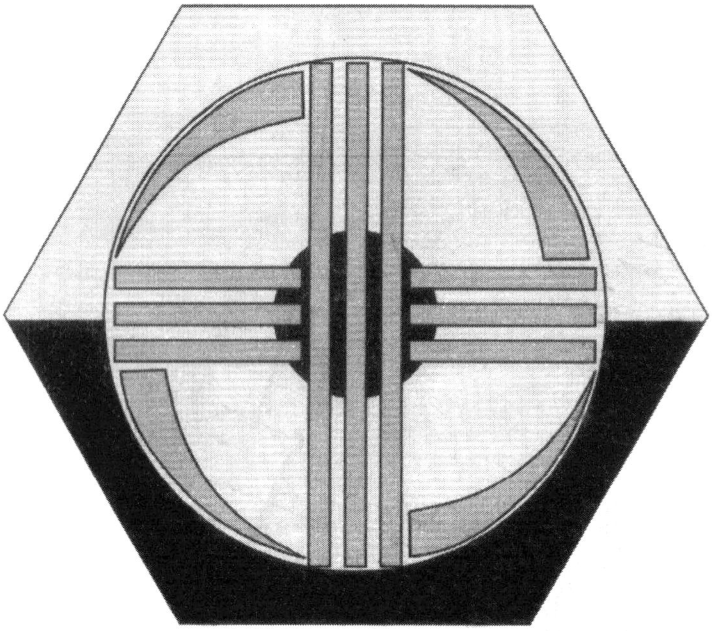

Fig. 1. The Gnostika is a hexagonal mandala enclosing the *Svastika* at its core. It is a universal meditation and centering device, representing various spiritual traditions, like, the I-Ching, Hinduism, Judaism, Christianity, Islam and Japanese Buddhism

Thus, we see that the *Svastika* was a symbol used by many different civilizations and religious sects for a variety of reasons and had a variety of interpretations. It is a symbol, which has often been studied by scholars, for its origin, significance, symbolism and uses. However, when we come to studying the areas where the *Svastika* is found, either as a religious symbol or just as a sign, we see that the area of Gandhāra is singularly lacking in examples of the *Svastika* in the prehistoric or Early Historic times (during the Historic times it entered this area in association with Buddhism, Hinduism or as an emblem of a king or dynasty). Hence in this study, I shall, for the most part, be dealing with the presence or rather the absence of the *Svastika* from the region of Gandhāra and its adjoining areas.

Gandhāra, intimately connected with India from prehistoric times, has always been conditioned by the variations that Indian history has gone through the course of centuries and even millenniums. In fact, it has many-a-time been a catalyst in bringing about sweeping changes, which have in more ways than one, influenced and contributed to the prolific culture of this country. These changes were, by and large, borne first by Gandhāra itself and then passed on to the other parts of the Indian subcontinent or vice-versa, owing to its geographical proximity location and is specifically true for the socio-cultural metamorphosis of the countries.

In prehistoric times, India shared its various cultures with Gandhāra and other areas of Afghanistan We have sites like Damb Sadaat and Kili-gul-Mohammad, which share affinities with other Indus valley sites in India. That India had trade and cultural relations with western Asia has been amply demonstrated by the discovery of Indus valley seals in Mesopotamia.[2] Some of the scenes shown on the tablets found from Mohenjodaro, has exact parallels in the seals from Susa, Crete and Palestine,[3] thus extending the cultural expanse beyond Gandhāra.

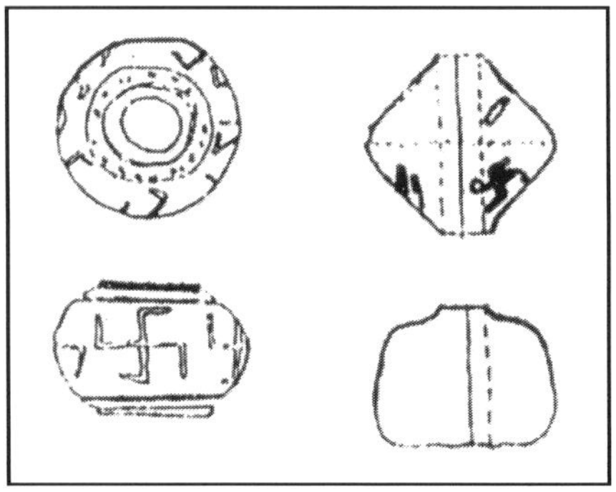

Fig. 2. Clay Whorls from Tarsus

Bearing in mind the above mentioned evincing examples of close contacts between India and West Asia, if we may, at this point confine our observations to the occurrence of the *Svastika*, we find that its most ancient examples come from Susa in Persia, Indus valley culture

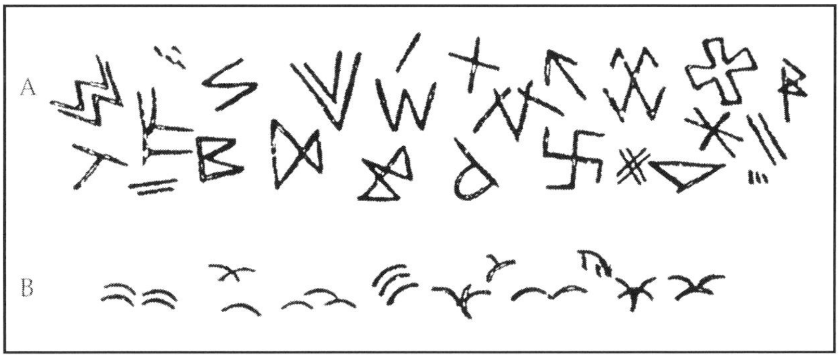

Fig. 3. Potters' marks from Damb Sadaat II-III levels, Damb Sadaat, Quetta, A–Incised, B–Fingernail-marked

sites in India and Pakistan and Samarra in Mesopotamia.[4] It has also been noticed in far-off places like Europe (Celts), Italy (Etruscans) and Turkey (Anatolia). It is found on the Christian catacombs. This was done to ensure safety of the departed soul and was later replaced by the Cross. In China the *Svastika* was used as a character symbolizing the notion of abundance, prosperity and long life. The Chinese empress Wu, in AD 68-70, made a law that the *Svastika* be used as a sign for the sun. In Japan, the number 10,000 are represented by the word *Svastika*.[5] Thus, we see that this graphic symbol is found in every ancient religion or cult of the world.

Ideas, beliefs and traditions are known to travel with travellers and invaders and possibly the ubiquitous *Svastika* owes its presence in far-off areas of the world to this phenomenon. It is impos-sible, considering the areas mentioned above, that these migrations and movements of cultures from India to the West or vice-versa could have taken place without affecting the area of Gandhāra. In spite of this, where we find the *Svastika* symbol closely associated with the worship of the sun, mother-goddesses or phallus-worship and even conceived as the Chatuṣpada Brahmā[6] (the four-fold form of the divine principle, spreading in the four directions) in places like Asia Minor, Italy[7] or India, or even Tarsus[8] and Troy[9] (see Fig. 2), it is merely found in the form of potters marks in the pot-shards discovered from Damb Sadaat, Quetta (see Fig. 3). To adduce further, some more examples of the *Svastika*, of the spiral tetraskelion type (see Fig. 4), have been found painted with black on buff or grey ware from Shahi Tump, Makran. But these seem to be samples of Iranian pottery, rather than Gandhāran.[10]

In the historical period, the *Svastika* is extensively found on Corinthian, Palestinian, Hindu, Danish and other coins of the world. In India, roughly around 600 BC, it was found on most of the varieties of punch-marked coins, especially those from Ujjain, Himachal Pradesh and Uttaranchal region. Certain coins bearing the *Svastika*, have been found in Gandhāra. But, one type of coin, bearing an inscription, belongs to Amoghabhuti, the Kuṇinda kings of Himachal Pradesh (1st century BC),[11] the other coin, of the uninscribed type, bearing lion with curved tail with *Svastika* at the back,[12] seems to be of foreign origin (see Fig. 5). Thus, these coins cannot be associated with the kingdom of Gandhāra or modern Afghanistan in any way.

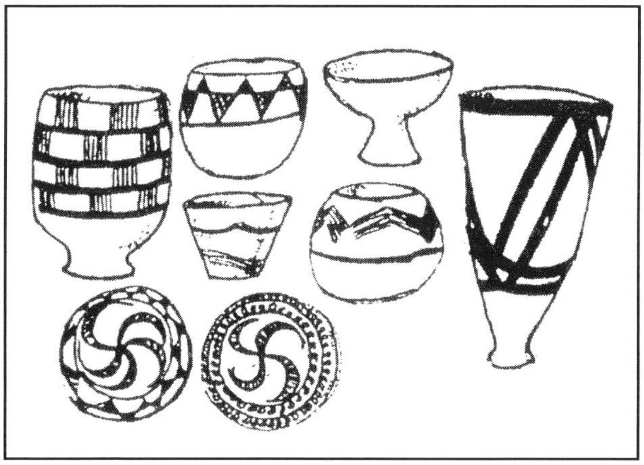

Fig. 4. Funerary pottery from Shahi Tump

In examining the history of migrations of symbols through religion, we see that Buddhism has played a key role in transporting the *Svastika* to the Extreme Orient, including Tibet, China, Japan, Korea,

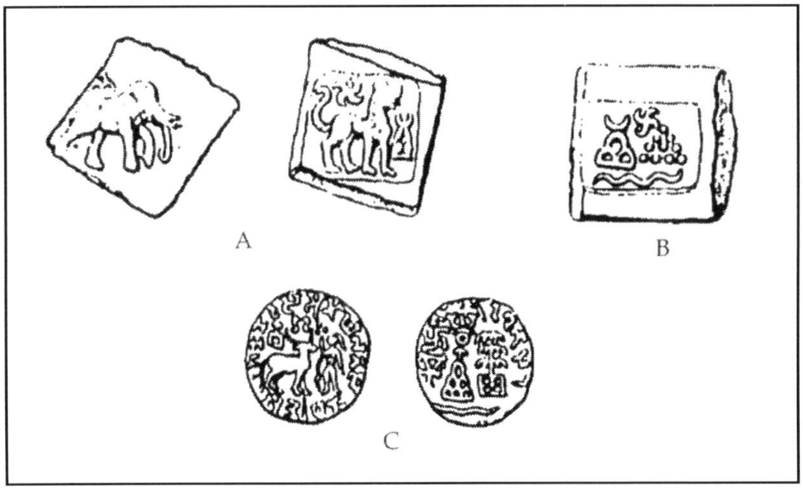

Fig. 5. A: Coin of foreign origin from Gandhāra; B: Punch-marked coin from Himachal Pradesh; C: Coin of King Amoghabhūti of Kuninda dynasty

etc. The *Svastika* is one of the prime symbols of Buddhism, found on most of the monuments associated with this religion, throughout the world. The art of Gandhāra, intimately associated with Buddhism, but sparingly depicts the *Svastika*, whereas it is extensively even in the far-off sculptures of China and Japan.[13]

Thus, we see that *Svastika*, the symbol of prosperity and well being, is the most varied and omnipresent symbol from ancient times. It is a symbol that has been discovered in almost all parts of the world, in a medley of forms, either expressing a meaning or just being used as a mark by potters or traders. Scholars have devoted considerable space and attention to this fascinating symbol, regarding its origin, variants, symbolism and dispersion. Its use in several parts of the world did not sustain through the centuries and fell away with the passage of time. Whereas it survived in countries like India, China, Japan, and also Lapland. The Shiite and the Bohri sects of the Muslims also probably perpetuate the use of a certain type of *Svastika*,[14] which read from any direction, means Ali ( ) the son-in-law of the Prophet (see Fig. 6). Shiites and Bohris consider Ali the Supreme Deity. Hence they may be using this symbol to show Ali-ka-Rudba, guarded on the four sides by the angels Jibrail, Israfil, Mekail and Israil.[15] Yet, the *Svastika* remains enigmatically absent from Gandhāra.

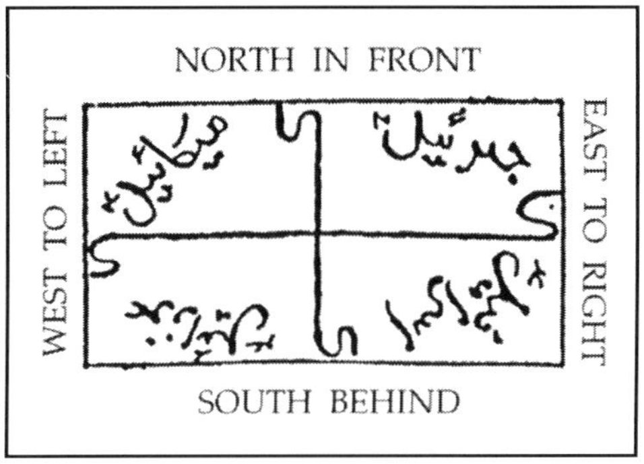

Fig. 6. Muslim *Svastika*

It is due to this lack of evidence of the *Svastika* in Gandhāra that scholars like Thomas Wilson, who have worked in detail on this symbol, refrain from associating it with this area. However, from the above-mentioned examples of pottery, seals and coins, we cannot absolutely negate the existence of *Svastika* in Gandhāra. The implausibility of this is further strengthened when we consider the geographical situation of Gandhāra, as a connecting point between India and West Asia. It is possible that, in future, further research and study may reveal to us the enigmatic *Svastika* of Gandhāra.

REFERENCE

1. David Bastow, *The Possibility of Symbolism in Indian Religion*, p. 191.
2. A.L. Basham, *The Wonder That Was India*, p. 21.

3. Heinz Mode, *The Harappan Culture and the West*, p. 7.
4. Henri Franfort, *The Pehcan History of Art : Art and Architecture of the Ancient Orient*, p. 17.
5. Padma Sudhi, *Symbols of Art Religion and Philosophy*, p. 147.
6. V.S. Agrawala, *Indian Art*, p. 49.
7. Thomas Wilson, *The Swastika*, p. 95.
8. Hetty Goldman, *Excavations at Gozlu Kule, Tarsus*, p. 447.
9. Dr. Schliemann, *Troy and its Remains*, p. 101.
10. W.A. Fairservis, *The Roots of Ancient India*, p. 222.
11. I wish to express my deep gratitude to Late Dr. Ajay Mitra Shastri, who kindly consented to read this coins for me, which was variously read as Krananda by T. Wilson and Ranakanadasa by H.H. Wilson.
12. H.H. Wilson, *A Descriptive Account of the Antiquities of Afghanistan*, p. 28, pl. I.
13. Thomas Wilson, *The Swastika*, p. 38, plate I.
14. Donald Mackenzie, *The Migration of Symbols*, p. 14.
15. I am grateful to Dr. Abbas Ali, eminent scholar of Arabic language, for having read this inscription for me and giving the interpretation of this *Svastika*-like emblem.

20

DECORATIVE ELEMENTS IN GANDHĀRA ART

S.D. TRIVEDI

Aesthetics is an important aspect of an art object; it enhances the charm of viewing. Artists in order to have proper aesthetic response beautify their creations through multifarious designs, motifs, symbols, accessory figures and patterns. All art styles have, in more or less degree, followed the integrated scheme of decoration visualizing the harmonious balance in various compositions. In our literature too *lāvaṇya* (loveliness) is described as an essential ingredient of *rūpa* (form). Coomaraswamy[1] rightly observed in one of his works: 'Mere narration (*nirvāha, itihāsa*), bare utility, are not art, or are only art in a rudimentary sense'.

By and large, the decorative element is assimilated in art objects to enhance their piquancy and charm. Apart from this some of the motifs are indicative of auspiciousness. It is believed that they can ward off evil if they are faithfully depicted in their manifold aspects of purpose and beautification. At times, the decorations are meant for support or filling space when the plain surface looks too plain or ugly.

What then is the role of a person who determines the nature of decoration in a particular composition? In all probability the master craftsman was mainly responsible for conceiving and deciding the decorative scheme, though collective indulgence at various stages is not ruled out.[2] Furthermore, it depends on the talent, skill, experience and imagination of the sculptor how he decorates his renderings and in which way the various decorative elements are arranged in the composition in order to achieve perfect relationship between theme and ornamentation.

Like other art idioms, a variety of decorative motifs were introduced in the Gandhāra School of Sculpture, which flourished in the early centuries of Christian era. Because of its political and cultural background, the assessment of origin of decorative motifs is quite complex. The inspiration might have come from the Achaemenians, Persians, Greeks, Indians, Indo-Bactrians, Śakas, Imperial Kuṣāṇas, Parthians or Sassanians. Many scholars are of the opinion that technique as well as motif have been borrowed from Greek and Western Asiatic art. Honeysuckle, grapevine, triton and acanthus mouldings are some of the Hellenistic features. The Indo-Persepolitan columns with false capitals surmounted by fabulous animals, ogee arches, the cupid garland bearers, the balconies with figures and dog-tooth ornament, are some of the West Asian decorations.[3]

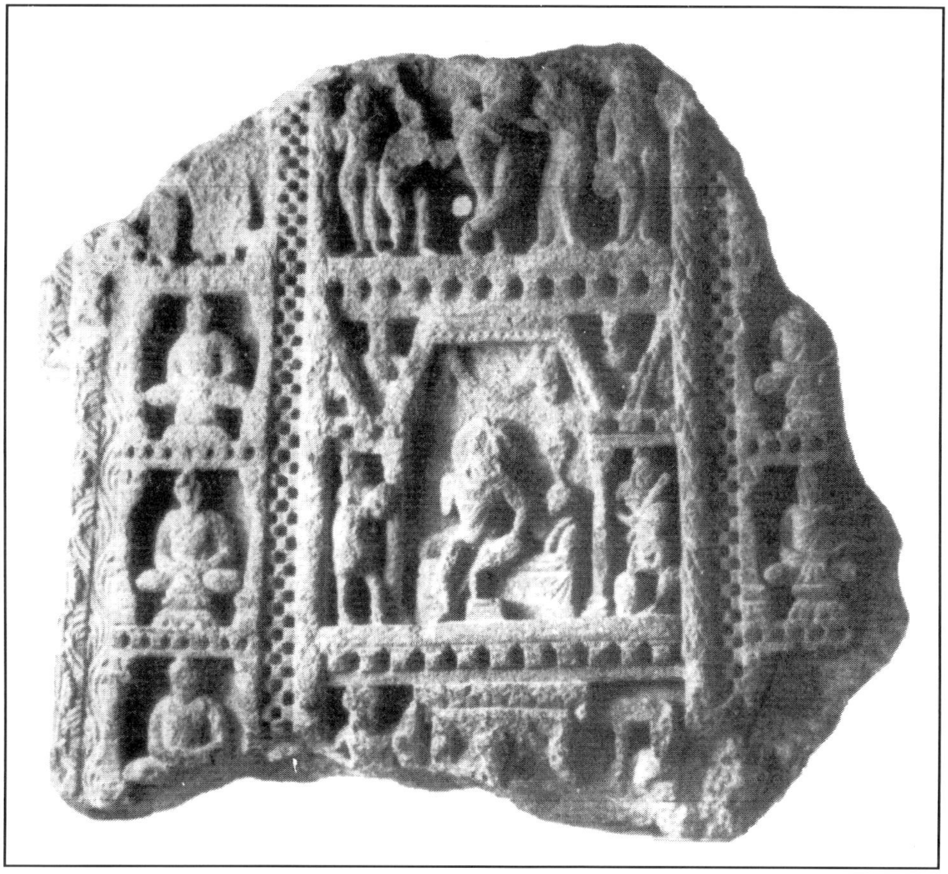

Fig. 1. Relief showing architectural, floral and geometrical decorations

Mathurā School of Sculpture was contemporary to Gandhāra art and it was but natural that the two would interact and be influenced by each other. For instance, Mathurā inspired the tradition of using *Garuḍa* as an ornamental motif. Several motifs are common in both arts.[4] Besides interaction, several other traditions also contributed to enrich the decoration of reliefs. With such a rich variety of choices available to him, the artist must have fully exercised the liberty and freedom to decide the perspective of ornamentation vis-à-vis each piece of artwork.

The question arises whether there was any standardization of decoration. Was it that a particular motif was always to be used in a particular theme or was it the choice and spontaneous decision of the sculptor. As appears from the study of a number of images, there were no set formulae of decorative techniques. However, in certain themes the common pattern of ornamentation does appear. Such decorative arrangements impart a feeling that the accomplished craftsmen favoured certain similar beautifications while dealing with specific subjects. At the same time, it is also true that the clever carver strove for novelty and new experiences and this was the reason for his applying separate patterns of decoration for similar subjects. We can thus safely establish that certain aesthetic principles were stereotyped in a particular class of subjects. The artists also had special preference for certain motifs and they were repeatedly used in varied compositions. For example, in majority of cases the Preaching Buddha was provided with a beautiful lotus seat. The lotus is full-blown flower

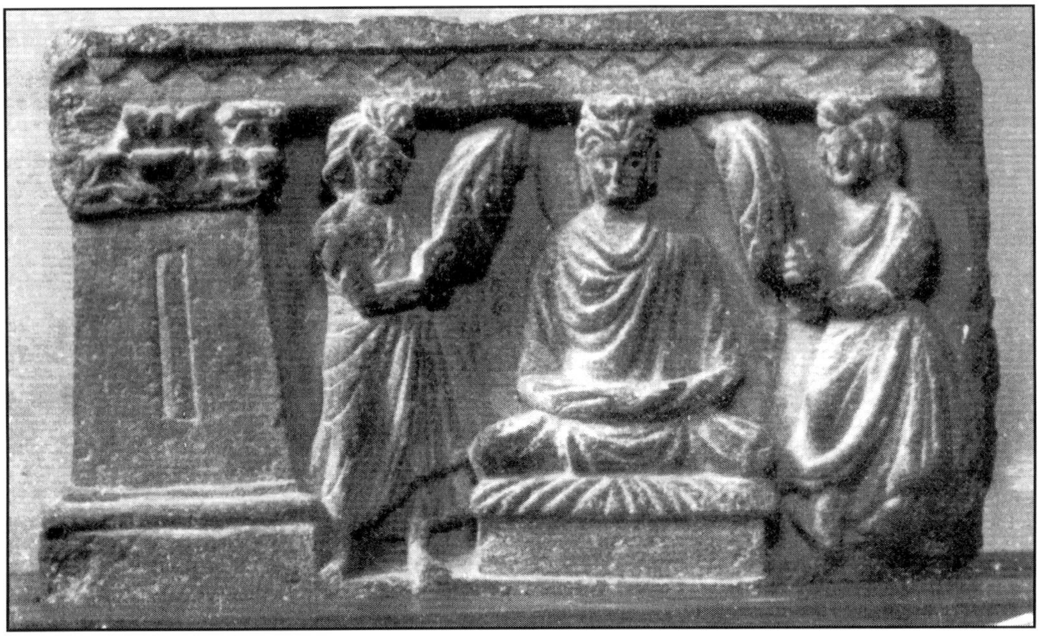

Fig. 2. Buddha with devotees. Pilaster with undercut mark. State Museum, Lucknow (47.38a)

raised on a long stem. The lotus is shown in such a way that its petals cover almost full plinth of the Lord. These are some of the finest specimens of the decorative relief work.[5]

The other very common pattern was the representation of Indo-Corinthian pilasters with medallions, shown on both sides of panels. Illustrating the events or episodes in separate niches, horizontal or vertical, generally adopts a common pattern forming a single element in the decorative and narrative scheme of a stele. Sunken panels enclosed with pilasters and decorated with geometrical patterns separate the scenes (Fig. 1).

We admire the richness of art motifs in Gandhāra School but if we go for comparison with other styles regarding soothing effect, the charm of artistry and aesthetic appeal, the decorations, taken in entirety, are not as good as we find in the Mathurā art or the art that flourished at Sanchi and Bharhut. It is possible that this is due to rough nature and hardness of schist stone. Of course, it may also be due to the dull colour of the stone. On the other hand, the medium of sandstone seems to be more favourable for chiselling and achieving delicate and exquisite refinement. It should also be borne in mind that some outstanding sculptures of Gandhāra School, adorned by fantastic decorations, are livelier than any Buddhist reliefs of other schools. For example, the 'Buddha with Donors' from Peshawar is extremely beautiful and is carved with multifarious decorative motifs.[6] Similarly, some reliefs depicting the Preaching Buddha are sumptuously decorated with several other patterns apart from the flowering lotus.[7]

Nature has been an integral part of Indian art from the very beginning. In Gandhāra art too, a number of animal figures, plants and creepers decorate the subjects and a variety in presentation can be seen in countless pieces. Grandeur of conception is, however, lacking and the spirited vitality is somewhat conventionalized. This becomes evident if we compare them with the products of other art schools, contemporary and of preceding period.

Generally, Gandhāra sculptures are meant for decoration of a *stūpa* or a Buddhist monument. Keeping this purpose in the mind, the delineation of artwork is done only on the front surface of the dome or stele. In Mathurā art of Kuṣāṇa period, several sculptures

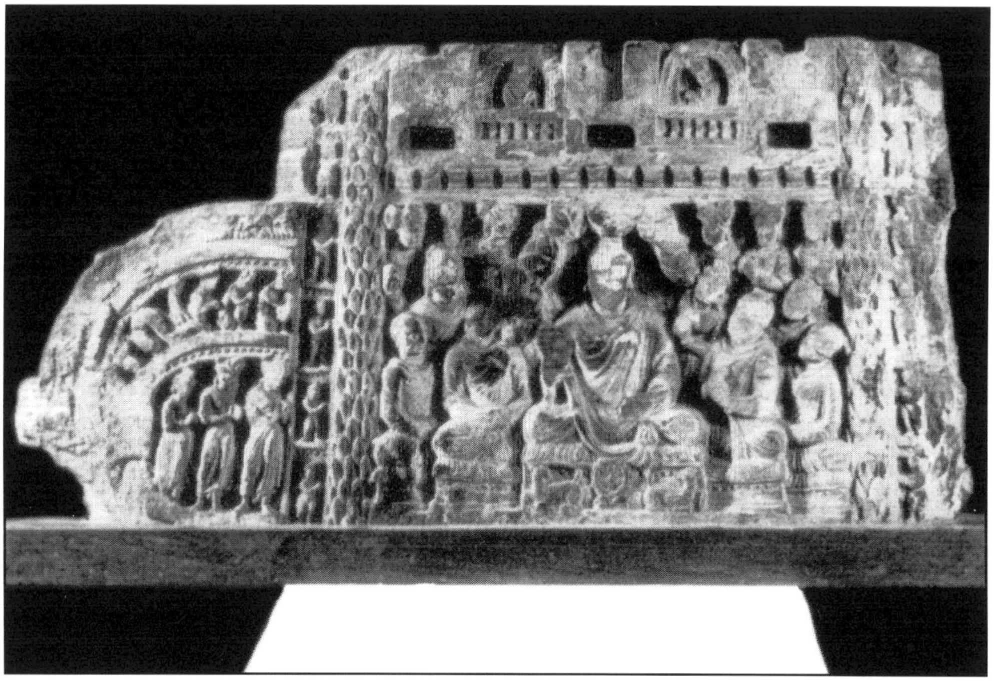

Fig. 3. Frieze decorated with architectural and floral motifs. State Museum, Lucknow (G.268)

are carved in round and many of them are decorated on their back with some motifs, mainly *Aśoka* tree. However, in Gandhāra, due to their specific use, there was little possibility of such decoration.

There may be an academic curiosity whether any chronology of decorative motifs can be established. Is it possible to trace the evolution of any particular pattern or can we on the basis of the shape, treatment or portrayal date the sculpture? I have not yet been able to work out such parameters. The dating of Gandhāra sculpture, on the whole, remains a problem though positive efforts have been made in the past and are still continuing. The dating on the basis of decorative motif may be even more difficult.

For the sake of convenience, the decorative elements are broadly classified in the following four groups: (1) Architectural (*sthāpatya*), (2) Floral (*patra-vallarī*), (3) Geometrical (*rekhākṛti*) and (4) Symbolical (*pratīkātmaka*).

Among all the decorative motifs, the depiction of pillar was most dear to the Gandhāran sculptor. Variety in shape and design can also be seen in the delineation of pillars and pilasters. Generally, the themes are carved in between the columns, which are placed on both sides of the main subject. Very often single pillar is also shown within an enclosure.[8] This way of presentation of a column clearly indicates that this architectural motif was used just to beautify the composition. A sculpture shows an Indo-Persepolitan tapering pillar within a rectangular frame with its base resting on a stepped plinth. At the capital are two bulls sitting back to back. Their bodies are in profile while their heads are in frontal view. Between them is placed a lion's head.[9]

The round pillars with Corinthian capital are common. They are flat and tapering towards the top with a deep-cut up-standing rectangular mark in the middle (Fig. 2).[10] Sometimes, the pillars are plain without this cut mark.[11] In some cases human figures are carved on the surface of these pillars instead of the plain cut mark.[12] In one sculpture, Indo-Corinthian

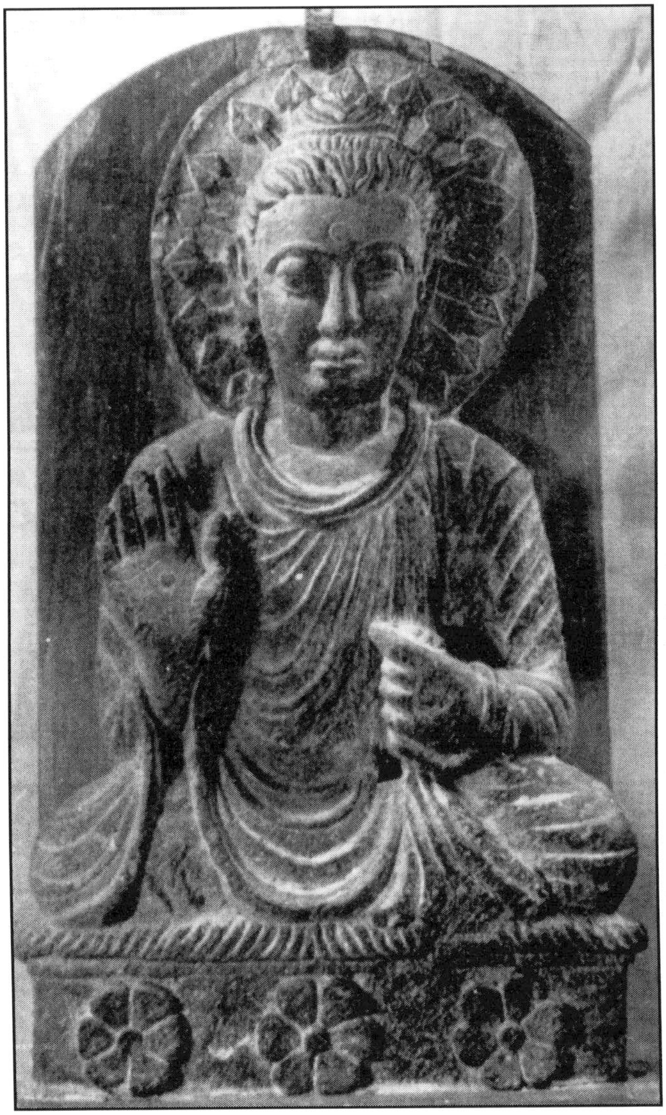

Fig. 4. Buddha in *abhaya* pose. Decorated base and halo. State Museum, Lucknow (47.37)

pilasters supporting an interrupted architrave and cornice with medallions flank each panel.[13] The Indo-Persepolitan pilasters crowned with animal capitals are portrayed facing the cardinal points of the sunken friezes as often found in Mathurā sculptures.[14] Indian pillars are also shown mainly on sunken friezes.[15]

The arch too has been variously represented in the reliefs. Generally they are ogee arches under which a figure or a scene is carved out in a depression.[16] Some of the friezes show purely Indian arches, in various shapes, richly decorated with many geometrical designs.[17] Enclosures and compartments are provided for the convenience of separating the themes and enhancing the decorative value of the visuals (Fig. 3). Decorated small boxes having figures of Amorini or worshippers are also made inside the compartments.[18]

False *jāli* work has fascinated the Indian artist right from 1st century AD to late medieval period as evidenced by numerous examples. Gandhāra masters had special inclination for incorporating this pattern in their creations.[19] Its beautiful display is discerned in several sculptures[20] housed in Peshawar and Lahore museums.

Bharhut seems to have been the first experiment in the pattern of railing. It greatly inspired artists of later period and its use as a decorative element is frequently found at Sanchi, Mathurā, Kauśāmbi and other places.[21] Gandhāra was not lagging behind and some beautiful specimens were found at Sikri.[22] An excellently executed *vedikā* and its placing has a similarity with many such images of Mathurā.[23] With the combination of upright pillar, crossbars, bases and coping stones, the main purpose of the railing was to protect the shrines from undesirable elements.[24] The artists adopted the same pattern in their compositions. Apart from its aesthetic appeal this motif was also used to divide the scenes. In Gandhāra art, medallions and half-medallions were also used to depict some scenes of other decorative motifs.[25]

Gandhāra artists were marvellously adept in producing countless attractive patterns and designs of floral decoration freely used in natural and conventional forms. The motifs include the depiction of leaves, buds, flowers, creepers, trees, etc. The scroll work (*patra-racanā*) was an important element in Gandhāra art. Its assimilation in the composition is considered sacred apart from being a mark of beauty.

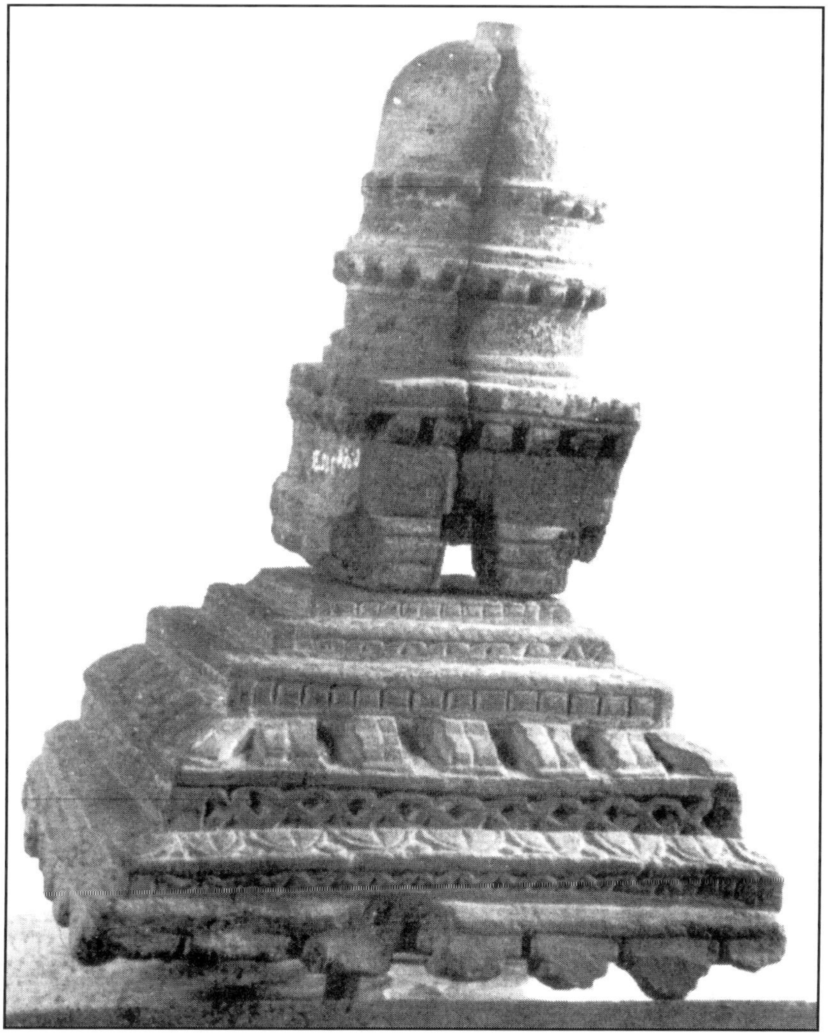

Fig. 5. Capital and votive *stūpa* decorated with various designs. State Museum, Lucknow (G.262 & G.264)

The scroll motifs are organic, geometrical or a combination of both. The organic motifs are purely vegetative and look fresh and natural while the geometrical floral designs in contrast are lightly etched on the surface to suggest their presence. They are decorated with the beads, dentil lotus leaves, lozenge and fillets.

Early Indian decorators have used lotus very frequently and it was easy for Gandhāran craftsmen to choose it from a wide range of floral symbols. This sweet-smelling flower is beautiful, attractive, pure and pious. It has been associated with Hindu, Buddhist and Jaina pantheons as a sacred and auspicious symbol. It is used to symbolize Buddha's miraculous nativity. The ornamental value of lotus is not less than its divine association. This is the reason for the remarkable diversity of this motif of early Indian art.

The medallions and half medallions show variants of compositions of lotus flower in Bharhut, Sanchi and Mathurā. In Gandhāra art such portrayals are conspicuous by their absence.[26] But the representation of lotus is frequent and the variety of its decoration is also rich. The lotus-seat is prescribed for many Hindu gods and goddesses like Brahmā, Lakṣmī also and the same is provided for several images representing the *Tīrthaṅkara* and Buddha. In Gandhāra style also the lotus motif was associated with Lord Buddha's seat. On some of the Preaching Buddha images, the rising lotus is carved to serve as a throne. Here some leaves and stalks are shown resting on the ground bearing the load. At times a large lotus seat is supported by two traditional *nāga* figures.[27] In some cases inverted lotus is also used to denote the *kamalāsana*. An excellent specimen[28] depicting full-blown inverted lotus below the seat comes from Loriyan Tangai and is presently housed in Indian Museum, Kolkata.[29] Such magnificent examples of lotus-thrones are not noticeable elsewhere.

A row of small lotus flowers is carved in relief on the base of a few Buddha images.[30] These rosettes are conventionalized. Three rosettes on the front of the seat of a Buddha image (Fig. 4) represent *triratna* of Buddhism. Some scholars are of the opinion that these are the flowers that the gods rained down over him at the enlightenment. The scrollwork on the outer surface of the seat was an accepted device of ornamentation. A lotus flower rising from a full vase (*pūrṇaghaṭa*) was frequently depicted at Bharhut, Sanchi, Amarāvatī and Mathurā in many designs but not in Gandhāra. However, in Gandhāra we have a rare depiction[31] showing the Tutelary Couple, with two vases on both sides of the base lying on their sides from which lotus petals are pouring out. A fragment[32] from Charsadda shows full-blown lotus flowers with tendrils and bells. This has close similarity with Bharhut[33] where a series of full-blown lotuses are found. Its portrayal must have been inspired by an Indian conception.

At Bharhut and Sanchi the unusual scrollwork termed *kalpalatā* and *kalpadruma* appear in varying forms. Generally, their root or source is not visble. Sometimes, the wish-fulfilling foliage also issues forth garments, ornaments, birds, animals, etc.[34] There are also some examples where the *kalpalatā* is shown issuing from the navel or mouth of a *yakṣa*.[35] However, wish-fulfilling creeper (*kalpalatā*) oozing the ornaments and other things is not found in Gandhāra art. More often, there are undulating garlands enclosing Amorini figures and other decorative ornamentation.[36] In another imaginative use of foliage, an artist has shown earth goddess rising from among a profusion of acanthi at the base of a Meditating Buddha panel in the Museum for Indian art, Berlin.[37]

The scrollwork containing acanthus leaves was very popular with sculptors and was generally applied on top of the friezes.[38] Its presence in Mathurā art of Kuṣāṇa period indicates both way interactions.[39] The grapevine and *pīpala* creeper were some scroll decorations which are sometimes used for multiple purposes—auspiciousness, ornamentation and separating the lower band from the upper. The sacred *pīpala* (*Ficus religiosa*) tree has a special significance in the Buddhist mythology and its creeper was also taken for decoration. A relief from Peshawar[40] shows a beautifully executed intricate design of *pīpala* leaves.

Certain friezes used on the drum of *stūpas* are decorated in a variety of undulating garlands, creepers, bunches of fruit, buds, etc. The nude figures are composed in different attitudes. In a fragment[41] of State Museum, Lucknow, the dwarf with his back view facing left holds an undulating vine creeper with twisted leaves and bunches of grapes. There are some friezes composed of floral scrolls mingled with animals and other figural motifs. A deeply undercut fragment[42] presents a horizontal portrayal of vine creeper with clusters of grapes, with a stag, a peacock and a monkey interwoven in it. Such decorative compositions are frequently found in Roman Imperial art as well as in Indian art.[43]

The honeysuckle[44] motif first appeared in the art of Mauryan period. Since then it came to be adopted as one of the important decorative motifs in subsequent artwork. Consequently, several forms of it emerged at various art centres.[45] In Gandhāran art, surprisingly, it was not so popular and only a few examples are known. A frieze[46] shows a stylized form of honeysuckle at its extreme left in a separate enclosure, its shape and placing resembling a Mathurā sculpture.[47] The pedestal of a Buddha image[48] also has linear decoration of honeysuckle.

The representation of tree has been a practice in various artworks through the ages for its religious perspective as also its decorative value. In Buddhism, certain types of trees are used as symbolic embodiments of great events of Buddha's life and his previous births. In Gandhāra art, the sculptor innovated a fanciful device of showing the trees associated with Buddha. Here the trunk is invisible and only leaves, at times along with stems also, are carved above and around the head of the Buddha. In another sculpture[49] the leaves of *pīpala* tree with stalks are shown within a halo as if these are issuing forth from the head itself (Fig. 4). Sometimes, this depiction is extremely stylized.[50] In yet another illustration of Māra's attack[51] the long leaves are stretched around the halo of the Buddha. There are some examples[52] where leaves can be seen emerging from the head of the Amorini couples and other subsidiary figures. In an interesting specimen[53] the leaves are seen sprouting from the head of a six-tusked elephant.

A few sculptures do incorporate the symbol of tree but the portrayal is neither natural nor very impressive.[54] In one scene of *Indraśālā* cave, an unexciting tree without leaves is depicted, probably to highlight the locale.

In comparison to other contemporary indigenous art, Gandhāra School seems to have used the geometric patterns in much more elaborate manner. The relationship between the subject matter and the arrangement of geometric motifs is complex. In general, the Gandhāran sculptors made it a point to incorporate some sort of linear designs here and there for multi-pronged purposes, viz., enhancing the beauty, filling the space, or strengthening the piece of art. Decoration, however, was the foremost motive and this urge led to the invention of a number of patterns and designs, e.g. bead-and-reel, criss-cross, leaf-and-dart, check-and-recess, saw-tooth, twisted rope, beading, fillets, circles, diagonals, rectangles, etc.

The saw-tooth motif was used for decorating compartments, small boxes, top sections of reliefs and pedestals.[55] A band[56] with criss-cross design appears in several panels. A frieze[57] depicting scenes from Buddha's life is adorned with railing, a laurel moulding and circle dots. Sometimes, the whole top or middle part of panel is crowned by a leaf-and dart moulding.[58] A fragment[59] of a doorjamb illustrates leaf-and-dart and a course of bead-and-reel decoration in the middle register used for separating the upper part from the lower. In a panel[60] below a single acanthus moulding, the base has a geometric decoration, which includes four squares, placed side by side, each divided into eight triangles, enclosing wedge-shaped points.

Buddha and his life events were represented by different symbols before and even after his anthropomorphic portrayal in the Indian art. Several other symbols had decorative value along with their religious association. In Gandhāra art only a limited number of Buddhist symbols were depicted. The cult of *stūpa* was the most popular in this region. The *stūpa* represents *Mahāparinirvāṇa*. Many sculptures depicting votive *stūpa* or worship of *stūpa* are found having different sets of decoration. A horizontal stone panel[61] from Peshawar shows two *stūpas* with a worshipper at right and another *stūpa* parted with an Indo-Persepolitan pilaster. Another small frieze[62] presents a *stūpa* flanked by a worshipper. The cult of Reliquary[63] is represented in an incomplete relief topped by a leaf-and-dart moulding. A small votive *stūpa*[64] decorated with floral and geometrical patterns is one of the best illustrations of symbolical representation. A square capital of a pillar and a votive *stūpa* illustrate the beautiful patterns of architectural and geometrical motys (Fig. 5). A couple of panels from Peshawar present a symbolic representation of the First Sermon, or Turning of the Wheel of Law. In the first[65] the symbol *triratna* is placed on a platform and *bhikṣus* are sitting around it. The *cakras* are decorated with lotus-petals. The other one[66] is much more decorated and the wheel is actually a stylized, full-blown lotus flower.

Faunal decoration in the plastic art was in practice since the days of Harappan culture. Gandhāra art also assimilated both types of birds and animals: natural and mythical. The elephant, horse, bull, camel, lion, bird—all were represented. The parrots perched on arches are seen on some friezes.[67] In Mathurā art, the lions on the extremities of the pedestal denote the *siṁhāsana* but Gandhāra artists rarely experimented with such devices. On such illustrations the lions are entirely stylized and look like an ornamental sketch.[68]

The portrayal of mythical animals is more forceful than the natural ones in Gandhāra art. Some Indo-Corinthian pilasters are crowned by fantastic animals as generally found in

West Asia. Crocodile faced horse with ornamental tail, winged crocodile with horse's face and coiled tail, winged dragon with human bodies, marine bull, centaur, leonine animals, are some of the fabulous creatures which were used by the Gandhāra artists. *Garuḍa*, a mythical bird, was also often used as an ornamental motif as in Mathurā art. *Garuḍa* with human ears has been represented in Mathurā[69] as well as in Gandhāra.[70]

The Gandhāra artists also favoured the triton motif. Greek influence on this decorative motif is obvious. A panel[71] presents two tritons between leonine feet. They are facing each other as if busy in conversation. Majority of the sculptors assimilated more than one kind of decoration, the aim being ultimately to enhance the beauty of the artwork.

A beautiful sculpture[72] from Takht-i-Bahi is heavily ornamented. The decoration here occupies more than half of the available space. The beauty of the relief lies in the blending of geometrical designs and floral patterns with the subject matter. The curvature of arches has a varied decorative scheme. The worshippers of meditating Buddha in upper frieze include the ichthyocentaurs in adoration, on extreme corners.

Sūrya and Candra were used as a decorative element by Indian artists.[73] The depiction of both is found on the Kaniṣka casket from Shahji-ki-dheri, Peshawar.[74] A figure of Sun-god is painted on vault of niche of 120-feet Buddha, Bamiyan.[75] It is a pictorial version of the relief of Sūrya at Bodh Gaya. Dr N.P. Joshi identified an image of Indian Museum, Kolkata as that of Candra generally mistaken for Sūrya by scholars.[76] In another richly decorated sculpture the busts of Sūrya and Candra are depicted on a balcony.[77] There are several toilet or cosmetic trays from Gandhāra region on which manifold decorative motifs appear.[78]

In sum, we find that the Indian artist worked with conventional motifs, motifs borrowed from Greek art, as well as images that were dear to his own heart like bull, or a pastoral scene and blended the whole into superbly crafted works of art.

NOTES AND REFERENCES

1. A.K. Coomaraswamy, *Transformation of Nature in Art*, p. 46.
2. S.D. Trivedi, "Decorative Elements in Mathurā Art", *Kalā: Journal of Indian Art History Congress*, Vol. V (1998-99), p. 169, fig. 1; The chief monk and chief architect of the *stūpa* must have their say in deciding the decorative scheme of the artefacts.
3. Almost all these features can be seen in one sculpture found at Loriyan Tangai, presently kept in Indian Museum, Calcutta.
4. N.P. Joshi and R.C. Sharma, *Catalogue of Gandhara Sculptures in the State Museum,* Lucknow (hereafter abbreviated as *GS-SML*), pp. 27-37; The interactions between Gandhara and the art of Sarnath and Andhra Pradesh are also noteworthy.
5. A. Foucher, *The Beginnings of Buddhist Art*..., pl. xxxiv-1; xxvi-1-2; xxvii, xxviii-1; The author has seen two images of Preaching Buddha in Sarnath Museum where flowering lotus has been shown as his lotus-seat.
6. Harald Ingholt, *Gandhāran Art in Pakistan* (hereafter abbreviated as *GAP*) fig. 188; Prof. Farid Khan, Chairman, Pakistan Heritage Society told me that the stone used in some of the sites of Uḍdyana and Gandhāra is soft and greenish. Naturally the result is much better in appearance. *GAP* figs. 71, 16, 90.
7. *GAP* figs. 254-257; S.J. Czuma, *Kushan Sculpture: Image from Early India Exhibition Catalogue* 91986), p. 198, fig. 109.
8. *GAP,* figs. 254-257.
9. *Gandhāran Art of Pakistan: The Exhibition Catalogue* (1984) (Hereafter referred to *GAP*-Exhibition Cat.) iv-9, p. 231.

10. *GAP* figs. 15, 76; *GS-SML*, fig. 22. Some scholars described it as 'oblong' but it does not seem to be actually that. It is true that it has different shapes.
11. *GAP* figs. 44, 12, 10, 9; *GA-SML*, fig. 20.
12. *GAP* figs. 61, 57 A-B (here pillars show Buddha's figure)
13. A. Foucher, *L'art Greco-Boudhique du Gandhara* (hereafter abbreviated as *AGBG*), p. 251, fig. 434.
14. Mathurā Museum Accn no. J.7, 76.40.
15. The flat-topped canopy rests on Indian pillars, *GAP* fig. 11.
16. *GAP* figs. 130, 131G.
17. *GAP* fig. 127, *GS-SML* fig. 37.
18. *GAP* figs. 160, 161, 409.
19. This is also mentioned as check-and recess motif.
20. *GAP*, Exhibition Cat. fig. li-6, *GAP* 238, 409.
21. S.D. Trivedi, *op.cit.*, p. 170.
22. A. Foucher, *AGBG*, I, fig. 297, 298, 300.
23. *GAP* fig. 132.
24. V.S. Agrawal, *Indian Art*, p. 150.
25. *GAP* figs. 479-480.
26. Dr F. Khan showed a slide at Varanasi Seminar wherein a worshipper is depicted within a medallion carved with lotus flower.
27. A. Foucher, *op.cit.*, xxv-2. Sometimes in place of *Nāgas*, two elephants are shown. This is probably due to dual meaning of word *'Nāga'*.
28. Burgess, *Journal of Indian Art and Indonesia*, No. 69 (1900) fig. 25; Examples of inverted lotus-seat- *GAP* figs. 8, 257, 259, 261, 262, etc.
29. A. Foucher, *op.cit.*, xxiv-1, xxv-2, xxvi-1-2, xxvii, xxviii; *GS-SML*, fig. 36; *GAP*, 253-256.
30. *GS-SML*, fig. 33; *GAP* figs. 68, 127. Generally three rosettes are shown horizontally on the pedestals which symbolize three jewels of the Buddhism.
31. H. Hargreaves, *Handbook to the Sculptures in the Peshawar Museum*, p. 60.
32. A. Foucher, *AGBG*, I, p. 221, fig. 97.
33. Pramod Chandra, *Stone Sculpture in Allahabad Museum*, fig. 40a.
34. See illustrations in *Stupa of Bharhut* by A. Cunningham, London, 1879.
35. Chandra, *op.cit.*, fig. 40a, b, 41a.
36. *Palast Der Gotter* (German Exhibition Cat. 1991-92), p. 34a, b.
37. *Ibid.*, fig. 25, p. 73.
38. *GAP* figs. 15, 119; *GS-SML* figs. 12, 37.
39. State Museum Lucknow Accn. Nos. J 577, J 580, J 614, B 132; Mathura Museum nos.
40. The *Pipal* tree was the one under which the Buddha received the Enlightenment. No wonder that its leaves came to play an important decorative role. *GAP*, p. 172, fig. 463.
41. *GS-SML*, p. 95, fig. 82.
42. *GAP* fig. 461; A frieze in Indian Museum, Calcutta, each loop of which has a playful child, a goat, or a couple of children. Majumdar, *Guide*, p. 114, No. 174.
43. The Gandhāra motif of the spiraling vine filled with human figures and animals is frequent in Roman art of the Antonine period and later. The vine-scroll symbolizes the eternal youth and immortality in after-life or paradise. B. Rowland, 'The Vine-scroll in Gandhara' *Artibus Asioe*, Vol. XIX (1956)m, pp. 253-261; *GAP*-Exhibition, iv-1, p. 231.
44. It is mainly found on abacus of Asokan pillars and ring stones. Its Sanskrit version is named as *'Nāgapuṣpa'*. Dr Agrawal says that it is same as *Muchakunda*, *Indian Art*, p. 78.
45. S.P. Gupta, *The Roots of Indian Art*, pp. 92, 111-14.
46. *GAP* fig. 390.
47. R.C. Sharma, *The Splendour of Mathura Art and Museum*, p. 133, fig. 49.
48. *GAP*, fig. 196.
49. *GS-SML*, p. 72, fig. 33.

50. Sometimes an undulating *pīpala* is framed between two projecting bands. *GAP*, fig. 30; *GS-SML*, figs. 4 & 9.
51. *GAP* fig. 66.
52. *Ibid.*, fig. 59, 359, 365, 370.
53. H. Hargreaves, *The Buddha Story in Stone*, pp. 3-4, fig. 1; *GAP* fig. 1.
54. *GAP* figs. 62, 04, 140, 142, 143, 431.
55. *GAP* figs. 194 A-B.
56. Band with criss-cross design, *GAP* figs. 30, 466; State Museum Lucknow Accn. No. B-208.
57. *GAP*, fig. 18.
58. *Ibid.*, figs. 156, 243.
59. *GAP*-Exhibition Cat. iv-6.
60. *GAP* fig. 197.
61. *Ibid.*, fig. 155.
62. *Ibid.*, fig. 157.
63. *Ibid.*, fig. 156.
64. G. 264, State Museum, Lucknow, fig. 5.
65. *GAP* fig. 79; There are other forms of *triratna*. In some images a pillar is surmounted with three wheels or three full blown lotuses. See the image of Bharat Kala Bhavan, Varanasi.
66. *GAP* fig. 78.
67. *Ibid.*, figs. 244, 259.
68. *Ibid.*, figs. 248, 299, 306, 308; In a sculpture of the Museum for Indian Art, Berlin (German Exhibition cat. fig. 25) a lion is shown seated in a fantastic pose on either side of the pedestal of the Buddha. Sometimes the lions have human faces.
69. R.C. Sharma, *Buddhist Art of India*, pp. 122-25.
70. *GAP*-Exhibition Cat. xv-1, xv-2, *GAP* figs. 350, 351, 352.
71. *GAP*, fig. 395.
72. *Ibid.*, fig. 188.
73. N.P. Joshi, *Brahmanical Sculptures in the State Museum*, Lucknow, pt. I, p. 27.
74. G.B. Spooner, *Archaeological Survey of Indian Annual Report* (*ASIAR*) 1909, pp. 49-93, pls. xii, a-b, xiii, a-b; A.K. Coomaraswamy, *History of Indian and Indonesian Art*, p. 54, pl. xxiv, fig. 89.
75. Benjamin Rouland, *The Art and Architecture of India: Buddhist-Hindu-Jain*, pp. 174-76, fig. 119.
76. *GAP* figs. 479-488, *Kushana Sculpture Exhibition* (1986), Pl. 63-71.
77. *Ibid.*, fig. 39 A-B.
78. *Ibid.*, figs. 479-488.

21

DECORATED TRAYS FROM THE GANDHĀRA REGION

KAMAL GIRI

Beside the most important and interesting Buddhist sculptures in the gamut of stone objects from the region of Gandhāra, a large number of utensils and articles of daily use have also been found. These are known mainly from the Bhir mound and Sirkap and belong to the period from about 300 BC to AD 100. These comprise pestles and mortars, grinding mills, household vessels of various kinds, lamps, burnishers, amulets, ring stones and also the so-called toilet trays with variety of decoration. In the present paper an attempt has been made to discuss the so-called toilet trays made of stone. Through this brief study of the objects of actual utility in more than one way, I intend to draw the attention on the point that along with the art objects of greater importance, several other areas of aesthetic expressions were created. In view of the multiple use of such toilet trays I propose to call them Decorated Trays.

The decorated trays are recovered mainly from different sites of Taxila, most important of all such spots being Bhir mound and Sirkap. The stones used for these are grey schist, yellowish brown steatite, greenish grey steatite, light grey claystone, micaceous schist, micaceous steatite, etc. These stones are of fine texture and because of that the trays could be carved so lavishly. Possibly this was the reason that a number of trays are embellished with fine figural carvings. These trays show the features of Śaka, Parthian and Kuṣāṇa styles.

In the typical Gandhāran composition the system to divide the panels into two tiers was common. Such sculptural examples are well known where the upper section of the panel depicts stories from the Buddha's life, in continuous narration, while the lower section shows identical scenes. In such examples the composition is conceived in the style of the continuous narratives of the early Indian tradition. The trays are usually divided into two, four, five or even more compartments and embellished with figures or scenes in relief. In some two tiered examples half inner portion of the tray is embellished with figures and the remaining half is used as compartment. However, there are examples where the compartments are divided through a particular motif. In one such example *svastika* divides the tray into four units. The subjects portrayed in these trays are not numerous. These comprise figure reclining on coach attended by females, drinking scene where male and female are holding wine cups in their hands, erotic scene, dancing scene, lions, horses, leogryphs, winged stag, hippocamps and other fish-tailed monsters with or without riders, etc. Some of the examples show geometrical and floral designs. However, the drinking and erotic scenes were the most favourite ones. Such scenes were more favourite in the Parthian art.

Most of the subjects represented on these trays are clearly Hellenistic. Not only the subjects but the treatment of the figures also show the Hellenistic influence, particularly in the examples of Śaka-Parthian period. It is apparent that different stylistic elements coexisted in the treatment of these trays, as found in the stone sculptures of the period. The trays distinctly represent an independent style although the interaction between the sculptural art and the trays is also visible in terms of iconographic and figural details. In the formation of Kuṣāṇa Gandhāra style there is a contributory role of several stylistic traditions, i.e. western classical, Indian and Parthian. A particular treatment of facial features, hairstyle and dress in the figures of trays are often indicative of alien influence. The Indian affiliations are also obvious. The motifs like *svastika*, lotus, rossettes or leaves are used for background of several of the reliefs. The *makara* like treatment of some of the sea-monsters make it more clear. The scenes of these trays mainly stress on the pleasures of life. The male and female figures holding drinking cups in these trays are familiar in the Mathurā School of Śuṅga-Kuṣāṇa art.

The figures displayed on these trays generally occupy the centres of the field and standout with effective simplicity against the plain background, which was an important feature of Gandhāra art. However, there are examples where the half upper portion is occupied by the figures. The figures mostly in bold relief are treated almost as if these were in the round, rather than being in relief. In few cases the figures are sketchy also. On the strength of style it is difficult to determine the respective ages of the decorative trays, except few. This difficulty arises from the fact that, with the passing of the Bactrian Greeks and coming of the Śakas, Hellenistic art in India rapidly declined, which revived again in the 1st century AD under the rule of Parthians. One such example belonging to 1st century BC reflects the increasing decadance of Hellenistic art under Śaka rule while other example, showing the Greek scene, shows the crudely modelled figures which are stiff and wooden in their appearance. Its composition reflects the older Hellenistic tradition. Some examples of 1st century AD show the figures of Greko-Roman art popularised at Taxila under Parthian rule.

In one such example the representation of host of figures distinctly reveal individuality of each figure and freedom of composition and drawing. In one example, the representation of host of figures distinctly reveal individuality of each figure and freedom of composition and drawing. In one example belonging to the Parthian period one can notice the blend of Mathurā art. After the advent of Parthians there is a marked improvement in the design and quality of the carvings on these trays. This improvement is well exemplified by the comparison between trays. Both of these trays depict drinking scenes but in the first Śaka period's example, the figures are stiff and tilted to some extent. Their faces are expressionless with wide open eyes and wooden like appearance. The folds of the garment are indicated by a multiplicity of parallel lines while the hairs are treated like a artificial wig. In the second example which belongs to the Parthian's period with elaborate and free design, the postures and movements of the figures are easy and natural. Such depictions could well be noticed in the Amarāvatī art. The details of hairs and drapery in the example are rendered with considerable skills.

The present study reveals that variety of subjects were represented on these trays which can broadly be divided as follows:

(1) **Trays with drinking scene**. Such examples represent couples mostly seated in balconies in different mood and offering drink to each other.

(2) **Trays with horse, lion and fabulous animals with or without riders**. In some interesting examples both the horse and the rider are provided with wings to suggest some mythology of the Hellenistic impact.

(3) **Trays with lion, stag, fish like animals.** Such animals are shown in the centre or upper compartment of the tray or even in four compartments all around.

(4) **Trays representing erotic scenes** showing couples either standing or seated in the centre.

(5) **Trays with miscellaneous scenes**. Such trays have two, four or even five compartments which contain some decorative designs or even as in one case, a reclining woman figure with attendants. One interesting tray is divided into four compartments through the *svastika* symbol.

On the basis of above brief study based on the available material we may surmise:

(1) Instead of calling all such trays toilet trays on the basis of their representations and forms, we should call them decorated trays with multi-purpose use.

(2) These trays non-Buddhist in content are related with material world, with special emphasis on pleasurous life.

(3) They were not merely used as the toilet trays but served the purpose of daily use also. Their domestic use is supported by the sculptural examples of female figures of the Kuṣāṇa period from Mathurā. Of these, one female figure is holding a tray with wine jar in her left hand. There are several ornamented examples which was possibly used for decoration purposes as they don't have any compartment with them. Such examples include the trays with animal figures, animal-riders and reclining female figure with attendants. The trays with decorative designs and motifs were also used for ornamental purposes.

(4) The compositional sense is particularly superb on such small trays which suggest that these were not the arbitrary product of art.

22

LADY HOLDING THE MIRROR
Beyond Archaeological Diggings

ANAMIKA ROY

The title of the paper may appear familiar. But there is a difference in approach for the treatment of the subject. E. Rosen in her remarkable work on the Begram ivories has taken great pains in drawing a parallel between the late Andhra tradition and Begram ivories. For this purpose she has quoted the famous Begram ivory coffer, now housed in the Kabul Museum.

She says (1985, 94) although it is well known that there was a classical influence in the Begram ivories and in the art of the north-west. We have demonstrated that there was also western influence in the art of the Sātavāhanas and Ikṣvākus, we believe that the Begram ivory carvers and the artists of Begram both had access to similar types of western materials.

The ivory coffer under discussion delineates a lady sitting with her toiletries, while the other is showing her a mirror. From Amarāvatī, at a drum slab in the left corner, Nanda's wife Sundarī with a beautiful mirror being shown to her is depicted. At a Nāgārjunakoṇḍā memorial pillar, deceased queen Varmabhaṭṭa, dressed as a foreigner, is represented with her cosmetics and holding a mirror. Karl Khandalavala cites comparative examples in the British Museum stating that such mirrors were in demand in India and they have been clearly represented on sculptures both at Nāgārjunakoṇḍā and Amarāvatī.

Time and again it is asserted that objects imported from the West had a direct influence upon composition of the Buddhist narrative reliefs from Amarāvatī and Nāgārjunakoṇḍā.

Rosen seeks a common classical prototype for this depiction from Begram to Bengi region. For Begram ivory she says (1984, 38): 'The whole notion of the mixture of Andhra classical style, combined with classical motifs has been seen in the ivories from Begram in Afghanistan. Here again on coffer IX from Begram, Venus is seen as seated in traditional Indian style surrounded by clearly classical motifs... these hybrid compositions persisted in India at least through the early part of the 4th century AD.'

These depictions may have taken an alien flavour, but such scenes were not limited to the north-western and southern India. They are found in the art of Mathurā of the 1st and 2nd century AD. A lady is depicted holding a mirror at a rail pillar at Sanghol (Gupta, 1985,

Pl. 61). Another such pillar is located at Bhūteśvara, Mathurā (Roy, 1979, Pl. 54). The sculpture shows a lady looking at her reflection in the mirror. These reliefs are treated as a vivid illustration of a feminine beauty holding a mirror and looking at herself.

The fact, however, cannot be denied that both Varmabhaṭṭa and Sundarī are shown in foreign dresses. Thus it needs a broader study. This was the period when Bengi region was feeling the pressure of foreign settlers. It shows the height of Indo-Roman trade, which had its bearing upon the art motifs (elsewhere I have discussed in detail). At this phase wine drinking scenes and *mithuna* couple were very common. Even Sumati, which was far away from south-east coast also succumbed to the same fate. Such scenes have even raised frowns for their relevance at a religious monument. It is unanimously asserted though that Indo-Roman trade was one of the strong factors for such depictions. Moreover the discoveries at Begram also confirm the importance of trade and cultural contacts between India and Afghanistan.

In Bengi region at south-east coast, quite a few foreigners were settled there. And a number of them must have been artists and artisans. There was a filtration of artists in this region. Elsewhere I have shown that a *yavana* artist 'Nagabu' has been identified as the 'Master Craftsman'. The three letters *na, ga* and *bh* occur on six plain stone pieces. In 1919-1920, Chandu has published three such inscriptions and in 1972 Sarkar has published three more plain slabs bearing these three letters.

This Nagabu was undoubtedly a sculptor and the frequent occurrence of his name tempts us to explore further. The native donors from Karle, Nasik and Junnar have very forcefully pronounced their profession, whereas the *yavana* donors are surprisingly silent over this issue. It leads to a speculation—perhaps they all were artists. Obviously, the sculptors of both Amarāvatī and Nāgārjunakoṇḍā were keenly aware of imported objects and styles from the West. So far as this motif from Begram and Bengi is concerned, there is a stark similarity. It naturally raises the query whether they were produced independently or were inspired by a common prototype. The simplest answer is obviously the both way traffic of artists.

The mingling of Begram treasure of Alexandrian, Indian and Chinese goods support it. Thus, the hybrid representation of the Begram coiffret arose from the fact that it grew out of the associations of many influences almost one can assert—from the conflict between opposing aesthetics.

Like for Begram it is said (J.M. Rosenfield, 1994-95, 58) that the style of the central portion of the coiffret and the details of jewellery, costume and coiffure suggest that this is the work of an Indian craftsman. For the Amarāvatī vine scroll shows a similar approach and yet there is a fundamental difference. The Begram example appears western, the Amarāvatī example does not. If the Amarāvatī artist had, in fact, been looking at a Roman vine scroll, he totally transformed it on his local knowledge and skill.

This dialogue between the Begram and Bengi motif and the artist becomes more meaningful, when we try to look beyond the archaeological diggings. It may give a romanticism or obsession towards the subject but shows a difference in approach.

It is the same motif—the lady holding the mirror—we enjoy in the narrations of the celebrated Buddhist poet, Aśvaghoṣa :

दत्त्वाथ सा दर्पणमस्य हस्ते ममाग्रतो धारय तावदेनम्
विशेषकं यावदहं करोमीत्युवाच कान्तं स च तं वभार ।।

Saundarananda. IV.13

धृतः प्रियेणायमभून्ममेति रुक्मत्सरूं दर्पणमालिलिङ्गे ।
यत्नाच्च विन्यस्ततमालपत्रौ रुष्टेव धृष्ट प्रममाज गण्डौ ॥

Saundarananda VI.29

The canto IV, verses 13-22 narrate the story of Sundarī, adoring herself before a mirror and Johnston (1932, 21-22) translates them under the caption—'Episode of Mirror'. One of the friezes at British Museum even depicts. Curiously enough, the fascinating depiction of mirror does not stop with the Buddhist art and philosophy. It does have an equally enchanting journey through the passage of time and space.

If a *nāyikā* is holding the mirror so is Pārvatī of Ardhanārīśvara image reported from Kashmir. If the pressure of trade developed a *yavana* colony at south-east coast of India and brought the art on a different horizon, the Gandhāra influence on Kashmir style was owing to geographical closeness. Actually, Kashmir style was an amalgam of various artistic traditions. It was during the Arab invasions that the Buddhist monk and artists migrated to Kashmir, where they got patronage under Korkota dynasty. Since the pronounced Gandhāran influence over Kashmir style is already much discussed subject, I am escaping the details (see, P. Lal, *Bronzes of Kashmir*, M.M.I., 1975). From the architecture of the Mārtaṇḍa temple to Maitreya at Los Angeles, a Gandhāran influence is visible. Thus the artistic tradition must have filtered into Kashmir from the land of modern Afghanistan. Come what may, the question artistic influence will remain unsolved with the historians working with their own prejudices.

Thus the motif from Venus to Pārvatī reveals a beauty of Indian art, philosophy, which does not know any dividing or demarcating line. Like Aśvaghoṣa, the *Śiva Purāṇa* also very beautifully narrates the pride of Pārvatī after having a glimpse of her beauty:

यथाऽदर्शस्वरूपे च स्वीयं प्रदृश्यते ।
तथा सर्वत्रगं शम्भु पश्यतीति सुनिश्चितम् ॥

Śiva Purāṇa IV.43.29

But such a simple explanation cannot bring out the beauty of Indian art. Stella Kramrisch considers the mirror '...a symbol and restatement of Siva's being. The objects seen in the mirror are neither separate from each other nor from the mirror'. Kramrisch here echoes what Abhinavagupta had already said, 'In a state of consciousness objects shine as one with the subject exactly in the manner a city shines in the mirror'. Nanda holding the mirror for Sundarī (B.M. No. 771). Thus one may call this delineation from Begram to Bengi—a hybrid, but for the theme one should not look at a common classical prototype. The subject itself is very much Indian and nowhere it tempts to use pick and shovel for the classical world for influence. It reveals a beautiful world and this is not the 'journey's end'. In fact it leads us much further from this material world to super mundane.

The mirror is erotic, exotic as well as symbolic. It is said that the first artist was a seer, but in Indian context he was a thinker also. The question is not whether there was a Hellenic prototype, but how this carving in stone opens a dialogue between what is seen and what is unseen. The hidden meaning the *'parokṣārtha'* is equally important.

Alex Wayman says 'Buddhism takes prestigious and imposing symbols of secular life and transforms them into religious symbols' (Wayman, *The Mirror as a Metaphor-Simile*, p. 63). Interpreting a passage from the *Saddharma Puṇḍarīka* Wayman refers to the necessity of obliterating the image in the mirror in the projection of this material world:

आदर्शपृष्ठे यथा बिम्बु पश्येत् लोकोऽस्य
काये अयु दृश्यते तथा ।

स्वयंभु सो पश्यति नान्यि सत्वाः
परिशुद्धि कायरिम इम एव रूपा ।।

Saddharma Puṇḍarīka, 18, .62

The Yogācāra School especially following the brothers Asaṅga and Vasubandhu expands philosophically upon a theory of the mind as mirror. Consistent with the theory of mind as mirror, it could be wiped off and washed. Interestingly, the *Svetāśvatara Upaniṣad* (2.14) echoes the same concept. 'Even as mirror stained by dust shines brilliantly when it had been cleansed; so the embodied one, seeing the nature of the self becomes unitary the end attained and from sorrow freed".

H.V. Dehejia in his monogram *Parvati Darpan* tries to find a more intense meaning than an ordinary syncretic ideology. The mirror in the hands of Pārvatī is not Pārvatī of *Kumārasambhava* and *Śiva Purāṇa*. It is an aesthetic perception leading Śiva to a state of creative sense. In the Pratyabhijñā School, there is concept of cognition through recognition. The Kashmir Saivites use the terms connected with light in their exposition. Thus, we come across terms like *prakāśa, ābhāsa, nibhāsa, bimba, pratibimba* and of course *darpaṇa*. The *darpaṇa* is not just another attribute, but a statement of togetherness of both.

Thus Begram, which was burning under Taliban, from that very land the artists carved a bewitching artefact. It produced the art object which inspired the art historians and the aesthetics alike. It picked up a tradition which was Venus, Sundarī, the deceased queen Varmabhaṭṭa, the daughter of mountains, Parvati. It created a problem for a common classical prototype or bemused the *rasika* to find a parallel into *Saundarananda* and *Śiva Purāṇa*. It compelled us to seek its roots from Buddhism to Śaivism.

The hybrid representations of Begram ivory was due to the many artistic forces working at the soil simultaneously. Thus the mirror reflects from the maritime activity to Buddhism and the land may again become a beauty it once created so that all that is beautiful bewitching may shine again and again.

BIBLIOGRAPHY

Chanda, R.P., 1925, "Some Unpublished Amaravati Inscriptions", *Epigraphia Indica*, XV, Government of India, Calcutta, pp. 258-75.

Dehejia, H.V., 1996, *The Advaita of Art*, Motilal Banarsidass, Delhi.

——, 1997, *Parvati Darpan*, Motilal Banarsidass, Delhi.

Gupta, S.P. (ed.), 1985, *Sculptures from Sanghol*, National Museum, New Delhi.

Johnston, E.H., 1936, (first ed.), 1995, *Buddhacarita*, Munshiram Manoharlal, Delhi.

Khandalwal, K., 1960, "Brahmapuri": A Consideration of Metal Objects Found in the Kundangar, *Lalit Kala*, Vol. 7, pp. 29-75.

Iyer, K.A. Subramania and K.C. Pandey, 1986, *Abhinavagupta, Īśvara Pratyabhijñā Vimarsinl*, Vol. I, Motilal Banarsidass, Delhi.

Kramarisch, Stella, 1981, *Presence of Śiva*, Princeton University Press, Princeton, p. 499.

Pal, Pratapaditya, 1975, *Bronzes of Kashmir*, Munshiram Manoharlal, Delhi.

Rosen, E., 1985, "A Dated Memorial Pillar from Nagrjunakonda", in *Indian Epigraphy and its Hearing on the History of Art*, eds. F.M. Asher and G.S. Gai, Delhi, pp. 35-40.

Rosen, E., 1994, *The Buddhist Art of Nagarjunakonda,* Motilal Banarsidass, Delhi.
Roy, U.N., 1975, *Śāla Bhañjikā,* Lokabharati, Allahabad.
Roy, Anamika, 1994, *Amarāvatī Stūpa,* Agam Kala Prakashan, Delhi.
Saddharma Pundarika, 1908-12 eds. H. Kern and Bunjiu Nanjio, Printed in Japan 2-15 Azabu-Jbn Minato ku, Tokyo.
Śiva Purāṇas, 1970, Ancient Indian Tradition and Mythology Series, Vols. I to IV, Motilal Banarsidass, Delhi.
Śvetāśvatara Upaniṣad, 1975, The Thirteen Principal Hume, Robert Ernest, Oxford University Press, London.
Wayman, A., 1974, "Mirror as a Pan Buddhist Mwtaphor–Simile", *History of Religions,* Vol. 13, pp. 251-69.

23

THE METAL CRAFT AND ART OF GANDHĀRA REGION

VIBHA TRIPATHI

Afghanistan is located at the cross-roads of civilizations. It has been alternatively called a 'bridgeland' connecting east and west. It is a melting pot of cultures from Europe, Central and Western Asia, China and India. Throughout the millennia, people with different socio-cultural, political and religious specificities have visited this land and some also made it their home. Thus Afghanistan has adopted and adapted to variety of cultural streams that have flowed into it from different directions from time to time. It may be interesting to take a closer look at the mosaic of culture that the land has sustained for thousands of years. It will be equally interesting to know the geo-ecological background that had the force to absorb an incessant flow of peoples and cultures. The present paper seeks to delineate the geographical factors that contributed to the make up of a cultural tradition more so in its metal craft and art known as Gandhāran. The questions that will have to be addressed in the process are: what are the primary regions of Gandhāra attracting hordes of people from time immemorial? Is there something in the geographical features of the land? Or conversely are there some precious treasures in this otherwise rugged land? Do incoming cultures sweep the local traits altogether? Is there a permanence in art and culture of Gandhāra or it undergoes change with new incoming elements? How can we interpret its art and technology as an important component in the context of the Gandhāra culture?

THE CULTURAL BACKGROUND

The archaeological background of Afghanistan may go upto prehistoric ages. But in the present context it may be traced back at least upto the Harappan phase that may be somewhat relevant to the present discussion. The Harappans had established important centres at Mundigak and Shortughai as important source of minerals and metals required by them. And perhaps also to guard this trade route leading to the Central Asia and West Asia. With decline of Harappan civilization these centres were also abandoned. On the western side, interactions with Iranian borderlands may be traced to Swat cemeteries, Shahi Tump in Makaran and Gandhāra grave culture in Pakistan in the 2nd millennium BC.

Literary evidence like the Vedas and epics of India refer to Gandhāra in very familiar terms. There were wars being waged on the riverbanks of this region. There were princesses married to kings in different parts of India. There appears to be a close relation with Gandhāra, almost like the two being parts of the same country. In the historical period Gandhāra was in fact a part of the Mauryan dynasty.

THE GEOPOLITICAL SETTING

The region of Gandhāra is located at such a point that it can be reached through various countries located around it in different directions. Within Afghanistan and adjacent north-west Pakistan that was ancient Gandhāra, there are geographical barriers separating one area from another. It needs to be looked into for a proper perspective.

Gandhāra does not have a homogenous ecological setting. There are bare mountain peaks interrupted by lush green river valleys and pastures. There are dry desolate deserts interspersed by orchards and oases. The peoples and their cultural traits match with its ecological setting, promoting a tribal/regional character. Yet the underlying trait of adaptability and warmth has given this land a character and culture of its own. The important places known from the ancient times may briefly be enumerated here because they have played an important role in the Gandhāran history.

From west, the Bactrians, Greeks, Śakas and Kuṣāṇas occupied Gandhāra and ruled over it bringing with them their culture and tradition. It was a seat from where they expanded their empire to mainland India whenever the central powers were weak there. Could it be a reason for the western neighbours to occupy Gandhāra? This cannot be denied altogether but Gandhāra itself had several attractions. Climatically also it had affinities with the Central Asiatic neighbourhood. We need to delve a bit on the geographical features of Gandhāra to understand this.

Balkh, referred in ancient Indian literature as Vāhīka was the northernmost important place. Situated some 12 miles west of Mazar-e-Sharif, it was used as a passage to India by western countries. Cyrus, Darius, Alexander and subsequently the Scythians, Parthians, Tukhars, Hūns and Turks entered India through this route. This was a passage also used by monks, travellers, traders and adventurers operating between East and West. This area was also famous for its horses, camels and jewels.

Bamiyan was the next important centre which became a famous Buddhist centre of learning and pilgrimage. Bamiyan is located midway between Bactrian and Peshawar. To its north lies the Hindukush and to its south Koh-i-Baba. Thus the location of Bamiyan is of crucial importance. No wonder the merchant class needed the divine grace for successful conclusion of their trips. They must have contributed to establishing the monastic set up here along with the gigantic statues of the Buddha on the hillside. The Buddha figure must have been visible from a long way and inspired and guided caravans taking the hazardous journey between Bactria and Peshawar.

Beyond Bamiyan there is a confluence of Helmand and Surkhab rivers leading towards the fertile plain of Ghorband and the Panjashir rivers in the north and by the Kabul-rud and Logar in the south. This was famous for its commerce in ancient times because of the passes to the Hindukush open in it. Passing through Kapisi the Central Asian commerce was carried to India' (Motichandra, 1977, p. 7). Hiuen Tsang comments that at Kapisi goods from all countries were available. It is fully corroborated by excavations at Begram where Kuṣāṇa, Indian and Roman goods have been found to be present. 'Because of its geographical situation (on the confluence of the Ghorbund & Panjshir) was bound to become the capital of that region' (Motichandra, *op.cit.*).

The next city of importance nearby is Kabul. The ancient Kabul of the Buddhist period is located on Logar River while the one belonging to the Muslim period is situated on Kabul-rud. The valley of River Kabul is divided into two parts: the one extending from Jalalabad to Attock is geographically part of the Indian subcontinent while the other one forms part of the Iranian plateau. Because of the varying heights, these two zones are even climatically different, affecting the people and the culture too. The routes from Kabul to the Indian subcontinent proceed along the Kabul and the Panjshir rivers.

The city of Jalalabad has been described by Hiuen Tsang as the frontier of India, under the Mauryan empire. It was conquered by Alexander from them and remained under one foreign rule or another till the Mughals conquered it back.

Between Jalalabad and Indus there is a mountain that separates the valleys of Kunar and Swat and forms a circle called Safed Koh. This limits the province of Jalalabad in the south and east. Nearby is the famous city of Puṣkarāvatī (Charsada) the old capital of Gandhāra. This passage between Jalalabad to Puṣkarāvatī upto Dakka is sandy and rocky. After crossing Indus one reaches Taxila. There might have been changes in river courses, especially from Kapisi to Puṣkarāvatī and Taxila that has many rivers.

The earliest historical empire of this region was probably the Achaemenid Persian empire expanding over larger parts of Indo-Iranian borderland. However, most of the control was loose. Baluchistan (Gedrosia), Archosia (included the mountains south of Afghanistan and Kandahar region) was home of the warlike tribes and hence difficult to control. Seistan or Drangiana was the centre of many Iranian traditions. Zoroaster came under the protection of Achaemenid chief Vishtaspa whose son Darius later became the greatest of the Achaemenid rulers. A large number of mounds may be located all over the plains around Mazar-e-Sharif including Bala Hissar, an ancient fortress of Timurid period. Kuṣaṇa remains were discovered in a bondage by Daniel Schlumberger (1946) and later by University of Pennsylvania (1953).

Interestingly, most of the ancient capitals were connected with one another through river or land route. Balkh, Bamiyan, Kapisi, Puṣkarāvatī, Udbhāṇḍa and Taxila were approachable through routes which were followed by kings, warriors and traders including by Alexander for his invasion. This had a far reaching impact on economic affluence of Gandhāra. It also assisted in movement of people and culture, promoting interaction within these cities.

GANDHĀRA, THE LAND OF PROMISE AND RICHES

Gandhāra opened the passage to India that was one of the coveted lands of the ancient world and a destination of invaders from the West. Gandhāra region itself was rich in a variety of minerals like copper, lead, tin, silver and zinc. Most of the deposits available locally bear traces of ancient working and mining activity. A quick look at position of metals may be in order here.

Copper

It is very commonly found throughout Afghanistan, viz., at Kabul, Herat, Badakhshan, Kandahar, Bamiyan, Kapisa and Ghazni also yield evidence of early mining along with slag heaps. The Achaemenian conquest of Gandhāra at close of 6th century BC and exploitation of copper at Safed Kohat Shah Maqsud, Nesh, etc., may be interlinked. In 3rd century BC to 1st century AD, Zanskara Valley was the source of copper. It contains lead and sulphur that went well with casting of copper alloy objects. Bronzes upto 21 to 25 per cent tin were used for utensils, ornaments and bells, etc.

Tin

Tin also occurs nearby at Badakhshan, Kapisa, Herat, Kandahar and Ghazni. Both stannite (sulphide form) and cassiterite (oxide form) are found. In Herat there are traces of ancient working too. This explains the presence of large-scale bronzes in Gandhāra right from the proto-historic times upto the historical times.

Since copper occurs side by side with tin, it was easy to make bronze here. Marshall feels that perhaps bronze was invented here (?)

Zinc

Several deposits of zinc have been located in Afghanistan, viz., at Ghor, Kandahar, Paktya. Smaller deposits were also noted at Badakhshan, Herat, Farah, Bamiyan, Ghazni and Takhar. Some of the occurrences have lead along with zinc. It explains the presence of zinc alloying at Taxila in 3rd century BC, one of the earliest utilizations of metallic zinc in the ancient world.

Lead

Lead deposits are scattered throughout Afghanistan. Many of these occur in association with zinc ore while others are independent. In the province of Ghor, Oruzghan, Lohar, Bamiyan and Ghazni there is a greater concentration. It occurs in both forms, that is cerussite (oxide form) and galena (a sulphate form). Extensive mining evidence has been noted with gallery system. In south Afghanistan at Faranjal and several other places argentiferous lead ore is found. Silver could be obtained from it. Parthians who occupied large parts here, according to Marshall, used these sources.

> No extensive copper, tin, zinc or lead ore bodies have been found in the Swat Valley, Gilgit or elsewhere in north west Pakistan, nor have any mine workings ever been reported in the area. Some very small occurrences of copper, zinc and lead minerals have been found but there is no evidence that they have ever been exploited .... Some copper and lead deposits are available further south, in Baluchistan and these were clearly exploited in the past. However, these deposits are much less numerous and extensive than those of Afghanistan (Reedy 1997, p. 268).

The above statement by one who has analysed and studied the metal sculptures of the region is significant indeed. Reedy asserts that not only Afghanistan is rich in copper, zinc, tin and lead mineralization but they have been extensively exploited over a long period.

> It would not have been difficult in the Gandhāran period for Afghanistan to supply all of its own needs and to have an excess of metal available for export to adjacent regions, particularly neighbouring areas in north-western Pakistan, which are rather poor in all of these minerals (Reedy, *op.cit.*, p. 269).

It may be added that Gandhāra not only exported the art style known by its name but the raw material as well to most of the contemporary centres of this region. Interestingly Gandhāra, with its location midway between west and east attracted invaders from both the directions for political supremacy and also to facilitate penetration in the lands beyond and also to have full control over the mineral resources of Afghanistan. The latter must have been of a great importance as many of these minerals are not available at least not in any noticeable amount in the adjacent lands. This minerally rich land, therefore, was vied by the Greeks, Roman, Bactrians and the Indians alike.

A MELTING POT OF CULTURES: REFLECTIONS IN METAL ART AND CRAFT

Any power worth the name chose to occupy Gandhāra whenever it could. It is fully reflected in the art style of Gandhāra. The metal sculptural art, though scarce, is to examine this assumption.

Coins, even though not from regular excavations have been found in good numbers in Afghanistan. While they indicate the political powers that ruled the land, they also manifest their art style. Coins of Bactrians bear classical motifs and Greek inscriptions. Later on there are Scythian and Indian influence which gradually displaced Hellenistic style. Kharoṣṭī joined Greek on the coins and eventually replaced it altogether. Elephant and humped bulls become common motifs. 'The coins thus represent one of the most graphic demonstration of the diffusion of styles and their integration with already established modes known to archaeologists' (Bacon, *op.cit.*, p. 276).

No metal sculptures are reported from the Greek period Taxila (Bhir mound). There are 11 pieces from Sirkap, 1 at Dharmarājikā and 1 at Julian. Most of these are thin repoussī metal. Solid cast in open modes are two pieces belonging to 1st century BC rest are datable to 1st century AD or even later. These have been classified by Marshall as Graeco-Roman, Quasi-Indian or Indian in style.

Afghanistan, especially Gandhāra had a specific style of modelling metal sculpture that could generally be distinguished from the north-western Pakistan. Two points may be underlined on the basis of technical study undertaken by Reedy (*op.cit.*). One, that the Gandhāra casting and decorating technology has the appearance of the early industry that was not fully developed and two, the local metal has been used for manufacturing of these pieces.

The copper based sculptures of Gandhāra are generally made with simple technology which is unlike the later ones made in north-west Indian, Greek, Hellenistic or Roman works in terms of casting and decorating techniques. Therefore, it may be deduced that Gandhāra casting could represent the beginning of a local sculpture tradition in the early stages of development (Reedy, *op.cit.*).

> Leaded bronzes are the predominant alloy, although zinc was also a frequent addition to Gandhāra alloy ... Abundant local sources were available in Afghanistan for all the alloy elements. North-west Pakistan, on the other hand, probably imported its metals and Afghanistan was the most logical source.

> Thus elemental analysis may not be much effective in determining and distinguishing the two ... statistical analysis of the technical data indicates that many works might well have been produced there. Given the presence of abundant ore sources throughout Afghanistan it is certainly logical to hypothesize that a number of casting workshops were in fact located there and that a major copper-based sculpture tradition could have developed in that region' (Reedy, *op.cit.*).

This observation fully justifies the name attributed to this style as Gandhāra. But it kept changing and evolving itself under different influences and conditions.

The Greek tradition with Gandhāra style in art and sculpture was later pushed aside by Śaka-Scythian and later the Kuṣāṇas. The point can more easily be demonstrated through stone sculptures because of their sheer number. Metal sculptures are just a few but nevertheless important.

The following copper sculptures have been described by Marshall:

No. 417 – Horus – the Egyptian Child-god – wearing a dress, a long sleeved tunic with finger pointing towards lips as if enjoining silence on votaries.

No. 418 – Aphrodik is solid bronze relief, goddess standing on lotus, clad in a himation only.

No. 419 – Winged Eros or possibly Harpocrates in the guise of Eros (on lotus) wearing a cloak.

No. 420 – Medallion of copper repoussÍ.

No. 421 – Women pig. (copper Quasi India)

Most of the subjects of these metal sculpture is non-Indian and indicates a presence of people from different cultural backgrounds. Horus, the Egyptian child god, the style of dress worn by it, similarly Aphrodite or winged Eros all manifest the elements other than Gandhāran or Indian. However, lotus is a typically Indian item showing admixture of two traditions (at least at Taxila).

Some private collections studied by Ingholt (1957) show copper-bronze and gold sculptures. There is a woman figurine in copper (3 1/8 inch, fig. 490) a bronze Harpocrates from Taxila (5 inch, fig. 492) bronze reliquary of Kaniṣka 7 inch, fig. 494 and a *stūpa* (15 inches fig. 496).

Gandhāra including Taxila has yielded a good number of silver object—pots, pans, jewellery and repoussÍ work. Though the technology is simple but it is effective in style and beauty. Reedy's analysis of silver objects shows a range unalloyed pure silver to a silver copper alloy (about 5%), gold also occurs in trace element from low to relatively higher level.

Even a quick look at Taxila objects (Marshall, 1951, pp. 162-196) is sufficient to prove the richness of metal objects both in quality and quantity. No where on Indian sites this can be matched. It may safely be attributed to easy availability of raw material, a constant inflow of inspiration from different cultures and peoples. The geographical location of Gandhāra rendered it the flexibility to adapt to changes and capability of the artisans to meet the demands put on them.

The question whether the metal objects have been imported or they were produced locally is not difficult to answer. Silver ware at Taxila, suggested Marshall, are a local product or made in north-west of India (Afghanistan-Gandhāra). Parthians, according to him imported some of the objects from Parthia or Yavana countries from west due to the dearth of craftsmen in Gandhāra. But by the 1st century AD, there were 'many craftsmen trained in Hellenistic tradition, some of whom were no doubt just as competent to work in gold or silver or copper as others were in terracotta or stucco' (Marshall 1975, p. 608). The imitation of Hellenistic prototypes indicate that there were many craftsmen in Taxila in 1st century AD who could produce Greek objects like *askos, phialai, Mesomphaloi*. Thus the artisan or craftsmen of the Gandhāra region had proficiency to produce art pieces on order. However, the local features had a way of creeping into that because of a characteristic trait of Gandhāra metal craft. On the basis of the foregoing we may conclude that :

1. The geographical location of Gandhāra played a vital role in shaping its character. It provided the culture a versatility that is typically Gandhāran.
2. The richness of Gandhāra in variety of metals and minerals added to its attraction as an important resource centre for neighbouring countries.

3. The metal craft and art style while absorbing the incoming cultural traits also maintained its individuality that has generally crept into its products.

It may be apt to conclude with Bacon's statement on Gandhāra art capturing its spirit. It becomes ironical today,

> It is no coincidence then that the styles, fashions and advances of much of Asia and the Mediterranean had their expression in the bridgeland countries. At Bamiyan one confined hundreds of examples of other cultures and civilizations whose contribution made of the hybrid culture of Mediaeval Afghanistan. Buddhism is of course an Indian faith and the floating *apsaras* and Bodhisattvas on some of the painted walls, full bodied and warm in aspect, have their parallels in the famous caves of Ajanta. But the stiff figures of, for example, the 120 feet Buddha, suggesting Byzantine mosaic, are Sassanian in style.... If there is such a thing as vocal stillness Bamiyan is a notable repository for such a quality. It is indeed a place of meditation and was meant to endure intact for ever.

Alas, it could no longer be so!

NOTES AND REFERENCES

1. Motichandra, 1977, *Trade and Trade Routes in Ancient India*, Abhinava Prakashan, New Delhi.
2. Edward Bacon, 1963, 'The New Knowledge of Early Afghanistan', *The Vanished Civilizations*, Edward Bacon (ed.), Thames and Hudson, London, pp. 251-278.
3. *Ibid.*
4. *Ibid.*
5. C.L. Reedy, 1997, 'Technical Studies of Gandhāran Art', *Gandhara Art in Context: East West Exchange at Cross-roads of Asia*, B. Allchin and R. Allchin, Neil Kreitman, Elizabeth Errington (eds.), Regency Publication, New Delhi, pp.267-281.
6. Bacon, *op.cit.*
7. Sir John Marshall, 1951, reprint 1975, *Taxila* (3 vols.), Motilal Banarsidass, New Delhi.
8. Ingholt H., 1957, *Gandhara Art in Pakistan*, New York.
9. Marshall, *op. cit.*

24

KUṢĀṆA PORTRAITS

T.K. BISWAS & SAVITA SHARMA

While writing on the Amarāvatī sculptures, Sri C. Sivaramamurti mentioned the existence of a portrait gallery with seven statues of the family of Sātakarṇī (almost destroyed) in the cave-shrine in a pass called Nanaghat, almost destroyed with the names of the members noted and declared these as representing the earliest Indian portraits. He also referred to Kondane where a portrait statue was fashioned by sculptor Balaka who was the pupil of a master called Kṛṣṇa.[1]

Did these really represent as the earliest examples of Indian portrait sculptures? Perhaps not! The above notion calls for a fresh review in the light of new discoveries of portrait sculptures of even earlier date. In a recently published small note in the Newsletter of *Circle of Inner Asian Art* (*CIAA*) Dr Pradhan of State Museum, Bhubaneswar, Orissa, referred to two inscribed statues of Aśoka discovered at Langudi Hill near Dharamsala in Jaipur district of Orissa.[2]

An inscribed bust was first found there at the entrance of the Aśokan *stūpa*. Prof. B.N. Mukherjee deciphered the Prākrit inscription on it as referring to '*Chhi karena rāñja Asokhena*' (sk. Śri Kareṇa rājñā Aśokena) and paleographically, the text has been dated to 2nd century BC.[3] Subsequently, from the same *stūpa* area another inscribed slab was discovered in which a crowned male figure is seen seated in *līlāsana* being flanked on either side by a female. Whether these females represent queens or simple attendants, cannot be conclusively identified. The inscription on this was examined by Prof. Mukherjee and Prof. Swamy. The latter found in this text a reference to 'rājño Aśoka'.[4] If the readings are accepted then the antiquity of the art of portraiture in India could be pushed back to the 2nd century BC.

However, from the available examples of portraits in ancient India, it appears that it was the Kuṣāṇa kings who were seriously interested in the art of portraiture. The rulers in this line maintained a sustained interest throughout to have their portraits projected. Such interest was not seen any dynastic family in ancient India.

Pandit Radha Krishna in 1912 discovered a temple site in the Õkrī īlā mound in the village of Māṭ, about 14.5 km north of the city of Mathurā on the left bank of river Yamuna. In Kuṣāṇa period this was a site of a dynastic sanctum (*devakula*).[5] The site yielded three monumental headless portraits in stone and some more in mutilated conditions. The three portraits are identified as representing Wima Kadphises, Kaniṣka and Caṣṭana.

The dynastic shrine discovered at Māṭ centred around the grandfather of Huviṣka. A badly mutilated portrait of Huviṣka (?) of which the left foot survived is found accompanied with a still badly damaged inscription. The inscription mentions about the temple of Wima and also mentioned that when the building fell in ruins, steps were taken to repair the *Devakula* by an official with the rank of Daṇḍanāyaka and it was done to increase the life and strength of Huviṣka.[6]

One of the three portraits found at Māṭ is the headless seated figure of Wema Kadphises. This colossal figure is 6′10′ high and is shown seated on a lion throne in European pose.[7] Costume of Wima includes a tunic and a top coat. The head and the upper part of the throne are missing. The figure holds with its right hand a sword of which the hilt is partially preserved. Its broken left hand is placed on a scabbard laid over the knees. His legs are covered with heavily folded trouser and his feet with thickly padded foots decorated with vine patterns. The costume is, in general, described as northern dress (*udīcya veśa*). There appears on the top of the foot stool (*pāda pīṭha*) an inscription *'mahārāja rājātirāja devaputro Kuṣāṇaputra sāhi Wima takṣama'*.[8] The word *takṣama* in old Iranian means strong or brave. This headless figure of Wima combines in it a 'rare dignity' and a 'matter fact style'. Wima also found seated in similar way with the profile of his face gazing to the left in one variety of his gold coins. His face is characterized by moustache, beard and a large nose. The headless stone portrait of Wima must have had a head with similar features. Incidentally, it may be mentioned here that the Kuṣāṇas were not Mongols, they were Caucasians and their ethnic features include narrow heads, prominent noses and abundant hair and beard growth.[9] Kuṣāṇa portraits with such features are quite conspicuous as found on their gold and copper coins.

The Archaeological Museum at Mathurā has in its collection the torso of standing portrait of King Kaniṣka. Carved in his lifetime, the portrait was apparently made at the climax of his military career. Visibly the portrait differs from the Hellenistic impressionism. It does not exhibit Hindu sensitivity either. The king wears a tunic that reaches down to the knees and is firmly held by a belt around the hips, above this appears a top coat, open at the front and turned back to the sides. The legs between which the stone has not been removed are covered with heavy boots made of felt and have spur straps. A legible neatly incised Brāhmī inscription runs across the lower part of the garment disregarding the folds. The inscription runs as *'mahārāja rājadhirāja devaputra Kaniṣko'*. Thus it becomes clear that the inscription raised Kaniṣka to a divine status. The rear side of this portrait statue which was not meant to be seen, there appears a regular and uninterrupted incision and therefore, it is believed that 'probably the torso once possessed a disc shaped numbus' that associates it with the idea of a *Devaputra* (son of god).[10] The portrait of Kaniṣka wears in this a Central Asian warrior's dress. His garments are found to be cut and stitched, his salwar under the tunic is tucked into his boots. These are un-Indian features. Kaniṣka holds in his left hand a metre long sword whose pommel is found shaped like a bird's neck and head while his right hand placed on a 104 cm long club, the top of which is round in shape, the middle part being sixteen sided and the lower part of it is eight sides. It looks as if it is wooden and its lower part is imbued with a makara motif. To some, this motif symbolizes the martial triumph of a victorious military commander. However, the portrait gives the idea that Kaniṣka was there for certain military engagements and to him, Mathurā was a military camp and not a princely court. Kaniṣka stands with his 'feet firmly planted on the ground in so masterful a manner that he seems to bestride his vast kingdom'.[11]

When studied from sculptural point of view, one finds that this portrait of Kaniṣka was carved in red Sīkrī sandstone with irregular structure and is found covered all over with light spots that literally impair its plastic qualities as they destroy the unity of surface. However, the figure as it stands, maintains a rigidity and strict symmetry. The pose of it is realistic and without any attempt at stylization. It is free standing and frontal and is conceived as a deified royal figure, a victorious prince of Central Asian Steppes.

A French Archaeological Mission excavated at Surkh-Kotal under the supervision of Prof. Daniel Schlumberger. The excavations laid bare a dynastic sanctum (*deva-kula*) like the temple of Wima Kadphises at Māṭ in Mathurā. The said temple is situated on the top of a hill in north-eastern Afghanistan and the temple is approached by five flights of stairs. Among the important remains, the excavations brought to light a massive stone inscription of 25 lines in curasive Greek letters and a Central Iranian language. In the said inscription, it is written that, 'this acropolis of the Kaniṣka Nikator sanctuary to which the lord king Kaniṣka gave his name'.[12] Five effigies were found from the site of Surkh-Kotal of which the most important was a limestone statue of Kaniṣka. Unfortunately, this is also a headless statue. It is shown wearing an ornate tunic with vine rincean pattern reaching below the knees and a heavy top-coat. It is provided with a wide full bloused salwar with the foot straps over the shoes. The hieratic symmetry of this statue calls upon a strong connection with the Kaniṣka figure from Mathurā. The only visible difference between the portrait of Kaniṣka at Mathurā and Surkh-Kotal is that while at Mathurā the king appears ready for a military engagement, the latter is seen wearing a festive robe in palace in time of peace.[13]

Incidentally, a reference needs to be mentioned here of the Kaniṣka Reliquary discovered by D.B. Spooner in 1908 at Shahji-ki-Ḍheri. On the middle part of this relic casket appears a royal figure who holds a lotus in his right hand and his feet are found covered with heavy boots and the position of feet in this recalls Kaniṣka's stone statue at Māṭ. The figure maintains the same vigour and imperious manifestation of power; the costume of it includes a tunic, a top coat and salwar and remind very much of Kaniṣka's portrait of Mathurā.

Reference may also be made here of a Kuṣāṇa portrait gallery found at Uzbekistan. Modelled in clay and then painted in colour, a number of heads were found from the main hall of a Kuṣāṇa palace at Kalchayan excavated by Soviet archaeologist Gulina Pugachenkova. These heads with evident portrait qualities present a cross-section of a people of a given area and these include a warrior, a bow-man, a jester or even a satyr.[14] With these heads was found an almost complete figure of a Kuṣāṇa prince. Seated cross-legged, this young prince looks straight. Covered fully with tunic and salwar and a top scarf, his bearings give an absolutely confident look. His simple headgear, his dressed moustache and his clean shaved face and above all with the dignity and nobility in him, he maintains a kind of an aristocratic aloofness.[15] The said figure reminds of the torso of a young prince discovered at Māṭ in Mathurā. This uninscribed torso has been identified as a portrait sculpture of ṣaṣṭana or Caṣṭana, the Śaka satrap of Ujjaini.[16] As it stands, the figure is found donned with a trouser and a long coat, the latter being comfortably secured by a beautiful belt made of square and circular plaques—a feature found associated with the Scythian equistrian figures. The presence of the portrait of a Śaka prince in the premises of Kuṣāṇa dynastic temple is somewhat significant. Either he was a junior contemporary of Kaniṣka or some take him as a relative of Kaniṣka. In this connection, a reference may also be made of two more portraits of similar dispositions of Mathurā and one of these is seen with folded hands.[17]

Portraits of Kuṣāṇa rulers in large numbers have come down to us on the coins struck during their reigns. Thousand of Kuṣāṇa coins, mostly in gold and copper, are now scattered all over the world in museums, art galleries and in personal collections. In 1830, Begram (ancient Kapiśā) alone is said to have yielded 30,000 Kuṣāṇa coins.[18] The exact locale of Kuṣāṇa mints is not known but in all probabilities, it was ancient Gandhārā which minted Kuṣāṇa coins thence, subsequently, migrated far and wide. An attempt is being made here to study the obverse of a few coins with particular reference to portraits on them. Though inspired initially by the Bactrian Greek coins, the Kuṣāṇa rulers soon overcame the impact and developed their own devices with distinctive Kuṣāṇa features.

Kujula Kadphises, the earlier Kuṣāṇa ruler issued only copper coins in imitation of the Parthian coins after Hermaeus death. One type of Kujula's coins shows on the obverse a diademed Roman male head generally taken to stand for Roman king Augustus. On the reverse of this type of coin there appears a male dressed in Indo-Scythian custom and seated on curule, probably represents Kujula Kadphises.[19] Wima Kadphises, next in the line issued not only copper coins but he introduced gold coins extensively in three denominations, i.e. double *dīnāra*, *dīnāra* and quarter *dīnāra*. Within the inadequately available space, the period witnessed admirable delineation of portraits. On the obverse of his gold coins, Wima generally appears in his advanced age, an elderly man with a heavy body but obviously looks accomplished and powerful. But there are coins in which he was projected comparatively young such as the coin that shows him through a squarish window. His younger look, sharp features, his conviction and resoluteness have also been found in a few other types. The divine connection of Wima is found projected on such coins where his bust evidently emerges out of cloud and flames emanate from his shoulder. In another type of coin Wima is seen seated on a coach. While in most of his coins his body is seen frontally, his face is delineated in strict profile and in the profiles of his face, his Caucasian features such as short head, long nose and bearded face become quite conspicuous. In yet another type, Wima is seen seated cross-legged posture; he holds in his right hand the branch of a tree while his left hand is placed on his thigh. From his coin types, it becomes evident that Wima developed a fascination to project himself in various attitudes. Thus he is seen riding an elephant or driving a big horse with mild gallop and finally, in his copper coins he is seen standing at an altar that served as the basic theme of the royal portraits of the subsequent Kuṣāṇa coins.[20]

Kaniṣka succeeded Wima and issued both gold and copper coins. For reasons unknown he opted only one type of portrait, i.e. standing and sacrificing at an altar with his right hand which at times, also displays a goad (*aṅkuśa*).[21] His left hand carries a spear. He is found attaired with a long tunic, salwar, a mantle held by a double clasp and a low round cap adorns his head. A small sword hangs from his left waist. In his standing stance, his legs are kept apart and are found covered by felt boots and this calls for a comparison with this lithic portrait found at Mathurā. In the portraits of Kaniṣka on coins one finds certain common mannerisms specially his dress and the stance. A close analysis of his faces would show his expressions differ from coin to coin. Some faces are imbued with happy smile, in some faces he looks reasonably serious while on others he maintains a powerful personality.

Among the Kuṣāṇa kings, it was Huviṣka who appeared quite concerned about the delineation of his portraits on his coins. For his coin types, he did not follow the coin type of Kaniṣka. He appears to have imbibed inspirations from the coin types of Wima Kadphises. On most of his coins, he gazes to the left but there are examples in which Huviṣka looks to the right. From his coins it appears further that he took fancy in wearing garments studded with jewels. His headgears likewise show several and distinguished types both high and flat topped and in many instances, his head is found nimbate. Curiously enough, the portraits showing his advance ages are depicted without a nimbus. This was, perhaps, the period he did not require it to proclaim his divine association. He normally holds either a sceptre or a club and a spear in his left hand. In other types of his coins, he is shown mounted on an elephant with a goad (*aṅkuśa*) in his left hand and a spear on the right. On yet another type, he appears seated cross-legged against either a rock or a cloud. His reclined figure is also known. Seated frontally or in profile his figure is also delineated on coins against a cushion. Differences in his age can be studied from the morphological changes in his faces, in the gradual growth of his beard and moustache and in the expressions of his eyes. In the portraits of Huviṣka, one finds that the artists paid more attention to work out the subtleties of his faces but they remained less careful in the depiction of his bust. Therefore, at times, it appears that a realistic head has been grafted to a clumsily conceived torso. His busts are generally conceived frontally but there are instances where his busts are found depicted in three quarter profiles. On some coins, his busts are found wrapped up in tightly fitted metal armour. In such coins while the face appears quite realistic and lively, the bust is found devoid of surging life breath.[22]

The art of portraiture on Kuṣāṇa coins laid bare a steady decline from the time of Vāsudeva I. Like Kaniṣka I, he opted for a single type of coin device where on the obverse he appears always standing and sacrificing at an altar. The only difference with Kaniṣka's figure is this that while Kaniṣka I holds a spear, he carries a trident. Otherwise, he appears attaired with northerner's dress and stands keeping his legs apart. His figure has been very summarily treated and faces reveal crude finish. His figure maintains the typical Kuṣāṇa mannerisms of standing types and his figures are found pervaded with pointedness and angularity. Crude and clumsy plastic qualities continued in the treatments of the portraits of Kaniṣka III and Vāsudeva II.

The next period, that is the Gupta period, which carved its riche as a notable dynasty, the so-called 'Golden Age' ushered in during this time. Excellence was achieved and the culture reached its acme during reigning of the imperial Guptas but the glorious chapter of the art of portraiture which one witnesses in the Kuṣāṇa period could not be continued with finer precision or further developed in the period of the Guptas. Stray instances of portraits have been searched out in Mahabalipuram or in Konark and in some other places and India had to wait to the arrival of the Mughals for a fresh interest in the art of portraiture.

NOTES AND REFERENCES

1. C. Sivaramamurti, 'Amaravati Sculptures in the Madras Government Museum', see *Bulletin of the Madras Government Museum*, Madras, 1942, p. 11 and also see *The Report of the Buddhist Cave Temples and Their Inscriptions* by Burgess, vide, Archaeological Survey of Western India, London, 1983, pp. 1-140.
2. D.R. Pradhan, 'Two Rare Statues of Asoka Discovered at Langudi Hill, Orissa, India', see Newsletter 13, *Circle of Inner Asian Art* (*CIAA*), London, 2001, page 15, pls. 1 and 2.
3. B.N. Mukherjee, see Newsletter 12, *Circle of Inner Asian Art* (*CIAA*), December, 2000, London, p. 16.
4. D.R. Pradhan, *op.cit*, p. 15.
5. The word *õkrī* possibly a corrupt form of Tokahrians, that loosely connect the Kuṣāṇas.
6. John M. Rosenfield, *Dynastic Art of the Kushanas*, New Delhi, 1993, p. 146.
7. Heimo Rau, *Reflections on Indian Art,* Bombay, 1976, p. 63.
8. John M. Rosenfield, *op.cit.*, p. 265.
9. Heimo Rau, *op.cit.*, p. 62.

10. *Ibid.*, p. 67.
11. V.S. Agrawal, *Indian Art*, Varanasi, 1965, pp. 249-250 and also see Heimo Rau, *op.cit.*, p. 65.
12. Bobojan, Gafurov, *The Great Civilization of the Kushanas*, Courier, February, 1969, U.K., p. 7.
13. Heimo Rau, *op.cit.*, p. 69.
14. *Ibid.*, p. 7 and also see *L' Afghanistan et son Art* by Jeanine Auboyer, published by Ed. circle d'Art and Arita, Prague.
15. Bobojan Gafurov, *op.cit.*, pp. 8-9 and pls. 3, 4, 5, 8, 9, 12.
16. John M. Rosenfield, *op.cit.*, p. 145, pl. 3.
17. *Ibid.*, pls. 8 and 12.
18. Bobojan, Gafurov, *op.cit.*, p. 13.
19. Parameswari Lal Gupta, *Coins, India—The Land and The People*, New Delhi, p. 28.
20. Savita Sharma, *Gold Coins of the Imperial Kushanas and Their Successors,* Varanasi, 1999, pp. 87-89.
21. A single specimen in gold in the collection of State Museum, Lucknow in which Kaniṣka appears with his bust and he looks quite elderly.
22. Mention may be made of Kuṣāṇa silver coins which are of course not much less in number and the portraits of Kuzula, Wima Kadphises, Kaniṣka I and Vāsudeva I appear on these. See *Kuṣana Numismatics*, Satya Shrava, New Delhi, 1985, pp. 58-61.

25

DIGITAL DOCUMENTATION OF GANDHĀRA ART IN CHANDIGARH MUSEUM

VIDYA NAND SINGH

Established after the partition of the country in August 1947, the Government Museum and Art Gallery, Chandigarh, is one of the premier institutions of India with its very rich collection of Gandhāra sculptures. Before the partition in 1947, these collections were housed in the Central Museum, Lahore, the then capital of Punjab.

On 10 April 1948, the division of collection took place by which sixty per cent of the objects were retained by Pakistan and the remaining forty per cent collections consisting mainly of Gandhāra sculptures and Indian miniature paintings of Mughal and Pahari schools, fell in the share of India. Received in the month of April 1949, this collection was first housed in Amritsar, then Shimla and Patiala and finally shifted to Chandigarh and displayed in the year 1967, in its present building which was specially designed by Le-Corbusier, a famous French architect, who designed Chandigarh – The City Beautiful. The Museum was formally inaugurated on 6 May 1968.

Museums document their collection in order to manage, exhibit and study them. This consists of creating a group of documentation records of the objects. The documentation record includes a series of different kinds of information called fields.

The Chandigarh Museum has digitized most of its collection on the computer based documentation system. In the beginning, for documentation works of art, the Museum was having only the main entry register with following columns:

(1) Serial number
(2) Accession number
(3) Title
(4) Artist
(5) Medium
(6) Size
(7) Source
(8) Period

(9) Price
(10) Signatures of Technical Assistant
(11) Signatures of Director

Later, the Museum's curatorial staff added the sectional, movement, reserve collection, conservation and photo-print record registers, catalogue and index-cum-location cards, black and white and colour photo-print albums and colour slides.

A few years back Museum established the Data Collection Management Section and the inputting of inventory data, object description and conservation data of the collection was started with a Pilot Project of 601 pieces of Gandhāra sculptures, which form an important collection of the Museum. Originally 627 pieces of Gandhāra sculptures were received from the Central Museum, Lahore as a share, out of which nineteen and seven Gandhāra sculptures were exchanged with Brahmanical and Jain sculptures from the National Museum, New Delhi and the State Museum, Lucknow, respectively. Gandhāra collection in the Government Museum and Art Gallery, Chandigarh is the second largest collection in the country, first is the Indian Museum, Kolkata.

Total collection of the Museum is about ten thousands, ranging from the prehistoric stone tools of Palaeolithic period to the paintings and sculptures of the medieval and contemporary period, out of which inputting of inventory data of about seven thousands of works of art has already been completed, remaining work will be completed by the end of the year.

There are two fundamental aspects to the digitization of the collection: creating and amending records and location coding:

Creating and amending records is achieved by transcribing information from the documentation record in the form of entry and sectional registers, index-cum-location and catalogue cards.

Location coding consists of noting down the location of the objects and ensuring that they are properly marked with their accession numbers.

Management of the museum collection through digitization is having the following advantages:

(1) it has complete inventory of collection and means of stock-checking;
(2) it is a first step towards automation of the information about the objects;
(3) it is an online system which means that the curatorial staff, conservators, librarians and photo and audio-visual sections can directly interact with data;
(4) it has a flexible record structures applicable to all the collection;
(5) it supports the security of the collection, by maintaining duplicate copies of information and enabling information to be made readily available to the outside agencies such as police and custom in the case of emergency;
(6) it has an easy access for researchers and scholars;
(7) it helps in layout and designing of the publicity materials of the exhibitions, seminars, conferences, lectures, etc., in the form of invitation cards, folders, brochures, captions, section labels, posters, banners and hoardings;
(8) it also retrieves data of the collection for preparation of general and scholarly publications, i.e. guide books, hand lists, catalogues, etc.;
(9) it enables information to be transferred to other museums, libraries and art and cultural organizations and also facilitates the development of common projects, i.e. research, exhibitions, training, etc., through fax and e-mail; and
(10) the image and data of the collection can also be displayed on the internet.

The data field of the computer based documentation system was developed by the museum's curatorial staff under the guidance of Prof. B.N. Goswamy and Prof. D.C. Bhattacharyya, known art historians with the technical support of the National Informatics Centre (NIC), Chandigarh UT Unit, Planning Commission, Government of India, the Regional Computer (a set up of the National Informatics Centre, Government of India) and Quark Media India Limited, a multinational software company based at Chandigarh.

The data structure is based on information collected, after surveying the leading institutions which are having an excellent digital documentation facilities available abroad i.e. the British Museum, the Museum of Mankind and the Victoria and Albert Museum, London; the National Museums of Scotland, Edinburgh (U.K.); the Museum Guimet, Paris (France); the Museum Rietberg, Zurich (Switzerland); and the National Museums of Kenya, Nairobi, Kenya (East Africa), National Gallery of Victoria, Melbourne (Australia), Asian Art Museum, San Francisco, California (U.S.A.) and in India i.e. the Indira Gandhi National Centre for the Arts, new Delhi; the Indian Museum, Kolkata; the Indira Gandhi Manav Sangrahalaya, Bhopal; and the Prince of Wales Museum of Western India, Mumbai.

Thus the museum information card consists of all the potential fields necessary for the documentation of the Museum's collection and known as 'MIC-GOMAG' – MASTER INFORMATION CARD OF THE GOVERNMENT MUSEUM AND ART GALLERY, CHANDIGARH' which includes the data fields in two main sections: academic and administrative. The academic and administrative sections have the following fifteen and thirteen sub-data fields respectively.

(A) ACADEMIC

(1) Accession no.
(2) Category of object
(3) Title
(4) Medium/material/technique
(5) Provenance
(60 Date/period
(7) Style/school
(8) Tribe/dynasty/community/patron
(9) Artists
(10) Dimensions/weight/denomination (coin)
(11) Brief description
(12) Inscription
(13) Original source information
(14) Published source references
(15) Remarks/comments

(B) ADMINISTRATIVE

(1) Unit No.
(2) Entry register No.
(3) Sectional register No.
(4) Source
(5) Mode of acquisition
(6) Price/value

(7) Photo-negative/slide no.
(8) Photo-album/video/audio cassette no.
(9) Location
(10) Condition of the object
(11) Restoration done, if any
(12) Last update
(13) Expert comments

The Master Information Card also carries digitized colour photo print of the image. The data and image is stored in the Digital Media System (DMS) software in the form of folder. The software allows scanning, cataloguing and storing as many pages as we desire. It is also possible to define our own set of data for a class of documents. The document stored in the system are organized in folders. The data and image can be stored in as many folders as required. Internally, the document is not duplicated only the references are maintained. The retrieval of each document can be done in seconds by giving a key word, i.e. accession number, unit number, title, school/style, date/period, artist's name, theme/title, medium/material/technique or category of objects. For accessing these documents, we can select a folder, look at the contents and then select the appropriate document. The software also uses a variety of standard compression techniques to store the document containing data and images so that they take very little space for storage and yet there is no loss of clarity either in data or in image. Online updating of remarks, comments or suggestions by research scholars and field specialists are done periodically, to keep the information of works of art update. Few samples of digital documented sheets are enclosed as annexure I, II and III.

Chandigarh Administration has launched its Home Page on 15th August 1997 during the occasion of the 50th anniversary of India's independence on the internet, making available the information about the Museum collection to the museologist, art historians, scholars, researchers, art lovers and tourists all over the world and the website can be visited at the following address: http//www.nic.in/chandigarh. An independent website of the Museum is under construction and will be launched shortly.

Annexure - I

MASTER INFORMATION CARD OF THE GOVERNMENT MUSEUM AND ART GALLERY (MIC-GOMAG), CHANDIGARH, INDIA

(A Digital Documentation of Works of Art in Multimedia)

ACADEMIC

(1) **Accession No.:** 1625.
(2) **Category of object:** Gandhāra sculpture.
(3) **Title:** Goddess Hārīti.
(4) **Medium/material/technique:** Grey Schist Stone.
(5) **Provenance:** Skarah Dheri.
(6) **Date/period:** *c.* 2nd century AD.
(7) **Style/school:** Gandhāra School.
(8) **Tribe/dynasty/community/patron:** Kuṣāṇa.
(9) **Artist**: Not known.
(10) **Dimensions/weight/denomination (coin):** Height: 132 cm Width: 54 cm.
(11) **Brief Description**: The heavily bejewelled female deity, mother goddess Hārīti carries three small children, one on each shoulder and the other standing in left palm holding on to the breast. The globular head with cheeks and chin are gently rounded. The narrow forehead projects with eyebrows in low relief over the protruding rounded eyes which have long narrowing corners. The drapery is having beaded ridges and deep folds.
(12) **Inscription**: The inscription is in Kharoṣṭī and consists of two lines, 16 in. and 13 in. long respectively, the height of individual letters varying from half inch to one and quarter inch. It bears a date.
Text: L.1. *vash(e*)ek (u) na (cha) dusatimae āṣāḍhasa māsasa divase 2011*
2.s(var)gapade dasama bharadu saẕ mam artha(e) tanay(e)sh(u)
Translation: In the four-hundredth year less one (i.e. 399), on the 22 day of the month Ashadha. In heaven may she carry the tenth. I ask for protection of the Children. (Konow, Sten)
(13) **Original source information**: G. Malalesekera, *Dictionary of Pali Proper Names.*
(14) **Published source references:**
   a) Sten Konow, *Corpus Inscriptionvm Indicarum*, Vol. II, Part I, Kharoṣṭī Inscriptions with exception of Aśoka, Calcutta, 1929.
   b) B.N. Mukherjee, A Note on the Skarah Dheri Hārīti Sculpture, National Museum Bulletin, 1991.
   c) Suwarcha Paul, Gandhāra Sculptures in Chandigarh Museum, Chandigarh, 1966.
   d) Zwalf W., *A Cataogue of the Gandhāra Sculpture in the British Museum*, Vols. I & II, London, 1996.
(15) **Remark/comments**: It is one of the eight known inscribed and dated sculpture from Gandhāra.

ADMINISTRATIVE

(1) **Unit no.** GS 432.
(2) **Accession register no.:** 1.
(3) **Sectional register no.:** 2.
(4) **Source:** Share from the Central Museum, Lahore (Pakistan).
(5) **Mode of acquisition:** Share from Central Museum, Lahore (Pakistan).
(6) **Price / value:** Not known.
(7) **Photo-negative:** B & W/colour no. and slide no.: GS-432.
(8) **Photo-album/video/audio cassette no.:** 9.
(9) **Location:** Displayed in Gandhāra Gallery.
(10) **Condition of the object:** The feet below the anklets are damaged Broken right hand was damaged but unevenly restored.
(11) **Restoration done, if any:** Technical examination is being done for proper restoration of uneven restored right hand.
(12) **Last update:** 31.1.1998.
(13) **Expert comments:** ______________

Annexure - II

MASTER INFORMATION CARD OF THE GOVERNMENT MUSEUM AND ART GALLERY (MIC-GOMAG), CHANDIGARH, INDIA

(A Digital Documentation of Works of Art in Multimedia)

ACADEMIC

(1) **Accession no.:** 2342.
(2) **Category of object:** Gandhāra Sculpture.
(3) **Title:** Bodhisattva Maitreya.
(4) **Medium/material/technique**: Grey Schist stone.
(5) **Provenance:** Sikri.
(6) **Date/period:** *c.* 2nd century AD.
(7) **Style/school:** Gandhāra School.
(8) **Tribe/dynasty/community/Patron:** Kushana.
(9) **Artist:** Not known.
(10) **Dimensions/weight/denomination (coin):** Height: 147 cm; Width: 61 cm.
(11) **Brief description**: Bodhisattva is wearing a heavy collar and a long necklace decorated with kneeling cherubs flanking a central bead and amulet strings pass over the left shoulder. The image is dressed in the attire of the typical Gandhāra period which consists of a lower garment with swallow-tailed folds and an upper garment swathed across the body and wound around the shoulder. The long hair is combed back, knotted in a loop over the head and falls over the shoulder in curls. A string of pearls is drawn across the head and circles the base of the hair loop. The plain halo is damaged. The right hand, now broken, probably had the palm facing the spectator in the gesture of granting freedom from fear (*abhaya mudrā*), while the left hand held an object, now missing.
(12) **Inscription:**____________
(13) **Original source information:** ____________
(14) **Published source references**: Chandra, Pramod: *The Sculpture of India* 3000 BC – AD 1300, National Gallery of Art, Washington (USA), 1985
(15) **Remarks/Comments**: Displayed in the 'Festival of India' exhibition at the National Gallery of Art, Washington (USA) in the year 1985.

ADMINISTRATIVE

(1) **Unit No.** GS 605.
(2) **Accession register no.:** 1.
(3) **Sectional register no.** 3.
(4) **Source:** Share from the Central Museum, Lahore (Pakistan).
(5) **Mode of acquisition:** Share from the Central Museum, Lahore (Pakistan).
(6) **Price/value:** Not mentioned.
(7) **Photo-negative/slide no.:** GS-605.

(8) **Photo-album/video/audio cassette no.:** 13.
(9) **Location:** Displayed in the Gandhāra Gallery at the main building.
(10) **Condition of the object:** There is surface incrustation on front- deep in design work; back – hard thick sandy deposition, obscuring the stone colour. Unevenly damaged both arms, both feet are also broken, halo partially broken but joined later, left arm is also broken.
(11) **Restoration done, if any:** Paper pulp treatment was given on April 10, 1995.
(12) **Last update:** 31.3.2000.
(13) **Expert comments:** ________________

26

EARLY EPIGRAPHS FROM GANDHĀRA AND ITS NEIGHBOURHOOD

KIRAN KUMAR THAPLYAL

The paper takes into consideration epigraphs ranging from the earliest times (Mauryan period) to the Gupta period, from Gandhāra and its neighbourhood, based on published materials available. It mentions briefly the main contents of the epigraphs and discusses the problem relating to the identification of kings, their genealogy and chronology, nature and significance of official designations, the errors used and the mood of dating followed and highlights various aspects of culture as glanced from them.

FOURTEEN ROCK EDICTS OF AŚOKA

Two sets of the fourteen rock edicts of Aśoka in Kharoṣṭī script have been found, one at Mansehra in the Hazara district in Pakistan,[1] and another at Shahbazgarhi in Peshawar district in Pakistan.[2] A brief summary of their contents is given below. In Rock Edict I, Aśoka prohibits killing of animals for sacrifice and also such festivities in which intoxicating drinks and meat were served and fight of animals, birds and men were arranged. It informs that instead of large number of animals, only three – two peacocks and a deer, were slaughtered for meat, in the royal kitchen. Rock Edict II tells us about the provisions of medical treatment that the king made for men and animals within his own kingdom in the territories of the Cholas, Pāṇḍyas, Satyaputras and Keralaputras and in the kingdom of Antiochus (Theos of Syria) and also that medicinal plants were brought and planted where they were not available. The third Rock Edict instructs high officials, *rājukas* and *prādeśikas*, to conduct tours every five years and preach to people proper treatment to parents, elders and relatives, charity to *brāhmaṇas* and *śramaṇas*, non-killing of animals and less hoarding and less spending.

Rock Edict IV tells that Aśoka arranged display of celestial chariots, divine elephants and ball of fire to inspire people to be good so that they may get these things in the next world. He claims that because of his efforts, killing of animals has been reduced and there had been an improvement in proper behaviour towards parents, friends and relatives. He expresses his wish that his progeny would follow his example. Rock Edict V mentions the creation of a new class of officers, *dharma-mahāmātras*, for the dissemination of *dhaṁma* in his own territory, among tribals and people of Greek colonies, Kambojas and the Gandharians. They had a role to play amongst different sects and were to induce the members of the royal family to make gifts and to help the prisoners in setting them free, inducing them to do meritorious acts so that they may reap the fruits in next life. Rock Edict VI says that the king had instructed his messengers to inform him important matters, including the difference of opinion that the *pariṣad* holds, even when he is eating, or in female apartment, or in inner chamber, or on horseback. Aśoka says he considers the welfare of his subjects as the most sacred duty and was relentlessly striving towards achieving it, as he thought by doing so he would free himself from the debt he owed to them.

In the Rock Edict VII, the king says people following any religion could settle anywhere in his kingdom, giving an inkling that there were areas occupied by people of one sect who did not allow the followers of other sects to settle there. The Rock Edict VIII says that instead of *vihāra-yātrās* practised by earlier kings in which hunting and other such acts were common, Aśoka went on *dhaṁma-yātrās* in which he gave gifts to *brāhmaṇas* and *śramaṇas* and paid visit to the learned people. He went on pilgrimage to Bodhi tree (Gaya). In Rock Edict IX he says that such rituals (*maṅgalas*) as people performed during illness, marriage, birth of child or proceeding on journey are of little value, while *dhaṁma-maṅgala*, which seeks proper behaviour towards slaves, servants, teachers, etc and non-violence is of great value. Rock Edict X also eulogizes *dhaṁma* and advises abstaining from committing sin. Rock Edict XI emphasizes on the importance of *dhaṁma* and tells that no *dāna* (gift) is so good as *dhaṁma-dāna* and no *maṅgala* (ritual) as *dhaṁma-maṅgala. Dhaṁma* again is explained in the same way as stated above. Rock Edict XII relates to religious toleration. It eulogizes concord and growth of essence among sects and lays emphasis on the control of speech. It says that praising one's own religion and condemning that of others, with a view to honouring one's own religion is not good. By doing so, one harms one's own religion, while by honouring others' religion, one honours one's own religion. People are advised to listen to the tenets of different religions, which would make them realize that all of them contain noble ideas and they would develop cosmopolitan outlook.

Rock Edict XIII refers to the horrors of war related to his conquest of Kaliṅga. It says that 1,50,000 people were captured, 1,00,000 killed and many times that number died (due to wounds, etc.). The king was greatly grieved and became inclined towards observing and disseminating *dhaṁma*. He vowed not to conquer any new territory and wished his progeny to follow this policy. He showed much tolerance towards forest tribes but warned them that it should not be taken as sign of weakness, as he could be ruthless if they did not behave. He wanted to conquer the heart of the people (*dhaṁma-vijaya*). He made provisions for conveying his message of *dhaṁma* not only in his own territory, but also in that of Antiochus [Theos of Syria, 266-46 BC], Ptolemy [Philadelphus of Egypt, 285-47 BC], Antigonus [Gonatas of Macedon, 278-39 BC], Megas [of Cyrene, 282-58 BC], Alexander [of Epirus, 272-55 BC, rather than the homonym who was the ruler of Corinth, 252-244 BC]. Nearer home, he did it in the kingdoms of the Cholas, Pāṇḍyas, Satyaputras, Tāmraparṇī (Śri Laṅka) and in the Yavana, Kamboja and Gandhāra territories. Rock Edict XIV is a comment on the style and contents of the edicts, stating justification for the detailed, medium or brief treatment and also for the deletion of some matter.

SHAR-I-KUNA MINOR ROCK EDICT OF AŚOKA[3]

An important Minor Rock Edict in Greek and Aramaic scripts, found at Shar-i-Kuna, Kandahar, is somewhat different in contents from the other Minor Rock Edict of Aśoka. There is slight difference even in the contents of the Greek and Aramaic versions. The Greek version says that after the tenth year of the coronation, the king embarked on the mission of disseminating the *dhaṁma*, which led to the increase in the righteousness and the welfare of the people. People gave up eating meat and huntsmen and fishermen gave up killing animals and fish and the uncontrolled ones became controlled and obedient to parents and elders. The Aramaic version says that due to the preaching of *dhaṁma*, after tenth year of coronation, illness and unfriendliness diminished and peace and harmony increased. There was little killing for king's meat and other people also followed his example. Even fishermen observed restraint and uncontrolled ones became controlled. People became obedient to parents and elders. The righteous ones did not need trial for [better] place in the next life. People began to follow *dhaṁma* and were hoped to do so thereafter. The Greek version was meant for the Greek-speaking people of the area, which had become part of the Mauryan empire after the cessation of four provinces by Seleucus to Chandragupta Maurya, grandfather of Aśoka.

TAXILA ARAMAIC INSCRIPTION OF AŚOKA[4]

The fragmentary inscription, found by John Marshall at Taxila (district Rawalpindi), refers to Lord (*Maran*) Priyadarśa, his queen and sons. Some scholars opine that the inscription could belong to any of the Maurya kings, but there is greater possibility that it belongs to Aśoka, who has been so very commonly referred to as Priyadarśī in his inscriptions. Herzfeld[5] rightly says that there is hardly any possibility of any king other than Aśoka, so well known for his keenness to propagate *dhaṁma*, to use an occidental script, Aramaic, for his epigraphs.

OTHER INSCRIPTIONS OF AŚOKA[6]

An inscription from Lampak in Aramaic script refers to the setting of pillar by Devānaṁpiya, in all probability, Aśoka. A Greek version of the Rock Edicts XII and XIII in condensed form and with omissions and an Aramaic version of Pillar Edict VII have been reported from Kandahar. The find of Pillar Edict VI in Brāhmī in Buner near Takht-i-Bahi is curious and of doubtful validity.

SHINKOT (BAJAUR) INSCRIPTION OF THE TIME OF MENANDER[7]

The steatite casket bearing the inscription comes from Shinkot in Bajaur territory, 20 miles north-west of the confluence of Panjkora and Swat rivers. It refers to the consecration of Buddha's relics by Apracharaja Viyakamitra in the fifth regnal year of the Indo-Greek king, Menander. Viyakamitra would have been a governor of Menander in Bajaur region. The relics have been referred to as full of life. It may be stated that in the *Mahāvaṁsa*, we are told that seeing Buddha's relics is seeing Buddha himself and that Buddha's relics took the form of Buddha and performed miracles.[8]

The relics thus consecrated decayed and because of it, the inscription states, the dead ancestors were not accepting food (*piṇḍa*) and water (*udaka*). They were reconsecrated by Apracharaja Vijayamitra, variously taken as son or grandson or descendant of Viyakamitra, some time later. Vijayamitra is known from coins from Taxila bearing legend in *c.* 1st century BC characters in Brāhmī and Kharoṣṭī.

The first consecration of the relics was done in the month of Kārttika and the second in that of Vaiśākha. Both months are sacred, as, according to one tradition, Buddha attained *nirvāṇa* on the full moon of Kārttika and according to another, on the full moon of Vaiśākha.

The Apracharāja was earlier rendered into Sanskrit as *apratyagrāja*, 'one who has no adversary', but now with the new evidence of even a prince of the family referred to as Apracharāja being available, it should be taken as a family name.

OTHER RELIC CASKET INSCRIPTIONS OF APRACHA FAMILY

Seven other relic casket inscriptions belonging to Apracha dynasty have been found.[9] One of them[10] refers to the consecration of Buddha's relics by the harem superintendent of the prince Viṣṇuvarman. This was done after honouring all the Buddhas, Pratyeka-Buddhas, Buddha's disciples, Brahmā Sahaṁpati, Śakra – the lord of gods, the Four Great Kings and all beings. Another inscription[11] mentions King Viṣṇuvarman's son, Prince Indravarman and bears the date year 63 which is taken to refer to the era commencing in 57 BC and would be equal to AD 6. Obviously, Viṣṇuvarman's date must be earlier than that. Of the eight reliquary caskets of the Apracha dynasty, the find spot of only one, Shinkot, is known, which would have been within the area of that dynasty. If another, as alleged, came from Charsadda, then possibly that area was also under their rule.[12]

THE SWAT INSCRIPTION OF *MERIDARKH* THEODORUS[13]

The inscription, on the vase containing relics, is one of the oldest inscriptions after Aśoka, pertaining to Indo-Greek rule. It says that one, Theodorus, a *Meridarkh* – a Greek title for district officer, established relics of the Buddha. Theodorus would have been administering the area around Kabul. Another inscription of a *Meridarkh,* whose name is missing, has been found near Taxila which refers to the erection of a *stūpa* in honour of his parents.[13a]

SOME GREEK INSCRIPTIONS[14]

Some Greek inscriptions have been found in course of excavations at the Bactrian city of Aikhanum (Afghanistan), which is taken by some as modern representation of Oxiana. One inscription says that as a child one should be well-behaved, as a young man, one should master oneself, when in middle age one should be just and when old one should be good counsel on death and be without chagrin. This was got engraved on the tomb of Kineas by one Clearchus, who is identified by some, though without much justification, with the homonym that was the disciple of Socrates. Another inscription from this site mentions one as a son of Strato. This Strato has been identified with one of the Indo-Greek rulers of that name. However, the absence of any royal titles in the epigraph makes the identification doubtful. Some epigraphs refer variously to personal names, place-names (like Taxila) and commodities deposited after counting or measuring. We have reference to the deposition of *drachms*, the Greek coin-type and *kārṣāpaṇas*, the Indian coins.

THE TAXILA COPPERPLATE OF PATIKA, YEAR 78[15]

The inscription records the consecration of Buddha's relics and erection of monastery by *Mahādānapati* Patika, son of *Kṣatrapa* Liaka Kusulaka. The consecration was done for the merit of his parents and relatives. The act was done in the month of Panemos (Greek month corresponding to Indian Āṣāḍha) during the reign of the Śaka king Moga, i.e. Maues. The date and identification of Patika has been a matter of controversy. The Mathurā Lion Capital Inscription of Śaka ruler Rājuvula refers to his son Śoḍāsa as *kṣatrapa* and to Patika as *mahākṣatrapa*, while the Mathurā inscription of Śoḍāsa, dated year 72, refers to him as *mahākṣatrapa*. Fleet[16] considers the era used in the Taxila copperplate and the Mathurā inscription as identical, but takes Patika mentioned in the Taxila plates and the homonym in the Mathurā Lion Capital Inscription as two separate persons, as, according to him, it is difficult to explain the reference to Patika as *mahākṣatrapa* before the year 72 and *mahādānapati* in the year 78. Marshall and Konow[17] take Patika in the Mathurā Lion Capital Inscription and the Taxila copperplate as one and the same person but consider the era used in them as different and such as to give the date of the Taxila copperplate as earlier than that on the Mathurā Stone Inscription (and also than Mathurā Lion Capital Inscription). H.C. Raychaudhuri,[18] however, opines that it is possible that the era used is one and the same and the two inscriptions refer to same Patika who earlier held the office of *mahākṣatrapa*, but was later reduced to the status of *mahādānapati*

Liaka Kusulaka has been referred to as *Kṣaharasa Cukhsasa ca Kṣatrapasa*. Indraji read the first word as *Kṣaharatasa* (Kṣaharāta, a branch of the Śakas),[19] but because of letter *ca*, it is better to take the expression to mean *kṣatrapa* of Kṣahara and Cukhsa. Cunningham[20] took *Kṣahara-Cukhṣa* for Sirsukh, but since in another Taxila inscription of year 191 (discussed below) we get the expression *Cukhsasa Kṣatrapasa*, *Cukhsa* appears as a name of a place. Buhler[21] suggests that *Cukhsa* may be read as *Cuskha* and be the same as *Coshka* in the *Trikāṇḍaśeṣa* means a horse from the district on the Indus and may be that Liaka Kusulaka was the *kṣatrapa* of that region. Liaka Kusulaka is also known from his coins.

THE TAKHT-I-BAHI INSCRIPTION OF GONDOPHARNES, YEARS 26 AND 203[22]

The inscription mentions that in the [regnal] year 26 of Gondopharnes and in the year [of an era] 103, Balasvāmi *Boyaṇa* (chief), along with his son Keṇamira *Boyaṇa*, gifted a railing after honouring *Erjhuṇa* (prince) KapaÖ and his parents. The date 103 should be referred to the era commencing in 57 BC, which comes to AD 47. Konow[23] read *Kapasa* and identified him with Kadphises I, which would mean that in AD 46, when Gondopharnes was king, Kadphises I was a prince.[24] The latter would have become king after driving out the Parthians from the Gandhāra region. Incidentally, the date AD 46 for Gondopharnes fits in well with the Christian tradition, which makes him contemporary of St. Thomas.

PANJTAR STONE INSCRIPTION OF A KUṢĀṆA KING, YEAR 122 (= AD 65)[25]

The inscription refers to the erection of a Śaiva shrine[25a] by one Moika, son of Urumuja in the reign of *Mahārāja* Guṣaṇa in the year 122. The king has been identified by some with Kujula Kadphises, the first king of the Kuṣāṇa dynasty. It is argued that even without the mention of name, people could know who the king was as he was the only king of that dynasty. Those who believe Kaniṣka founded the era in AD 78 suggest that Vima Kadphises was the king, it being the last year of his reign.

KALAWAN COPPERPLATE INSCRIPTION, YEAR 134[26]

The plate was found at Kalawan, near Taxila and records that *Upāsikā* Candrābhī established Buddha's relics along with her sons, daughter-in-laws, (mentioned by name as Lajjā and Indrā) and her grandson in the hope that it would be conducive to attaining *nirvāṇa*. The inscription is dated year 134. The date of the inscription and related matter has been discussed in the context of the following inscription.

TAXILA SILVER SCROLL INSCRIPTION, YEAR 136[27]

This inscription bearing date 136 (= AD 78) records the consecration of Buddha's relics in a Bodhisattva chapel of the Dharmarājikā *stūpa* at Taxila. The consecration was done by one, Bāhlīka, hailing from Uraska (or Uraska hailing from Bāhlīka) and scion of Iṁtavrihyas and inhabitant of the town Ṁoaca. This was done honouring the *arhats*, the Buddhas, Pratyeka-Buddhas and parents, friends and kinsmen of the consecrator and all beings. The consecration was for the health and welfare of *Mahārāja Rājātirāja Devaputra* Khuṣaṇa (Kuṣāṇa). The Kuṣāṇa king has been identified variously with Kujula Kadphises (arguing that he being first Kuṣāṇa king, it was not deemed necessary to mention his name), or Vima Kadphises (taking AD 78 as the last year of his reign), or Kaniṣka (taking AD 78 as the first year of his reign and also the first year of the Śaka era of which he is considered the founder). The *stūpa* is called Dharmarājikā, either because it was originally established by Aśoka who has been referred to in literature as *Dharmarāja*, or because it contained the relics of the Buddha who was a *Dharmarāja*. The Chira *stūpa* in which the silver scroll bearing the inscription was found has been identified by Boyer with Kuṇāla *stūpa* referred to by Hiuen Tsang.

The first few words of the Kalawan inscription and those of the Taxila Silver Scroll inscription are considerably similar. The former has *savatsariye 134 ayasa śravaṇasa masasa*, while the latter has *sa 136 ajasa asaḍhasa masasa*. Of the two inscriptions, the Taxila inscription was found first. Some scholars suggested that *aya* could stand for 'this' and the meaning would be 'this month of āṣāḍha'. Some suggested that *aya* stands for *ādya*, 'the first' and āṣāḍha has been so referred to because at that time, the year began with this month. A few opined that āṣāḍha month has been referred to as 'first' as there were two āṣāḍhas in that year, one being intercalary. But with the find of the Kalawan plate with the expression *ayasa śravaṇasa masasa*, it was clear that *ajasa* and *ayasa* should mean the same. Now, it does not seem that in the year 134, the year began with the month Śrāvaṇa and two years later, in the year 136, with āṣāḍha. Nor is it possible that there were two Śrāvaṇas in the year 134 and two āṣāḍhas in the year 136. The most reasonable and the commonly accepted view is that *ayasa / ajasa* should be taken to mean 'of Azes', i.e., '[the era]of Azes', which was so named either because it was founded by him, or because of his using it extensively. The era is taken to be the one which commenced in 57 BC.

RABTAK INSCRIPTION OF KANIṢKA I, YEAR 1[28]

The inscription, found near Surkh Kotal, gives the genealogy of the Kuṣāṇa kings from Kujula Kadphises to Kaniṣka as below:

Kujula Kadphises
|
Vima Taktu (?)
|
Vima Kadphises
|
Kaniṣka

Before the discovery of this inscription, the genealogy of the Kuṣāṇa kings, in the absence of any tangible evidence, was a matter of speculation. Some scholars believed that Kuṣāṇa kings belonged to two different families, one comprising two kings whose name ended in

Kadphises – Kujula and Vima and another of Kaniṣka and his successors most of whom bear names ending in *iṣka* – Kaniṣka, Vāsiṣka and Huviṣka. The view that was once held by some that 'Kaniṣka group' preceded 'Kadphises group' has been shown as erroneous by John Marshall's excavations at Taxila which showed that coins of the Kadphises kings were found in layers lower (hence earlier) than those of Kaniṣka. It was, however, believed that Vima was the son of Kujula. The present inscription shows that he was not the son but the grandson of Kujula and his father was Vima Taktu (?), whose rule intervened those of Kujula and Vima Kadphises. This king was not known before the discovery of the inscription under discussion. The inscription conclusively establishes that Kaniṣka did not belong to a family different from that of Kadphises kings, but to that very family. It has been suggested that since coins of Vima Taktu have not been found, he might have ruled as a junior partner of his father and predeceased him. Some suggest that Vima Taktu (?) may be the king who issued coins bearing the legend *Soter Megas* which have been found in fairly large number and some also suggest that the statue bearing inscription *Vima Takṣa* from Māṭ, now in Mathurā Museum, may be his representation.

ZEDA INSCRIPTION OF KANIṢKA, YEAR 11[29]

The Kharoṣṭī inscription is on a rock near village Zeda in Rawalpindi district, Pakistan. It is dated 20th āṣāḍha, Uttara Phalguni *nakṣatra*, year 11, in the reign of *Muroḍa* (lord) and *Marjhaka (gṛhapati)* Kaniṣka. It records the digging of well and providing of water shed by Hipeyadhiya (Indian form of Greek Hippeos or Hippias, as Sten Konow suggests) for the Sarvāstivādin monks. The act was done for the merit of *Kṣatrapa* Liaka and that of the mother of the donor. This was done by the grace of Monk Saṅghamitrarāja. The titles *muroḍa* and *marjhaka* are of Central Asian origin, probably Khotanese.

MANIKIALA STONE INSCRIPTION OF KANIṢKA, YEAR 18[30]

The Kharoṣṭī inscription from Manikiala in Rawalpindi district records the erection of several *stūpas* by Lala, the *daṇḍanāyaka* (general) and increaser of the glory of Guṣaṇa (Kuṣāṇa) family. The act was done on the 20th Kārttika of the year 18 (= AD 96). Lala was *horamurta* of *Kṣatrapa* Veśpasi. He associated a few others in this act, which was for the merit of his brother and the architect of the monastery. *Horamurta* is compared with *horamuruṇḍaga* of a Mathurā inscription and *muroḍa* of the Zeda inscription. Senart takes *horamurta* and the following *satasa* as one word of which the Sanskrit form *horamūrtasattvasya*, would mean 'an incarnate image of Ahuramazda'. But Lūders' interpretation of *horamurta* as *dānapati* is preferable. Kaniṣka appointed a member of his own clan on the office of *daṇḍanāyaka*.

SHERTALA INSCRIPTION, YEAR 39[31]

The Kharoṣṭī epigraph was found in Shertala plain in north Waziristan. According to the reading and interpretation of B.N. Mukherjee, the inscription records in the year 39, in the month of Avadunaga (Macedonian Audunaios, equal to Indian Pausha-Māgha), a cave was excavated by the order of the *daṇḍanāyaka* of Kuṣāṇa āhi for the welfare of all beings. The name of the Kuṣāṇa king is not mentioned, but the date 39 (= AD 117) falls during the reign of Huviṣka.[32]

GARHI MATANI INSCRIPTION OF KANIṢKA[33]

This Kharoṣṭī inscription from Garhi Matani, 13 miles east of Campbellpur, Pakistan, records the gift (not specified) of Monk Budhavarman and others during the reign of *Maharaja Rajatiraja Devaputra* Kaniṣka.

KURRAM COPPERPLATE INSCRIPTION, YEAR 21[34]

The provenance of the casket bearing Kharoṣṭī inscription is not known. It was given to a *tehsildar* of honour of Kurram (near Peshawar) by a villager. The inscription is dated 20th day of Avadunaka (Macedonian Audunaios, equivalent to Indian Pauṣa-Māgha), Year 21 (= AD 99). It records the consecration of the relics of the Buddha in the monastery belonging to the Sarvāstivādins, for the welfare of all beings. It contains the *Nidāna-sūtra* in Prākṛta, of which we have given the Sanskrit forms below: (i) ignorance *(avidyā)*, (ii) impressions (*saṁskāra*), (iii) consciousness (*vijñāna*), (iv) name-and-form (*nāma-rūpa*), (v) six provinces (of six senses, *ṣaḍāyatana*), (vi) contact *(sparśa)*, (vii) sensation (*vedanā*), (viii) thirst or desire (*tṛṣṇā*), (ix) attachment *(upādānam)*, (x) existence *(bhava)*, (xi) birth (*jāti*), (xii) old age, death, great lamentation, suffering, dejection and despair *(jarā-maraṇa-śoka-parideya-duîkha-daurmanasya)*. Only two other inscriptions are known to contain *Nidāna-sūtra* – one from Gopalapur (district Gorakhpur) on a brick in Gupta script,[35] and another from Kushinagar on a copperplate, partly engraved and partly written in ink.[36] Buddha taught in Prākṛta and turned down the request of some disciples to allow them to preach in Sanskrit. The Kurram version of the *Nidāna-sūtra* is nearer to the original version both in terms of time and language than the other two versions, mentioned above.

SURKH-KOTAL INSCRIPTION OF KANIṢKA, YEAR 31[37]

It is a large inscription of 25 lines in cursive Greek script and Tocharian language, found at Surkh-Kotal on Kabul – Mazar-i-Sharif road. It refers to the repair of the acropolis of Kaniṣka *Nikator* sanctuary by Nokonzoko, an official of the emperor. He, with the help of other officials, strengthened the wall of the fort, dug a well and perhaps also a canal. The inscription was engraved by Mihirman and Burzmihrpuhr, who also signed it.

Kaniṣka sanctuary was inaugurated with the worship of Mithra and performance of *homa*. Either two statues, one of king and another of Mithra, were established, or only a statue of king as Mithra. The year 31 for Kaniṣka creates problem. His known dates range between 1 and 23 and Vāsiṣka's date between 24 and 28 and Huviṣka's reign began in year 28. It has been suggested that Kaniṣka might have shifted to Bactria, leaving eastern kingdom to Vāsiṣka and later to Huviṣka. It is also suggested that he may be identical with Kaniṣka of Ara inscription, year 41. Hanning[38] is of the view that the sanctuary was made during the time of Kaniṣka, but the inscription was engraved during the reign of Huviṣka. But there is also a view that the way the official is mentioned as devoted to king suggests that Kaniṣka was alive at that point of time.

The statues of the Kuṣāṇa kings from Surkh-Kotal sanctuary remind one of the Kuṣāṇa statues from Māṭ (Mathurā). The statues at both the places were meant to be worshipped. These sanctuaries are like the *devakula* of the *Pratimānāṭaka* of Bhāsa and *Raghuvaṁśa* of Kālidāsa. Incidentally, both the statues of Kaniṣka – the one found at Surkh-Kotal and that from Māṭ, are now headless. It has been pointed out that while Kaniṣka statue at Māṭ shows him dressed as a warrior, that from Surkh-Kotal depicts him in a dress befitting festive occasion.

ARA STONE INSCRIPTION OF KANIṢKA, YEAR 41[39]

The epigraph from Ara, near Attock, Pakistan, records the digging of a well by a person in honour of his parents, for the benefit of himself, his wife and son and for the welfare of all beings. The reord was engraved by one Madhu, in the year 4l, during the reign of *Maharaja Rajatiraja Devaputra Kaisara* Kaniṣka. The title *maharaja (mahārāja)* is Indian, *rajatiraja* is based on Iranian mode, *devaputra* is based on Chinese title and *kaisara* (Caesar) is Roman.

The dates for Kuṣāṇa kings, as stated above, are known as 1 to 23 for Kaniṣka, 24 to 28 for Vāsiṣka and 28 to 60 for Huviṣka. The year 4l of Kaniṣka of this inscription falls in between the reign of Huviṣka. Some scholars held the view that there was division of the Kuṣāṇa empire with Vāsiṣka and later Huviṣka ruling the eastern part and Kaniṣka in the north-western part. Some suggested the chronology as below: Kaniṣka, Vāsiṣka, Huviṣka, Kaniṣka II and Huviṣka II. A few scholars identified Kaniṣka of Ara inscription with the homonym whose dates range between l to 23. The fact that the name of the father of Kaniṣka of Ara inscription is mentioned as Vajheṣpa is significant. It was suggested that Kaniṣka I did not mention the name of his father as it was not deemed necessary as he was the only king of that name. But when there was second king of that name, to avoid confusion regarding the identity of the two, his father's name, Vajheṣpa, was given. Vajheṣpa is generally identified with Vāsiṣka. One could argue that he was Vāsiṣka II and there was another king of that name who was father of Kaniṣka I. But with the discovery of Rabtak inscription, it is known for certain that Vima Kadphises was the father of Kaniṣka and so this possibility is entirely ruled out.

We may mention another possibility. The Ara inscription is of private individual who by mistake wrote Kaniṣka for Huviṣka. If this is accepted, then there would be only one Kaniṣka, who ruled between years l to 23. Vajheṣpa would then be the father of Huviṣka, of which there is every possibility as the latter succeeded the former. There would be no interregnum in Huviṣka's reign-period. However, the find of Surkh-Kotal inscription of Kaniṣka, discussed above, has again created the problem of explaining his rule in the year 3l, unless the view of Hanning is accepted that the work mentioned in the epigraph was done between years l and 23, but was recorded in the year 3l during the reign of Huviṣka.

KHAWAT (WARDAK) BRONZE VASE INSCRIPTION OF HUVIṢKA, YEAR 51[40]

The Kharoṣṭī inscription on a vase found at Khawat (Wardak) in Afghanistan mentions that in the year 5l, i.e. (51+ 78=) AD 129 in the month of Arthamisiya (Macedonian Artemesios, equivalent to Indian Vaiśākha-Jyeṣṭha), Vagra Marega, son of Kamagulya, established relics of Buddha in Vagra Marega *stūpa* (named after the donor) for the acceptance of the Mahāsāṅghika teachers. The merit accruing from this work was to go to *Maharaja Rajatiraja* Huviṣka. This was done for the welfare of donor's parents, brother, friends, relations, kinsmen and the donor himself.

KHALATSE STONE INSCRIPTION OF UVIMIKASTU, YEAR 187[41]

The Kharoṣṭī inscription records the date year l87 (= AD l30) in the reign of *Maharaja* Uvimikastu. Konow read Uvima-Kavthisasa and identified the king with Vima Kadphises. He believes that Kaniṣka era began even after that date and not in AD 78, as majority of the scholars believe.

TAXILA SILVER VASE INSCRIPTION OF JIHONIKA, YEAR 191[42]

The Kharoṣṭī inscription dated year 191 was found at Taxila, district Rawalpindi. It reads *Maharaja ... sa putrasa Jihoṇikasa Cukhsasa kṣatrapasa.* Konow restores the missing portion as – *bhrata Maṇigula* –, which would make Jihoṇika as son of Maṇigula who was a brother of a great king. Jihoṇika has been identified with *Kṣatrapa* Zeionises of the coins who was son of the *Kṣatrapa* Maṇigula, supposed to be a contemporary of Azes II. D C Sircar thinks Jihoṇika was the son of a *mahārāja* and perhaps grandson of Zeionises. The year 191 is taken to refer to the era, which began in 57 BC and the date would come to AD 134.

KHAROṢṬĪ INSCRIPTION OF THE KUṢĀṆA AGE,YEAR 56[43]

The inscription is on a Gandhāra sculpture. The text, as translated by B.N. Mukherjee, refers to two years – year 4, which appears to be regnal one and year 56, which is taken to refer to the era beginning in AD 78. The date would thus come to AD 134, which fits in well with the date of the sculpture based on stylistic grounds.

AN INSCRIPTION OF THE KUṢĀṆA AGE[44]

The inscription on a Gandhāran sculpture, according to B.N. Mukherjee, records the installation of an image of the Buddha at Dharmarāja monastery founded by Aśoka, with the hope that it will lead to *nirvāṇa.* The epigraph is of Kuṣāṇa age and it is interesting that even during this period, the Dharmarājikā *stūpa* was known as originally created by Aśoka, who has been referred to as Dharmarāja in the Buddhist literature.

MISCELLANEOUS SHORT KHAROṢṬĪ INSCRIPTIONS

A Bajaur (south-east of Jalalabad) inscription of 1st century AD bears the legend *Su Theudama* i.e. 'King Theudama'.[45] A rock inscription from village Tirth on the border of the Swat Kohistan has an inscription in 1st century BC characters *Buddhasa Śakamunisa padāni,* i.e. 'footprints of Buddha Śākyamuni'.[46] The Shadpur (Agror Valley) inscription[47] of Damajada refers to some pious act in the year 60. Another inscription from the same site[48] refers to a pious act which cost ten thousand *kārṣāpaṇas.* An epigraph from Mansehra[49] refers to the donation of an *ārāma.* An inscription from village Majhia (Attock district)[50] refers to some gift in the year 68. The Bajang inscription.[51] now in the Lahore Museum, records the gift of a well in the Vajra-*stūpa* by a private individual. The Paja (a village in the Yusufzai) inscription[52] mentions the gift of a well by Saṅghamitra in honour of his parents and for the welfare and happiness of all beings. An inscription from Kaladarra in Swat refers to the gift of a tank by a person in honour of all beings in the year 113.[53] A Peshawar Museum inscription[54] of an unknown provenance records the gift of a well to a monastery in the year 168. An inscription on a vase from Taxila refers to the erection of a *stūpa* at Taxila in honour of the Buddha.[55] An inscription on a laddle[56] mentions a gift to *saṅgha* of the four quarters in the Uttarārāma of Taxila for the acceptance of the Kāśyapīyas (a branch of the Sarvāstivādins). An inscription from a village near Mansehra records the gift to the monks of the four quarters.[57] An inscription from the Dharmarājikā *stūpa* (Taxila) refers to some gift of the monk Dharmadāsa in the Dharmarājikā compound.[58] Some inscriptions refer to the gift of the Greek coins – *staters* and *drachms.*[59] A seal inscription refers to Śivasena, the *kṣatrapa* of Abhisāraprastha (hilly region between Jhelum and Chenab).[60] An inscription from Palatu Dheri mound[61] mentions gifts for the acceptance of the Bhadranikāyikas and Kāśyapīya *śramaṇas.* From the Shahji-ki-dheri, near the city of Peshawar, an inscription[62] records the gift in Kaniṣka-*vihāra* of which Agisala was the architect, for the acceptance of the Sarvāstivādins. Agisala is taken to be an Indian form of Greek Agesilaos and this would show that Kaniṣka appointed a Greek as an architect.[63] A boxlid inscription[64] mentions consecration of Buddha's relics in year 18, in the month of Artemisios. An inscription from Hadda, near Jalalabad,[65] records the consecration of Buddha's relics in year 28, in the month of Apelae (Macedonian Apellaios) for the *nirvāṇa* of all the beings. An inscription on a potsherd from Tor Dheri (district Loralai, Baluchistan) records the gift of a water-hall by Shāhi Yola Mira in the *vihāra* named after him for the acceptance of the Sarvāstivādins and for the merit of his parents and all beings.[66]

GUPTA INSCRIPTIONS FROM CHILAS[67]

A number of inscriptions from Chilas in Hunza district of Kashmir bear the name of king, with or without the epithet Vikramāditya, variously as *Śrī Candra, Devaśrī Candra, Śrī Deva Candra, Śri Candra Deva, Candraśrī Deva Śri Vikramāditya* and *Śrī Vikramāditya Śrī Candra* in Gupta characters, together with the date 143. Some inscriptions record the name Hariṣeṇa. The date 143 could not be in Vikrama era or in Śaka era as the letters are of Gupta period. It could not even be in Gupta era as counting by this era, the date would come to AD 462, when Skandagupta and not Candragupta II, was ruling. The Kalacuri era would suit Candragupta's date (143 + 248 =) AD 391. But the use of Kalacuri era for a Gupta ruler in this area would be extremely unusual. There is a possibility that a local era has been used. A.H. Dani refers the date to Harṣa era, which converted to Christian era would give the date (606 + 143 =) AD 749 and he identifies King Candra with his homonym of local Patola Shahi dynasty. According to him, in such a remote area as Chilas, the use of Gupta characters might have continued, without much change, even long after the end of the Gupta rule. He also points out that the title *Vikramāditya* was popular with this dynasty also. There is a view that the date is in the Gupta era, but the epigraphs relating to Candragupta II were recorded in the reign of Skandagupta (AD 455-67). Besides the script being Gupta, there are other points which favour the identification with Candragupta II. The form of the name as *Devaśrī* occurs in the Archer type of coins of that king bearing legend *Devaśrī-mahārājādhirāja-Śrī-Candraguptaî.* He has been referred to as *Devarāja* in his Sanchi inscription and *Devagupta* in a Vākāṭaka record and Vikramāditya was his title. The name as *Candra* occurs on his copper coins. Candra also occurs as the form of the name in the Mehrauli Pillar Inscription, which has generally and rightly been ascribed to him.

Hariṣeṇa of the Chilas inscriptions should be identified with his homonym of the Allahabad Pillar Inscription of Samudragupta in which he has been referred to as *sāndhivigrahika, mahādaṇḍanāyaka* and *kumārāmātya* of that Gupta ruler. The Kuṣāṇas ruling in the north-western India acknowledged the suzerainty of Samudragupta, as per evidence of the Allahabad Pillar Inscription and it seems quite natural for his successor, Candragupta II, to lead an expedition to Bactria. Hariṣeṇa would have continued to serve Samudragupta's son and successor, Candragupta II, in the same or similar capacity and he might have led the Gupta army in that expedition. In short, the form of the name as *Candra*, the epithet *Deva*, the title *Vikramāditya,* the name Hariṣeṇa and the use of Gupta script provide sufficient proof of the identification of the king with Candragupta II and also of the conquest of that region by him.

KHAROṢṬĪ AND BRĀHMĪ INSCRIPTIONS FROM KARA TEPE[68]

Some Brāhmī and Kharoṣṭī inscriptions have been found at Kara Tepe, Termez, near ancient Bactria on the Oxus. One bearing the legend *Māheśvara dharmasya* shows the presence of Śaivism in otherwise Buddhist area. It reminds of the dedication of Śaiva caves at Udaigiri during the reign of Candragupta II. Trident and Brāhmī letters on the coins of Sassanian kings Yezdergard (accession AD 399) indicate Indian influence. A Sassanian seal shows a king offering round objects to a person smaller than his size. This motif seems to have been inspired by Cakravikrama type of coins of Candragupta II in which Viṣṇu is shown offering three objects, perhaps symbolizing sovereignty, exertion and counsel, or three worlds. These pieces of evidence also support the view of Candragupta II's expedition in that area, as arrived at on the basis of the Chilas inscriptions.

KURA STONE INSCRIPTION OF THE TIME OF TORAMĀṆA[69]

The Brāhmī inscription found in Kura Salt Range was engraved during the reign of Toramāṇa Śāhi Jaūvla. It contained date but the letters mentioning it have been mutilated. Some scholars believe that first year of the reign of the king was mentioned. It records the construction of a Buddhist monastery by Roṭṭa Siddhavṛddhi, son of Roṭṭa Jayavṛddhi, for the monks of the Mahīśāsaka school. Būhler and Kielhorn opine that the title Jaūvla (literally falcon) is a feudatory title or tribal name and therefore, Toramāṇa of this inscription should not be identified with the Hūṇa king who was the father of Mihirakula. Most scholars, however, take the two as identical, pointing out that there are examples of the use of subordinate titles even for the independent kings, of which the use of *senāpati* for Puṣyamitra Śuṅga even after his assuming kingship is an example. The inscription would show that the area around the Salt Range formed part of the empire of Toramāṇa. In this inscription, Buddha has been referred to as *Devātideva*, 'god of gods', *Sarva-vatsala*, 'affectionate towards all', *Sarva-pāpa-parikṣīṇa sarva-puṇya-parigata*, 'free from all sins and endowed with all holiness', *Mahākāruṇika*, 'full of great kindness', *Tīrṇa-pārāṇava-sattvanāṁtārayitā*, 'saviour of those who have crossed ocean of birth',[70] *Daśabalabalī*, 'possessors of power of ten powers', *Cāturvaiśāradya*, 'master of four subjects of confidence or fearlessness' and *Catuî-pratisambhida*, 'master of four analytical sciences' and 'one who has attained *Aṣṭādaśa-veṇikā-dharma* (eighteen independent conditions).[70]

CONCLUSIONS

There are some common points between the art and the inscriptions of the Gandhāra region and its neighbourhood. Gandhāra art has foreign form and Kharoṣṭī script, which is the most common script used for the inscriptions of the region, is generally taken to be of foreign origin. Both are primarily Buddhistic, the former depicting Buddhist themes and the latter mentioning acts relating to Buddhism. The Gandhāra art flourished mostly under the Indo-Greeks, Śakas, Kuṣāṇas and the Parthians and a large number of Kharoṣṭī inscriptions were engraved during the rule of these dynasties and some directly pertain to them. The Gandhāra art shows decline in the Gupta period and the Kharoṣṭī script goes out of use in about the same period.

Some inscriptions are dated. The date generally comprises the year [of an era], the month and the day within month. Rarely, the fortnight (*pakṣa*) as in the Takht-i-Bahi inscription, which refers to dark fortnight and nakṣatra as in Zeda inscription, which refers to Uttara-phalguni, find mention. Except in the case of the Kalawan copperplate inscription and Taxila silver scroll inscription, which contains *Ayasa* and *Ajasa* respectively, both of which have been taken to mean '[the era] of Azes', the name of the era is not mentioned. Naturally, often there is difference of opinion regarding the identification of the era. The Azes era commenced in 57 BC, which incidentally is also the initial year of the Vikrama era. Kaniṣka certainly founded an era, which most scholars take to be the same as the Śaka era commencing with his accession in AD 78, but the founding of which others place in the 2nd century AD. Barring the date 143 met with at Chilas, all other dates have been, according to merit, referred either to the era beginning in 57 BC or to that beginning in AD 78.

In some cases, regnal year has been mentioned. All the dates in Aśokan epigraphs are with reference to his accession. In the Shinkot (Bajaur) inscription, 5th regnal year of Menander is mentioned and in the Takht-i-Bahi inscription, along with the date 103 of an era (probably Azes era), 26th regnal year of Gondopharnes is also mentioned. Quite interesting is the mention of the Macedonian months, which obviously was the result of the influence of the Indo-Greeks. We come across Arthamisa (Macedonian Artemisios, equivalent to Indian Vaiśākha-Jyeṣṭha) in Khawat (Wardak) inscription, Panemasa (Macedonian Panemos, equivalent to Indian āṣāḍha-Śrāvaṇa) in Taxila copperplate inscription of Patika; Avadunaga in the Shertala inscription and Avadunaka in Kurram copper-casket inscription stand for Macedonian Audunaios (equivalent to Indian Pauṣa-Māgha). It may be stated, in passing, that the Sui Vihar inscription of the time of Kaniṣka mentions Daiṁsaka (Macedonian Daisios, equivalent to Indian Jyeṣṭha-āṣāḍha) and the Mathurā stone inscription of Huviṣka refers to Gurppiya (Macedonian Gorpiaios, equivalent to Indian Bhādra-āśvina).

The Aśokan inscriptions exhort people to show proper treatment and charitable disposition towards various categories of people – parents, teachers, old men, slaves, servants, poor, orphans, *brāhmaṇas* and *śramaṇas*. They appeal to the people to show religious tolerance and refer to the acts of public welfare done by the king, such as digging of wells, planting of trees and provisions for medical treatment for men and animals.

Barring a couple of Śaiva inscriptions, the epigraphs generally refer to pious acts mostly related to Buddhism, such as consecration of relics of Buddha and construction of *stūpas* and monasteries. The reference to *stūpas* as Dharmarājikā, as in Taxila silver scroll inscription, is either because of its association with Aśoka who is known as Dharmarāja (righteous king), or even because the *stūpa* symbolizes Buddha who too was a Dharmarāja. In one Kuṣāṇa inscription Aśoka is associated with the Dharmarājikā *stūpa*. It is occasionally specified that the pious act was meant for the followers of a particular school of Buddhism (and not for the Buddhists in general), such as for Sarvāstivādins in the Kurram casket inscription and the Zeda inscription, for Mahāsāṅghikas in Khawat bronze vase inscription and for Mahīśāsakas in Kura stone inscription of Toramāṇa. The Kurram casket inscription is significant as it is one of the three inscriptions known so far recording the twelve *nidānas* and the only one in Prakrit—the language in which the Buddha preached.

The donors associated in their pious acts their family members—parents, wife, brothers, sisters, etc, kinsmen, friends, teachers and others. In the Kalawan inscription, a lady associated in such act, amongst others, her two daughter-in-laws, mentioned by name as Lajjā and Indrā. In such epigraphs, a wish is generally expressed that the merit of the act should be for the welfare and *nirvāṇa* of such people as family members, teachers, kings, officials, queens, princes and even all sentient beings.

A number of epigraphs mention names of kings, most of them of foreign origin, such as Menander in the Shinkot inscription, Guduvhara, i.e. Gondopharnes, in the Takht-i-Bahi inscription, Moga, i.e. Maues, in the Taxila copperplate inscription, Kujula Kadphises, Vima

Taktu and Vima Kadphises in Rabtak inscription, Kaniṣka in Rabtak, Zeda and Manikiala inscriptions, Vajheṣpa, i.e. Vasiṣka and Kaniṣka II in Ara inscription, Huviṣka in Khawat inscription and Toramāṇa in Kura inscription. The kingly titles include *maharaja* (mahārāja) of Indian origin, *rajatiraja* in Iranian mode, *devaputra* based on the Chinese *t'ien-tzu* – all these have been used for Kaniṣka and some of his successors. *Maharaja* is also used for Menander in the Shinkot inscription and for Maues in the Taxila copperplate inscription, which, latter, also contains the title *mahata* for that king. The title *Kaisara* is met with only for Kaniṣka II in the Ara inscription and is based on Roman *Caesar*.

Certain offices and officers also find reference in the epigraphs. Theodorus, a Greek, is referred to as *meridarkha* (Greek title meaning a district officer) in the Swat relic vase inscription. Liaka in Taxila copperplate inscription and Jihonika in the Taxila silver vase inscription have been referred to as *kṣatrapa*. Patika in the Taxila copperplate inscription has been referred to as *mahādānapati*. Lala of the Kuṣāṇa family has been mentioned as *daṇḍanāyaka* in the Manikiala inscription.

Kaniṣka has been referred to as *muroḍa* (lord) and *marjhaka (gṛhapati)* and Kapa. . . (identified with Kujula Kadphises by Sten Konow) has been referred to as *erjhuṇa* (prince). The terms *muroḍa, marjhaka* and *erjhuṇa* are all of Central Asian origin. Toramāṇa has been called *jaūvla* in the Kura stone inscription. Quite interesting are the forms *Guṣaṇa* in Manikiala inscription and Panjtar inscription and *Khuṣaṇa* in Taxila silver scroll inscription, instead of the more common form, Kuṣāṇa.

At times, there has been some problem regarding the interpretation of certain terms and identification of certain kings. In Aśokan inscriptions the Maurya king has been referred to as *Devānaṁpiya*. It took a long time to establish that *Devānaṁpiya* of the epigraphs is definitely Aśoka, this could done only when an epigraph with his name (Aśoka) together with this title was found. There has been and still is, difference of opinion whether Alexander of Aśoka's Rock Edict XIII should be identified with a king of that name who was ruler of Epirus or the one who was ruler of Corinth. Some scholars consider Viyakamitra and Vijayamitra of Shinkot inscription as identical while others take them as two different persons. Similarly, opinion is divided whether or not *Mahādānapati* Patika of Taxila copperplate inscription is identical with *Mahakṣatrapa* Patika of Mathurā lion capital inscription. The Kuṣāṇa king of the Panjtar inscription is identified with Kujula Kadphises by some and with Vima Kadphises by others. The *Maharaja Rajatiraja Devaputra* Khuṣaṇa of the Taxila silver scroll inscription has been variously identified with Kujula Kadphises, Vima Kadphises and Kaniṣka I. The Rabtak inscription has for the first time settled the extremely controversial issue of the genealogy and chronology of the early Kuṣāna kings, which, according to it, runs – Kujula Kadphises, Vima Taktu, Vima Kadphises and Kaniṣka.

NOTES AND REFERENCES

1. For the text of these rock edicts, see Hultzsch, *Corpus Inscriptionum Indicarum*, I, pp. 7lff.
2. For the text of these rock edicts, see *ibid.*, pp. 50ff.
3. J. Filliozat, *EI*, XXXIII, pp. 333ff; *EI*, XXXIV, pp. lff.
4. E. Herzfeld, *EI*, XIX, pp. 25lff; D.C. Sircar, *Select Inscriptions*, I, pp. 78-79.
5. *Ibid.*
6. For references, see Romila Thapar, *Aśoka and the Decline of the Mauryas*, p. 271.
7. N. G. Majumdar, *EI*, XXIV, pp. lff; D.C. Sircar, *EI*, XXVI, pp. 3l8ff; Sten Konow, *EI*, XXVII, pp. 52ff.

8. See references quoted by N.G. Majumdar, *EI*, XXIV, p. 3. Sten Konow (*EI*, XXVII, p. 54) suggests that *praṇasameda* may mean 'lifelong'.
9. For references, see R. Solomon, 'A Kharoshṭhī Reliquary Inscription of the Time of Apraca Prince Visṇuvarman', in *South Asian Studies*, 11, 1995, pp. 27ff.
10. *Ibid.*, p. 30.
11. *Ibid.*, pp. 27ff.
12. *Ibid.*, p. 28.
13. Sten Konow, *CII*, II (i), p. 1ff; D.C. Sircar, *Select Inscriptions*, I, p. 101.
13a. *Ibid.*, pp. 4ff.
14. A.K. Narain has discussed these inscriptions afresh.
15. G. Būhler, *EI*, IV, p. 54; Sten Konow, *CII*, II (i), pp. 23ff ; D.C. Sircar, *Select Inscriptions*, p. 124.
16. J.F. Fleet, *JRAS*, 1907 , p. 1035.
17. *Vide* H. C. Raychaudhuri, *Political History of Ancient India* (6th ed), p. 448.
18. *Ibid.*, pp. 448-49.
19. Bhagwanlal Indraji, *JRAS*, XX, pp. 551ff.
20. *ASR*, V, p. 68, *vide EI*, IV, p. 56.
21. G. Būhler, *EI*, IV, pp. 56-57.
22. Sten Konow, *EI*, XVIII, p. 282; *CII*, II (i), pp 57- 62; D.C. Sircar, *Select Inscriptions*, p. 125.
23. *Ibid.*, p. 62.
24. *Ibid.*, pp. 61-62.
25. Sten Konow, *EI*, XIV, p. 136; *CII*, II (i), pp. 67-70; D.C. Sircar, *Select Inscriptions*, p. 130.
25a. Sten Konow,*CII*, II (I), p. 70, takes *sivathala* to mean 'auspicious ground'.
26. Sten Konow, *EI*, XXI, p. 251f; D.C. Sircar, *Select Inscriptions*, pp. 131-32.
27. Sten Konow, *EI*, XIV, pp. 285ff; *CII*, II (i), pp. 70-77.
28. N. Sims Williams, *Silk Road Art and Archaeology*.
29. Sten Konow, *EI*, XIX, pp. 1ff; *CII*, II (i), pp. 142-145; D.C. Sircar, *Select Inscriptions*, p. 140.
30. Sten Konow, *CII*, II (i), pp. 145-150.
31. B.N. Mukherjee, 'Shertala Kharoshṭhī Inscription of the Year 39 of the Kaniṣka Era', *Journal of the Epigraphical Society of India* (hereafter *JESI*), XIV, pp. 35ff.
32. *Ibid.*
33. B.N. Mukherjee, 'Garhi Matani Inscription of Kaniṣka [I]', *JESI*, V, pp. 113-14.
34. V. Natesa Aiyar and F.W. Thomas, *EI*, XVIII, pp. 16f; Sten Konow, *CII*, II (i), pp. 152-55.
35. For the text of the brick inscription, see *EI*, XVIII, pp. 19-20.
36. *Ibid.*, p. 19.
37. W.B. Hanning, *Bulletin of School of Oriental and African Studies*, XXIII, 1960, pp. 47ff.
38. *Ibid.*
39. Sten Konow, *EI*, XIV, pp. 130ff; CII, II (i), pp. 162-65; D.C. Sircar, *Select Inscriptions*, p. 154.
40. F.E. Pargiter, *EI*, XI, pp. 210f; Sten Konow, *CII*, II (i), pp. 165- 170.
41. Sten Konow, *CII*, II (i), pp. 79-81.
42. Sten Konow, *ibid.*, pp. 81-82; D.C. Sircar, *Select Inscriptions*, p. 135.
43. B.N. Mukherjee, 'A Kharoṣṭī Inscription on an Image of Gandhāra Art', *JESI*, XV, pp. 78ff.
44. B.N. Mukherjee, 'A Kharoṣṭī Inscription of the Kuṣāṇa Age referring to Aśoka', *JESI*, XVI, 1960, pp. 32-33.
45. Sten Konow, CII, II (i), pp. 4ff.
46. *Ibid.*, pp. 8-9.
47. *Ibid.*, pp. 13-14.
48. *Ibid.*, pp. 16-17.
49. *Ibid.*, pp. 18-20.
50. *Ibid.*, pp. 21-22.
51. *Ibid.*, pp. 55-57.
52. *Ibid.*, pp. 63-65.

53. *Ibid.*, pp. 65-66.
54. *Ibid.*, pp. 77-79.
55. *Ibid.*, p. 87.
56. *Ibid.*, pp. 87-88.
57. *Ibid.*, pp. 88-89.
58. *Ibid.*, p. 90.
59. *Ibid.*, pp. 88-89.
60. *Ibid.*, p. 103.
61. *Ibid.*, pp. 121-22.
62. *Ibid.*, pp. 135-37.
63. H.C. Raychaudhari, *PHAI*, VIth ed., p. 476.
64. Sten Konow, *CII* (i), pp. 151-52.
65. *Ibid.*, pp. 158-59.
66. *Ibid.*, pp. 173-76.
67. For the text of the inscriptions, see M.C. Joshi and S.K. Gupta (eds.), *King Candra and the Mehrauli Pillar*, Meerut, 1989, pp. 58-59.
68. V.S. Pathak and V.B. Rao in *King Candra and the Mehrauli Pillar,* Meerut, 1989. pp. 191ff.
69. G. Būhler, *EI*, I, pp. 239ff.
70. For references to these various terms, see *ibid.*

27

COIN HOARDS FROM AFGHANISTAN
Their Bearing on Art History

DEVENDRA HANDA

There is enough archaeological evidence which links the north-western region, called Gandhāra, with the proto-historic (particularly the early and mature Harappan) cultures of India and Pakistan. The geographical perspective of the Ṛgvedic India also extends from the river Kubbā (Kabul) to the Gaṅgā. The origin of the term may be traced to 'Gandhārī', the name of the tribe settled in the extreme North West Frontier Province of the subcontinent. Gandhārī is mentioned in the *Ṛgveda*[1] and *Atharvaveda*.[2] The former mentions the good wool of the sheep of Gandhārī and the later mentions them with the Mūjavats. The Brāhmaṇa texts refer to Nagnajit, king of Gandhāra and his son Svarjit.[3] In later times, Gandhāra developed as a great seat of learning and a resort of scholars of all classes who flocked to its capital for instructions in the Vedas and eighteen branches of knowledge.[4] The *Chāndogya Upaniṣad*[5] also indicates Gandhāra and Takṣaśilā to be the centres of learning. Pāṇini was also a native of Gandhāra and refers to the city of Takṣaśilā.[6] It is listed as one of the sixteen *Mahājanapadas* 'Great States' in the Buddhist chronicles.[7] Pukkusati (Puṣkarasārin), the king of Gandhāra, was a contemporary of King Bimbisāra of Magadha and is known to have sent an embassy with a letter of friendship to his Magadhan counterpart. In the Behistun Inscription of Darius, *c.* 520-18 BC, Gadara (Gandhāra) is referred to as one of the kingdoms subject to the Persian Empire. Later Candragupta Maurya annexed it to his kingdom. The University of Takṣaśilā (Taxila), situated in this *janapada*, attracted students from distant places. Kauṭilya was also a celebrity of this city. In ancient times, Gandhāra included the NWFP and the adjoining portions of north-western Punjab (now in Pakistan) having the two royal cities of Takṣaśilā (modern Taxila) and Puṣkalāvatī (modern Charsadda near Peshawar).

Gandhāra occupies a very strategic position between the India and West Asia. The silk route also passed through it. It has been India's window towards the West and all intercourse of the country with the West via the land-route has been taking place through this region only. It has thus been the meeting place of the East and the West. As such, not only the invaders from the West have been coming to India via this route, but also all overland trade with the West has been taking place through Gandhāra. It is thus natural to expect rich archaeological material in Gandhāra. Some very important coin-hoards have also been discovered from Gandhāra from time to time, which are listed below.

IMPORTANT COIN HOARDS

(i-iv) Ai Khanum Hoards of 1970, 1973, 1973/74 and the 1980s,[8]
(v) Attock Hoard,[9]
(vi-viii) Bajaur Hoards,[10]
(ix) Begram Hoard,[11]
(x-xii) Bhir Mound,[12]
(xiii) Chaman Huzuri Hoard,[13]
(xiv) Haripur Hoard,[14]
(xv) Hazrajat Hoard (now in the Fitzwilliam Museum),[15]
(xvi) Khauzikhelai Hoard,[16]
(xvii) Kunduz/Qunduz Hoard, found by chance on 23 August 1946 at Tepe Khisht on the Afghan side of Amou Daria, about 90 km from Qunduz in Afghanistan.[17]
(xviii) Mian Khan Sanghou Hoard discovered accidentally by a peasant from Mian Khan Sanghou in the Mardan district, while ploughing his fields. He found an earthen pot with 83 silver coins.[18]
(xix-xx) Mir Zakah Hoards of 1947 and 1992.[19]

Beside these, Mac Dowall published articles on coins from excavations at Kandahar,[20] 'Two Azes Hoards from Afghanistan',[21] and R.C. Senior published 'Indo-Scythian and Indo-Parthian Coin Hoards from the Northwest'.[22] Hoards have been discovered from Shaikhan Dheri,[23] Malakand,[24] Wesa, Sarai Saleh, Swat, Siranwali (between Gujranwala and Sialkot, two hoards), Daska, Charsadda, Peshawar, etc., in Pakistan and in Kashmir also.[25]

The Chaman Huzuri (Kabul) hoard, also known as 'tresors de Caboul' (found in 1933) provided very important evidence regarding the origin and antiquity of coins in India.[26] It comprised the following—

(a) Thirty coins of diverse Greek city states, early 6th-5th centuries BC.
(b) Thirty-four Athenian Owls and their imitations (5th century BC), some in mint state, but the latest coin in the hoard is dated to 393/4 BC also.
(c) Eight sigloi of the Persian Empire, *c.* 450 BC.
(d) Fourteen Gandhāran bent-bar punch-marked coins.
(e) Twenty-nine coins of otherwise unknown type on globular flans heavily stamped with a geometric-like mark on one side and with traces of a design on the reverse.

We are concerned here with some important and recently found hoards obtained from Afghanistan. Two hoards were discovered from Bajaur in 1942 and their coins have been discussed well by scholars. In October 1993, another hoard containing 800 Indo-Greek drachms was found accidentally in Khar village near Pandyaly in the Bajaur area of the NWFP of Pakistan. All the three hoards contained silver coins of Apollodotus I, Antimachus II and Menander I. Most of the coins of the 1993 hoard have been sold in the western markets. The Mian Khan Sanghou hoard contained eight tetradrachms and seventy-five drachms of Apollodotus I, Antimachus II Menander I and Zoilus I. Khauzikhelai (a small village near Saidu-Sharif in the Swat valley) hoard was discovered accidentally in 1992 in a broken vase from the bed of the Swat river. It contained 800 coins, all exclusively of the Indo-Greek rulers: silver coins of Apollodotus I, Antimachus II, Menander I, Lysias, Antialcidas, Philoxenus and

Nicias. Besides the drachms, it contained a good number of tetradrachms also: 200 tetradrachms of Menander I and four of Antialcidas. It has yielded a unique Attic tetradrachm of Diomedes with helmeted bust.[27] The unique tetradrachm of Nicias, now forming part of Amar Ur Rehman's collection in Pakistan, was also found in this hoard.[28] The Attock hoard seems to have contained 93 tetradrachms (3 of Antialcidas and 90 of Menander I) and 600 drachms of Menander I, Zoilus I, Lysias, Antialcidas and Amyntas.

A hoard of ancient coins was discovered in May 1947 from Mir Zakah, situated 53 km north-east from the city of Gardez in Afghanistan, very close to the Pakistan border. At that time, the Afghan authorities were able to procure the hoard and entrust it to a French Archaeological Delegation in Afghanistan, which prepared its brief inventory. It contained 5837 Indian coins of bent-bar and punch-marked types, five Greek coins, 2757 Graeco-Bactrian and Indo-Greek coins, 4390 Indo-Scythian coins, 29 Indo-Parthian coins and 37 Kuṣāṇa coins.

The Indo-Greek, Indo-Scythian and Indo-Parthian coins carry a good amount of information through their style, overstrikes, minting techniques, metrology, iconography and portraiture, monograms and find-spots. Various scholars, however, have discussed the earlier hoards but the recent hoards are not that well known, particularly in India. The evidence obtained from Ai Khanum, a vast Greek city situated at the junction of the Amu and the Kokcha rivers in northern Afghanistan, however, is extremely important and has resolved many puzzling problems of the history of the Bactrian period besides throwing fresh light on the art and iconography of some Hindu deities.

The first hoard at Ai Khanum was found in 1970, in room no. 20 of the administrative bloc of the palace situated in the centre of the lower city. Curiously enough, it was hidden at this place after the destruction of the building. The hoard contained 677 silver punch-marked coins and six bilingual drachms of Agathocles. Coins of other Graeco-Bactrian kings were completely absent.[29] The second hoard was discovered in 1973 in the ruins of the kitchen of a large private house situated outside the northern wall of the city. It comprised 63 silver tetradrachms of Attic standard, 49 of which are Graeco-Bactrian coins: 7 Diodotus in the name of Antiochus, one Diodotus in his own name, 27 pieces of Euthydemus I, three of Demetrius I, one of Euthydemus II, three belonging to Agathocles, two of Antimachus (I) Theos, one each of Apollodotus and Eucratides I.[30]

The third hoard was found in the winter of 1973-74 by an Afghan farmer near the excavated site itself. It was quickly disposed of in Kabul and when a large part of it passed through New York by commerce, the former curator of the American Numismatic Society, Dr N. Waggoner, prepared a rapid inventory on the basis of which Fr. Holt published its details in 1981.[31] Though there may be some doubts about some of the coins, yet the contents betray a good amount of similarity to the composition of the second hoard. This third hoard may have comprised 142 silver coins of Attic standard of which 120 were Graeco-Bactria: 7 Diodotus in the name of Antiochus, 4 Diodotus in the name of Diodotus, 81 belonging to Euthydemus I, 8 of Demetrius I, 3 of Euthydemus II, 6 pieces of Agathocles, 2 of Antimachus (I) Theos and 9 of Eucratides I. The excavations at Ai Khanoum yielded 274 coins of which 224 were legible. Seventy-seven of these belonged to Graeco-Bactrian and Indo-Greek rulers. The stray finds included only bronze pieces. Of the 68 Seleucid coins, 62 belonged to Antimachus I, followed by 49 coins of Euthydemus I, 26 of Diodotus and 12 of Eucratides I of which 11 were bilingual.[32] The fourth hoard may have contained more than 1000 coins comprising gold, silver and bronze coins of Eucratides I and his Bactrian predecessors Diodotus, Euthydemus I and II, Demetrius I, Agathocles, Pantaleon, Antimachus I and Apollodotus I.[33] The site has been looted and pillaged badly during the last decade.

Aman Ur Rehman possesses a unique Attic standard tetradrachm of Diodotus from Ai Khanum IV in the name of Antiochus II showing the diademed head to right on the obverse and Zeus striding to left, naked, hurling thunderbolt, Aegis on left arm and eagle with outstretched wings at his feet and monogram to left with the Greek legend ANTIOXOY/ NIKATOPOΣ.[34] The portrait on the obverse of this coin is not of Antiochus II, but that of Diodotus. The reverse has the type of 'Diodotus: Zeus' and not that of 'Antimachus: Apollo' seated on the Omphalos. Bopearachchi takes this coin as decisive 'to support the view that it was under Antiochus II that Bactria became an independent kingdom'.[35] Aman Ur Rehman's collection, made mostly from Pakistan and Afghanistan, contains two more interesting coins, probably from Mir Zakah II, in the name of Euthydemus I (nos. 119 and 120). The first is a reduced Attic standard tetradrachm depicting on the obverse the bust of Mithridates to left, wearing a Parthian bonnet and on the reverse, traces of the type of Euthydemus I's coins, with the type of Herakles seated on a rock and the legend ΒΑΣΙΛΕΩΣ ΕΥΘΥΔΗΜΟΥ. It is interesting to note that only drachms of Mithridates I with this obverse type are known so far. The coin seems to have been struck with an obverse die of Mithridates I and a reverse die of the first series of Euthydemus I's imitations. The coin has actually received three strikes and has a blackish patina which is a characteristic of most of the coins of the Mir Zakah II deposit. It may be placed in the early years of Mithridates' reign, about 170 BC. The second coin is a double stater struck in the name of Euthydemus I and is a mint error. It shows on one side the negative and incuse image of Herakles, seated on a rock, holding club against his right thigh and the negative incused legend ΒΑΣΙΛΕΩΣ / ΕΥΘΥΔΗΜΟΥ, while the reverse shows the same image and legend in relief.

Agathocles (*c.* 180-165 BC) and Pantaleon seem to have been the earliest rulers to introduce bilingual coinage. The bilingual silver coins of Agathocles found in the excavations at Ai Khanum range from 2.32 to 3.30 g corresponding to the weight of the punch-marked coins of India.[36] The technical aspects of minting methods and the irregular shape of the rectangular bronze coins is also comparable to the early Indian coins. The most important feature of these coins, however, is their purely indigenous iconography. The most remarkable types, of course, are the ones represented on the bilingual coins of Agathocles. The obverse and reverse of these coins show two masculine personages standing in front, dressed identically in Indian *dhotī* and *uttarīya*, wearing large earrings, helmeted headgear adorned with two floating ribbons and half-boots, with swords hanging on a cross-belt in a long sheath, one carries a six-spoked *cakra* and a conch while the other carries a pestle and a plough. Bernard identified the two figures as those of Viṣṇu and Śiva but Filliozat and Narain have rightly identified them with Vāsudeva and Saṃkarṣaṇa.[37] Another important type shows the image of a goddess holding a lotus on the bronzes of Agathocles and Pantaleon,[38] which has been identified by certain art historians to be Ekānaṃśā or Subhadrā, Kṛṣṇa's sister, or Lakṣmī.[39] These images are the earliest iconographic representations of the Indian deities.

The study of monograms on Greek and allied coins is very fascinating. In 1965, A.N. Lahiri proposed a list of 441 monograms.[40] Bopearachchi, however, has reduced their number to about 300 by eliminating certain derivative and modified forms from the basic monograms and feels that by excluding the monograms of the posthumous issues struck by nomads in the name of Indo-Greek kings this number will be around 250.[41] Cunningham believed that the monograms represented names of cities,[42] Whitehead took them to be the names of the local magistrates responsible for issuing the coins or as mint-names,[43] Tarn regarded them as those of moneyers, mint-masters or city magistrates, Mitchiner attributes each monogram to a mint city without giving any convincing argument.[44] Bopearachchi's analysis brings out an interesting fact that except for one or two very rare cases, the coins of most of the Indo-Greek kings do not bear more than ten monograms with their variants and that some of the principal monograms can be localized in different geographical regions. Since bronze coins are normally intended for local transactions and not for wide circulation like silver issues, which could travel to distant places, such coins can be more relied to know the significance and use of the monograms. Having studied various collections, he agrees with Bivar that the monogram composed of two Greek letters *Kappa* and *Rho* ( ) can be attributed to Gardez-Ghazni and that the monogram , which is preponderant on Masson's collection from Kabul may be associated with that place and the monogram noticed on a majority of coins found in the Taxila excavations may represent that city.[45] The following figure would give some idea of the connections.[46]

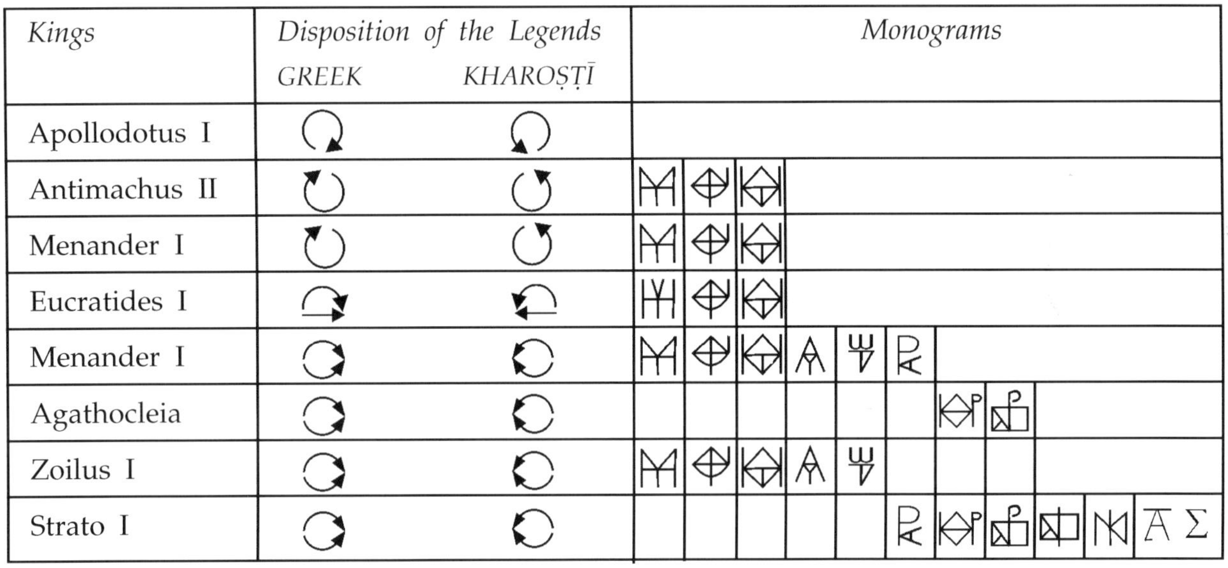

In the absence of exhaustive archaeological excavations and proper documentation of all collections, it is, however, very difficult to attribute each and every monogram to a city. It is interesting to note that on the basis of his study of the monogram of a triangle with a semicircle in the centre of its base line, enclosed in a circle as found on some Ai Khanum coins and bricks used in the first of the three architectural phases of Period I at Ai Khanum, Narain has deduced the antiquity of the foundation of Ai Khanoum to the middle of the third century BC.[47] The Greek city came to an end with the nomadic invasion of *c.* 145 BC and once driven away, the Greeks never returned to the city.[48] Bopearachchi has demonstrated as to how the Ai Khanum and Qunduz hoards corroborate the different stages of the large-scale movement and advance of the Chinese hoards and that Heliocles I was the last Greek ruler of Bactria.[49]

Justin (XLI.6) tells us that a usurper named Eucratides who became a powerful king in Bactria invaded India. This fact is corroborated by his bilingual silver drachms also which bear a peculiar legend arrangement: for the Greek and for the Kharoṣṭī, which can be integrated without any difficulty in between the two groups of Menander's coins where the legends are disposed as and . Bopearachchi feels that this new legend adjustment may have resulted from the disposition of the legend adopted accidentally while engraving the legend on the unique and interesting 20-stater gold piece now in the Cabinet des Medailles of Paris.[50] This piece has the peculiar disposition of the legend ΒΑΣΙΛΕΩΣ ΜΕΓΑΛΟΥ / ΕΥΚΡΑΤΙΔΟΥ which is different from the first group of his coins where the simple legend ΒΑΣΙΛΕΩΣ ΕΥΚΡΑΤΙΔΟΥ is adjusted in two parallel lines. Many numismatists are of the view that this piece, because of its exceptional value, may not have been an ordinary coin but a prestigious medallion that Eucratides may have struck to commemorate his victory over the Indian territories. Having become the master of the new territory of India, Eucratides called himself *megas* 'the great'. The second hoard of Ai Khanum contained only one coin of Eucratides I giving the title *megas* with the name of the king and the legend adjusted contrary to his first issues where the legend is without epithet and adjusted in two parallel horizontal lines.[51] Ai Khanum IV, however, contains a very interesting piece of helmeted bust and mounted Dioscuri type, second of its kind, which shows the legend ΒΑΣΙΛΕΩΣ ΜΕΓΑΛΟΥ / ΕΥΚΡΑΤΙΔΟΥ in two parallel lines. One can notice that the two words of the title are crouched together. This thus provides us an important link between the two series of legend arrangements. On the basis of an inscription found in the destruction stratum of Ai Khanum, bearing the date of the year 24th of an unknown reign, which Bernard identified as the reign of Eucratides I, the French scholar was able to fix exactly the end of Eucratides reign. It is believed that the Greek city of Ai Khanum may have been destroyed as a result of the first Yuezhi attack which probably took place immediately after the assassination of Eucratides by his own son, around 145 BC. It is interesting to note that the second and third hoards of Ai Khanum did not contain any coins of the successors of Eucratides.

Very few people, however, know that the biggest ever haul of ancient coins ever attested in the history of mankind was discovered accidentally in 1992 in the village of Mir Zakah. The hoard consisted of two to three tons of gold, silver and bronze coins, between 300,000 to 400,000 pieces and over 250 kilos of gold objects, dating from the fifth century BC to second century AD. Since this discovery was made at a time of political instability and insecurity, it did not receive the publicity it deserved and much of this heritage has been lost.

The people of Mir Zakah romanticize the event of the discovery of this hoard. According to a popular rumour going around, one day a woman of Mir Zakah, while fetching water from a particular spring famous for its sweet water, found a gold coin in her pitcher. The news spread like a wildfire and inhabitants of Mir Zakah and neighbouring villages hurried to the find-spot and started digging it. Many were killed when claiming the looted property of the deposit. Much of the treasure has been sold in bits across the border in the city of Peshawar and from there to the Japanese, English and American collectors who pay very high prices for antiquities. The best items in gold – jewellery and coins – seem to have been disposed in this way and the leftovers were sold in the bazaars of Peshawar openly. Dr Osmund Bopearachchi, a Sri Lankan numismatist, now settled in France and one of the foremost authorities on Indo-Greek coins, made several visits to Pakistan (Peshawar in particular) to see and study the coins put for sale in the bazaar in Peshawar taking notes on them and published some articles on what he saw. He gave a lecture in the British Museum, London on this find and asked various museums and even UNESCO to intervene to save this huge cultural heritage but nothing substantial could be done because of the paucity of funds.[52] Now the whole treasure has practically been exhausted and lost in bits. Let us hope, the collectors will preserve items of this hoard for the posterity and allow access to scholars to bring them to light. Most of the coins of this hoard were covered with a blackish layer of sulphide or mud.[53]

This lost hoard may be presumed to have comprised the same categories of coins as the first (Mir Zakah 1947) hoard and some others. Needless to say that the earliest issues in this deposit were the silver bent-bar and punch-marked coins of India and the Greek gold darics. An important coin belonged to Nasten, a great Iranian king, about whom nothing was known earlier. The coin bearing the portrait of the ruler on the obverse gives us an insight into his personality and the legend indicates that he probably lived about fifty years before the beginning of the Christian era. The important Indo-Greek coins from Mir Zakah include pieces struck in the name of Alexander, Diodotus, Demetrius I, Euthydemus II, Agathocles (unreported variety), Pantaleon (second known specimen), Antimachus I, Eucratides I (many new varieties in silver and one gold unique), Eucratides II (unreported), Heliocles, Antialcidas, etc. Most of the coins, however, belong to the Indo-Scythians. More than 3000 tetradrachms of Azes II and nearly 2000 specimens of posthumous imitations of Hermaeus, the last Indo-Greek king, many of which are characterized by a hitherto unreported Kharoṣṭī letter, have been noticed. Coins of the first century BC and the following two centuries are the most abundant. Bronze coins of Soter Meas, Vima Kadphises and especially of Kaniṣka are attested in thousands. The latest in the hoard were a few coins of Vāsudeva, the last important Kuṣāṇa ruler of India.[54]

People in the Indo-Pak subcontinent have a custom to throw coins and other various small (sometimes also big and precious) objects as offerings in the sacred rivers and basins. The first Mir Zakah find actually came from two such sacred basins. Many people believe that the case for the second and the biggest ever treasure is also similar. It may, however, be mentioned that this latter find also contained statuettes, cups and jewellery of solid gold. Also no traces of any ancient site or architectural structure exist anywhere near the find-spot. Some people believe that some unknown looters may have hidden the booty in a well after having pillaged the treasuries of temples and palaces, but could never return to retrieve it.[55]

Relying mainly on numismatic data, Bopearachchi considers Apollodotus I as the immediate successor of Agathocles, Pantaleon and Antimachus Theos in the Indian territories.[56] Contrary to his predecessors, Apollodotus I ruled only in the Indian territories. He may be credited with an innovation with far-reaching consequences in the field of monetary politics, by issuing bilingual silver coins of Indian standard. When his round silver coins of Attic standard of 2.12 g did not become popular with his Indian subjects, he introduced square form of the native punch-marked coins associated with the characteristic Indian symbols (sun, six-armed or *ṣaḍara-cakra*, three-arched hill with sun at the top, undulating line representing a river and taurine symbol) usually found on punch-marked coins. The first coin of this series appeared in the Mir Zakah deposit.[57] Since the low weight coins did not become popular, ultimately he was obliged to issue coins of slightly higher weight of 2.45 g, which remained popular even after the extinction of the Greek rule in India.

According to A.D.H. Bivar,[58] Apollodotus I was succeeded by Antimachus (II) Nikephorus who reintroduced the round shape in his silver coins and a new disposition of the legend: the Greek legend beginning at I and ending at XII and the Kharoṣṭī from XII to I. Antimachus (II) Nikephorus was succeeded by Menander (I) Soter, as is revealed by the latter's early coins which betray the same disposition of the legends in Greek and Kharoṣṭī, as noted above. Justin[59] refers to Apollodotos and Menander as kings of India and the *Periplus of the Erythraean Sea* mentions the drachms of Apollodotus' and Menander circulating in Barygaza. Since a tetradrachm of the Attic standard with the portrait of Apollodotus I has been found in excavations at Ai Khanum,[60] the king represented on this coin has to be placed before the destruction of Ai Khanum in 145 BC, i.e. different from Menander who overstruck the coins of Maues, the Scythian king who ruled from *c.* 85 BC.[61] Menander II struck Indian standard drachms of about 2.45 g and 17 mm diameter with obverse having diademed bust of king to r., wearing a crested helmet and bearing the legend ΒΑΣΙΛΕΩΣ ΔΙΑΚΑΙΟΥ / ΜΕΝΑΝΔΡΟΥ and the reverse depicting the king, wearing a crested helmet, on prancing horse to right with Kharoṣṭī legend *Maharajasa dhramikas / Menaṁdrasa* with a monogram to right. Menander I was a contemporary of the Indian king Puṣyamitra Śuṅga and is well known through literature. His coins are the commonest in most hoards of Indo-Greek coins. An Indian-standard tetradrachm of Menander from Mir Zakah II in the collection of Aman Ur Rehman (No. 307) is a unique piece from the point of view of the legend arrangement. Menander had introduced Indian-standard tetradrachms in the second group of his coins. His silver coins can be divided into two groups: the first group showing the disposition of the Greek and Kharoṣṭī legends as 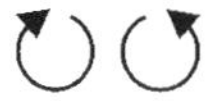 and with three monograms: 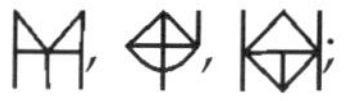; the second characterized by a different disposition of legends like  for the Greek and 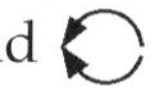 for the Kharoṣṭī and accompanied by new mint marks 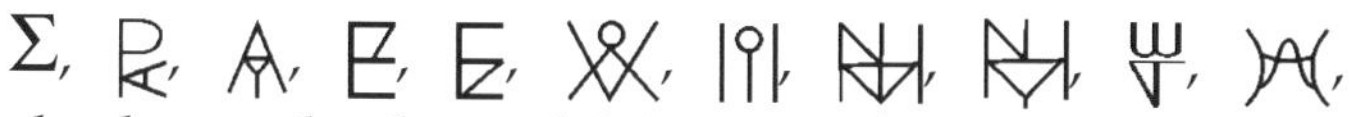, and by the introduction of an Indian-standard tetradrachm of 9.80 g, as below:

Kings	*Disposition of Legends*	*Monograms*
Antimachus II	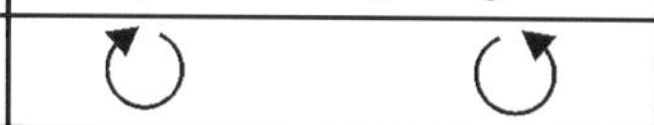	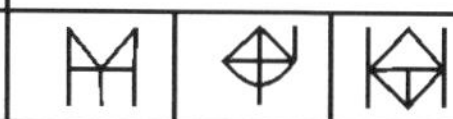
Menander I	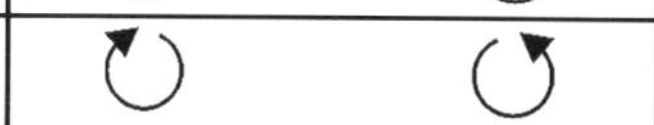	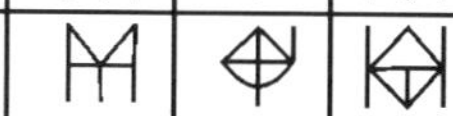
Eucratides I	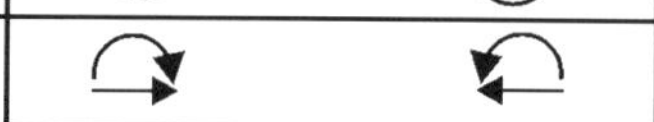	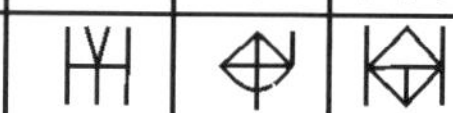
Menander I	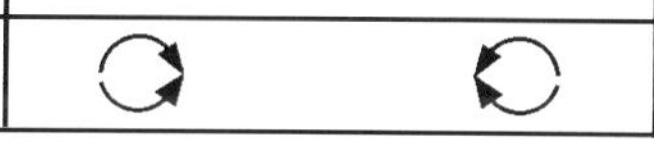	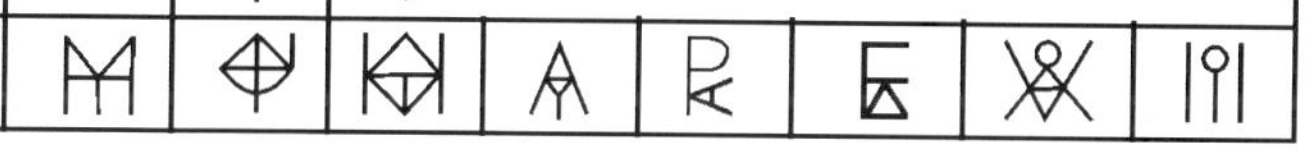

The new coin under discussion bears the portrait of the king on the obverse but the Greek legend is disposed like the twenty stater coin of Eucratides I. The Kharoṣṭī legend on the reverse is disposed without interruption. The next development in the coinage of Menander is to show both legends separately and this innovation was adopted by all his successors. This new coin may, thus, have been struck when the new denomination was introduced in Menander's second group of coins.

Greek power in Bactria ended with Heliocles I. In Propamisadae, Hermaios was the last Greek king to reign south of the Hindukush mountains. He was a contemporary of archebius but in different territories, as revealed by his mongrams. While Archebius was ruling in Gandhāra (Taxila 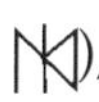), Hermaios occupied Paropamisadae (Alexandria of the Caucasus 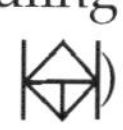) and the western Gandhāra (Charsadda 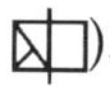). Hermaios was the last Greek ruler to use the mint of Alexandria of the Caucasus represented by the monogram 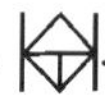. The monogram and many others 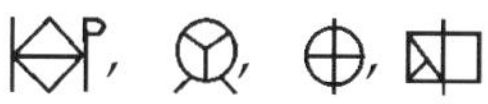 disappear after him. The coins show gradual debasement of silver.

His currency was, however, imitated after his death and it is very difficult to differentiate his lifetime issues from the posthumous imitations. On the basis of style, monograms, legend and metal, Bopearachchi has found that (1) The flans of his lifetime issues are very regular in shape whereas those of the imitations are irregular, (2) The dies of some of the imitations are adjusted at 3 O'clock instead of the usual 12 O'clock and (3) The limitations show extremely poor quality of engraving.[62] Coins of Hermaios have been divided into ten groups of which the last one is the so-called joint coinage of Su Hermaios and Kujula Kadphises. On the obverse

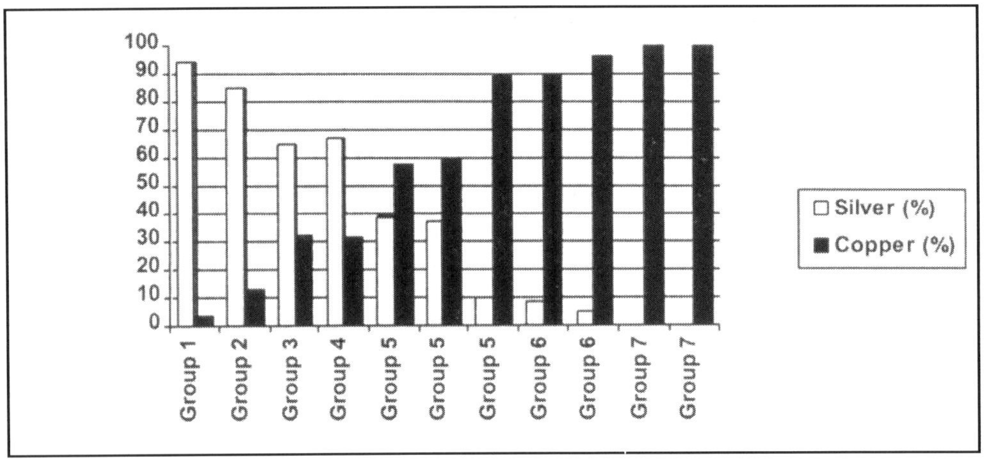

we find a larger bust of the king and on the reverse Heracles standing, facing, holding club in the right hand with the legend *Kujulakasa kushana Yavugasa dhramatidasa*. The reverse type as well as the legend is new. A.K. Narain considered all seven coins of the first seven groups as lifetime issues, the ninth as an issue of one of the Śaka or Parthian rulers and the tenth as minted by Kujula himself when he conquered the Kabul valley from the Pahlavas to whom Hermaios lost his kingdom.[63]

We come to another interesting aspect of the coins of Hermaios. It was in 1955 that a Pakistani numismatist Agha Inayat Ali Shah published a silver drachm issued in the name of Hermaios and averred that the Greek god Zeus on the reverse has been Indianized by wearing an elephant trunk like the Hindu deity Gaṇeśa.[64] Probably unaware of this publication, Narain presented similar idea in 1973 in his paper presented at the Paris session of the International Congress of Orientalists and in his presidential address at the Diamond Jubilee Conference of the Numismatic Society of India, 1973.[65] In 1978, following the same argument he said that 'The Pi-lo-sho-lo mountain in Kapisi was so-called after its presiding deity who had the Greek god Zeus of the Indo-Greeks and the elephant deity of the local population of a part of Afghanistan'.[66] Joe Cribb contested this view and showed that the photograph of the same coin, lit from a different angle, gives a different picture. He argued that what Narain took as the trunk of an elephant is a badly copied Zeus-Mithra's nose, beard and a fold in his gown.[67] Without caring for Cribb's criticism, Narain repeated the same argument in 1984[68] and 1988[69] declared the so-called 'elephant'headed' divinity on Hermaios' coin as a well-established fact.[70] In two of his articles, Bopearachchi has shown the untenability of this view saying that the illusory 'elephant-trunk' effect is the result of the engraver's hand and that other coins with the same monogram and showing the enthroned deity do not carry this effect.[71]

Of all the coin-hoards found in the recent years, the Sarai Saleh hoard is one of the most significant because of its composition, the very high frequency of certain monograms and its provenance which are extremely helpful in understanding the chronological sequence of the Greek and Scythian kings who were the successors of Maues in Taxila and Puṣkalāvatī. Among the Greek kings, only those who reigned over the territories of Gandhāra and west Punjab are represented in this hoard as evidenced by the monograms 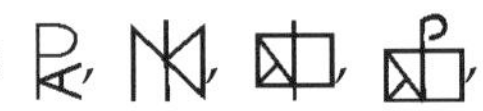 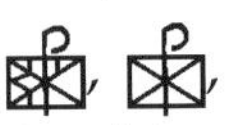 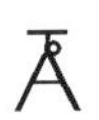 and , which are usually attributed to these regions. None of the Greek or Scythian kings of the east Punjab (e.g. Dionysius, Apollophanes, Zoilus II, Strato II and III,

Rajuvula) is attested in the hoard. The hoard contained only one posthumous coin of Hermaios and the coins stop at Azes I, indicating the date of the burial of this hoard.[72] Artemidorus, probably the immediate predecessor of Archebius, was known only from 36 coins earlier but this hoard contained more than fifty drachms and tetradrachms, some of the unreported series and some others with new monograms.[73] Coins of Artemidorus depicting the king on prancing horse may be compared with the same reverse type depicted on Menander II Dikaios' coin, probably by the same engraver,[74] indicating the two to be close contemporaries (*c.* 90-85 BC) ruling in the Taxila region. A coin of Artemidorus overstruck on a coin of Hermaeus and Calliope from this hoard published by R.C. Senior is very important as it also establishes the close contemporaneity of the two.[75] This coin is overstruck on a coin of Hermaios and Calliope betraying the fact of their being close contemporaries. Beside about twenty lifetime issues of Hermaios, this hoard contains one of his posthumous coin which bears the monogram . A slightly variant shape of this monogram  is found on a coin of Apollodotus II, also contained in this hoard. This coin would have been struck after the death of Apollodotus II and Hippostratus and before the conquest of Azes I whose coins, along with the posthumous coin of Hermaios, would have been the last additions to this hoard before its burial. Jenkins[76] had pointed out long back that the Greeks under the leadership of Apollodotus II had subsequently regained the territories of the Punjab, which they had earlier lost to Maues. If we take the date 78th year of an unspecified era of the great king Moga (Maues) in Patika's Taxila copperplate to the 155 BC era of Menander I, as noted above, the date of Maues' reign may be fixed in 90-80 BC. The Greeks were, however, finally expelled from this region in *c.* 55 BC by another Scythian price, Azes I, who dethroned Hippostratus, the last Greek king to reign in the west Punjab, including Taxila and Puṣkalāvatī. It is interesting to note that Apollodotus II had overstruck a bronze coin of Maues and Azes I had overstruck the bronzes of Apollodotus II and his successor Hippostratus.[77] Azes was succeeded by Azilises and Azes II as revealed by their coins. The Peshawar hoard[78] contains coins of Azes I, Azilises, Azes II and Gondopharnes and takes the story further. The Malakand hoard[79] confirms and corroborates the evidence. The numismatic evidence thus indicates that Gondopharnes may be dated *c.* 20-46 and Kujula Kadphises *c.* AD 30-78.

The hoard evidence thus throws important and significant light on the chronology of pre-Kuṣāṇa or rather pre-Kaniṣka period.

Some coins of Maues probably carried a representation, which is regarded by some scholars as that of Buddha/Bodhisattva.[80] These coins have remained somewhat controversial and different scholars have been writing in favour of or against the representation of Buddha on them. Recent re-examination, particularly by Joe Cribb[81] and the discovery of a figure inscribed *Budhaotasa* (*Bodhisattvasa*) in the Karakorum rocks,[82] however, leave little doubt that Buddha/Bodhisattva came to be represented in iconic form during the time of Maues, if not earlier.[83] This view, however, is contested by R.C. Sharma who traces the origin of the Buddha image to Mathurā in the first century AD.[84]

We thus see that the coin hoards from Afghanistan are immensely helpful in solving some knotty chronological problems and the earliest depiction of some divinities and throw a very welcome light on the art and history of the Indo-Pak subcontinent.

NOTES AND REFERENCES

1. *Ṛgveda* I.126, 7.
2. *Atharvaveda* V.22, 14.
3. *Aitareya Brāhmaṇa* VIII.34; *Śatapatha Brāhmaṇa* VIII.1, 4, 10; Vedic Index, I, p. 432.
4. Cf. Rhys Davids and Stede, *Pali-English Dictionary*, p. 76; *Milinda-Pañho* I.9; *Vāyu Purāṇa* 61.79; *Brahmāṇḍa* 67.82, etc.
5. *Chāndogya UP.* VI.14.
6. *Aṣṭādhyāyī* IV.3, 99.
7. For details see Hemchandra Raychaudhuri, *Political History of Ancient India*, 6th ed., Calcutta, 1953, pp. 59 ff.
8. R. Audouin and P. Bernard, 'Tresor de monnaies indienness et indogrecques d'Ai Khanoum (Afghanistan)', *Revue Numismatique*, XV (1973), pp. 238-39; XVI (1974), pp. 7-41, C.Y. Petitot-Biehler, 'Le tresors d' Ai Khanoum', *Ibid.*, XVII (1975), pp. 23-57; Fr. Holt, 'The Euthydemid Coinage of Bactria: Further Hoard Evidence from Ai Khanum', *Revue Numismatique*, 1980, pp. 7-44; P. Bernard, *Fouilles d' Ai Khanoum IV. Les Monnaies hors tresors. Questions d'histoire Greco-bactrienne,* MDAFA, xxvii, Paris, 1985; Cl. Rapin, 'La tresorie hellenistique d'Ai Khanoum', *Revue Archeologique*, 1987, pp. 41-70; Osmund Bopearachchi, 'Recent Discoveries: hoards and finds of ancient coins from Afghanistan and Pakistan', *Yavanika, Journal of the Indian Society for Greek and Roman Studies*, Vol. 4 (1994), pp. 3-30.
9. Osmund Bopearachchi, 'Recent Coin Hoard Evidence on Pre-Kushana Chronology', *Coins, Art and Chronology*, edited by Michael Alram and Deborah E. Klimburg-Salter, Wein, 1999, p. 112.
10. M. Thompason, O. Morkholm and G.M. Kray, *An Inventory of Greek Coin Hoards,* New York, 1973, nos. 1845-46; H.L. Haughton, 'Notes on Greek and Kushan Coins from North-West India: a) The Bajaur Hoard of 1942, b) Some Rare Copper Coins from the north-west Frontier of India', *Numismatic Chronicle*, Cambridge, 1946, pp. 141-45; Bopearachchi (1999), pp. 99-147.
11. Charles Masson, 'Memoir on the Ancient Coins Found at Begram in the Kohistan of Kabul', *Journal of the Asiatic Society of Bengal*, Calcutta, Vol. III (1834), pp. 152-75; 'Second Memoir on the Ancient Coins Found at Begram in the Kohistan of Kabul', *Ibid.*, Vol. V (1936), pp. 1-28; 'Third Memoir on the Ancient Coins Found at Begram in the Koistan of Kabul', *Ibid.*, pp. 537-47; R. Ghirshman, *Begram. Recherches archeologiques et historiques sur les Kouchans*, MDAFA, XII, Cairo, 1946.
12. Taxila Hoards of 1912-13, 1924 and 1946: P.L. Gupta, 'The Silver Punch-Marked Coins from Taxila (the Hoard of 1924): A Critical and Comparative Study', *Journal of the Numismatic Society of India*, Vol. XI (1949), pp. 14 ff; 'Some Observations on the Punch-Marked Coins Based on the Study of Taxila Hoard of 1924', *ibid.*, Vol. XII, pp. 136 ff.; 'A New Hoard of Silver Punch-Marked Coins from Taxila', *Ibid..*, Vol. XIII, pp. 53 ff.; 'Punch-Marked Coins from Taxila (Bhir-Mound Hoard of 1912-23)', *Ibid.*, Vol. XV, pp. 172 ff; E.H.C. Walsh, *Punch-Marked Coins from Taxila*, Delhi, 1939; 'Two Hoards of Silver Punch-Marked Coins Found in the Bhir Mound', in John Marshall, *Taxila*, 3 vols., Cambridge, 1951.
13. A.H.D. Bivar, 'The Chaman Huzuri Hoard: Countermarked Greek Flans as the Proto-types of the Indian Punch-marked Coinage', *Numismatic Chronicle*, 1954, pp. 163-72.
14. R.C. Senior, 'Vonones, Maues and the Early Indo-Scythian Succession', *Oriental Numismatic Studies*, Vol. 1, Delhi 1996, pp. 11 ff.
15. Thompson, *et al.*, *op.cit.*, No. 1842.
16. Osmund Bopearachchi, (1999), *op.cit.*, p. 111.
17. A.D.H. Bivar, 'The Qunduz Treasure', *Numismatic Circular*, May 1953; A.D.H. Bivar, *The Bactrian Treasure of Qunduz*, Numismatic Notes and Monograph, Numismatic Society of India, No. 3, Varanasi 1955, pp. 4-12; R. Curiel and G. Fussman, *Le Tresor Monetaire de Qunduz, Memoires de la Delegation Archeologique Francaise en Afghanistan* (MDAFA), Paris, Vol. XX, 1965.
18. Osmund Bopearachchi (1999), pp. 99-147.
19. R. Curiel and D. Schlumberger, *Tresors Monetaires d' Afghanistan, Memoire de le Delegation Archeologique Francaise en Afghanistan*, Paris, 1953; Osmund Bopearachchi, 'Coins from Mir Zakah

in Private Collections', *Indian Numismatics, History, Art and Culture (Essays in the honour of Dr P.L. Gupta)*, Delhi, 1992, pp. 87-94; 'Le depot de Mir Zakah', *Numismatique Grecque, Romaine et Celte*, November 1999, pp. 36-43; Osmund Bopearachchi and Aman Ur Rehman, *Pre-Kushana Coins in Pakistan*, Karachi, 1995; Osmund Bopearachchi and Wilfred Pieper, *Ancient Indian Coins*, Brepols, turnhout, Belgique, 1998, Indicopleustoi, Vol. II, p. 289, pl. 59; R.C. Senior, 'Punch-Marked Coins from Mir Zakah II', *ONS Newsletter*, No. 150, 1996.

20. D.W. MacDowall, 'Excavations at Kandahar 1975: Coin Finds', *Afghanistan Studies*, Vol. I, 1978, pp. 50ff., 'Pre-Islamic Coins in Herat Museum', *Ibid.*, Vol. II, 1979, pp.45-53.
21. In *South Asian Studies*, Vol. I (1985), pp. 51-55, etc.
22. *ONS Newsletter*, No. 107 (1987), pp. 2-3 and No. 115 (1988), pp. 3-5.
23. H.L. Haughton, 'The Shaikhano Dheri Hoard, March 1940', *Numismatic Chronicle*, 1940, pp. 123-126. See also A.H. Dani, 'Shaikhan Dheri Excavation: 1963 and 1964 Seasons', *Ancient Pakistan*, 1965-66, pp. 17-214.
24. Osmund Bopearachchi, *Indo-Greek, Indo-Scythian and Indo-Parthian Coins in the Smithsonian Institution*, Washington, 1993.
25. Thompson *et al.*, *op.cit.*; Bopearachchi and Rehman, *op.cit.*; Senior (1996), pp. 11ff. The Kosam Hoard also consists of coins of the bent-bar type but seems to have come to Kosam by way of trade.
26. *Tresors Monetaires d'Afghanistan*, pp. 1-64.
27. Osmund Bopearachchi (1999), pp. 111-12. It is now in the private collection of Prof. A. Hollis.
28. Bopearachchi and Rehman, *op.cit.*, No. 495.
29. R. Audouin and P. Bernard, *Revue Numismatique*, 1973, pp. 238-39; *Ibid.*, 1974, pp. 7-41.
30. C.Y. Petitot-Biehler, *Revue Numismatique*, 1975, pp. 23-57.
31. *RN*, 1981, pp. 7-43.
32. P. Bernard, *Monnaies hors tresors*, pp. 17-71.
33. Bopearachchi and Rehman, *op.cit.*, p. 13.
34. *Ibid.*, p. 2116, No. 1057.
35. *Ibid.*, p. 56.
36. Audouin and Bernard, *RN*, 1974, 7-41.
37. J. Filliozat, 'Representation de Vāsudeva et Saṃkarṣaṇa au lie siecle av. J.C.', *Arts Asiatiques*, XXVI (1973), pp. 113-21 and A.K. Narain, 'The Two Hindu Divinities on the Coins of Agathocles from Ai-Khanum', *JNSI*, XXXV (1973), pp. 73-77, pl. VII.
38. Bopearachchi (1993), *op.cit.*, pl. I.3.
39. *RN*, 1974, p. 25.
40. A.N. Lahiri, *Corpus of Indo-Greek Coins*, Calcutta, 1965, pls. A-C.
41. Monnaies Greco-bactriennes et indo-grecques. Catalogue raissonne, Bibliotheque Nationale, Paris, 1991 (*BN*), p. 451.
42. Alexander Cunningham, *Coins of Alexander's Successors in the East*, London, 1884 (reprint: Delhi-Varanasi, 1970), pp. 52-77.
43. R.B. Whitehead, 'Notes on Indo-Greek Numismatics', *Numismatic Chronicle*, 1923, p. 311.
44. Michael Mitchiner, *Indo-Greek and Indo-Scythian Coinage*, 9 vols., London, 1975-76, pp. 333-363.
45. Bopearachchi and Rehman, *op.cit.*, pp. 18f.
46. Collated from the works of Bopearachchi.
47. A.K. Narain, 'The Greek Monogram and Ai-Khanum—The Bactrian Greek City', *Numismatic Digest*, Vol. X (1986), pp. 4-15.
48. Bernard (1985), pp. 97-105.
49. There is not a single coin of Eucratides II, Plato and Heliocles I in the Ai Khanum IV hoard. See Osmund Bopearachchi, 'Graeco-Bactria Issues of Later Indo-Greek Kings', *Numismatic Chronicle*, 1990, pp. 79-103.
50. Bopearachchi (1993), *op.cit.*, p. 27.
51. *BN*, Eucratides I, serie 1.
52. Francesca Pierantozzi, 'Running After Ancient Coins', *Gulf News*, Tuesday, 30 May 1995, p. 12; Bopearachchi and Rehman, *op.cit.*, pp. 11f.

53. Bopearachchi and Rehman, *op.cit.*, pp. 55ff.
54. *Ibid.*, pp. 11-12.
55. *Ibid.*
56. Bopearachchi (1993), p. 24.
57. *Tresors Monetaires*, pp. 76, 86, 87. Three coins of this type from Mir Zakah deposit are housed in the Cabinet des Medailles, Paris; one exists in a private collection and one lies in the Smithsonian Collection.
58. *JRAS*, 1970, pp. 123-26.
59. *Prologue*, XLI.
60. *RN*, 1975, pp. 37-39.
61. Cf. G.K. Jenkins, 'The Apollodotus Question: Another View', *Journal of the Numismatic Society of India*, XX (1959), pp. 20-23. See also *JNSI*, 1955, p. 14.
62. Osmund Bopearachchi, 'On the So-Called Earliest Representation of Gaṇeśa', *Topoi*, Vol. 3/2 (1993), p. 432.
63. *The Indo-Greeks*, p. 161.
64. Agha Inayat Ali Shah, 'A Notable Numismatic Discovery', *The Museums Journal, Organ of the Museums Association of Pakistan*, August 1955, pp. 16-17.
65. *JNSI*, XXXVI (1974), pp. 180-91.
66. A.K. Narain, 'On the Earliest Gaṇeśa', *Senerat Paranavitana Commemoration Volume*, Leiden, 1978, pp. 142-44. The coin which Narain illustrated belonged to the British Museum and was donated in 1961 by A.D.H. Bivar (no. 1961, 3.2.1).
67. Joe Cribb, 'The Earliest Gaṇeśa: A Case of Mistaken Identity', *Numismatic Digest*, 1982, pp. 30-32.
68. A.K. Narain, 'Some Brahmanical Divinities on the Indo-Greek Coinage Revisited', *Inaugural Seminar, Indian Institute of Research in Numismatic Studies*, January 8-10, 1984, Nasik, pp. 9-14.
69. A.K. Narain, 'Iconographic Origins of Gaṇeśa and the Evidence of the Indo-Greek Coinage', in *Orientalia Iosephi Tucci Memoriae Dicta*, edited by G. Gnoli and L. Lanciotti, *Serie Orientale Roma*, LVI, 3 (1988), pp. 1007-1019.
70. A.K. Narain, 'Gaṇeśa: A Protohistory of the Idea and the Icon', in *Ganesh: Studies of an Asian God*, edited by R.L. Brown, New York, 1991, pp. 19-48.
71. Osmund Bopearachchi, 'Elephant-Headed Gaṇeśa or Zeus-Mithra', *Yavanika*, Vol. 2, 1992 and *Topoi*, Vol. 3/2 (1993), *op.cit.*, pp. 425-53; Bopearachchi (1999), p. 123.
72. Bopearachchi, *BN*, pp. 316-18.
73. Bopearachchi (1994). *Yavanika*, Vol. 4, 1994, pp. 3-30.
74. Bopearachchi and Rehman, No. 510.
75. Senior Consultants, List No. 1, No. 65, pl. I.4; Bopearachchi (1994), *Yavanika*, Vol. 4, No. 4.
76. G.K. Jenkins, 'Indo-Scythian Mints', *JNSI*, XVII (1955), pp. 22-23.
77. Osmund Bopearachchi, 'Monnaies Indo-Grecques Surfrappees', *RN*, XXXI (1990), pp. 49-79.
78. Joe Cribb,'Indo-Scythian Silver Coins from Pakistan', *Coin Hoards*, III, 1977, pp.108-13.
79. Bopearachchi (1993), *op.cit.*
80. See Percy Gardner, *Catalogue of Coins of the Greek and Scythic Kings of Bactria and India in the British Museum*, Chicago, 1967 (reprint), p. 17, pl. XVII. 5; V.A. Smith, *Catalogue of Coins in the Indian Museum*, Vol. I, Calcutta 1908, p. 40; R.B. Whitehead, *Catalogue of Coins in the Punjab Museum*, Lahore, Vol. I, etc.
81. Joe Cribb, 'The Origin of the Buddha Image—The Numismatic Evidence', in *South Asian Archaeology*, 1981, ed. by Bridget Allchin, Cambridge, 1984, pp. 231-44.
82. Rock carving no. 81 of Chilas II vide A.H. Dani, *Chilas, the City of Nanga Parvat (Dyamar)*, Islamabad, 1983, pp. 103ff.
83. See also A.K. Narain (ed.), *Studies in Buddhist Art of South Asia*, New Delhi, 1985.
84. R.C. Sharma, *The Buddhist Art of Mathura*, Delhi, 1984, pp. 149-67.